5.60

THE MAGPIES

THE MAGPIES

DAY-TO-DAY LIFE AT ST JAMES' PARK

MICHAEL BOLAM

MAINSTREAM
PUBLISHING

EDINBURGH AND LONDON

First published in Great Britain in 1998 by
MAINSTREAM PUBLISHING COMPANY (EDINBURGH) LTD
7 Albany Street
Edinburgh EH1 3UG

ISBN 1 84018 034 X

A catalogue record for this book is available from the British Library

Typeset in 9½ on 12 pt Times
Printed and bound in Great Britain by Butler and Tanner Ltd, Frome

INTRODUCTION AND ACKNOWLEDGEMENTS

When I started jotting down pieces of Newcastle-related trivia in old diaries many months ago, I had a vague idea of trying to publish something that was slightly different from the usual material available about the club. Years of digesting local-newspaper exclusives, badly written programmes and fanzines, and, of course, watching the team at God-forsaken places like the Manor Ground have resulted in this attempt at an alternative history. As well as the usual scores and scorers, you will find the odd match report and snippet of trivia, as well as some thinly veiled abuse of certain other teams. I hope that it will remind you of some bygone players and matches, even if many of them were better left forgotten.

For anyone who is looking for a balanced and comprehensive history of Newcastle United, I would refer you to the excellent set of publications by Paul Joannau, which along with the Local Studies section of Newcastle Central Library provided the backbone of the information contained in this book. Grateful thanks are also due to Danny Brannigan for the use of some of his excellent photographic work. Family and friends far too numerous to mention played a massive part in the creation of this book, as did the Internet mailing list known only as the 'blatherers'. Should you wish to contact me, you will find an e-mail link from the best unofficial Newcastle website bar none, www.nufc.com.

This book is dedicated to the many Newcastle supporters who have unwittingly contributed to it by their humour and loyalty to the cause.

JANUARY 1ST

1889	Angus Douglas born, Lochmaben, Scotland.				
1894	Lincoln City	(h) 5–1	Division Two	Bartlett 3, Thompson, Quinn	4000
1895	Lincoln City	(h) 4–2	Division Two	Dickson, Willis, Thompson 2	4000
1896	Leicester Fosse	(h) 1–0	Division Two	Aitken	7000

Debuts for John McDonald and John Warburton.

| 1897 | Newton Heath | (h) 2–0 | Division Two | Wardrope, Aitken | 16125 |

Later to become our friends from Old Trafford, Manchester United. Played at Bank Street in the Clayton district of Manchester.

| 1898 | Walsall | (h) 2–1 | Division Two | Peddie, R. Allen | 16000 |
| 1900 | Glossop | (h) 2–3 | Division One | Macfarlane, Peddie | 1500 |

Called off after 72 minutes due to fog. In the replayed match Peddie scored the only goal.

1901	Woolwich Arsenal	(h) 5–1	Friendly	Niblo 2, Fraser (pen), Laidlaw, Macfarlane	5000
1902	Third Lanark	(h) 2–1	Friendly	Ghee, Veitch (pen)	2000
1903	Third Lanark	(h) 4–0	Friendly	Veitch, Carr, Gardner, OG	2500
1904	Sunderland	(a) 1–1	Division One	Orr	40000

Andy McCombie played in his tenth and final Tyne–Wear derby for Sunderland. The next time the sides met, he was playing for United, for whom he made seven derby appearances.

1906	Blackburn Rovers	(a) 0–1	Division One	No Scorer	30000
1907	Derby County	(h) 2–0	Division One	Orr, Speedie	30000
1908	Sheffield United	(a) 1–1	Division One	Appleyard	20000
1909	Everton	(a) 1–0	Division One	Howie	40000
1910	Chelsea	(h) 1–0	Division One	Shepherd	30000
1912	Sheffield United	(a) 1–2	Division One	Stewart	40000
1913	Liverpool	(h) 0–0	Division One	No Scorer	30000

A clean sheet on his United debut for local lad James Wilson. However, eight goals passed by him in his other three first-team appearances.

1914	Manchester City	(h) 0-1	Division One	No Scorer	20000
1915	Sheffield Wednesday	(a) 1–2	Division One	King	11000
1920	Aston Villa	(h) 2–0	Division One	Smailes 2	40000
1921	Manchester United	(h) 6–3	Division One	Seymour 2, Smailes, Harris 2, Phillipson	40000
1923	Oldham Athletic	(h) 1–0	Division One	McDonald (pen)	30000
1924	Aston Villa	(h) 4–1	Division One	Seymour 2, McDonald, Harris	30000
1925	Sheffield United	(h) 0–0	Division One	No Scorer	20000
1926	Burnley	(h) 1–3	Division One	Urwin	
1927	Leeds United	(h) 1–0	Division One	Gallacher	40000
1929	Blackburn Rovers	(h) 0–2	Division One	No Scorer	40000
1930	Corinthians	(h) 4–4	Friendly	Hutchison 2, Richardson, McCurley	4000
1931	Aston Villa	(h) 2–0	Division One	Starling, Wilkinson	50000
1932	Aston Villa	(h) 3–1	Division One	Lang, J.R. Richardson, Cape	46000
1934	Liverpool	(h) 9–2	Division One	Boyd, Lang, Williams, J.R. Richardson 3, Weaver 3	18000

A debut for goalkeeper Bill McPhillips. One of the club's greatest ever second-half performances, as United centre-half Alec Betton had put through his own goal to make it 2–2 just before the break. Seven goals were notched without reply in the second half.

| 1935 | Bury | (h) 5–1 | Division Two | Bott 3, Pearson, Smith | 28000 |

Debutant Wilf Bott struck a memorable hat-trick from the right wing, while fellow newcomer Billy Cairns was to leave United fans waiting for his first league goal until mid-February, when he also struck a hat-trick.

1936	Plymouth Argyle	(h) 5–0	Division Two	Weaver 2 (1 pen), J. Smith 2, Ware	20000
1937	Bradford	(h) 1–1	Division Two	Leighton	29000
1938	Manchester United	(h) 2–2	Division Two	Smith 2	40000
1947	Nottingham Forest	(h) 3–0	Division Two	Bentley, Wayman, Woodburn	56827

Bob Fraser made his debut.

1948	West Bromwich Albion	(h) 3–1	Division Two	Dodgin, Milburn 2	61301
1949	Preston North End	(a) 1–2	Division One	Taylor	37000
1953	West Bromwich Albion	(h) 3–5	Division Onc	Davies, Milburn, Mitchell	48944
1954	Blackpool	(h) 2–1	Division One	Milburn 2	44343
1955	Sheffield United	(a) 2–6	Division One	Keeble, R. Mitchell	32000

Debut for Harry Taylor, at outside-right. The Blades started the New Year with a bang, cutting through their visitors to score four times in the opening eight minutes.

1957	Birmingham City	(h) 3–2	Division One	Tait, Casey 2 (1 pen)	29383
1966	Aston Villa	(a) 2–4	Division One	Bennett 2	19402
1969	Real Zaragoza (Spain)	(a) 2–3	Fairs Cup 3rd Round 1st Leg	Davies, Robson	22000
1972	Wolverhampton Wanderers	(a) 0–2	Division One	No Scorer	26571

Parkin and Richards on target for the Wolves.

1973	Leicester City	(h) 2–2	Division One	Tudor, Smith	30868
1974	Arsenal	(a) 1–0	Division One	Hibbitt	29258
1975	The home game with Liverpool was postponed due to inclement weather.				
1980	Sunderland	(h) 3–1	Division Two	Cartwright, Shoulder (pen), Cassidy	38784

What a day, as Peter Withe climbed out of a hospital bed to lead the United attack against the old enemy. Even an opening goal by mackem midget Stan Cummins couldn't prevent United prevailing. The events of the day are now immortalised in a version of 'Hark, the Herald Angels Sing' that you wouldn't hear in church . . .

| 1983 | Carlisle United | (h) 2–2 | Division Two | Keegan 2 | 28578 |

A lucky point as Carlisle twice took the lead. Although he didn't know it at the time, this was to be John Cragg's last appearance at St James' in his second spell with the club.

| 1985 | Sunderland | (h) 3–1 | Division One | Beardsley 3 (1 pen) | 36529 |

'Happy New Year,' the United fans sang as referee David Scott sent off Gayle and Bennett for the visitors and Beardsley claimed a memorable hat-trick, even missing another penalty. Colin West scored with an acrobatic volley at the Leazes end, but who cares?

| 1986 | Everton | (h) 2–2 | Division One | Beardsley, Gascoigne | 28031 |

Newcastle fan Trevor Steven gave the defending League champions a half-time advantage that United overturned within 17 minutes thanks to a couple of quality strikes. However, a late penalty from Graeme Sharp gave Everton a share of the points.

| 1987 | Manchester United | (a) 1–4 | Division One | D. Jackson | 43334 |

The usual Old Trafford hammering was initiated by a fourth-minute Peter Jackson own goal before Whiteside, Stapleton and Olsen joined the party.

| 1988 | Nottingham Forest | (a) 2–0 | Division Two | Gascoigne, Mirandinha | 28583 |

Delight at the City ground as Mira celebrated by dancing a jig of delight round the corner flag in front of the jubilant travelling Magpies. He would have been booked for it these days.

| 1990 | Wolves | (h) 1–4 | Division Two | Brock | 21937 |

Mick Quinn saw an early penalty saved by Mark Kendall before a one-man demolition by Steve Bull, who put four past former Wolves keeper Burridge. The large away following, many of whom travelled by charter plane, celebrated as one home fan remonstrated with Brock on the pitch and another invaded the dugout to hurl abuse at Jim Smith.

| 1991 | Oldham Athletic | (a) 1–1 | Division Two | Quinn | 14550 |

Comedy of errors as Newcastle, inspired by full debutant 17-year-old Steve Watson, looked to have secured the points until Stimpson rolled a backpass agonisingly out of reach of Burridge in the last seconds. Along with the 5–5 draw at QPR, this was the closest we ever came to winning on an artifical pitch in a competitive fixture.

1992   Southend United   (a) 0–4   Division Two   No Scorer   9458
Rock bottom for United, played off the park and in freefall towards Division Three oblivion.

1994   Manchester City   (h) 2–0   Premier League   Cole 2   35585
Brian Kilcline and Mark Robinson made their first appearances of the season, the latter after a career-threatening injury suffered pre-season. A pair from Cole wrapped things up nicely, while Beardsley saw a great individual effort mysteriously chalked off.

1997   Leeds United   (h) 3–0   Premier League   Shearer 2, Ferdinand   36489
How we laughed as Ian Rush played for Leeds and looked old, slow and finished. Little did we know . . .

JANUARY 2ND

Year	Opponent		Competition	Scorers	Att
1893	Everton	(h) 4–2	Friendly	Thompson 2, Sorley, Graham	4000
1894	Middlesbrough Ironopolis	(h) 7–2	Division Two	Law, Thompson, Willis 2, Quinn 2, Graham	3000
1896	Lincoln City	(h) 5–0	Division Two	Aitken, Lennox 2, Stott, Collins	5000
1897	Lincoln City	(h) 2–1	Division Two	Aitken, Smellie	12000
1899	Burnley	(h) 1–4	Friendly	Stevenson	8000
1900	Death of James Collins, 28. Following an injury sustained playing for Chatham, James contracted tetanus and died.				
1900	Sam Russell born, Downpatrick, Northern Ireland.				
1902	Corinthians	(h) 2–2	Friendly	Roberts, Veitch	6000
1904	West Bromwich Albion	(h) 1–0	Division One	Orr	16000
1905	Notts County	(h) 1–0	Division One	Orr	18000
1906	Corinthians	(h) 5–7	Friendly	Orr 2, Higgins, Hardinge, OG	3000
1907	Corinthians	(h) 3–0	Friendly	McClarence 2, Orr	5000
1909	Leicester Fosse	(a) 4–0	Division One	Higgins 2, Shepherd, Stewart	15000
1911	Everton	(a) 5–1	Division One	Randall, Shepherd 2, Stewart, Duncan	40000
1915	Everton	(a) 0–3	Division One	No Scorer	20000
1922	Liverpool	(h) 1–1	Division One	Harris	43000
1926	Bolton Wanderers	(h) 5–1	Division One	Gallacher 4, Urwin	35000
1928	Birmingham	(h) 1–1	Division One	Gallacher	40000
1932	Liverpool	(a) 2–4	Division One	Cape, Hutchinson	30000
1933	Middlesbrough	(a) 3–2	Division One	Allen, Boyd, McMenemy	27000
1937	Sheffield United	(h) 4–0	Division Two	Cairns, Mooney, Smith 2	33000
1939	Chesterfield	(h) 0–1	Division Two	No Scorer	34000
1954	Manchester United	(h) 1–2	Division One	Broadis	56034
1956	West Bromwich Albion	(h) 0–3	Division One	No Scorer	50768
1960	Manchester United	(h) 7–3	Division One	Allchurch, White 3, Eastham (pen), Hughes, Bell	57200
1965	Huddersfield Town	(h) 2–1	Division Two	McGarry 2	45315
1968	Paul Stephenson born, Wallsend. Winger who failed to live up to his early promise.				
1978	Leeds United	(a) 2–0	Division One	Burns 2	36643
	Debuts for 'Dick' Barton and Mark McGhee.				
1984	Barnsley	(h) 1–0	Division Two	Waddle	29842

1988 Sheffield Wednesday (h) 2–2   Division One   Goddard 2   25503
Lee Chapman and Brian Marwood were on target for the Owls, all the goals coming in the second half.

1989 Derby County   (h) 0–1   Division One   No Scorer   31079
A goal from Mark Wright left United at rock bottom, 20th in the First Division.

1993 Port Vale   (h) 4–0   FA Cup 3rd Round   Peacock 2, Lee, Sheedy   29873
United eventually overcame their third-round opponents with four second-half goals.

1995 Manchester City   (h) 0–0   Premier League   No Scorer   34437
Peter Beardsley returned to the team following injury, but Fox continued as penalty-taker following his success at Norwich days earlier. Unfortunately Andy Dibble saved this time.

1996 Arsenal   (h) 2–0   Premier League   Ginola, Ferdinand   36530
Ginola blasted an early effort into the Leazes end goal past a helpless Seaman. Ferdinand increased the lead with a second-half effort.

JANUARY 3RD

1893 Glasgow Rangers   (h) 4–0   Friendly   Reay, Creilly, Thompson,   3000
                                                         Sorley
1898 Loughborough   (h) 3–1   Division Two   Peddie, Ostler, OG   4000
     Town
1899 Hearts   (h) 4–1   Friendly   Macfarlane 3, Rogers   4000
1903 Stoke   (a) 0–5   Division One   No Scorer   6000
1905 Corinthians   (h) 1–2   Friendly   McWilliam   5000
1910 Preston North End   (h) 5–2   Division One   Shepherd 4, OG   26000
     Debut for Henry Thompson, at left-back.
1911 Preston North End   (h) 1–1   Division One   Wilson   30000
1914 Everton   (a) 0–2   Division One   No Scorer   25000
1920 Oldham Athletic   (h) 0–1   Division One   No Scorer   35000
1923 Corinthians   (h) 3–0   Friendly   Dixon 2, Clark   2000
     United's third goal came from Bob Clark, who played before being registered as a player for Newcastle. The club were later censured by the Football Association.
1925 Aston Villa   (h) 4–1   Division One   Cowan 3, McDonald   28000
1931 Grimsby Town   (a) 2–2   Division One   Boyd, Hutchinson   10000
1948 Luton Town   (h) 4–1   Division Two   Milburn 3, Stobbart   64931
1953 Tottenham Hotspur   (a) 2–3   Division One   Davies, Milburn   52648
1959 Everton   (h) 4–0   Division One   White 2, Allchurch 2   42475
1961 Bruce Halliday born, Sunderland. Joined as an apprentice, made 34 senior appearances.
1962 Albert Craig born, Glasgow. In a short-lived United career, his major achievement was being Peter Beardsley's best man!
1966 Sunderland   (a) 0–2   Division One   No Scorer   54668
     George Herd and John O'Hare scored and not-so-slim Jim Baxter made his debut for the home side.
1970 Southampton   (a) 0–3   FA Cup 3rd Round   No Scorer   19010
1975 Manchester City   (a) 2–0   FA Cup 3rd Round   Nulty, Burns   37625
     Following the disturbances during the Forest tie the previous season, United were forced to concede home advantage in this game despite being drawn first.
1976 Queens Park   (a) 0–0   FA Cup 3rd Round   No Scorer   20102
     Rangers
1981 Sheffield Wednesday (h) 2–1   FA Cup 3rd Round   Waddle 2   22458
     The emergence of Chris Waddle began in this memorable third-round encounter, as he struck his first senior goals to end United's barren run of four goalless games. Pearson replied for Wednesday, who could have forced a replay had Terry Curran fallen less acrobatically when tackled in the area. Owls boss Jack Charlton was not amused.
1983 Bolton Wanderers   (h) 2–2   Division Two   Waddle, Martin   23533
     An early sending-off for Terry McDermott was merely the start of the fun, as Bolton led

for virtually all of the game until a last-minute Waddle equaliser. The visitors then went straight back up the field to snatch the winner, or so it seemed. Cue Zico Martin with another equaliser. Those spectators who popped out for the early bus missed it all. Early in the game McCreery sustained a horrific leg injury, which required 60 stitches.

1987   Coventry City   (h) 1–2   Division One   McDonald   22366
Conceding a goal after 42 seconds (Dave Bennett) is never the ideal way to try and climb out of a five-match losing rut. Despite a second on the hour from Regis, however, the Sky Blues hung on for a victory after a late Neil McDonald strike gave Newcastle hope.

1995   Death of Geordie Stobbart, 73.

JANUARY 4TH

Year	Opponent	Venue & Score	Competition	Scorers	Att
1874	James Lockey born, Newcastle.				
1896	Manchester City	(a) 2–5	Division Two	McKay, Lennox	10000
1898	South Shields	(a) 6–2	Friendly	Peddie 4, Campbell 2	2000

A mid-season friendly against local opposition who by 1930 had moved along the Tyne to become Gateshead.

Year	Opponent	Venue & Score	Competition	Scorers	Att
1902	Blackburn Rovers	(h) 0–3	Division One	No Scorer	12000
1908	Sheffield Wednesday	(h) 2–1	Division One	Appleyard 2	30000
1913	Oldham Athletic	(h) 4–1	Division One	McDonald, Stewart, Higgins 2	25000
1930	Grimsby Town	(h) 3–1	Division One	Gallacher, Hutchinson, Scott	20000
1936	Tottenham Hotspur	(h) 1–4	Division Two	Bott	35000
1936	Jimmy Fell born, Cleethorpes.				
1947	Swansea Town	(a) 2–1	Division Two	Shackleton, Wayman	32000
1958	Plymouth Argyle	(a) 6–1	FA Cup 3rd Round	Eastham 2, Mitchell, White 3	40000
1964	Bedford Town	(h) 1–2	FA Cup 3rd Round	Anderson	34585

Non-league opposition provided third-round cup humiliation, having even been two goals ahead, one an own goal from Bill McKinney. In goal for Bedford was Jock Wallace, later to manage Berwick and Leicester, amongst others.

Year	Opponent	Venue & Score	Competition	Scorers	Att
1969	Reading	(h) 4–0	FA Cup 3rd Round	Craig, Dyson, Robson, Scott	41255
1982	Colchester United	(h) 1–1	FA Cup 3rd Round	Varadi	16977
1986	Brighton and Hove Albion	(h) 0–2	FA Cup 3rd Round	No Scorer	25112

An uphill battle when the visitors took the lead after 50 seconds through Eric Young, a meek United bowing out at the third-round stage for the fourth consecutive year. Dean Saunders scored the other goal.

Year	Opponent	Venue & Score	Competition	Scorers	Att
1992	Bournemouth	(a) 0–0	FA Cup 3rd Round	No Scorer	10651

Traffic jams and driving rain made it a gruelling trip to the south coast, and a poor performance from all of the outfield players resulted in their being booed at the end. One honourable exception was Tommy Wright, who denied Bournemouth with a series of spectacular saves, despite hobbling badly with a leg injury.

Year	Opponent	Venue & Score	Competition	Scorers	Att
1994	Norwich City	(a) 2–1	Division One	Beardsley, Cole	19564

Future United winger Ruel Fox set up Mark Bowen for a Norwich lead, but Beardsley moved swiftly to net his 200th career goal and Cole hit the winner. Paul Bracewell missed out and lost his ever-present record for the season, but stand-in Robbie Elliott had a storming game in an attacking sweeper role.

Year	Opponent	Venue & Score	Competition	Scorers	Att
1998	Everton	(a) 1–0	FA Cup 3rd Round	Rush	20885

The sheer inevitability of Rush scoring the winner made it all the more enjoyable as he forced home a Barnes centre from all of 18 inches. He had replaced the departing Asprilla, who looked a sorry figure as he was substituted and never played for United again. A thoroughly miserable game, televised live by ITV, which was banished from the memory once the cup draw was made. Within minutes of the final whistle, we were paired with Stevenage Borough, and journalists worked through the night polishing their 'giantkiller' clichés.

JANUARY 5TH

1895	Burton Swifts	(a) 3–5	Division Two	Thompson, O'Brien, Unknown Scorer	3000
1901	Blackburn Rovers	(h) 1–0	Division One	Peddie	10000
1903	Glasgow Rangers	(a) 1–3	Friendly	McColl	10000
1907	Birmingham	(h) 2–0	Division One	Rutherford 2	26000

1923 George King born, Amble.

1924	Nottingham Forest	(h) 4–0	Division One	Harris 2, Cowan 2	
1929	Sheffield United	(h) 4–2	Division One	Boyd, Carlton, McCurley, OG	20000
1935	Brentford	(a) 0–3	Division Two	No Scorer	28000

1940 Bill Thompson born, Bedlington. A centre-half on United's books for a decade from 1957.

| 1946 | Barnsley | (h) 4–2 | FA Cup 3rd Round 1st Leg | Hair, Stubbins, Milburn 2 | 60284 |

Full debuts for Bobby Corbett, Bobby Cowell, Charlie Crowe, Joe Harvey, Ray King, Tot Smith, Charlie Wayman and goalscorers George Hair and Jackie Milburn. To complete the side, Henry Clifton and Albert Stubbins represented the pre-war era.

| 1952 | Preston North End | (h) 3–0 | Division One | Foulkes, Milburn, G. Robledo | 42410 |
| 1957 | Manchester City | (h) 1–1 | FA Cup 3rd Round | White | 57921 |

1964 Chris Hedworth born, Wallsend. Central defender who graduated from the youth side.

1972 Malcolm Macdonald scored for England Under-23 as they defeated Wales 2–0 at Swindon.

| 1974 | Hendon | (h) 1–1 | FA Cup 3rd Round | Howard | 33840 |

A first-half opener from Howard, deservedly equalised by Rod Haider, set up a replay at Watford rather than Hendon's compact Claremont Road ground.

| 1980 | Chester City | (h) 0–2 | FA Cup 3rd Round | No Scorer | 24548 |

A young Ian Rush marked his first appearance at St James' Park by hitting the second goal in his team's thoroughly deserved cup victory.

1990 Swindon chairman Brian Hillier and manager Lou Macari were charged by the FA over allegations of match betting. The match in question was Swindon's 5–0 FA Cup defeat at St James' Park in January 1988.

| 1991 | Derby County | (h) 2–0 | FA Cup 3rd Round | Quinn, Stimson | 19748 |

Cup joy for United: John Anderson showed inspirational form and set up an opening goal for Quinn, who lobbed Peter Shilton. Stimpson scored from a free-kick to partially atone for his nightmare in the previous game. The only low point was the racial abuse that Rams striker Kevin Francis had to endure from home fans. Steve Watson became the youngest United player to feature in an FA Cup match, at 16 years and 279 days.

| 1997 | Charlton Athletic | (a) 1–1 | FA Cup 3rd Round | Lee | 14980 |

Keegan's last game as manager. Former Charlton turnstile-operator Robert Lee scored on his first return to The Valley since September 1985, having scored the Addicks' last goal before they abandoned the ground. A splendid equaliser from Mark Kinsella ensured a replay, but strange things were afoot at the after-match press conference . . .

JANUARY 6TH

1894	Ardwick	(h) 2–1	Division Two	Thompson, Graham	1200
1900	Everton	(a) 2–3	Division One	Fraser, Peddie	5000
1903	Moffatt	(a) 7–0	Friendly	McColl 4, Stenhouse, Caie, McWilliam	1000
1906	Birmingham	(a) 1–0	Division One	Gosnell	8000
1912	Bradford City	(a) 0–0	FA Cup 3rd Round	No Scorer	8000

Another atrocious day in Yorkshire, where the teams battled on for 51 minutes, until poor light and snow forced an abandonment.

| 1923 | Nottingham Forest | (h) 1–0 | Division One | McDonald | 20000 |
| 1934 | Leeds United | (h) 2–0 | Division One | Weaver, Williams | 22000 |

| 1951 | Bury | (h) 4–1 | FA Cup 3rd Round | Milburn, G. Robledo, Taylor, Walker | 33944 |

1952 Bobby Shinton born, West Bromwich.

| 1962 | Peterborough United | (h) 0–1 | FA Cup 3rd Round | No Scorer | 42782 |

1964 Death of Ray Robinson, 68.

| 1968 | Stoke City | (a) 1–2 | Division One | Davies | 17623 |

1972 Death of Albert Gosnell, 91.

1973	Ipswich Town	(a) 0–1	Division One	No Scorer	19609
1984	Liverpool	(a) 0–4	FA Cup 3rd Round	No Scorer	33566
1985	Nottingham Forest	(a) 1–1	FA Cup 3rd Round	Megson	23582

Sweet revenge for Gary Megson on his return to the City Ground. He had been bought by Brian Clough, who then voiced the opinion that he couldn't trap a medicine ball and refused to pick him for the first team. Despite being played on a Sunday, the game wasn't televised, simply delayed 24 hours to allow the pitch conditions to improve.

| 1990 | Hull City | (a) 1–0 | FA Cup 3rd Round | O'Brien | 10743 |

The Magpies regained a measure of pride with this narrow victory over the Tigers at Boothferry Park, following the New Year's Day mauling from the Wolves.

1992 Newcastle sent a team to Federation Park, home of Dunston Federation, to mark the switching on of their new floodlights. A mixture of juniors and reserves were aided by a three-man defence of Ossie Ardiles, Tony Galvin and Derek Fazackerley. Dunston won 2–1 in front of a crowd of around 500, David Robinson netting for United. The highlight of the evening was a one-woman complaint about the new lights, by a female neighbour who stood in her garden and yelled abuse at the amused spectators.

1993 A strong reserve side beat Alnwick Town 10–0 in a home tie in the Northumberland Senior Cup. Alan Thompson and Steve Watson both hit hat-tricks, Andy Hunt got two, McDonough netted a rare goal and Belisle of Alnwick put one past his own keeper.

JANUARY 7TH

1862 John Auld born, Cumnock, Scotland. First player to join United from Sunderland, October 1896.

| 1893 | Bolton Wanderers | (h) 3–1 | Friendly | Reay 2, Thompson | 2000 |
| 1899 | Everton | (h) 2–2 | Division One | Aitken, Stevenson | 15000 |

1901 Jimmy Nelson born, Greenock, Scotland.

| 1905 | Derby County | (h) 2–0 | Division One | Veitch, Gardner | 20000 |
| 1911 | Oldham Athletic | (h) 3–0 | Division One | Shepherd, Stewart, Duncan | 20000 |

1917 George Bradley born, Maltby, Yorkshire.

1922	Newport County	(h) 6–0	FA Cup 1st Round	McDonald 2, Harris, Dixon 2, Mooney	28567
1928	Tottenham Hotspur	(a) 2–5	Division One	McKay, Hudspeth (pen)	34710
1933	Liverpool	(a) 0–3	Division One	No Scorer	25000

Debut for William Gallantree at outside-right.

| 1939 | Brentford | (a) 2–0 | FA Cup 3rd Round | Clifton, Mooney | 27551 |

Debut for Willie Scott, who had been signed by United from Aberdeen after he scored five goals in a reserve match for the Dons.

| 1950 | Oldham Athletic | (a) 7–2 | FA Cup 3rd Round | Milburn 3, Mitchell, Walker 2, OG | 41706 |

1950 Malcolm Macdonald born, Fulham.

| 1956 | Sheffield Wednesday | (a) 3–1 | FA Cup 3rd Round | Curry, Keeble, Milburn | 48198 |

The cup winners began their defence against the Owls, who offered token resistance in the shape of a Don Gibson effort.

| 1961 | Fulham | (h) 5–0 | FA Cup 3rd Round | Allchurch, Neale 3, Woods | 36037 |
| 1976 | Queens Park Rangers | (h) 2–1 | FA Cup 3rd Round Replay | Gowling, T. Craig (pen) | 37225 |

Third-round replay success caught by the *Sportsnight* cameras. After Don Masson had equalised for Rangers, a Tommy Craig penalty took United through. For Gowling, it was the end of an 11-match goalscoring drought, and he went on to stick three past Everton in the next league match.

| 1978 | Peterborough United | (a) 1–1 | FA Cup 3rd Round | Hudson | 17621 |

1985 Death of Albert McInroy, 83.

| 1989 | Watford | (h) 0–0 | FA Cup 3rd Round | No Scorer | 24217 |

The start of a four-match FA Cup marathon, with out-of-form Mirandinha demoted to sub.

1991 Forty-eight hours after his FA Cup baptism, it was back to FA Youth Cup action for Steve Watson. Unfortunately, United lost 2–1 to West Bromwich Albion, watched by their first-team manager Brian Talbot. It didn't do him much good, though, being informed of his dismissal at half-time . . .

| 1996 | Chelsea | (a) 1–1 | FA Cup 3rd Round | Ferdinand | 25151 |

Les Ferdinand conjured up a 93rd-minute equaliser to force a replay after Mark Hughes had put the Blues ahead. Live TV showed the travelling fans exchanging pleasantries with Ken Bates and others in the directors' box as the final whistle blew. Hughes went through his full repertoire of shirt and hair pulling, diving and kicking before finally being deservedly booked.

| 1998 | Liverpool | (h) 0–2 | League Cup Quarter-Final | No Scorer | 33207 |

JANUARY 8TH

1884	Bob Blanthorne born, Rock Ferry, Birkenhead.				
1898	Manchester City	(a) 1–1	Division Two	R. Allen	20000
1910	Blackburn Rovers	(h) 4–1	Division one	Higgins, Shepherd 2, Howie	35000
1921	Nottingham Forest	(h) 1–1	FA Cup 1st Round	Harris	47652

The draw for the FA Cup had seen Forest out of the bag first, but the game was switched to Gallowgate at their request.

1927	Notts County	(h) 8–1	FA Cup 3rd Round	Gallacher 3, McDonald 3, Seymour, Urwin	32564
1938	West Bromwich Albion	(a) 0–1	FA Cup 3rd Round	No Scorer	33932
1938	Bobby Ferguson born, Dudley.				
1949	Bradford Park Avenue	(h) 0–2	FA Cup 3rd Round	No Scorer	47196
1949	John Cowan born, Belfast.				
1950	Gordon Hindson born, Quaking Houses, Durham.				
1955	Plymouth Argyle	(a) 1–0	FA Cup 3rd Round	Keeble	28685
1966	West Ham United	(h) 2–1	Division One	Bennett, Suddick	31754

Debut of Keith Kettleborough, in midfield.

1969 Jim Iley appointed manager of Peterborough United.

1972	Coventry City	(h) 4–2	Division One	Hibbitt, Tudor 2, Macdonald (pen)	25875
1977	Sheffield United	(a) 0–0	FA Cup 3rd Round	No Scorer	30513
1983	Brighton and Hove Albion	(a) 1–1	FA Cup 3rd Round	McDermott	17711
1994	Coventry City	(h) 2–0	FA Cup 3rd Round	Cole, Beardsley	35444

Cup time again, and a trouble-free victory once Cole had reacted first to Beardsley's rebound off a post. Mickey Quinn appeared as a second-half substitute for the Sky Blues.

| 1995 | Blackburn Rovers | (h) 1–1 | FA Cup 3rd Round | Lee | 31721 |

A late Lee equaliser in this Sky Television Sunday game, after Sutton had given Rovers the lead, set up an Ewood replay. However, by then Andy Cole had been sold to Manchester United, having struck 68 goals in 84 appearances for Newcastle. This was his final appearance.

1997 In a prepared statement, Newcastle announced that Kevin Keegan had resigned as manager. Speculation over his replacement included his former Liverpool team-mate John Toshack, and virtually anyone you could think of.

JANUARY 9TH

1897	Leicester Fosse	(a) 0–5	Division Two	No Scorer	3000
1904	Small Heath	(a) 0–3	Division One	No Scorer	8000
1909	Woolwich Arsenal	(h) 3–1	Division One	Anderson, Shepherd, Veitch (pen)	30000

1913 Ralph Birkett born, Newton Abbot, Devon.

1915 West Ham United (a) 2–2 FA Cup 1st Round Goodwill 2 15000
Two second-half goals from Alf Leafe took this third-round tie back to Tyneside.

1921 Geordie Stobbart born, Pegswood.

1926	Aberdare Athletic	(h) 4–1	FA Cup 3rd Round	Cowan, Gallacher 2, Gibson	38452
1932	Blackpool	(a) 1–1	FA Cup 3rd Round	Lang	14000
1937	Tottenham Hotspur	(a) 1–0	Division One	Rogers	31129
1946	Barnsley	(a) 0–3	FA Cup 3rd Round 2nd Leg	No Scorer	27000

United lost this unique third-round game on aggregate, the only time the FA Cup third-round format ever altered from single-game knockout. In the immediate post-war period there was an urgent need for the revenue earned from additional fixtures, hence the doubling up. Ernie Taylor made his United debut.

| 1954 | Wigan Athletic | (h) 2–2 | FA Cup 3rd Round | Broadis, Milburn | 52222 |
| 1957 | Manchester City | (a) 5–4 | FA Cup 3rd Round | Casey (pen), Tait, Curry, White 2 | 46990 |

A genuine cup classic at Maine Road. United came back from a 3–0 half-time deficit (the opener a Bob Stokoe OG) to force extra time. Bobby Johnstone again gave City the lead, but two Len White screamers settled it.

1960	Wolverhampton Wanderers	(h) 2–2	FA Cup 3rd Round	Allchurch, Eastham	62443
1965	Swansea Town	(a) 0–1	FA Cup 3rd Round	No Scorer	18951
1971	Stoke City	(h) 0–2	Division One	No Scorer	25708

1971 Paul Kitson born, Murton, Durham. Forward who left for West Ham frustrated at a lack of first-team football.

1974 Hendon (n) 4–0 FA Cup 3rd Round Replay Hibbitt, Tudor, Macdonald, McDermott (pen) 15385
An afternoon kick-off at Vicarage Road for this replay, due to the miners' strike and power restrictions on using floodlights. BBC cameras were on hand, hoping for another Hereford debacle, but the Isthmian League side were swept aside at the second attempt.

1985 Nottingham Forest (h) 1–3 FA Cup 3rd Round Replay Waddle 26383
How this third-round replay slipped away will for ever remain a mystery. A United onslaught direct from the kick-off resulted in a Beardsley penalty saved on four minutes by Hans Segers. Waddle then missed a hat-trick of chances before finally opening the scoring – all this in the first 14 minutes. A Peter Davenport penalty levelled the scores until extra time, when Ian Bowyer and United fan Trevor Christie wrapped it up for the visitors.

1988 Crystal Palace (h) 1–0 FA Cup 3rd Round Gascoigne 20415
Only one goal in it, but a memorable strike which rocketed into the Gallowgate end net.

1988 Death of Billy Cairns, 75.

1993 Bristol City (a) 2–1 Division Two Kelly, Scott 15446
United's first win at Ashton Gate since 1910 was achieved against a City side featuring the burgeoning talents of Andy Cole and the brilliantly named Junior Bent. Their manager Denis Smith said of United after the game, 'They are a team at peace with themselves.' He left the club shortly after . . .

1997 Press speculation over the vacant United manager's job now tipped Dalglish to take over.

JANUARY 10TH

1914	Sheffield United	(h) 0–5	FA Cup 1st Round	No Scorer	28185

Injuries sustained during this cup-tie meant that Newcastle ended with only eight players on the field.

1920	Crystal Palace	(h) 2–0	FA Cup 1st Round	Dixon, Hall	15000
1925	Hartlepools United	(h) 4–1	FA Cup 1st Round	Cowan, Harris, McDonald, MacKenzie	36632
1931	Nottingham Forest	(h) 4–0	FA Cup 3rd Round	Bedford, Hutchinson 3	34219

1945 Death of Tony Whitson. A member of the 1910 cup final team, born in South Africa.

1948	Charlton Athletic	(a) 1–2	FA Cup 3rd Round	Pearson	53428
1953	Swansea Town	(h) 0–0	FA Cup 3rd Round	No Scorer	63499

A whole eight minutes of play were possible in this cup game, before the referee called a halt due to the thick fog enveloping the ground.

1965 Paul Sweeney born, Glasgow. Signed from Raith, he was an uncompromising player, i.e. he liked kicking people.

1976	Everton	(h) 5–0	Division One	Gowling 3, Nulty, Nattrass	31726
1981	Wrexham	(a) 0–0	Division Two	No Scorer	6437
1989	Watford	(a) 2–2	FA Cup 3rd Round 1st Replay	Brock, Mirandinha (pen)	16431

Match two against the Hornets, who took the lead within two minutes, United not having even touched the ball. However, the visitors forged ahead only for a late penalty to level it again.

1990 Roy Aitken joined United from Celtic for a fee of £500,000 after a protracted chase.

1995 In a move that shocked football and forced Keegan to defend his actions on the steps of St James' Park to a crowd of bemused fans, Andy Cole was sold to Manchester United for £7 million, with Keith Gillespie moving the opposite way, valued at £1 million.

1996	Arsenal	(a) 0–2	League Cup Quarter-Final	No Scorer	37857

Disgraceful refereeing saw savage tackles on Ginola go unpunished and even result in a booking for the Frenchman when brought down! His frustration resulted in a dismissal for elbowing Lee Dixon in the face. Ian Wright scored a goal in each half to the unbridled delight of commentator Brian Moore, covering the game live for ITV. Man of the match was referee Gerald Ashby (Arsenal).

1997 Bobby Robson was allegedly offered the Newcastle job, according to reports in the now-hysterical media.

1998	Sheffield Wednesday	(a) 1–2	Premier League	Tomasson	29446

United's game plan appeared to be to stonewall Wednesday for a point. Unfortunately this lasted about a minute before Carbone waltzed in from the right to set up Di Canio. After Tomasson levelled courtesy of a rebound, Des Hamilton inexplicably gave the ball away in front of goal for Newsome to hit the winner. Another outing for the lucky dark blue away strip with the orange stripe.

JANUARY 11TH

1896	Grimsby Town	(h) 1–5	Division Two	Collins	5000
1902	Stoke	(a) 0–0	Division One	No Scorer	5000
1908	Nottingham Forest	(h) 2–0	FA Cup 1st Round	Appleyard, Rutherford	41637
1913	Bradford City	(h) 1–0	FA Cup 1st Round	G. Wilson	15928

This FA Cup match had to be called off at half-time, due to a combination of bad light and falling snow.

1925 Jimmy Scoular born, Livingstone, Scotland.

1930	York City	(h) 1–1	FA Cup 3rd Round	Gallacher	38674
1936	Walsall	(a) 2–0	FA Cup 3rd Round	Connelly, J. Smith	19882

Eddie Connelly opened the scoring on his first-team debut.

1947	Crystal Palace	(h) 6–2	FA Cup 3rd Round	Bentley, Pearson, Shackleton 2, Stobbart, Wayman	43183
1958	Birmingham City	(h) 1–2	Division One	White	34825
1964	Charlton Athletic	(a) 2–1	Division Two	McGarry, Thomas	18588
1969	Leicester City	(a) 1–2	Division One	Robson	21673
1971	Ipswich Town	(h) 1–1	FA Cup 3rd Round	Mitchell	32150

The only goal scored by Scotsman Ian Mitchell while at St James' seemed to have earned his team a fourth-round place, only for McFaul to fumble a speculative effort from Mick Mills into his own net.

1973 Lee Makel born, Washington, Tyne and Wear. Midfielder who appeared briefly before joining Blackburn.

| 1975 | Tottenham Hotspur | (h) 2–5 | Division One | T. Craig, Burns | 39679 |

A memorable first-team debut for Alfie Conn, who struck a hat-trick for the visitors.

| 1978 | Peterborough United | (h) 2–0 | FA Cup 3rd Round Replay | T. Craig (pen) Blackhall | 26837 |
| 1986 | West Bromwich Albion | (a) 1–1 | Division Two | Wharton | 9100 |

That man Varadi again, who netted the Baggies' equaliser. His strike partner, George Reilly, had just joined them from Newcastle.

| 1992 | Watford | (a) 2–2 | Division Two | Kelly, Hunt | 9811 |

The home team took precisely 40 seconds to score through David Holdsworth, and when Tommy Wright had given away a penalty within three minutes, a hammering seemed on the cards. Gary Porter converted it for 2–0 but then the home side lost their way. Even so, David Kelly's goal on 22 minutes was a major surprise to the crowd as well as Waugh, the Watford keeper, who let it through his legs. A second-half goal from substitute Andy Hunt could even have been followed by a winner, as Watford faded badly, much to the dismay of their fans.

1996 Death of Bobby Cowell, 73, member of all three victorious 1950s FA Cup final teams.

| 1997 | Aston Villa | (a) 2–2 | Premier League | Shearer, Clark | 39339 |

Caretaker managers Arthur Cox and Terry Mac took charge after the shock departure of Keegan. Shaka saved a penalty from his childhood pal Dwight Yorke, after Yorke and Milosevic had levelled for the Villa. United had gone two ahead thanks to a Shearer strike and a Clark lob, the latter after Bosnich fell over and dropped the ball.

1997 Another day, another new name for the vacant manager's job – Luis Van Gaal of Ajax.

JANUARY 12TH

1895	Woolwich Arsenal	(a) 2–3	Division Two	Dickson, Willis	5000
1901	Stoke	(a) 0–2	Division One	No Scorer	6000
1907	Crystal Palace	(h) 0–1	FA Cup 1st Round	No Scorer	28000

An early giantkilling act, as non-league Palace knocked out the previous season's finalists at the first hurdle. Former Magpie Richard Roberts was in the victorious Palace side.

1921	Nottingham Forest	(h) 2–0	FA Cup 1st Round Replay	Seymour, Harris	30278
1924	Portsmouth	(a) 4–2	FA Cup 1st Round	Seymour, Harris, J. Low, Gibson	26422
1929	Swindon Town	(a) 0–2	FA Cup 3rd Round	No Scorer	17689
1935	Hull City	(a) 5–1	FA Cup 3rd Round	Bott 2, Cairns, Pearson, OG	23000
1952	Aston Villa	(h) 4–2	FA Cup 3rd Round	Foulkes, Mitchell 2, G. Robledo	56897

With 80 minutes played United were 2–1 down, before Mitchell exploded into life with two late goals and created the fourth for Robledo.

| 1957 | Manchester United | (a) 1–6 | Division One | Milburn | 44911 |

Debut for Malcolm Scott, standing in for the injured Bob Stokoe at centre-half.

| 1974 | Wolverhampton Wanderers | (a) 0–1 | Division One | No Scorer | 22235 |

Only goal struck by John Richards in the first half.

| 1980 | Chelsea | (a) 0–4 | Division Two | No Scorer | 32281 |
| 1983 | Brighton and Hove Albion | (h) 0–1 | FA Cup 3rd Round Replay | No Scorer | 32687 |

Bedlam at St James', as Barnsley referee Trelford Mills disallowed two legitimate United goals in the dying minutes of this third-round cup replay. Peter Ward put the Seagulls ahead before Varadi and Keegan struck in vain.

1985	Everton	(a) 0–4	Division One	No Scorer	32156
1989	It's goodbye to Dave Beasant, who lurched off to join Chelsea for £750,000.				
1991	Blackburn Rovers	(h) 1–0	Division Two	Mitchell	16382

The only goal of Dave Mitchell's short career on Tyneside came on his debut.

| 1996 | Amid much press speculation, Kevin Keegan ruled himself of the running for the vacant position of England manager. | | | | |

JANUARY 13TH

1894	Northwich Victoria	(h) 3–0	Division Two	Crate 3	2000
1900	Blackburn Rovers	(h) 4–1	Division One	MacFarlane, Peddie 2, Carr	11000
1906	Grimsby Town	(h) 6–0	FA Cup 1st Round	Gosnell, Orr 2, Appleyard 2, J. Rutherford	23672

The Mariners were first out of the bag, but elected to play the game on Tyneside for financial reasons.

1912	Derby County	(a) 0–3	FA Cup 1st Round	No Scorer	21500
1923	Southampton	(h) 0–0	FA Cup 1st Round	No Scorer	28287
1932	Blackpool	(h) 1–0	FA Cup 3rd Round Replay	Boyd	46104
1934	Wolverhampton Wanderers	(a) 0–1	FA Cup 3rd Round	No Scorer	33850
1951	Chelsea	(a) 1–3	Division One	Mitchell	43840
1954	Wigan Athletic	(a) 3–2	FA Cup 3rd Round Replay	Broadis, Keeble, White	26500
1960	Wolverhampton Wanderers	(a) 2–4	FA Cup 3rd Round Replay	Eastham, White	39082

The Wolves went on to beat Blackburn in what was remembered as one of the worst Wembley finals.

| 1962 | Plymouth Argyle | (a) 1–1 | Division Two | Allchurch | 17457 |
| 1968 | Nottingham Forest | (h) 0–0 | Division One | No Scorer | 43274 |

Debut for Jackie Sinclair.

| 1971 | Ipswich Town | (a) 1–2 | FA Cup 3rd Round Replay | Robson | 21449 |

Colin Viljoen and Mick Hill cancelled out a scrambled Pop Robson effort, with Peter Morris prompting the home team from midfield. Morris was later to coach United under the reign of McGarry.

| 1973 | Bournemouth | (h) 2–0 | FA Cup 3rd Round | Macdonald, OG | 33930 |
| 1990 | Leicester City | (h) 5–4 | Division Two | McGhee 2, Quinn 2, Gallacher | 20785 |

A memorable introduction to English football for debutant Roy Aitken, United coming back from a 4–2 deficit with only minutes left to take all the points. Tommy Wright (not that one) having given the Foxes the lead, McGhee's header was adjudged to have crossed the line and Anderson had a penalty well saved by Martin Hodge. Further goals by Steve Walsh, Gary McAllister and on-loan Kevin Campbell appeared to have won it, but substitute John Gallagher began the fightback on 80 minutes. A typical Quinn finish levelled it before McGhee's trademark turn on the edge of the box and crisp shot at the Gallowgate end completed the revival.

JANUARY 14TH

1893	Sheffield United	(h) 1–1	Friendly	OG	3000
1899	Notts County	(a) 1–3	Division One	Peddie	12000
1905	Everton	(a) 1–2	Division One	Howie	27000
1911	Bury	(h) 6–1	FA Cup 1st Round	Shepherd 3, Stewart, Duncan, McWilliam	32000
1922	Manchester United	(a) 1–0	Division One	McDonald	20000
1928	Blackburn Rovers	(a) 1–4	FA Cup 3rd Round	Seymour	27652

A convincing third-round defeat by the eventual FA Cup winners.

| 1933 | Leeds United | (h) 0–3 | FA Cup 3rd Round | No Scorer | 47554 |

A debut for Johnny Dryden couldn't prevent the FA Cup holders being comprehensively beaten in their first defence.

1939	Burnley	(a) 0–2	Division Two	No Scorer	11098
1950	Charlton Athletic	(h) 1–0	Division One	G. Robledo	48557
1953	Swansea Town	(h) 3–0	FA Cup 3rd Round	Davies, Keeble, Mitchell	61064
1956	Luton Town	(h) 4–0	Division One	Curry, Davies, Keeble 2	21464

1958 Death of Bill Appleyard, United's battering ram of the early 1900s who averaged a goal every other game, many of them involving the goalkeeper being propelled into the net still clutching the ball.

| 1961 | Nottingham Forest | (h) 2–2 | Division One | White, Woods | 25845 |

Debut for Ken Hodgson, standing in for Gordon Hughes.

| 1967 | Burnley | (a) 2–0 | Division One | Bennett, Robson | 17369 |

1968 Ruel Fox born, Ipswich.

| 1970 | Southampton | (a) 1–1 | Fairs Cup 3rd Round 2nd Leg | Robson | 25182 |
| 1976 | Tottenham Hotspur | (a) 0–1 | League Cup Semi-Final 1st Leg | No Scorer | 40215 |

A battling performance in the capital saw United bring a single-goal deficit back to Gallowgate in this first leg of the League Cup semi-final. Only a remarkable save from Jennings to a Craig shot prevented an even better outcome.

| 1978 | Middlesbrough | (h) 2–4 | Division One | McGhee, Cassidy | 34460 |

Stuart Boam, Stan Cummins and a pair from Billy Ashcroft put another nail in United's First Division coffin. The game marked the last appearances of Aidan McCaffery and Tony Smith, while youngster Kevin Carr made way for Mahoney until near the end of the season.

| 1989 | Aston Villa | (a) 1–3 | Division One | Mirandinha (pen) | 21010 |

At the height of West Midlands police paranoia, United fans were lectured before kick-off and told that 'raising your hands above your head will result in ejection'. The fans failed this test when Wharton earned a penalty and Mirandinha converted it in front of the joyous away section. Reality intervened as debutant Tommy Wright picked efforts from Andy Gray, Tony Daley and Alan McInally out of his net. Frank Pingel came on as a substitute and looked utterly lost.

| 1996 | Coventry | (a) 1–0 | Premier League | Watson | 20547 |

A third away trip within eight days (all of them live on TV) and at last a victory. Highfield Road resembled Cullercoats beach and the donkey was one-time Newcastle target John Salako, who lost possession to Steve Watson. He scored from close range and a nervous three points were collected.

1997 At a 6 p.m. press conference, Kenny Dalglish was confirmed as Newcastle manager.

JANUARY 15TH

1897 Bert Chandler born, Carlisle.

| 1898 | Darwen | (h) 1–0 | Division Two | OG | 10000 |

Only senior appearance for Bishop Auckland-born John Allen, who played at centre-forward. Newcastle were fined £10 after illegally poaching him from his hometown club.

| 1910 | Stoke | (a) 1–1 | FA Cup 1st Round | Howie | 18080 |

A creditable draw at The Victoria Ground, especially as United's players were suffering from the effects of a gas leak in the train carriage that had brought them down from Newcastle.

1921	Bradford City	(h) 4–0	Division One	Smailes 2, Harris, Aitken	40000
1927	Aston Villa	(a) 2–1	Division One	Gallacher, McDonald	50000
1930	York City	(a) 2–1	FA Cup 3rd Round Replay	Gallacher, Hutchinson	12583
1938	Sheffield United	(a) 0–4	Division Two	No Scorer	15000
1949	Burnley	(h) 1–1	Division One	Houghton	33439
1966	Tottenham Hotspur	(a) 2–2	Division One	Bennett, Suddick	26683
1969	Real Zaragoza (Spain)	(h) 2–1	Fairs Cup 3rd Round 2nd Leg	Gibb, Robson	56055
1983	Queens Park Rangers	(a) 0–2	Division Two	No Scorer	13972
1992	Bournemouth	(h) 0–0	FA Cup 3rd Round Replay	No Scorer	20000

Referee Vic Callow called a halt after 17 minutes of this fog-bound farce and abandoned the tie some 40 minutes later after conducting fruitless tests with an orange ball and allowing the police to take up their pitchside positions. Suggestions that the match should never have started and consequently the spectators would have been entitled to a refund were rebuffed by United. However, they did bow to public pressure and reduced ticket prices for the restaged game.

| 1995 | Manchester United | (h) 1–1 | Premier League | Kitson | 34471 |

Feelings were running so high on Tyneside that the recently departed Andy Cole and newly arrived Keith Gillespie missed the game on police advice. Cole's predecessor Mark Hughes opened the scoring, but in doing so collided with Srnicek and was stretchered off. Kitson equalised with a six-yarder through Schmeichel's legs. A traumatic week ended with the St James' crowd chanting Keegan's name. The match was played on a Sunday and covered live by Sky.

| 1997 | Charlton Athletic | (h) 2–1 | FA Cup 3rd Round Replay | Clark, Shearer | 36398 |

Kenny Dalglish was introduced to the crowd as the new manager. Clark forced in the first goal of the post-Keegan era but Mark Robson beat Hislop to bring Charlton level. With extra time looming and the mists descending, Shearer ensured a happy ending with a free-kick at the Leazes end that was a replica of his home-debut strike against Wimbledon.

JANUARY 16TH

1897	Blackpool	(h) 4–1	Division Two	Wardrope, Smellie, Collins, Auld	8000
1904	Everton	(h) 1–0	Division One	Appleyard	16000
1909	Clapton Orient	(h) 5–0	FA Cup 1st Round	Anderson, Shepherd, Wilson 3	23670
1913	Bradford City	(h) 1–0	FA Cup 3rd Round	G. Wilson	11953
1915	West Ham United	(h) 3–2	FA Cup 3rd Round Replay	Pailor 2, Hibbert	28130

Newcastle triumphed narrowly in this third-round replay, Alf Leafe and Casey netting for the visitors.

| 1926 | Notts County | (a) 3–1 | Division One | Gallacher 2, McDonald | 15000 |
| 1932 | Grimsby Town | (h) 2–0 | Division One | Cape 2 | 28000 |

The only appearance of striker Joe Ford, who sustained a double fracture of the leg on his debut and never played for the Magpies again.

| 1937 | Preston North End | (a) 0–2 | FA Cup 3rd Round | No Scorer | 25387 |

1951	Alex Cropley born, Aldershot.				
1954	Bolton Wanderers	(a) 2–2	Division One	Keeble, Broadis	30000
1959	Stuart Robinson born, Middlesbrough.				
1960	Preston North End	(a) 2–1	Division One	Eastham, OG	24355
1965	Coventry City	(a) 4–5	Division Two	McGarry 2, Hilley 2	28038

1967 Middlesbrough defeated Carlisle United 4–1 at St James' Park in a second replay of their third-round FA Cup tie. Future Magpie Arthur Horsfield scored the final 'Boro goal in front of 21347.

1971	Nottingham Forest	(a) 1–2	Division One	Robson	21978

Following the midweek FA Cup exit to Ipswich Town, Joe Harvey missed this defeat as he was elsewhere scouting for new talent to add to his squad, including a young centre-forward playing for Luton Town named Macdonald.

1979	Torquay United	(h) 3–1	FA Cup 3rd Round	Robinson, Withe, Nattrass (pen)	21366
1982	Watford	(a) 3–2	Division Two	Varadi, Todd 2	12333

A pair for Wearsider Kevin Todd in his first start for Newcastle.

1989	Watford	(h) 0–0	FA Cup 3rd Round 2nd Replay	No Scorer	28498

Stalemate again, despite another bout of extra time.

1991	Brighton and Hove Albion	(a) 2–4	Division Two	Quinn, Brock	7684

1991 The first appearance of goalkeeper Pavel Srnicek, in a home reserve match against Rotherham. On loan from Banik Ostrava initially for a month and only knowing a couple of words of English, he didn't have the best of debuts as United lost 3–1. The only goal for the home side was scored by Neil Simpson.

1993	Peterborough United	(h) 3–0	Division Two	Lee 2, Kelly	29155

High winds battered Tyneside as Newcastle battered a Posh side including on-loan David Roche making his debut.

1994	Queens Park Rangers	(a) 2–1	Premier League	Clark, Beardsley	15774

Lee Clark set United on their way to victory when he shot through Rangers defender Darren Peacock's legs. Gary Penrice equalised by half-time, but a memorable volley from Beardsley sealed it for the visitors. Another Sunday afternoon game, covered live by Sky.

JANUARY 17TH

1903	Sheffield Wednesday	(a) 0–3	Division One	No Scorer	12000
1914	West Bromwich Albion	(h) 3–3	Division One	Hardy, McDonald, Shepherd	18200

Debuts for Bill Mellor in goal and Jimmy Spink at right-half.

1920	Oldham Athletic	(a) 0–1	Division One	No Scorer	20460
1921	Charlie Mitten born, Rangoon, Burma. Former manager.				
1923	Southampton	(a) 1–3	FA Cup 1st Round Replay	Harris	20060
1925	Arsenal	(a) 2–0	Division One	Harris, Seymour	30000
1931	Manchester United	(h) 4–3	Division One	Bedford 2, Boyd, Hutchinson	20000

Interesting debut for locally born centre-half James Robinson, who never played again.

1948	Brentford	(a) 0–1	Division Two	No Scorer	32000

Debut for Wille McCall, at outside-left.

1953	Burnley	(h) 0–0	Division One	No Scorer	49366
1959	Tottenham Hotspur	(h) 1–2	Division One	White	32503
1970	Wolverhampton Wanderers	(a) 1–1	Division One	Guthrie	29665
1976	Aston Villa	(a) 1–1	Division One	Gowling	36389

1981   Luton Town   (a) 1–0   Division One   Harford   10774
A rare away win after Harford's soft shot somehow went in and Kevin Carr saved a Moses penalty. After 491 barren minutes, the goal drought was finally over.

1996   Chelsea   (h) 2–2   FA Cup 3rd Round   Albert, Beardsley (pen)   36535
                               Replay
Penalty shoot-out debacle part 87. Yet another cup exit on penalties as Chelsea triumphed in this replay, equalising right at the end of extra time through Gullit. Darren Peacock was dismissed following a tackle on Wise, who recovered to score the resultant penalty, but debutant substitute Darren Huckerby showed glimpses of his talent and nearly settled it with a mazy run and shot at the Leazes end. In the shoot-out at the same end, Beardsley hit the bar, Watson had his saved, Beresford and Albert netted, but Chelsea scored all theirs, Eddie Newton settling it. Former Magpie Gavin Peacock also beat Srnicek.

1998   Bolton Wanderers   (h) 2–1   Premier League   Barnes, Ketsbaia   36767
When Nathan Blake equalised for the visitors, the celebrations of the travelling fans were drowned out by the ovation that greeted Alan Shearer returning to the team as a substitute, former captain Peter Beardsley leading the applause. Shearer then headed the ball down for Ketsbaia to net a late winner, the Georgian celebrating as if possessed by demons, tossing his shirt into the Gallowgate end and kicking seven bells out an advertising hoarding. Bemused team-mates eventually calmed him down long enough to play out the last seconds.

JANUARY 18TH

1896   Woolwich Arsenal   (h) 3–1   Division Two   McKay, Stott, Miller   6000
1902   Everton   (h) 1–1   Division One   Roberts   17000
1908   Bristol City   (h) 2–0   Division One   McClarence, Soye   30000
1913   Chelsea   (a) 0–1   Division One   No Scorer   45000
1930   Leicester City   (a) 1–6   Division One   Hutchinson   15000
       Jackie Cape made his debut, at outside-right.
1936   Manchester United   (a) 1–3   Division Two   Ware   22000
1947   Tottenham Hotspur   (h) 1–0   Division Two   Shackleton   62873
1954   Jeff Clarke born, Hemsworth, Pontefract. Free transfer defender who suffered numerous spells sidelined through injury at United and eventually joined the backroom staff.
1958   Chelsea   (a) 1–2   Division One   White   37327
1961   Peter Beardsley MBE born, Longbenton. Two inspirational spells at United.
1964   Grimsby Town   (h) 4–0   Division Two   Thomas 2, Anderson 2   23681
1969   Arsenal   (h) 2–1   Division One   Davies, Robson   34227
       Arsenal's consolation came from Bobby Gould.
1975   Manchester City   (a) 1–5   Division One   Macdonald   32021
1981   Death of Duggie Livingstone, 82. Former manager.
1982   Colchester   (a) 4–3   FA Cup 3rd Round   Waddle, Saunders, Brownlie,   7505
                               Replay   Varadi
An absolute battle, with spectacular goals from Waddle, Saunders and Brownlie and Kevin Carr conceding two penalties. The majority of Newcastle fans attempted to keep track of the evening's events via a local-radio commentator who gave the impression of never having seen a football before, never mind a microphone. Both Saunders and Brownlie had previously failed to score in a competitive match for United, in Brownlie's case after nearly 100 games.

1982   Death of Benny Craig, 66. A great servant to Newcastle in 40 years of service. Initially a full-back, he then coached the juniors, including their 1962 Youth Cup success.

1986   Queens Park   (a) 1–3   Division One   Gascoigne   13159
       Rangers
1988   Queen of the South   (a) 4–0   Friendly   Goddard 2, Lormor, P. Jackson   2500
1989   Watford   (a) 0–1   FA Cup 3rd Round   No Scorer   24065
                               3rd Replay
Fourth time unlucky, as Glenn Roeder diverted a shot past the helpless Tommy Wright to win it for Watford deep into extra time.

1992 Charlton Athletic (h) 3–4 Division Two Clark, Hunt, Brock 15663
For 79 minutes of this game Newcastle were in control and comfortably leading 3–1. Ten minutes later they were drawing 3–3 and Liam O'Brien was in the act of deflecting the ball past his own keeper to win it for Charlton. Even by Newcastle's standards, this was a spectacular capitulation.

1995 Blackburn Rovers (a) 2–1 FA Cup 3rd Round Hottiger, Clark 22658
Replay
A storming cup replay televised live by Sky saw a memorable free-kick struck by Hottiger and a late winner from Lee Clark send the travelling fans in the Darwen Stand wild. Sutton scored for Rovers.

1997 Southampton (a) 2–2 Premier League Ferdinand, Clark 15251
Beardsley led out the team on his 36th birthday, but going two up with only eight minutes remaining simply inspired the Saints, and Maddison pulled one back straight away. A last-minute equaliser from guess who spoiled Kenny's first Premier League game in charge and continued to remind us all by being included in the BBC *Match of the Day* opening titles.

JANUARY 19TH

1895 Sunderland (h) 1–4 Friendly Smith 8000
1901 West Bromwich (h) 1–1 Division One Peddie 10500
Albion
1907 Everton (a) 0–3 Division One No Scorer 45000
1910 Stoke (h) 2–1 FA Cup 1st Round Higgins, Howie 14545
Replay
1924 Tottenham Hotspur (a) 0–2 Division One No Scorer 25649
1929 Bury (a) 0–2 Division One No Scorer 12000
Debut for George Mathison, at right-half.
1935 Fulham (h) 1–1 Division Two OG 25000
Debut for Stan Docking at inside-left.
1942 Ken Hodgson born, Newcastle.
1945 Bobby Moncur born, Perth, Scotland.
1952 Burnley (a) 1–2 Division One Milburn 33719
1957 Arsenal (h) 3–1 Division One Curry, White 2 46815
1959 Chelsea (h) 1–4 FA Cup 3rd Round Eastham 57038
1963 Plymouth Argyle (a) 2–0 Division Two Thomas, McGarry 11940
1974 West Ham United (h) 1–1 Division One Macdonald 27217
The points were shared after Pat Holland equalised for the visitors.
1980 Orient (h) 2–0 Division Two Connolly, Barton 20954
The two points gained from this victory put United back on top of Division Two, but a steady decline and loss of form in front of goal saw them dwindle away to ninth by the end of the season.
1985 United's home game with Leicester fell victim to heavy snowfalls on Tyneside, and Jack Charlton and the team jetted off to Spain for a few days.
1991 Millwall (a) 1–0 Division Two Peacock 11478
The usual warm welcome at Cold Blow Lane, but once Gavin Peacock had netted the whole team defended well – including substitute Darren Bradshaw, for once. On-trial striker Dave Mitchell missed the game through injury and never got another chance to win a contract. He was eventually to sign for Millwall.
1993 Former Newcastle striker Peter Withe was sacked as manager of Wimbledon, after only 105 days in charge.

JANUARY 20TH

1894 Rotherham Town (a) 1–2 Division Two Wallace 1000
1900 Derby County (a) 1–2 Division One Stevenson 10000

Goals from John Boag and, inevitably, Steve Bloomer gave Derby the points but United still finished one place ahead of them, in fifth spot.

1906	Everton	(h) 4–2	Division One	Orr, Appleyard, Howie, J. Rutherford	22000
1912	Woolwich Arsenal	(h) 1–2	Division One	Stewart	10000
1923	Chelsea	(a) 0–3	Division One	No Scorer	30000
1934	Derby County	(a) 1–1	Division One	J.R. Richardson	19989

1947 Jimmy Smith born, Glasgow.

1948 Tot Winstanley born, Croxdale, Durham. Centre-half whose finest performance came in the away leg of the Fairs Cup encounter with Sporting Lisbon, deputising for John McNamee.

1951	Burnley	(h) 2–1	Division One	Milburn 2	40666
1962	Huddersfield Town	(h) 1–1	Division Two	Wilson	31950

Debut for Barrie Thomas.

1968	Coventry City	(a) 4–1	Division One	Davies, T. Robson, Scott, Sinclair	33760

Triumph for Newcastle but tragedy for Albert Bennett, who was helped from the field after damaging a cartilage in the first 20 minutes. England manager Sir Alf Ramsey was sitting in the stand, having travelled to watch Bennett with a view to granting him an England Under-23 cap.

1971 Peter Garland born, Croydon, Surrey. Diminutive midfielder who never made an impact. Last seen playing for non-league Dulwich Hamlet, who were managed by his father . . .

1973	Crystal Palace	(h) 2–0	Division One	Hibbitt, Nattrass	24676

1979 Death of Bill McCracken, nine days short of his 96th birthday. A Newcastle legend, famed for popularising the offside trap, Bill won three League championships and an FA Cup winners' medal during his 19 years of service with the club.

1990	Oldham Athletic	(a) 1–1	Division Two	McGhee	11190

A dark and gloomy afternoon at Boundary Park on the plastic pitch, where Andy Ritchie scored the opener and McGhee replied.

1993	Southend United	(a) 1–1	Division Two	Peacock	8246

Stan Collymore equalised and former Magpie John Cornwell played for the Shrimpers in this rearranged match, brought forward from February to avoid clashing with a Young Conservatives Conference!

1996	Bolton Wanderers	(h) 2–1	Premier League	Kitson, Beardsley	36543

Kitson opened the Scorer with a header in the mould of the absent Ferdinand. Bolton, prompted by Scott Sellars (who received a good reception), levelled through Bergsson. Beardsley hit a a typical late winner, his 100th goal in a black-and-white shirt. The three points sent United 12 points clear of their Premiership pursuers.

1998	Liverpool	(a) 0–1	Premier League	No Scorer	42791

'Young' Michael Owen scored.

JANUARY 21ST

1892	Middlesbrough	(h) 2–3	FA Cup 1st Round	Reay, Thompson	4000

The first time the club had competed in the FA Cup under the name 'Newcastle United'. Rumours of bribery surrounded this match, with accusations of Newcastle players not trying and 'Boro offering incentives to switch the tie to Teeside. In the final, West Bromwich Albion defeated neighbours Aston Villa at the Kennington Oval, the last time the original final venue hosted the match.

1899	Stoke	(h) 3–0	Division One	Peddie 2, Rogers	12000

1901 Harry Wake born, Seaton Delaval. After a limited run at right-half, he moved to Cardiff City for £200 in 1923 where he appeared in the 1925 FA Cup final (and gave the winning goal away).

1905	Small Heath	(h) 0–1	Division One	No Scorer	24000
1911	Tottenham Hotspur	(h) 1–1	Division One	Low	22000

| 1922 | Birmingham | (a) 4–0 | Division One | Dixon, Finlay, Low, Hudspeth (pen) | 20000 |
| 1928 | Manchester United | (h) 4–1 | Division One | McKay, Seymour, Wilkinson 2 | 25000 |

Debut for Willie Gillespie.

| 1933 | Leicester City | (h) 2–1 | Division One | Boyd, J. Richardson | 20000 |
| 1939 | Cardiff City | (a) 0–0 | FA Cup 4th Round | No Scorer | 42060 |

Debut for goalkeeper Cam Theaker.

| 1950 | Manchester City | (a) 1–1 | Division One | Hannah | 42986 |

The sole appearance of reserve centre-forward Andy Graver, who moved to Lincoln City where he became a Sincil Bank legend. An executive suite in the South Park Stand is now named after him.

1956	Charlton Athletic	(a) 2–0	Division One	Casey, Mitchell	34414
1961	Manchester City	(a) 3–3	Division One	Allchurch, White, Woods	19746
1967	Nottingham Forest	(h) 0–0	Division One	No Scorer	37079
1976	Tottenham Hotspur	(h) 3–1	League Cup Semi-Final 2nd Leg	Gowling, Keeley, Nulty	49902

United qualified for their first League Cup final 3–2 on aggregate, getting off to a flyer as the Londoners waited for an offside that never came and Gowling beat Pat Jennings. A fine header from Keeley put United on their way and Nulty finished it before Don McAllister pulled one back. Joyous scenes followed the final whistle as the players embarked on a lap of honour in front of delirious supporters. Even Gordon Lee was seen to smile, allegedly.

1978	West Ham United	(a) 0–1	Division One	No Scorer	25461
1984	Crystal Palace	(a) 1–3	Division Two	Beardsley	9464
1984	Heavy metal shouter and United fan Brian Johnson was turned down as he attempted to buy his way onto the United Board.				
1987	Northampton Town	(h) 2–1	FA Cup 3rd Round	A. Thomas, Goddard	23177

The Fourth Division leaders were managed by Geordie Graham Carr, who once had a trial for United. They brought a good following but never really threatened an upset, thankfully.

| 1989 | Charlton Athletic | (h) 0–2 | Division One | No Scorer | 19076 |

The ground echoed to the chant of 'Sack the Board' as future Magpies star Robert Lee scored a goal in each half, assisted by fellow striker Garth Crooks.

| 1995 | Sheffield Wednesday | (a) 0–0 | Premier League | No Scorer | 31215 |

The second and final outing for the green away strip was a totally forgettable bore draw. Former Magpie favourite Chris Waddle appeared for the home side and received the usual abuse, while the only bright spot was the form of debutant substitute Keith Gillespie. Chris Woods had a rare outing in goal for the Owls but was never tested, while Paul Kitson received such abuse from callers to BBC Radio's '606' programme that Keegan turned off the radio on the team bus to spare his embarrassment.

JANUARY 22ND

1898	Leicester Fosse	(h) 4–2	Division Two	Aitken, Peddie 3	10000
1910	Nottingham Forest	(a) 1–0	Division One	McWilliam	8000
1921	Bradford City	(a) 1–1	Division One	Ward	19000
1927	Bolton Wanderers	(h) 1–0	Division One	McKay	57000
1938	Grimsby Town	(h) 3–3	Friendly	Imrie 2, Cairns	19000
1948	Dennis Laughton born, Dingwall, Scotland.				
1949	Stoke City	(a) 1–1	Division One	Milburn	25000
1955	Burnley	(a) 1–0	Division One	Hannah	23460
1959	Rob Macdonald born, Hull. Widely travelled striker who thankfully continued to travel . . .				
1966	Chester City	(a) 3–1	FA Cup 3rd Round	Robson, McGarry, Craig	18251
1969	Shaka Hislop born, Hackney.				
1972	Tottenham Hotspur	(h) 3–1	Division One	Tudor, Macdonald, Nattrass	30113
1977	Derby County	(a) 2–4	Division One	T. Craig (pen), Gowling	23036

The Rams chose to issue a newspaper for this fixture rather than the usual programme. Rams scorers were two for Derek Hales, and one each for Roy McFarland and Steve Powell.

1983 Shrewsbury Town (h) 4–0 Division One Wharton 2, Varadi, 19333
Keegan (pen)

1992 AFC Bournemouth (h) 2–2 FA Cup 3rd Round Hunt 2 25954
Replay

An early goal from Gavin Peacock, later given to Andy Hunt who followed the ball in, was equalised with seven minutes remaining to set up extra time. By then United were down to ten men, Thompson having been dismissed for dancing on an opponent's ankles. The extra half-hour mirrored the first 90 minutes as Hunt struck straight away and Kevin Bond equalised in the last seconds to force a penalty shoot-out. Inevitably, Newcastle lost 4–3, O'Brien and Brock missing, Watson, Peacock and Matty Appleby netting. Tommy Wright failed to save any of Bournemouth's efforts.

1994 Southampton (h) 1–2 Premier League Cole 32067

Andy Cole struck to become the quickest Newcastle player ever to reach 30 goals. However, the new Saints management team of Alan Ball and Lawrie McMenemy got off to a winning start, thanks to a header by Darlington-born Neill Maddison and a late free-kick by some bloke from the Channel Islands, who left Hooper rooted to the spot.

JANUARY 23RD

1897 Woolwich Arsenal (h) 2–0 Division Two Aitken, Auld 6000
1901 Jerry Best born, Mickley, Northumberland. After failing to break into the first team other than odd runouts, Best emigrated to the USA and played for a variety of fledgling soccer outfits, including Pawtucket Rangers and New Bedford Whalers.
1904 Stoke (a) 3–2 Division One McColl, Appleyard 2 8000
1907 Ron Williams born, Llansamlet, Wales. Welsh international forward and cricketer.
1909 Notts County (a) 4–0 Division One Shepherd 4 20000
Amazingly, Albert Shepherd had agreed prior to the game that he would leave the pitch early to catch a train, had he completed a hat-trick. In the event he hit four and left the game after 80 minutes.
1915 Bradford City (a) 1–1 Division One Pailor 12000
1917 Bob Fraser born, Glasgow. Right-back for United and subsequently a scout.
1926 Aston Villa (h) 2–2 Division One McDonald, Hudspeth (pen) 40000
1932 Southport (h) 1–1 FA Cup 4th Round Boyd 50155
1937 Blackpool (h) 1–2 Division Two Pearson 34000
1954 Preston North End (h) 0–4 Division One No Scorer 40340
1960 Leicester City (h) 0–2 Division One No Scorer 32353
1965 Cardiff City (h) 2–0 Division Two Hilley, Anderson 37291
1971 Sunderland (h) 1–1 Friendly Moncur 16650
Willie McFaul saved a penalty at the Gallowgate end from Gordon Harris.
1978 Tommy Craig left United as the internal divisions at the club grew wider, signing for Aston Villa for £270,000.
1982 Grimsby Town (h) 1–2 FA Cup 4th Round OG 25632
Mariner Phil Crosby netted a late consolation for the Magpies in this hugely disappointing fourth-round encounter. Bearded keeper Nigel Batch kept out countless efforts from Waddle and Varadi, the latter hitting the bat in a frantic finale.
1988 Tottenham Hotspur (h) 2–0 Division One Gascoigne 2 24616
The start of a brief Newcastle career for substitute Anth Lormor.
1990 Middlesbrough (a) 0–1 Zenith Data No Scorer 16948
Systems Cup
Cooper struck a last-minute winner to seal a place in the Zenith Data Systems Northern area final, which later led to 'Boro's first Wembley cup final. In common with their subsequent appearances, they were well beaten.
1993 Rotherham United (a) 1–1 FA Cup 4th Round Lee 13405

United fans fought with locals on the Tivoli end in this dramatic cup-tie, played in front of Millmoor's first full house since 1971. The home side sought to cash in by increasing ticket prices for the away fans, but Newcastle refused to charge the extra £2.50 to their fans and reported Rotherham to the FA. Nigel Johnson equalised with his knee as an indirect free-kick rebounded off Srnicek's post, while 35-year-old Tony Cunningham led the line for the Millers against one of his former clubs.

JANUARY 24TH

Year	Opponent	Venue	Score	Competition	Scorer	Attendance
1903	West Bromwich Albion	(h)	1–0	Division One	Andrew Gardner	22000
1914	Sheffield Wednesday	(a)	0–0	Division One	No Scorer	30000

A successful debut at right-back for Billy Hampson, who made 174 appearances before moving to South Shields.

Year	Opponent	Venue	Score	Competition	Scorer	Attendance
1920	Everton	(a)	0–4	Division One	No Scorer	20000

Sadly the youthful goalscoring exploits of debutant Tom Phillipson were lost in this roasting. Fellow debutant Alex Rainnie was never called upon again.

Year	Opponent	Venue	Score	Competition	Scorer	Attendance
1925	Manchester City	(h)	2–0	Division One	Cowan, Urwin	26000
1931	Leeds United	(a)	1–4	FA Cup 4th Round	Hutchinson (pen)	40261
1942	Herbert Garrow born, Elgin, Scotland.					
1948	Leeds United	(a)	1–3	Division Two	Milburn	35000
1953	Preston North End	(a)	1–2	Division One	Brander	26394

One of only two goals for George Brander, and a debut for Stan Keery.

Year	Opponent	Venue	Score	Competition	Scorer	Attendance
1959	Liverpool	(a)	2–2	Friendly	White, Allchurch	18449
1970	Everton	(a)	0–0	Division One	No Scorer	42845
1972	Hereford United	(h)	2–2	FA Cup 3rd Round	Tudor, Macdonald	39381
1974	Alex Bruce signed from Preston for £150,000, as cover for Tudor and Macdonald.					
1976	Coventry City	(a)	1–1	FA Cup 4th Round	Gowling	32004
1976	Death of Bob Pailor, 88. Forward who joined United from West Bromwich Albion as the Great War loomed.					
1977	Sheffield United	(h)	3–0	FA Cup 3rd Round Replay	T. Craig, Burns, McCaffery	36375
1981	Luton Town	(h)	2–1	FA Cup 4th Round	Clarke, Martin	29211
1986	Nottingham Forest	(a)	0–3	Friendly	No Scorer	4000

A friendly match between two clubs dumped out the FA Cup, which took place in Bermuda!

Year	Opponent	Venue	Score	Competition	Scorer	Attendance
1987	Liverpool	(a)	0–2	Division One	No Scorer	38054

JANUARY 25TH

Year	Opponent	Venue	Score	Competition	Scorer	Attendance
1896	Crewe Alexandra	(a)	0–3	Division Two	No Scorer	8000
1902	Woolwich Arsenal	(a)	2–0	FA Cup 1st Round	Veitch, A. Gardner	15000
1908	Nottingham Forest	(a)	0–0	Division One	No Scorer	12000
1913	Woolwich Arsenal	(h)	3–1	Division One	Stewart, Higgins, Hudspeth (pen)	20000

This game marked the only appearance of goalkeeper Jack Alderson, who eventually played for England, following his move to Crystal Palace after the Great War.

Year	Opponent	Venue	Score	Competition	Scorer	Attendance
1930	Clapton Orient	(h)	3–1	FA Cup 4th Round	J.R. Richardson 3	48141
1936	Sheffield Wednesday	(a)	1–1	FA Cup 4th Round	Pearson	25355
1939	Cardiff City	(h)	4–1	FA Cup 3rd Round Replay	Clifton, Gordon, Mooney, Park	44649
1947	Southampton	(h)	3–1	FA Cup 4th Round	Wayman 3	55878
1949	In preparation for the imminent arrival of George Robledo, reserve forward Andy Donaldson was offloaded to 'Boro.					
1958	Scunthorpe	(h)	1–3	FA Cup 4th Round	Paterson	39234
1964	Middlesbrough	(h)	4–3	Friendly	Mahon, Thomas, Burton, McGarry	14455

Two goals for Gibson and one for Peacock as both teams celebrated being out of the FA Cup with a friendly match.

1967   David Ginola born, Gassin, France. Spectacular skills but questionable commitment while wearing a black-and-white shirt. Rotten match summariser during the 1998 World Cup, rivalling Chris Waddle for incoherence.

1969   Manchester City   (h) 0–0   FA Cup 4th Round   No Scorer   57994

1973   Former United player Stan Anderson announced he was stepping down as Middlesbrough manager.

1975   Walsall   (a) 0–1   FA Cup 4th Round   No Scorer   19998
A fruitless trip to Fellows Park, as a first-half George Andrews goal dashed hopes of an early Wembley return. The absence of Tudor through injury gave Paul Cannell an FA Cup debut.

1995   Wimbledon   (h) 2–1   Premier League   Fox, Kitson   34374
A wet and windy night on Tyneside saw Gillespie dazzle on his home debut to such an extent that his marker Kimble was withdrawn at half-time. A nail-biting last ten minutes followed Efan Ekoku's goal, with referee Mike Reed ruling out what would have been a last-minute equaliser from Elkins in dubious circumstances. An incensed Vinnie Jones was later fined by the FA for swearing at Keegan in a tunnel flare-up which required police intervention.

1996   Death of Tim Rogers, 86.

1998   Stevenage Borough (a) 1–1   FA Cup 4th Round   Shearer   8040
After all the bad press, this game eventually took place at Broadhall Way with United fans housed in a wobbly temporary stand behind one goal and a small terrace in front. An early Shearer header gained the initiative, but Stevenage hit back and after having one goal disallowed forced a replay through Grazioli. The final whistle saw a pitch invasion and numerous scuffles broke out as a few United fans clashed with 'home fans' wearing various shirts including Manchester United and West Ham. Sky televised both this and the home replay.

JANUARY 26TH

1907   Woolwich Arsenal   (h) 1–0   Division One   Howie   35000
1924   Tottenham Hotspur   (h) 2–2   Division One   Seymour, McDonald   34000
Debut for James Hunter at left-back.
1931   West Ham United   (a) 2–3   Division One   Bedford, Weaver   10000
Debut for Alec Betton, in defence.
1932   Southport   (a) 1–1   FA Cup 4th Round   Boyd   20010
Replay
The record attendance was set at the home side's Haig Avenue ground in this first replay.
1935   Tottenham Hotspur   (a) 0–2   FA Cup 4th Round   No Scorer   61195
1952   Charlton Athletic   (h) 6–0   Division One   Foulkes, Milburn 2,   45905
G. Robledo 2, Walker
1957   Millwall   (a) 1–2   FA Cup 4th Round   Tait   45646
A cup humbling at the Den by the Lions of the Third Division (South). Both their goals were scored by Stan Anslow, a full-back turned centre-forward.
1969   John Gallacher born, Glasgow. Gifted winger who saw his career curtailed by a shin injury.
1974   Scunthorpe United   (h) 1–1   FA Cup 4th Round   McDermott   38913
Having dealt with Hendon in the previous round, Newcastle again had to resort to a replay after being a goal down following a mistake from Alan Kennedy. With Hibbitt suspended, United struggled against the Fourth Division team until Terry Mac spared their blushes.
1996   Tyneside's first sighting of Faustino Asprilla, who appeared at St James' Park in a fur coat to be greeted by cheering fans and a snow shower. A deal was agreed, but Tino flew back to Italy without having signed a contract.
1997   Nottingham Forest   (h) 1–2   FA Cup 4th Round   Ferdinand   36434

Yet again Ian Woan sunk United, with two long-range strikes in four minutes. Ironically, these were his first goals since the Newcastle game at the City Ground the previous May.

1998 Newcastle reserves lost 3–0 to Barnsley at Gateshead in the Pontins Cup, which managed to be even more unpopular than the Pontins League. French defender David Terrier had a nightmare in the centre of defence, while on-trial Jorge Bohme from TSV Munich 1860 looked a forlorn figure wide on the left.

JANUARY 27TH

Year	Opponent		Competition	Scorer	Attendance
1894	Sheffield United	(h) 2–0	FA Cup 1st Round	Wallace 2	7000
1900	Reading	(h) 2–1	FA Cup 1st Round	Stevenson, Rogers	11259
1906	Derby County	(a) 1–2	Division One	McClarence	7000

Yet another goal for Steve Bloomer.

| 1912 | Manchester City | (a) 1–1 | Division One | Lowes | 28000 |

Sole appearance of inside-right Jack Thomas.

| 1923 | Chelsea | (h) 0–0 | Division One | No Scorer | 15000 |

Debut for James Clark.

| 1934 | West Bromwich Albion | (h) 1–2 | Division One | J.R. Richardson | 22000 |

Debut for John Hughes, a former Durham miner, who had five appearances at left-half.

1949 Newcastle secured the services of both Robledo brothers from Barnsley.

1950 The eve of a fourth-round FA Cup tie away at Chelsea and, as was the practice at the time, the Newcastle team had a night out, at the circus, rather than the usual show. Also in the crowd were the Chelsea team, as well as the Sunderland and Spurs teams, who met each other the day after. There's a joke about clowns here I just can't get right.

1951	Bolton Wanderers	(h) 3–2	FA Cup 4th Round	Milburn 2, Mitchell	67596
1962	Leeds United	(a) 1–0	Division Two	Tuohy	17209
1968	Carlisle United	(h) 0–1	FA Cup 3rd Round	No Scorer	56569

Carlisle keeper Alan Ross guessed correctly and saved a late penalty from Ollie Burton.

| 1973 | Arsenal | (a) 2–2 | Division One | Macdonald, Smith | 37906 |

Ray Kennedy and Alan Ball on target for the Gunners. United sub was full-back Ray Ellison, who wasn't called upon and within a month had moved to Roker Park for £10,000.

| 1979 | Wolverhampton Wanderers | (h) 1–1 | FA Cup 4th Round | Withe | 29561 |

The two Hibbitt brothers faced each other in this tie, with Kenny getting an equalising goal in the final seconds.

| 1990 | Reading | (a) 3–3 | FA Cup 4th Round | McGhee 2, Quinn | 11989 |

United fans threw pies at home supporters as the Royals came from behind to draw level three times, the second and third directly as a result of suicidal backpasses, Michael Gilkes netting courtesy of John Gallacher with the referee about to blow for full-time.

| 1993 | Luton Town | (a) 0–0 | Division One | No Scorer | 10237 |

An uninspiring midweek encounter, which neither side deserved anything from.

1998 Andreas Andersson signed from AC Milan, at a cost of £3 million, to boost an ailing Newcastle attack.

JANUARY 28TH

Year	Opponent		Competition	Scorer	Attendance
1893	Stockton	(a) 2–3	Friendly	Sorley 2	2000
1895	Hulford Comb	(h) 6–1	Friendly	Thompson 2, Willis 2, McNee 2	1000
1899	Glossop	(a) 1–0	FA Cup 1st Round	Peddie	7000
1905	Manchester City	(a) 2–3	Division One	Howie 2	35000
1911	Middlesbrough	(a) 2–0	Division One	Randall, Stewart	20000
1922	Preston North End	(a) 1–3	FA Cup 2nd Round	Seymour	33000
1933	Portsmouth	(a) 0–2	Division One	No Scorer	13000
1939	Southampton	(a) 0–0	Division Two	No Scorer	13000

| 1947 | Burnley | (a) 0–3 | Division Two | No Scorer | 25309 |

1948 Stuart Boam born, Kirkby in Ashfield, Notts.

| 1950 | Chelsea | (a) 0–3 | FA Cup 4th Round | No Scorer | 64446 |
| 1956 | Fulham | (a) 5–4 | FA Cup 4th Round | Casey, Keeble 2, Milburn, Stokoe | 39200 |

A remarkable cup-tie at Craven Cottage. United had a seemingly unassailable lead at 3–0, let it slip to go behind 4–3, then recovered to win it. Fulham's fourth goal was scored by a young Jimmy Hill, complete with beard, while Bobby Robson also appeared for the Cottagers.

1963 Death of Bert Chandler, 66.

| 1967 | Coventry City | (a) 4–3 | FA Cup 3rd Round | Davies 3, Robson | 35569 |

1968 Tony Nesbit born, Sunderland. Former apprentice who made one appearance in midfield.

| 1976 | Coventry City | (h) 5–0 | FA Cup 4th Round Replay | Gowling, Macdonald 2, Cassidy, Burns | 44676 |

Fourth-round replay joy for the Magpies with Supermac at the fore, scoring two and making two. With a League Cup final place secured the previous Wednesday, this was the nearest we've been to a double Wembley appearance.

| 1978 | Wrexham | (h) 2–2 | FA Cup 4th Round | Bird, Blackhall | 29344 |
| 1995 | Swansea City | (h) 3–0 | FA Cup 4th Round | Kitson 3 | 34372 |

A large contingent of travelling Swans and former mackem John Cornforth were on the receiving end of Kitson, who reacted to universal criticism with two headers and a delicate lob to put Newcastle into the fifth round.

JANUARY 29TH

1884 Bill McCracken born, Belfast.

| 1898 | Preston North End | (a) 2–1 | FA Cup 1st Round | Peddie 2 | 15000 |

1917 Jimmy Woodburn born, Rutherglen, Scotland.

| 1921 | Liverpool | (h) 1–0 | FA Cup 2nd Round | Harris | 62073 |
| 1927 | Corinthians | (a) 3–1 | FA Cup 4th Round | McDonald 2, McKay | 56338 |

United triumphed against famed amateur opponents at Selhurst Park. Three late goals booked a fifth-round place after Claude Ashton had given Corinthians the lead in the first half. The match was the first FA Cup tie to be broadcast on radio by the BBC, who helpfully printed a grid of the pitch divided into eight sections in that week's *Radio Times*. Listeners then followed play as the relevant square was announced.

1936	Sheffield Wednesday (h) 3–1		FA Cup 4th Round Replay	Bott 2, J. Smith	27680
1938	Burnley	(a) 1–2	Division Two	Park	9000
1949	Bristol Rovers	(a) 1–1	Friendly	Taylor	25855

With the scores level, Eastville was shrouded in fog after 65 minutes which forced the game to be abandoned.

| 1955 | Brentford | (h) 3–2 | FA Cup 4th Round | Curry, Hannah, Mitchell | 46574 |

1963 Tommy Gaynor born, Limerick, Ireland. Loaned from Forest, Tommy played four games when McGhee was ruled out through injury, but wasn't retained.

| 1966 | Nottingham Forest | (a) 2–1 | Division One | Suddick, Hilley | 21659 |
| 1969 | Manchester City | (a) 0–2 | FA Cup 4th Round Replay | No Scorer | 60844 |

City went on to defeat Leicester City at Wembley.

| 1972 | Huddersfield Town | (a) 0–0 | Division One | No Scorer | 12829 |
| 1977 | Manchester City | (h) 1–3 | FA Cup 4th Round | Gowling | 45300 |

Crowd trouble blighted this fourth-round tie played out as rumours of manager Gordon Lee's departure grew. A clearly demoralised home team went through the motions and angry home fans staged a pitch invasion which held the game up for some time. David Craig put through his own goal to add to the misery.

1986 Peter Beardsley gained his first England cap as Bobby Robson brought him on as a substitute in a 4–0 friendly defeat of Egypt in Cairo.

1994   Luton Town   (h) 1–1   FA Cup 4th Round   Beardsley (pen)   32216
Previously unknown Tony Thorpe looked to have put United out of the cup for another
year until Beardsley was tripped in the box and levelled from the spot. Keegan's post-
match press conference was held on the pitch to highlight its poor state, which was
hampering his team's attempts to play flowing football.

1997   Everton   (h) 4–1   Premier League   Lee, Shearer, Ferdinand,   36143
                                                           Elliott
Another late show at the Park, as Everton held a lead courtesy of a Gary Speed effort until
well into the second half. Then Lee broke the deadlock, swiftly followed by Alan and Les.
To cap it all, Elliott managed to scrape a fourth past stand-in keeper Paul Gerrard after
having struggled all afternoon to hit a pass to a team-mate. Shearer was presented with an
award before the game to celebrate his being voted third-best player in the world in a FIFA
poll.

JANUARY 30TH

1897   Aston Villa   (a) 0–5   FA Cup 1st Round   No Scorer   7000
Villa went on to beat Everton 3–2 in the final to claim the FA Cup.

1904   Derby County   (h) 0–0   Division One   No Scorer   16000
1909   Sheffield Wednesday (h) 1–0   Division One   Veitch   33000
1915   Swansea Town   (h) 1–1   FA Cup 2nd Round   McCracken (pen)   30005
1926   Cardiff City   (a) 2–0   FA Cup 4th Round   Seymour 2   38270
1932   West Ham United   (h) 2–2   Division One   Weaver 2   32000
Debut for Wilf Feeney, at inside-left.

1935   Bradford   (a) 3–1   Division Two   Bott, Williams, Wilson   5000
1937   Blackburn Rovers   (a) 1–6   Division Two   Park   7000
1954   Burnley   (a) 1–1   FA Cup 4th Round   Broadis   53000
1971   Burnley   (a) 1–1   Division One   Barrowclough   12521
First appearance of John Tudor for United.

1974   Scunthorpe United   (a) 3–0   FA Cup 4th Round   Macdonald 2, Barrowclough 19028
                                       Replay
This fourth-round replay at the Old Showground was to be United's last visit to this venue.
By the time they met again in 1993, Scunthorpe played at Glanford Park on the outskirts
of the town and the Old Showground was a supermarket.

1977   Gordon Lee announced he was leaving United to take up a lucrative contract as Everton
manager. His decision was to prompt the sorry player power episode that eventually saw
the club slip down the league and into Division Two.

1982   Norwich City   (h) 2–1   Division Two   Varadi, Mills   14492
Goalscoring debut for on-loan David Mills, who bucked the trend by eventually signing
permanently for United.

1988   Swindon Town   (h) 5–0   FA Cup 4th Round   D. Jackson, Goddard, O'Neill, 28699
                                                           Gascoigne 2 (1 pen)
Laugh if you may, but this victory indirectly resulted in Sunderland's promotion two years
later. An inquiry into alleged betting by then Swindon manager Lou Macari, who put money
on Newcastle to win this match, spread to encompass all financial aspects of the Wiltshire
club. Further irregularities came to light, and Swindon were then refused entry to the First
Division, despite beating Sunderland in a one-sided Wembley play-off final. For reasons never
explained, Sunderland then took their place (but not for long). In the match itself, Neil
McDonald missed one penalty and refused to take another, leaving it to Gazza, who scored.

1998   Newcastle signed Andrew Griffin from cash-strapped Stoke City in a £1.5 million deal,
plus the promise to play a friendly at the new Britannia Stadium.

JANUARY 31ST

1890   Andy Cunningham born, Galston, Scotland.
1903   Notts County   (a) 2–2   Division One   Andrew Gardner, Orr   11000

Debut for Archie Turner, at outside-right.

1903 Jack Allen born, Newburn.

1920 Huddersfield Town (h) 0–1 FA Cup 2nd Round No Scorer 46462
Peter Mooney made his debut in this cup-tie against the eventual losing finalists.

1925 Leicester City (h) 2–2 FA Cup 2nd Round McDonald (pen), Cowan 58713

1931 Bolton Wanderers (h) 4–0 Division One Starling, Hutchinson, Boyd 210000

1934 Ron Greener born, Easington.

1948 Leicester City (h) 2–0 Division Two McCall, Sibley 51675
Debut for Frank Houghton.

1953 Rotherham United (h) 1–3 FA Cup 4th Round Keeble 54356
This cup exit, engineered by the forward play of Len White, prompted Seymour to invest £12,500 in him within days.

1959 Manchester United (a) 4–4 Division One
Allchurch, McGuigan, White 2 48777

1970 Crystal Palace (h) 0–0 Division One No Scorer 36008

1976 Middlesbrough (a) 3–3 Division One Gowling, Nattrass, Kennedy 31000
Willie Maddren, David Mills and a Glen Keeley own goal looked to have won it with only three minutes left but a goal from each of the United full-backs secured a point.

1981 Bolton Wanderers (h) 2–1 Division Two Clarke, Martin 19143

1987 Preston North End (h) 2–0 FA Cup 4th Round Roeder, Goddard 30495

1990 Reading (h) 4–1 FA Cup 4th Round McGhee 2, Quinn, Robinson 26658
Replay revenge over the Royals, Wallsend-born veteran Mick Tait getting a consolation and Walkergate-born David Robinson scoring the only goal of his Newcastle career.

1993 Derby County (h) 1–1 Division One O'Brien 27285
Newcastle fan Tommy Johnson put the Rams ahead after only two minutes of this Sunday televised game. O'Brien equalised in the dying seconds, but United's lead in Division Two was cut to 11 points. Johnson was attacked later in the evening when drinking in the Bigg Market area of the city.

FEBRUARY 1ST

1896 Chesterfield (a) 4–0 FA Cup 1st Round Wardrope 2, Aitken, 5000
Thompson

1902 Small Heath (h) 2–0 Division One Veitch, Carr 13000

1908 West Ham United (h) 2–0 FA Cup 2nd Round Appleyard 2 47285

1913 Hull City (a) 0–0 FA Cup 2nd Round No Scorer 18250

1927 Hugh Cameron born, Burnbank, Scotland.

1930 Huddersfield Town (a) 0–2 Division One No Scorer 15000
Debuts for Dave Davidson and Joe Devine, as United desperately tried to find a winning formula to lift them from the bottom of Division One.

1932 Southport (n) 9–0 FA Cup 4th Round Lang, McMenemy, Cape 2, 19350
2nd Replay Weaver, J.R. Richardson 3,
Boyd
A remarkable end to the three-match tie played at a neutral Hillsborough, where the score was still 0–0 after 41 minutes. Among the defeated Southport team was former Magpie Jack Little.

1936 Fulham (a) 1–3 Division Two Ware 30000

1947 Barnsley (h) 4–2 Division Two Bentley, Shackleton, 40182
Stobbart, Wayman

1958 Sunderland (h) 2–2 Division One Curry, Tait 47739
A second-half revival by the visitors saw them claim a point with goals from Billy Elliott and Alan O'Neill.

1961 Stockport County (h) 4–0 FA Cup 4th Round Allchurch, White, Woods 2 48715

1964 Preston North End (a) 0–3 Division Two No Scorer 18982

1966 Robert Lee born, Plaistow.

1969 Manchester City   (a) 1–1   Division One   Horsfield   30160
Arthur Horsfield marked his United debut with an early goal, but unfortunately torrential rain caused the match to be abandoned shortly before half-time. United lost the rescheduled match 1–0.

1975 Middlesbrough   (h) 2–1   Division One   Macdonald, Burns   42514

1986 Coventry City   (h) 3–2   Division One   Wharton, Beardsley, Allon   16785
The jeers that greeted Coventry debutant and former Sunderland player Nick Pickering were replaced by cheers after 13 minutes when Joe Allon set up Beardsley to open the scoring. Allon himself then curled a beauty in for 2–0 before Cyrille Regis pulled one back as half-time approached. Fellow City debutant Alan Brazil capitalised on an Anderson foul-up before Wharton netted a late winner at the Gallowgate end.

1992 Oxford United   (a) 2–5   Division Two   Scott, Peacock (pen)   5872
Debut for Terry Wilson, on loan from Nottingham Forest. The swirling mists descended on the Manor Ground and neither myself nor Newcastle keeper Tommy Wright could see the ball. My excuse was that my hands were in the way of my eyes, but as for Tommy . . . Rock bottom had been reached, and the final whistle wasn't greeted with any catcalls or jeering from the travelling fans, just a numb silence.

1994 Kevin Scott left St James' after over eight years with the club, signing for Tottenham for a fee of £850,000.

1995 Everton   (h) 2–0   Premier League   Fox, Beardsley (pen)   34465

1998 Aston Villa   (a) 1–0   Premier League   Batty   38266
Debut for striker Andreas Andersson in this Sunday televised Sky match.

FEBRUARY 2ND

1894 William Aitken born, Peterhead, Scotland.

1895 Burnley   (h) 2–1   FA Cup 1st Round   Rendell 2   8000

1903 Hughie Gallacher born, Bellshill, Scotland.

1907 Manchester United (h) 5–0   Division One   Gosnell, Orr, Rutherford,   35000
                                                    Veitch 2

1923 Tot Smith born, Horden.

1924 Derby County   (a) 2–2   FA Cup 2nd Round   McDonald 2   27873

1929 Leicester City   (a) 1–1   Division One   Gallacher   19000
First appearance of Andy Cunningham in a black-and-white shirt, at the age of 38. Within a year he had become United's first manager.

1935 Plymouth Argyle   (h) 3–0   Division Two   McMenemy, Pearson, Smith 22000

1938 Tottenham Hotspur (h) 1–0   Division Two   Cairns   12000

1951 Martin Burleigh born, Durham.

1952 Tottenham Hotspur (a) 3–0   FA Cup 4th Round   Mitchell, G. Robledo   69009
A comprehensive victory at a swamp-like White Hart Lane in this fourth-round tie. Bobby Mitchell was again the inspiration, beating Alf Ramsay on the wing at will.

1957 Burnley   (a) 2–3   Division One   Milburn, Tait   26778

1962 Swansea Town   (a) 2–3   Division Two   Thomas, Wright   20000

1974 Derby County   (a) 0–1   Division One   No Scorer   24992

1980 Leicester City   (a) 0–1   Division Two   No Scorer   24549

1985 West Ham United   (a) 1–1   Division One   Waddle   17723

1991 Port Vale   (h) 2–0   Division Two   Peacock, Quinn   14602

1994 Ruel Fox became the latest recruit to Kevin Keegan's dream team, coming from Norwich for £2.25 million.

1997 Leicester City   (h) 4–3   Premier League   Elliott, Shearer 3   36396

FEBRUARY 3RD

1894 Burslem Port Vale (a) 1–1   Division Two   Wallace   2000

1900 Bury   (h) 2–1   Division One   Stevenson, OG   10000

1906 Derby County   (a) 0–0   FA Cup 2nd Round   No Scorer   18000

1911	Death of Jock Smith, 43 (approximately).				
1934	Birmingham	(a) 2–1	Division One	Weaver, Williams	18000
1951	Arsenal	(a) 0–0	Division One	No Scorer	55073
1954	Burnley	(h) 1–0	FA Cup 4th Round Replay	Mitchell (pen)	48284
1968	Sheffield United	(h) 1–0	Division One	Davies	32191
1968	Darren Peacock born, Bristol.				
1973	Luton Town	(h) 0–2	FA Cup 4th Round	No Scorer	42276

The new East Stand was open for this game, and former popular-siders could now watch their team from an angle previously only available to those who scrambled on to the rooftops of Leazes Terrace. Former Manchester United player John Aston hit both goals as United slipped out of the cup.

1975	Former Magpie Stan Anderson was appointed manager of Doncaster Rovers.				
1979	Orient	(a) 0–2	Division Two	No Scorer	7251
1982	Bolton Wanderers	(h) 2–0	Division Two	Wharton, Trewick (pen)	14714
1993	Rotherham United	(h) 2–0	FA Cup 3rd Round Replay	Kelly, Clark	29005
1996	Sheffield Wednesday	(h) 2–0	Premier League	Ferdinand, Clark	36567

FEBRUARY 4TH

1893	Stockton	(a) 3–1	Friendly	Reay, Crate, Unknown Scorer	1500
1899	Burnley	(h) 4–1	Division One	Peddie, Rogers 2, Lindsay	20000
1904	United signed Andy McCombie from rivals Sunderland.				
1905	Plymouth Argyle	(h) 1–1	FA Cup 1st Round	Gosnell	28385
1911	Northampton	(h) 1–1	FA Cup 2nd Round	Higgins	42023
1922	Arsenal	(a) 1–2	Division One	McDonald	30000

Debut for Harry Woods, at inside-right.

1928	Cardiff City	(h) 2–0	Division One	McKay, Wilkinson	15000
1933	Chelsea	(h) 2–0	Division One	Lang (pen), Allen	30000

Debut for Billy Leighton.

1938	Dave Hollins born, Bangor, Wales.				
1939	Coventry City	(h) 0–4	Division Two	No Scorer	45000

Forgettable debut at centre-half for Dom Kelly. He was never tried again.

1948	Len Shackleton moved from St James' to Roker for a fee of £20,050.				
1950	Fulham	(h) 3–1	Division One	Hannah, G. Robledo, Thompson	41120
1953	Alan Shoulder born, Bishop Auckland.				
1956	Tottenham Hotspur	(h) 1–2	Division One	Paterson	29597
1961	Arsenal	(h) 3–3	Division One	Hughes, Scanlon, White	34394
1967	Fulham	(a) 1–5	Division One	Robson	21612
1984	Portsmouth	(a) 4–1	Division Two	Beardsley 2, Keegan 2	18686
1989	Liverpool	(h) 2–2	Division One	Mirandinha, Pingel	30983

A match played on Saturday afternoon but beamed live to various Scandinavian countries, which accounted for the unpronounceable advertising hoardings for cooked meats circling the Gallowgate pitch. Frank Pingel scored the only goal of his unmemorable time on Tyneside.

1990	Sunderland	(h) 1–1	Division Two	McGhee	31665

Gabbiadini for the mackems.

1992	Death of Alan Davies, 30. An inquest later ruled he had taken his own life.				
1995	Queens Park Rangers	(a) 0–3	Premier League	No Scorer	16576
1998	Stevenage Borough	(h) 2–1	FA Cup 4th Round Replay	Shearer 2	36705

Crawshaw scored for the non-leaguers as a nervous Newcastle advanced into the fifth round after a hotly disputed first goal, which Stevenage claimed had never crossed the line.

FEBRUARY 5TH

1896	Robert Roxburgh born, Morpeth.				
1896	Tom Urwin born, Haswell.				
1898	Derby County	(h) 4–4	Friendly	Aitken, Peddie, Ostler, Allan	7000
1910	Fulham	(h) 4–0	FA Cup 2nd Round	Higgins 2, Rutherford, McCracken (pen)	35846
1913	Hull City	(h) 3–0	FA Cup 2nd Round Replay	Hibbert, Rutherford, Hudspeth (pen)	32278
1921	Chelsea	(a) 0–2	Division One	No Scorer	50000

Debut for Tom Mitchell, at outside-left.

1925	Leicester	(a) 0–1	FA Cup 2nd Round Replay	No Scorer	40350
1927	Derby County	(h) 3–0	Division One	Gallacher, McDonald, Urwin	30000
1936	Port Vale	(h) 2–2	Division Two	J. Smith, Ware	12000
1938	Bury	(h) 1–0	Division Two	Cairns (pen)	20000
1949	Charlton Athletic	(h) 2–0	Division One	Walker 2	56143

Debut for George Robledo, at inside-forward.

1953	Death of Finlay Speedie, 72.				
1955	Leicester City	(h) 2–0	Division One	Hannah, Milburn	36061
1964	England Under-23 defeated Scotland Under-23 3–2 at St James' Park in front of 35,032.				
1966	Sheffield Wednesday	(h) 2–0	Division One	Suddick 2	31207
1972	Hereford United	(a) 1–2	FA Cup 3rd Round Replay	Macdonald	14313

Nightmare on Edgar Street, starring Ronnie Radford, Ricky George, lots of small boys wearing snorkel parkas and United's hellish all-red away strip. Unfortunately John Motson was present to commentate on this match for the BBC and made a whole career from his new-found fame.

1974	Southampton	(a) 1–3	Division One	Macdonald	16497

Debut for Alex Bruce.

1977	Bristol City	(a) 1–1	Division One	Burns	28000
1978	David Burt born, Blyth. A forward player currently appearing for the reserve team.				
1983	Middlesbrough	(a) 1–1	Division Two	Keegan	25184
1991	Pavel Srnicek joined Newcastle for a fee of £350,000 following a successful trial period in the reserves.				

FEBRUARY 6TH

1897	Manchester City	(h) 3–0	Division Two	Wardrope 2, Aitken	9000
1903	Bob Clark born, Newburn.				
1904	Bury	(a) 1–2	FA Cup 1st Round	Templeton	12635
1909	Blackpool	(h) 2–1	FA Cup 2nd Round	Howie, Rutherford	32137
1915	Swansea Town	(a) 2–0	FA Cup 2nd Round Replay	King, Pailor	15000
1924	Derby County	(h) 2–2	FA Cup 2nd Round 1st Replay	Harris, Cowan	50393
1926	West Ham United	(h) 4–1	Division One	Cowan, Gallacher 2, Seymour	28000
1932	Sheffield Wednesday	(a) 0–2	Division One	No Scorer	14000
1937	Bury	(h) 1–3	Division Two	Leighton	22000
1952	West Bromwich Albion triumphed 2–0 at Gallowgate, in a fourth-round cup-tie against Gateshead, in front of 40,000 fans. Such was the interest in the tie that it had been switched from Redheugh Park across the Tyne.				
1954	Tottenham Hotspur	(a) 0–3	Division One	No Scorer	35798
1955	Geordie actor Kevin Whately born. Whately came to prominence playing the part of wimpish Newcastle fan Nev in the hit series *Auf Wiedersehen Pet*.				

1958   Munich air disaster, which claimed the life of former Newcastle player Tom Curry, by then coaching the Busby Babes. Albert Scanlon, later to join Newcastle, escaped with a broken leg.

1960	Burnley	(a) 1–2	Division One	Allchurch	6998
1965	Preston North End	(a) 0–2	Division Two	No Scorer	18961
1970	West Bromwich Albion	(h) 1–0	Division One	Dyson	32054
1971	Chelsea	(h) 0–1	Division One	No Scorer	34336
1978	Wrexham	(a) 1–4	FA Cup 4th Round Replay	Burns	18676

Victory in this replay would have set up a fifth-round meeting with non-league Blyth Spartans.

1982	Cambridge United	(a) 0–1	Division Two	No Scorer	5092
1988	Wimbledon	(a) 0–0	Division One	No Scorer	10505

The most memorable image of this match was Vinnie Jones tightly marking Paul Gascoigne by grabbing hold of his testicles.

1997   Paul Kitson signed for West Ham United at a cost of £2.3 million, to form a striking partnership with the considerably more expensive John Hartson.

1998   Gary Speed signed for United for the outrageous sum of £5.5 million, after a 'reluctant' Everton manager Howard Kendall had held out as United's offers increased.

FEBRUARY 7TH

1903	Grimsby Town	(a) 1–2	FA Cup 1st Round	McColl	6000
1905	Ossie Park born, Darlington.				
1906	Derby County	(h) 2–1	FA Cup 2nd Round 2nd Replay	Appleyard, J. Rutherford	28257
1914	Bolton Wanderers	(h) 4–3	Division One	G. Wilson 2, Shepherd 2 (1 pen)	35000
1920	Bradford City	(a) 0–1	Division One	No Scorer	25000
1925	Nottingham Forest	(h) 4–1	Division One	Harris 2, McDonald, Urwin	21000
1930	Tommy Urwin moved to Sunderland from United, having previously played for Middlesbrough.				
1931	Liverpool	(a) 2–4	Division One	Hutchinson, Wilkinson	35000
1943	Joe Butler born, Newcastle.				
1948	Aston Villa	(a) 2–1	Friendly	McCall, Taylor	25000
1953	Stoke City	(h) 1–2	Division One	G. Robledo	31426
1959	Wolverhampton Wanderers	(h) 3–4	Division One	Eastham 2 (2 pens), White	42377
1976	Derby County	(h) 4–3	Division One	T. Craig (pen), Nulty, OG, Macdonald	45770

Stirring stuff as the visitors twice came from behind to tie the scores with only eight minutes remaining. A headed goal from Supermac won it for United. Scorers for the Rams were Rioch, George and Powell.

1979	Death of Billy Foulkes, 52.				
1981	Queens Park Rangers	(h) 1–0	Division Two	Waddle	20404

A stormy afternoon as the visitors employed strong-arm tactics once Waddle's header had put United ahead.

1987	Luton Town	(h) 2–2	Division One	P. Jackson, Goddard	22437

Debut for Albert Craig.

1992   Death of Cam Theaker, 79.

1996   United completed the signing of Tino Asprilla from Italian club Parma at a cost of £7.5 million.

1998	West Ham United	(h) 0–1	Premier League	No Scorer	36763

Lazaridis hit an outstanding shot which Given in the Gallowgate goal could only watch soar past him for the only goal. There were debuts for Andy Griffin and Gary Speed.

FEBRUARY 8TH

1896 Burton Wanderers (h) 4–0 Division Two Lennox 2, Graham 2 7000
United took a 1–0 lead in this game opposed by only eight players, this after holding up the kick-off some for 45 minutes. Eventually the other three players appeared, and conceded another three goals.

1902 Arctic conditions forced the postponement of the eagerly awaited United v Sunderland FA Cup second-round tie.

1905 Plymouth Argyle (a) 1–1 FA Cup 1st Round Gosnell 20000
Replay

1908 Manchester United (a) 1–1 Division One Howie 50000

1909 Sammy Weaver born, Pilsley, Derbyshire.

1911 Northampton (h) 1–0 FA Cup 2nd Round Shepherd (pen) 28200
Replay
Although the first tie had been staged at St James', the replay was also staged there at the request of Northampton.

1911 Jimmy Richardson born, Ashington.

1913 Bradford City (a) 0–2 Division One No Scorer 20000
Debut for South Hetton-born Tom Hughes at inside-left. Sadly, after only one game for the first team he joined the army and was killed in France.

1919 Dave Hamilton born, Carlisle.

1922 Birmingham (h) 0–1 Division One No Scorer 25000

1930 Sheffield United (h) 3–5 Division One Devine, Gallacher, 35000
Hutchinson

1936 Burnley (h) 1–1 Division Two Imrie 17000
Debuts for William Forster at right-back and Dave Smith at outside-right.

1947 Leicester City (h) 1–1 FA Cup 5th Round Shackleton 50301

1963 Death of Frank Hudspeth, 72.

1964 Leyton Orient (h) 3–0 Division One Cummings, Penman, 20670
McKinney
A dispiriting day for the visitors, for whom amateur international goalkeeper Mike Pinner was in inspirational form. McKinney's goal came from a header after he had been injured and pushed forward into the centre-forward position.

1969 Terry Wilson born, Broxburn, Scotland.

1975 Luton Town (a) 0–1 Division One No Scorer 18019

1986 Nottingham Forest (a) 2–1 Division One Beardsley 2 15388

1992 Bristol City (h) 3–0 Division Two Kelly 2, O'Brien 29263
A momentous day for Newcastle United as Kevin Keegan returned as manager and led his new charges to victory, backed by a crowd that had virtually doubled from the previous home game. On-loan Terry Wilson celebrated his 23rd birthday in a state of shock, having made his debut in the previous week's slaughter at Oxford. Sadly for him, Keegan didn't rate the midfielder and he was packed off back to Forest, where he was forced to retire with a knee injury two years later.

FEBRUARY 9TH

1883 Bob Benson born, Whitehaven, Cumbria. Right-back who appeared once before joining Southampton. Later moves took him to Sheffield United and Woolwich Arsenal, where he tragically died in the dressing-room following a wartime game.

1895 Manchester City (a) 0–4 Division Two No Scorer 3500

1901 Middlesbrough (a) 1–3 FA Cup 1st Round Aitken 16000

1907 Bury (h) 3–2 Division One Brown, Howie, Rutherford 25000

1921 Chelsea (h) 1–0 Division One Smailes 40000

1924 Huddersfield Town (h) 0–1 Division One No Scorer 25000
Debut for Bert Keating.

1927	Manchester United	(a) 1–3	Division One	McDonald	25402
1929	Manchester United	(h) 5–0	Division One	Lang, Gallacher 3 (1 pen), Urwin	40000

1934   Death of Harry Brown, 50.

| 1935 | Norwich City | (a) 0–2 | Division Two | No Scorer | 16000 |

1936   Death of Arthur Metcalfe, 46. After only 12 games he departed from Gallowgate and played for a number of clubs before settling on Merseyside upon his retirement from the game. At the time of his death he was employed as a gateman with Liverpool.

| 1952 | Fulham | (a) 1–1 | Division One | G. Robledo | 46000 |

1953   Death of Charlie Spencer, 53.

1957	Preston North End	(h) 1–2	Division One	Milburn	43086
1974	Coventry City	(h) 5–1	Division One	Tudor, Macdonald, Bruce, OG 2	27371
1980	Wrexham	(a) 0–1	Division Two	No Scorer	13299

Debut for on-loan Alex Cropley.

| 1985 | Manchester United | (h) 1–1 | Division One | Beardsley | 32555 |

Tony Cunningham made his debut in blizzard conditions, which had enveloped the ground shortly before kick-off. The rapid snowfall required the introduction of an orange ball, which Peter Beardsley duly slotted past Pears for a deserved late equaliser. Ron Atkinson's team had taken a half-time lead through Kevin Moran. Gordon Strachan played for the reds on his 28th birthday.

| 1993 | Portsmouth | (a) 0–2 | Division Two | No Scorer | 21028 |

A game United never got to grips with. Pompey were ahead within 13 minutes from Guy Whittingham and increased their lead just before half-time through Kit Symons. The best the visitors could manage was an 85th-minute penalty, which David Kelly smashed against the bar and into the crowd.

| 1994 | Luton Town | (a) 0–2 | FA Cup 4th Round Replay | No Scorer | 12503 |

Cup dreams dashed by John Hartson and Scott Oakes as Mike Hooper had a game to forget. A miraculous goal-line clearance by Venison merely delayed the inevitable exit.

FEBRUARY 10TH

1880   Albert Gosnell born, Colchester.

| 1894 | Bolton Wanderers | (h) 1–2 | FA Cup 2nd Round | Crate | 10000 |
| 1900 | Southampton | (a) 1–4 | FA Cup 2nd Round | Peddie | 8000 |

1903   Ed Wood born, Stairley, Warwickshire.

1906	Nottingham Forest	(a) 1–2	Division One	Gosnell	7000
1912	West Bromwich Albion	(a) 1–3	Division One	Lowes	25000
1923	Cardiff City	(a) 0–5	Division One	No Scorer	18000
1934	Sheffield Wednesday	(h) 0–0	Division One	No Scorer	14169

1945   Dave Elliott born, Tantobie, Durham.

1948   Tommy Pearson left United to sign for Aberdeen, the third striker to have requested a transfer within weeks, after Roy Bentley and Len Shackleton. Despite losing these three, United still gained promotion back to Division One.

1950   Keith Dyson born, Blackhill, Durham.

| 1951 | Stoke City | (a) 4–2 | FA Cup 5th Round | Milburn, Mitchell, G. Robledo 2 | 48500 |
| 1962 | Southampton | (h) 3–2 | Division Two | Thomas, Kerray, Neale | 30564 |

An instant impact for debutant Jimmy Kerray, scoring once.

1964   Mike Hooper born, Bristol.

| 1968 | Arsenal | (a) 0–0 | Division One | No Scorer | 36996 |

Joe Harvey gave 17-year-old Alan Foggon his debut, but it wasn't until the following season that he was given a run in the team, culminating in his memorable Fairs Cup final goal. Moncur took over the captaincy from Iley for the first time and John McGrath was recalled from a five-month exile. However, it was to be his final game in a black-and-white shirt as Southampton manager Ted Bates was at the game and agreed a transfer with him immediately after.

1973	Coventry City	(h) 1–1	Division One	Barrowclough	23051
1988	Monaco	(h) 1–2	Friendly	Gascoigne	8003
1990	Portsmouth	(a) 1–1	Division Two	Quinn	14204
1996	Middlesbrough	(a) 2–1	Premier League	Watson, Ferdinand	30011

Newcastle made their Riverside debut and Beresford turned a Juninho cross into his own net to give the smoggies a half-time advantage. With time running out, Keegan brought on Asprilla for his debut and his first action was to charge down the left wing, totally bamboozle the lumbering Vickers and cross for Watson to equalise. Ferdinand then won it for United when goalkeeper Walsh fumbled an easy shot into the net. Malcolm Allison, commentating for local radio, was sacked after describing the goal in somewhat coarse language.

FEBRUARY 11TH

1899	Liverpool	(a) 1–3	FA Cup 2nd Round	Peddie	7000
1905	Sheffield United	(a) 3–1	Division One	Gosnell, McClarence, OG	15000
1911	Notts County	(a) 2–2	Division One	Randall, Stewart	10000
1920	Everton	(h) 3–0	Division One	Robinson, Smailes 2	20000
1922	Arsenal	(h) 3–1	Division One	Harris 2, McDonald	30000
1924	Derby County	(n) 2–2	FA Cup 3rd Round 2nd Replay	Seymour, Hudspeth (pen)	17300

A third attempt at settling this second-round tie, both previous games having ended 2–2. After Derby had gone ahead in extra time at Burnden Park, Bolton, Stan Seymour sent the game to a fourth tie with a last-minute equaliser. He then called correctly on the toss of a coin to take the game to Gallowgate.

1925	Bury	(a) 0–0	Division One	No Scorer	6000
1928	Blackburn Rovers	(a) 0–1	Division One	No Scorer	10000
1933	Huddersfield Town	(a) 0–4	Division One	No Scorer	11000

Debut for Harry Heward at left-half.

1939	Preston North End	(h) 1–2	FA Cup 5th Round	Cairns	62327
1950	Middlesbrough	(h) 3–2	Friendly	Milburn 2, Taylor	17000
1956	Everton	(a) 0–0	Division One	No Scorer	35653
1961	Leicester City	(a) 3–5	Division One	Allchurch, White 2	26449

Eventful debut for local lad George Dalton, who had the misfortune to put through his own goal after only six minutes of play. Fellow newcomer John McGrath fared a little better.

1967	Everton	(h) 0–3	Division One	No Scorer	31214
1970	Southampton	(h) 2–1	Division One	Davies, Smith	30738
1984	Grimsby Town	(h) 0–1	Division Two	No Scorer	28633
1989	Coventry City	(a) 2–1	Division One	Hendrie, Mirandinha (pen)	16577

Debut for Gary Brazil as Pingel put through his own goal to equalise for City before Brian Kilcline handled in the area and Mirandinha again scored the winner from the spot.

| 1994 | Barry Venison, Steve Howey and Alex Mathie were all fined by Keegan after breaking a drinking ban by going to a wine bar. | | | | |
| 1995 | Nottingham Forest | (h) 2–1 | Premier League | Fox, Lee | 34471 |

FEBRUARY 12TH

1898	Southampton St Mary's	(a) 0–1	FA Cup 2nd Round	No Scorer	14000
1902	Sunderland	(h) 1–0	FA Cup 2nd Round	Orr	23000
1910	Manchester United	(h) 3–4	Division One	Wilson, Higgins 2	30000
1921	Huddersfield Town	(h) 1–0	Division One	Smailes	45000

1927	Sheffield United	(a) 1–2	Division One	Seymour	40000
1938	Coventry City	(a) 0–1	Division Two	No Scorer	21000
1949	Middlesbrough	(a) 3–3	Friendly	Stobbart, G. Robledo	36000
1955	Chelsea	(a) 3–4	Division One	Keeble 2, Milburn	50667

Another three goals for ex-Newcastle striker Roy Bentley.

1959 Mick Harford born, Sunderland.

1966	Sheffield Wednesday	(h) 1–2	FA Cup 4th Round	Suddick	39495
1972	Manchester United	(a) 2–0	Division One	Tudor, Barrowclough	44983

If any result encapsulated a club it was this one. Seven days after falling to non-league Hereford, Newcastle came to Old Trafford and recorded a rare victory. The home fans reacted badly and a knife-throwing incident was to lead to the ground being closed for two weeks at the start of the following season.

1975	Liverpool	(h) 4–1	Division One	Tudor, Macdonald 2, Barrowclough	38115

Revenge for the cup final humiliation, Liverpool's consolation coming from a Brian Hall header.

1994	Wimbledon	(a) 2–4	Premier League	Beardsley 2 (2 pens)	13358

Even the debut of Ruel Fox could do nothing to prevent the usual Dons destruction, thanks in part to a goalkeeping performance from Hooper which left something to be desired. Two dubious penalty awards late in the game for United made for a flattering final score.

FEBRUARY 13TH

1897	Grimsby Town	(h) 4–0	Friendly	Aitken 2, Connell, Blyth	4000
1904	Notts County	(h) 4–1	Division One	Orr 2, Appleyard, Howie	16000

Winning debut for Andy McCombie, at right-back, following his transfer from Sunderland.

1905	Plymouth Argyle	(n) 2–0	FA Cup 1st Round 2nd Replay	Orr 2 (1 pen)	11570

Played at the Manor Ground in Plumstead, the home of Woolwich Arsenal.

1909	Preston North End	(a) 1–0	Division One	Anderson	10000
1915	Manchester City	(h) 2–1	Division One	King, Hibbert	18000
1924	Derby County	(h) 5–3	FA Cup 2nd Round 3rd Replay	Seymour, Harris 3, Cowan	32496

At last a decisive result after three 2–2 draws in the second-round epic. The match was held at St James' on the toss of a coin after the previous game. Two goals up, Derby were spectacularly pegged back by a 24th-minute hat-trick from Neil Harris.

1926	Arsenal	(a) 0–3	Division One	No Scorer	40000
1932	Leicester City	(h) 3–1	FA Cup 5th Round	Allen, Lang, Weaver	43354
1937	Leicester City	(a) 2–3	Division Two	Cairns, Smith	25000

1949 Geoff Nulty born, Prescot, Liverpool.

1954	Burnley	(h) 3–1	Division One	Broadis 2, Milburn	29114
1959	Vienna SC (Austria)	(h) 1–1	Friendly	McGuigan	25370
1960	Leeds United	(h) 2–1	Division One	Hughes, White	16148
1965	Ipswich Town	(h) 2–2	Division Two	Suddick, Anderson	29459
1971	Huddersfield Town	(a) 1–1	Division One	Smith	15580

1973 England Under-23 triumphed 2–1 at Rugby Park, Kilmarnock, over their Scottish counterparts. Newcastle's Stewart Barrowclough netted for England on an icy pitch.

1982	Cardiff City	(h) 2–1	Division Two	Varadi, Trewick	15129
1988	Norwich City	(h) 1–3	Division One	Gascoigne	21068
1991	Nottingham Forest	(h) 2–2	FA Cup 4th Round	Quinn, McGhee	29231
1993	Blackburn Rovers	(a) 0–1	FA Cup 5th Round	No Scorer	19972

The Jack Walker revolution at Ewood began, as United fans stood on a roofless Darwen end. Manager Kevin Keegan was confined to home with the flu, and *Match of the Day* cameras were on hand to record an unadventurous display that nearly secured a replay at

St James'. Roy Wegerle struck with only a minute remaining to send Rovers into the sixth round.

1998   Former Magpies striker Ian Baird hit a hat-trick as his latest team recorded their best victory of the season. The score? Instant-Dict 6, Rangers 1 in a Hong Kong League match.

FEBRUARY 14TH

1899	Sunderland	(a) 4–3	Friendly	Peddie, Niblo, Stevenson	5000
1903	Middlesbrough	(a) 0–1	Division One	No Scorer	20000

This match took place at the Linthorpe Road ground.

1914	Chelsea	(a) 1–0	Division One	Shepherd	35000
1920	Bradford City	(h) 0–1	Division One	No Scorer	45000
1923	West Bromwich Albion	(h) 2–0	Division One	Seymour, J. Clark	10000
1925	Liverpool	(a) 1–1	Division One	Clark	35000
1931	Middlesbrough	(h) 0–5	Division One	No Scorer	35000

Two goals from George Camsell helped 'Boro to an easy victory, but their manager, ex-United player Peter McWilliam, stayed away due the nerves he suffered from when his team played big games.

1948	Liverpool	(h) 0–3	Friendly	No Scorer	44830
1951	Kevin Keegan born, Armthorpe, Yorkshire.				
1953	Manchester City	(a) 1–2	Division One	Milburn	24898
1976	Bolton Wanderers	(a) 3–3	FA Cup 5th Round	Gowling, Maconald 2	46880
1981	Exeter City	(h) 1–1	FA Cup 5th Round	Shoulder	36984

Large numbers of Exeter fans had journeyed on special trains to cheer their heroes on, but once substitute Alan Shoulder had put the home side ahead, cardboard FA cups were waved with abandon by the jubilant home fans in a deafening atmosphere. A last-gasp equaliser from Tony Kellow silenced the celebrations and set up what became a catastrophic replay at the other St James' Park.

1984   At a press conference held on his 33rd birthday, Kevin Keegan announced his intention to retire from playing football at the end of the current season. When pressed he revealed that being beaten to the ball by Mark Lawrenson in the FA Cup match at Anfield earlier in the season made him realise his powers were fading.

1987	Queens Park Rangers	(a) 1–2	Division One	Goddard	10731
1998	Tranmere Rovers	(h) 1–0	FA Cup 5th Round	Shearer	36675

FEBRUARY 15TH

1893	Bedlington Wednesday	(a) 8–1	Friendly	Crate 3, Crielly, Miller, Reay, Wallace	
1896	Bury	(h) 1–3	FA Cup 2nd Round	Thompson	14250
1902	Sheffield Wednesday	(h) 2–1	Division One	Roberts, Veitch	15000
1908	Manchester City	(h) 1–1	Division One	Willis	27000
1913	Manchester City	(h) 0–1	Division One	No Scorer	35000
1926	Frank Houghton born, Preston.				
1930	Brighton and Hove Albion	(h) 3–0	FA Cup 5th Round	Gallacher 3	56469

Debut for Joe Richardson, at right-back.

1936	Arsenal	(h) 3–3	FA Cup 5th Round	Pearson, J. Smith 2	65484
1939	Nottingham Forest	(a) 0–2	Division Two	No Scorer	7000
1947	Southampton	(h) 1–3	Division Two	Pearson	50516

Debut for Albert Sibley, at outside-right.

1955	Death of Andy Aitken, 77.				
1964	St Johnstone	(a) 3–1	Friendly	Burton, Cummings, Hilley	7000

The only competitive appearance that John Pickering ever made came in this friendly.

After leaving United to play for Halifax and Barnsley, he eventually returned in June 1986 as a coach to Wille McFaul. Saints welcomed new signing Ken Brownlee from Third Lanark and he opened the scoring. Ollie Burton then equalised with a curling shot from all of 35 yards. Late goals from Cummings and Hilley won it as the home side tired.

| 1969 | Southampton | (a) 0–0 | Division One | No Scorer | 22213 |

Debuts for Gordon Hindson and, at the second attempt, Arthur Horsfield. Arthur had scored a debut goal in the previous game at Maine Road, but the game was abandoned due to rain and replayed.

1975	Burnley	(h) 3–0	Division One	Macdonald 2, Barrowclough	40602
1980	Dundee	(a) 3–1	Friendly	Mitchell, Withe, Rafferty	3596
1992	Blackburn Rovers	(a) 1–3	Division Two	Kelly	19511

FEBRUARY 16TH

| 1885 | Jimmy Lawrence born, Glasgow. | | | | |
| 1895 | Aston Villa | (a) 1–7 | FA Cup 2nd Round | Thompson | 10000 |

Villa went on to win the cup, defeating neighbours West Bromwich Albion 1–0.

| 1901 | Derby County | (a) 1–1 | Division One | Peddie | 7000 |

Lancastrian Frederick Heywood made his debut, at inside-left. Steve Bloomer scored for Derby, again.

| 1904 | Bradford City | (a) 2–2 | Friendly | Fraser 2 | 6000 |
| 1907 | Manchester City | (a) 1–1 | Division One | Brown | 35000 |

The only senior appearance of Ashington-born Ben Nicholson, at left-back. At the time City were playing at the cramped Hyde Road ground, bordered by heavy industry, terraced houses and a railway line.

1916 Death of Bob Benson, 33. Tragically Bob died after making up the numbers for his former club Woolwich Arsenal in a wartime encounter with Reading, having turned up as a spectator following his retirement two seasons previously. His lack of fitness cost him his life as he was led from the field in obvious distress only to die minutes later in the Highbury dressing-room.

1924	Notts County	(a) 0–1	Division One	No Scorer	10000
1929	Leeds United	(a) 0–0	Division One	No Scorer	20000
1935	Swansea Town	(h) 5–1	Division Two	Cairns 3, Imrie, Murray	9000
1952	Wolverhampton Wanderers	(a) 0–3	Division One	No Scorer	42000
1957	Luton Town	(a) 1–4	Division One	Milburn	21003

Debut of Albert Franks.

1968 Graham Mitchell born, Shipley, Yorkshire. While playing for Huddersfield, Mitchell was watched several times by United and a deal to bring him to Tyneside had been agreed but collapsed when Ardiles was sacked. The incoming Kevin Keegan decided against the signing, and Mitchell remained with Huddersfield.

1970	Liverpool	(a) 0–0	Division One	No Scorer	38218
1974	West Bromwich Albion	(a) 3–0	FA Cup 5th Round	Tudor, Macdonald, Barrowclough	42699
1977	Manchester City	(h) 2–2	Division One	Burns 2	28954

Debut for Kenny Mitchell.

| 1985 | Chelsea | (a) 0–1 | Division One | No Scorer | 21806 |
| 1990 | Death of Eddie Connelly, 73. | | | | |

FEBRUARY 17TH

1894	Rotherham Town	(h) 4–0	Division Two	Wallace, Crate, Quinn, Graham	6000
1900	Southampton	(a) 1–4	FA Cup 3rd Round	Peddie	8000
1912	Sunderland	(h) 3–1	Division One	Anderson, Lowes, Stewart	45000
1915	Jack Smith born, Batley, Yorkshire.				

1932	Bolton Wanderers	(h) 3–1	Division One	Cape, Lang, Weaver	25000
1934	Manchester United	(a) 4–3	Friendly	Williams 2, Richardson, Weaver (pen)	7000
1951	Sheffield Wednesday	(h) 2–0	Division One	G. Robledo, Taylor	47075
1962	Luton Town	(a) 0–1	Division Two	No Scorer	9040
1968	Celtic	(h) 1–0	Friendly	No Scorer	38836

1972 Death of Jack Alderson, 80.

| 1973 | Wolverhampton Wanderers | (a) 1–1 | Division One | Hibbitt | 22147 |
| 1979 | Leicester City | (a) 1–2 | Division Two | Nattrass | 15106 |

1993 Newcastle reserves beat Wolves 4–0, with trialist Salou scoring twice. The other goals came from Hunt and Elliott.

FEBRUARY 18TH

1893	Notts County	(h) 3–2	Friendly	Thompson, Sorley 2	3000
1899	Bury	(h) 2–0	Division One	Peddie 2	16000
1905	Tottenham Hotspur	(a) 1–1	FA Cup 2nd Round	Howie	19013

Spurs were still a Southern League club when this match was played.

| 1911 | Manchester United | (h) 0–1 | Division One | No Scorer | 45000 |
| 1928 | Bolton Wanderers | (h) 2–2 | Division One | McCurley, Urwin | 29000 |

Goalscoring debut for John McCurley, at inside-forward.

| 1933 | Sheffield United | (h) 2–0 | Division One | Betton, J.R. Richardson | 8000 |

Only goal of Alec Betton's United career, some 61 games at centre-half. Bob Dennsion made his debut.

1934 Death of Robert Bradley, 27. Died in his sleep following an appearance at Chester the previous evening for his club Carlisle.

1939	Tranmere Rovers	(a) 3–0	Division Two	Clifton, Stubbins, Gordon	
1950	Stoke City	(a) 0–1	Division One	No Scorer	28000
1956	Stoke City	(h) 2–1	FA Cup 5th Round	Curry, Mitchell	61550
1961	Stoke City	(h) 3–1	FA Cup 5th Round	Scanlon, Allchurch, McKinney (pen)	46253

1962 John Ryan born, Ashton-under-Lyme.

| 1967 | Nottingham Forest | (a) 0–3 | FA Cup 4th Round | No Scorer | 45962 |

Cup dreams over for another year, thanks to goals from Frank Wignall, John Barnwell and Ian Storey-Moore.

1975 Keith Gillespie born, Larne, Northern Ireland.

| 1976 | Bolton Wanderers | (h) 0–0 | FA Cup 5th Round 1st Replay | No Scorer | 52760 |

1977 Paul Dalglish born, Glasgow. Brought to Newcastle on a free transfer from Liverpool by his dad and loaned to Bury for the rest of the 1997–98 season.

1981	Exeter City	(a) 0–4	FA Cup 5th Round Replay	No Scorer	17668
1984	Manchester City	(a) 2–1	Division Two	Beardsley, Keegan	41767
1989	Boston United	(a) 1–0	Friendly	Pingel	3588
1990	Manchester United	(h) 2–3	FA Cup 5th Round	McGhee (pen), Scott	31805

Manchester United went on to win the FA Cup and under-fire boss Alex Ferguson kept his job. The match was shown live on BBC on a Sunday afternoon.

| 1991 | Nottingham Forest | (a) 0–3 | FA Cup 4th Round Replay | No Scorer | 28962 |

No second chance for the Magpies, as Forest ruthlessly exposed the shortcomings of Dillon and Aitken. A young Roy Keane infuriated the United fans by making various gestures when Forest took the lead. As police moved in to prevent a mini pitch invasion, Forest boss Brian Clough commendably defused the situation by substituting Keane within seconds.

FEBRUARY 19TH

1870   Johnny Campbell born, Renton, Scotland. A centre-forward, he played for both United and Sunderland in their inaugural First Division fixtures.

1898   Luton   (a) 1–3   Division Two   R. Allen   3500
Debut for Scottish inside-left William Smith, who was brought in from Hibernian to augment the club's successful promotion campaign. Before this game, United were unbeaten in the league and went on to qualify for the test matches (forerunners of the modern-day play-offs).

1910   Blackburn Rovers   (h) 3–1   FA Cup 3rd Round   Higgins, Howie, Rutherford 54772
1921   Everton   (a) 0–3   FA Cup 3rd Round   No Scorer   54205
1927   Southampton   (a) 1–2   FA Cup 5th Round   McDonald (pen)   21406
1936   Arsenal   (a) 0–3   FA Cup 5th Round   No Scorer   62391
                                        Replay
A decisive victory for the eventual cup winners. Two goals came from Cliff Bastin, both from the spot.

1938   Nottingham Forest   (h) 3–1   Division Two   Bowden, J.R. Richardson, 17000
                                                            Imrie (pen)
1949   Manchester City   (a) 0–1   Division One   No Scorer   48624
1955   Nottingham Forest   (a) 1–1   FA Cup 5th Round   Milburn   25252
A smaller than expected crowd at the City Ground was partly explained by the counter-attraction of neighbouring Notts County entertaining Chelsea in another cup-tie at the same time. Peter Small looked to have won it for the home side when he scored with only five minutes remaining, but Milburn latched on to a Simpson clearance and beat keeper Farmer to force a replay. Small had scored not long after returning to the field, having been to hospital for an X-ray after a heavy tackle earlier in the game.

1957   Belenenses   (a) 1–2   Friendly   Mitchell (pen)
        (Portugal)
1957   Ray Blackhall born, Ashington.
1961   Justin Fashanu born, Hackney.
1966   Northampton Town   (a) 1–3   Division One   Iley   14541
1972   Everton   (h) 0–0   Division One   No Scorer   29584
1977   Manchester United   (a) 1–3   Division One   Nulty   51828
A Jimmy Greenhoff hat-trick sealed the victory for the home side.

1983   Oldham Athletic   (h) 1–0   Division Two   McDermott   20689
1994   Blackburn Rovers   (a) 0–1   Premier League   No Scorer   20798
A defensive performance almost secured a point, but after Srnicek had clawed a shot away for a corner, the ball was played back in and Batty set up May for the only goal.

1995   Manchester City   (h) 3–1   FA Cup 5th Round   Gillespie 2, Beresford 33219
1997   Torrential rain forced the away game at Upton Park to be postponed minutes before kick-off with the crowd already in the ground.

FEBRUARY 20TH

1897   Loughborough   (a) 0–3   Division Two   No Scorer   2000
        Town
1904   Everton   (h) 2–0   Friendly   Rutherford, McWilliam 4000
1909   West Ham United   (a) 0–0   FA Cup 3rd Round   No Scorer   17000
1915   Sheffield Wednesday (a) 2–1   FA Cup 3rd Round   King, Hibbert   25971
1926   Clapton Orient   (a) 0–2   FA Cup 5th Round   No Scorer   31400
        Played at Millfields Road.
1932   Middlesbrough   (a) 1–2   Division One   Feeney   20000
1937   Chesterfield   (a) 0–4   Division Two   No Scorer   10000
1947   Leicester City   (a) 2–1   FA Cup 5th Round   Pearson, Bentley   28424
                                        Replay

A light covering of snow on the Filbert Street pitch indirectly cost the home side the tie when an attempted clearance from Walter Harrison stuck on the penalty spot and Roy Bentley poked it home. City were reduced to ten men for part of the second half when George Dewes came off second best in a collison with Frank Brennan. He eventually returned swathed in bandages and tried to keep out of Brennan's way by taking a wide left position.

1954   West Bromwich   (a) 2–3   FA Cup 5th Round   Milburn, Mitchell   61088
       Albion
A game marked by a Ronnie Allen hat-trick, completed with a 45-yard volley that even the United players applauded. The Baggies went on to defeat Preston North End at Wembley.

1957   Tony Smith born, Sunderland.

1960   West Ham United   (a) 5–3   Division One   Allchurch, Eastham, Hughes, 27000
                                                         White 2

1965   Leyton Orient   (a) 1–2   Division Two   McGarry (pen)   8319
Tommy Knox made his debut on a Brisbane Road pitch ankle-deep in mud. A youthful Frank Bough commentated on the game which marked United's first appearance on BBC's *Match of the Day*.

1970   Dundee United   (h) 3–2   Friendly   Moncur, Robson, Dyson   8685
1971   Tottenham Hotspur (h) 1–0   Division One   Robson   31718
1980   Birmingham City   (h) 0–0   Division Two   No Scorer   27069
1982   Shrewsbury Town   (a) 0–0   Division Two   No Scorer   4636
1988   Wimbledon   (h) 1–3   FA Cup 5th Round   McDonald   28796
Undoubtedly the highlight of this cup humiliation was the post-match kick Mirandinha aimed at Dons keeper Dave Beasant's backside. Unlike any of his shots during the game, it was on target.

1996   Former United defender Glenn Roeder left his job as Watford manager 'by mutual consent'. He subsequently spent some time as assistant to Chris Waddle at Burnley and then joined the list of failed managers who sat in tracksuits behind Glenn Hoddle at Wembley internationals. Also in this exclusive club were Phil Neal and John Gorman.

FEBRUARY 21ST

1903   Sunderland   (h) 1–0   Friendly   Rutherford   3000
1914   Oldham Athletic   (h) 0–0   Division One   No Scorer   30000
1914   Norman Tapken born, Wallsend.
1920   Bolton Wanderers   (a) 3–0   Division One   Booth 2, Smailes   25000
1925   Sunderland   (h) 2–0   Division One   Cowan, Urwin   52000
1931   Derby County   (a) 5–1   Division One   Bedford, Hutchinson,   17831
                                                         Wilkinson 3
1948   Coventry City   (a) 1–1   Division Two   McCall (pen)   22047
       Debut for Tommy Thompson.
1953   Liverpool   (h) 1–2   Division One   Mitchell   40345
       Debut for Len White.
1959   Aston Villa   (h) 1–0   Division One   Taylor   20182
1973   Roma   (a) 2–0   Anglo-Italian Cup Tudor 2   18919
1976   Liverpool   (a) 0–2   Division One   No Scorer   43304
1981   Bristol Rovers   (h) 0–0   Division Two   No Scorer   14364
1987   Tottenham Hotspur (a) 0–1   FA Cup 5th Round   No Scorer   38033
Two years before Hillsborough, Newcastle fans were almost the victims of callous policing by the Met, as the Park Lane end was allowed to become dangerously overcrowded while adjacent paddocks remained closed. The first few United fans to climb over the fences were arrested but gradually dozens joined in and fought with stewards to open gates onto the pitch. In an eerie portent of the Hillsborough tragedy, seated fans pulled some of those below to safety and disaster was averted. The police's reaction was to stretch a line of officers in front of the away section which blotted out any view of the

match. After the final whistle, a vain attempt at holding the United fans back resulted in gates being forced and running battles taking place near the ground as furious fans vented their anger. Press reports subsequently estimated the travelling support at 14,000.

1993	West Ham United	(a) 0–0	Division One	No Scorer	24159
1996	West Ham United	(a) 0–2	Premier League	No Scorer	23843

Goals came from Danny Williamson and Tony Cottee on a night when little went right for the away team.

FEBRUARY 22ND

1896	Burton Wanderers	(a) 3–0	Division Two	Thompson, Lennox 2	3000
1902	Sheffield United	(h) 1–1	FA Cup 3rd Round	Stewart	20000
1905	Tottenham	(h) 4–0	FA Cup 2nd Round Replay	Orr 2, Appleyard, Howie	26755
1908	Liverpool	(h) 3–1	FA Cup 3rd Round	Speedie, Appleyard, Rutherford	45987
1913	Liverpool	(a) 1–1	FA Cup 3rd Round	Shepherd	37093
1926	Leicester City	(a) 2–3	Division One	Gallacher 2	20000
1930	Sunderland	(h) 3–0	Division One	Boyd, Hutchinson, Lang	60000
1936	Leicester City	(a) 1–2	Division Two	Weaver (pen)	

Abandoned after 80 minutes.

1950 United hosted an England 'B' international, 43,068 watching a 1–0 victory over Holland.

1956	Portsmouth	(a) 2–0	Division One	Curry, Keeble	15100
1958	Everton	(a) 2–1	Division One	Bottom 2	22448

A debut brace for Arthur Bottom.

1961	Cardiff City	(a) 2–3	Division One	Allchurch, White	30000
1964	Rotherham United	(a) 3–2	Division Two	Suddick 2, Penman	9727

1971 Pop Robson moved to Ron Greenwood's West Ham for a fee of £125,000, four months after publicly criticising United's tactics and lack of professionalism in a press conference held in a Newcastle hotel.

1975	Chelsea	(a) 2–3	Division One	Tudor, Macdonald	26770
1979	Wolverhampton Wanderers	(a) 0–1	FA Cup 4th Round Replay	No Scorer	19588
1992	Barnsley	(h) 1–1	Division Two	Kelly	27670

Debuts for Brian Kilcline and Kevin Sheedy. David Curry scored for the visitors.

1997	Middlesbrough	(a) 1–0	Premier League	Ferdinand	30063

'Boro's expensively imported Italian cheat Ravanelli had a goal chalked off when the referee spotted an earlier foul he had committed.

1998	Leeds United	(h) 1–1	Premier League	Ketsbaia	36519

Rod Wallace scored for Leeds, with substitute Ketsbaia seeing his hopeful punt wriggle through Nigel Martyn's grasp and into the net for a late equaliser.

FEBRUARY 23RD

1895	Blyth	(a) 2–2	Friendly	Wallace, Graham (pen)	3000
1901	Derby County	(h) 2–1	Friendly	MacFarlane, Peddie	6000
1907	Middlesbrough	(h) 4–0	Division One	Appleyard 2, McWilliam, McCracken (pen)	47000
1921	Huddersfield Town	(a) 3–1	Division One	Smailes 2, Harris	30000
1924	Watford	(a) 1–0	FA Cup 3rd Round	Seymour	23444
1929	Liverpool	(h) 2–2	Division One	Lang 2	45000
1935	West Ham United	(h) 3–0	Division Two	Murray, Pearson 2	28000

1950 Alan Foggon born, West Pelton, Durham.

1952	Swansea Town	(a) 1–0	FA Cup 5th Round	Mitchell	27801

The cup run continued with this fifth-round victory, despite the presence of future Magpie Ivor Allchurch in the home ranks.

1957	Charlton Athletic	(h) 3–1	Division One	Casey, Eastham, Scoular	21721
1959	Linfield	(a) 3–3	Friendly	Taylor, Allchurch, White	12000

1963   Wes Saunders born, Boldon, Durham.

1966   Death of Billy Hampson, 81. After a long career at United, FA Cup winner Billy became manager of Carlisle, bringing a young Bill Shankly to Brunton Park.

1968   Brian Tinnion born, Burnopfield, Durham.

1974	Liverpool	(h) 0–0	Division One	No Scorer	45192
1976	Bolton Wanderers	(n) 2–1	FA Cup 3rd Round 2nd Replay	Gowling, Burns	43448

Elland Road was the venue as the deadlock was finally broken.

1980	Shrewsbury Town	(a) 1–3	Division Two	Shoulder (pen)	10833

Third and final appearance of loaned midfielder Alex Cropley. As United had taken one point and scored one goal during his brief spell, and he had been substituted in all but one of the games, it was inevitable he was packed off back to Villa Park.

1985	Luton Town	(h) 1–0	Division Two	Wharton	24515

A Wharton effort lifted United to the dizzy heights of 14th place in Division Two, which was to be their finishing position. Ironically, on a day George Reilly made his debut, the defence kept their first clean sheet in 19 attempts.

1991	Wolverhampton Wanderers	(h) 0–0	Division Two	No Scorer	18612

The infamous Paul Moran was in the team for the only time, on loan from Spurs. His non-performance was allegedly attributable to a late night spent 'sightseeing' in Newcastle with his local tour guide, a Mr Paul Gascoigne. Mark Stimpson was dismissed late in the game after he and Kevin Scott tangled with Steve Bull.

1994	Coventry City	(h) 4–0	Premier League	Cole 3, Mathie	32210

1996   Newcastle completed the signing of midfielder David Batty in a £3.75 million move. United had been alerted to the fact Batty was unsettled at Ewood Park after he had been demoted to training with the juniors. Belting his team-mate Le Saux during a Champions' League match was also a bit of a giveaway.

FEBRUARY 24TH

1894	Grimsby Town	(h) 4–1	Division Two	Crate, Thompson, Quinn, Jeffery	4000
1906	Blackpool	(h) 5–0	FA Cup 3rd Round	Orr 2, Appleyard, Gardner, OG	34405
1909	West Ham United	(h) 2–1	FA Cup 3rd Round Replay	Anderson, Shepherd (pen)	36526
1912	Preston North End	(h) 1–0	Division One	Hay	25000
1934	Arsenal	(h) 0–1	Division One	No Scorer	35000
1951	Bristol Rovers	(h) 0–0	FA Cup 6th Round	No Scorer	63000
1962	Charlton Athletic	(a) 1–1	Division Two	Allchurch	16935

Allchurch put United ahead, but the points were shared after a brilliant strike from Sam Lawrie.

1968	Wolverhampton Wanderers	(h) 2–0	Division One	Elliott, T. Robson	35431

1971   Forty-eight hours after moving from Newcastle, Pop Robson scored on his debut as West Ham beat Nottingham Forest 2–0 at Upton Park.

1973	Norwich City	(a) 1–0	Division One	Macdonald	26411
1979	Sunderland	(h) 1–4	Division Two	Connolly	34733

A black day as Gary Rowell hit a hat-trick and Wayne Entwhistle the other goal in Sunderland's first league win on Tyneside for over a decade.

1982	Sheffield Wednesday	(h) 1–0	Division Two	Varadi	19174

1989   Death of Joe Harvey, 71.

1990	Sheffield United	(a) 1–1	Division Two	OG	21035

Brock's goal was later credited as an OG to Mark Morris, while a hugely unimpressive home side with lumbering Billy Whitehurst up front somehow snatched a late equaliser. McGhee mirrored the disgust of the travelling fans by volleying a plastic chair into the crowd as he left the field.

1993 Bristol Rovers (h) 0–0 Division Two No Scorer 29372
Journeyman Malcolm Allison brought his Rovers team to Tyneside on a night when United could do little right in front of goal. Such was the frustration of the crowd, used to seeing sweeping home wins, that the players were booed as they left the field at the end of both halves.

1995 Farewell to the barrel-chested Alex Mathie, off to Ipswich Town – where he kept up his sterling work by scoring a hat-trick against the mackems.

1996 Manchester City (a) 3–3 Premier League Albert 2, Asprilla 31115
A busy day as Asprilla scored his first goal for United and celebrated with a trademark cartwheel, but twice tangled with City defender Keith Curle and was later charged by the FA. Meanwhile, in a restaurant at Maine Road, David Batty was agreeing to become a Newcastle player.

FEBRUARY 25TH

1886 Harry Hardinge born, Greenwich.
1893 Sunderland (h) 1–6 Friendly Graham 7000
1898 Lawrie Crown born, Fulwell, Sunderland.
1898 Duggie Livingstone born, Alexandria, Scotland.
1899 Preston North End (h) 2–1 Division One MacFarlane, Peddie (pen) 15000
1905 Preston North End (h) 1–0 Division One Appleyard 20000
1905 Absentees from the United team Carr and McCracken faced each other at Ayresome Park as England and Ireland drew 1–1.
1911 Hull City (h) 3–2 FA Cup 3rd Round Shepherd 2, Veitch 46531
1922 Blackburn Rovers (h) 2–0 Division One J. Low, Woods 25000
1928 Sheffield Wednesday (a) 0–0 Division One No Scorer 20000
1930 Bill Paterson born, Kinlochleven, Scotland.
1939 West Ham United (h) 2–0 Division Two Pearson (pen), Cairns 30000
1950 Burnley (h) 0–0 Division One No Scorer 30032
1953 Celtic (h) 2–0 Friendly G. Robledo 2 41888
Floodlights inauguration at St James' Park.
1954 Charlton Athletic (a) 0–0 Division One No Scorer 13441
1956 Arsenal (h) 2–0 Division One Curry, Milburn 50822
1961 Aston Villa (h) 2–1 Division One White 2 21275
1967 Arsenal (h) 2–1 Division One Davies, Hilley 27463
1970 Chelsea (a) 0–0 Division One No Scorer 35341
1978 Ipswich Town (h) 0–1 Division One No Scorer 22264
1981 Cardiff City (a) 0–1 Division Two No Scorer 4235
1984 Cardiff City (h) 3–1 Division Two Waddle, Keegan 2 (1 pen) 27964
1995 Aston Villa (h) 3–1 Premier League Venison, Beardsley 2 34637
The only goal that Barry managed was a beauty at the Leazes end, while at the other end Andy Townsend hit an equally memorable effort for the visitors.

FEBRUARY 26TH

1898 Lincoln City (h) 3–0 Division Two Wardrope 2, Smith 10000
Debut for Billy Lindsay.
1910 Sheffield Wednesday (h) 3–1 Division One Shepherd, Howie, McWilliam 8000
1913 Liverpool (h) 1–0 FA Cup 3rd Round Replay Hudspeth (pen) 39769
1921 Middlesbrough (h) 2–0 Division One Smailes, Aitken 40000
1927 Liverpool (h) 2–1 Division One Seymour 2 34000

1936	Charlton Athletic	(a) 2–4	Division Two	J. Smith, Imrie (pen)	15000
1938	Aston Villa	(h) 2–0	Division Two	Cairns, Park	48000
1949	Liverpool	(h) 1–1	Friendly	Milburn	29980
1955	Sunderland	(h) 1–2	Division One	Milburn	62835
1966	Stoke City	(h) 3–1	Division One	Suddick 2, Hilley	26201
1972	Southampton	(a) 2–1	Division One	Macdonald (pen), Barrowclough	18884
1977	Tottenham Hotspur	(h) 2–0	Division One	Gowling, Burns	30230
1979	Bjarni Gudjonsson born, Akranes, Iceland.				
1983	Fulham	(a) 2–2	Division Two	McDermott, Varadi	14277
1989	Middlesbrough	(a) 1–1	Division One	O'Brien	24385

Another goal for Bernie Slaven, in front of the Holgate End he loved so much he bought a piece of fence from the ground and put it in his back garden.

FEBRUARY 27TH

| 1897 | Leith Athletic | (h) 5–0 | Friendly | Connell 2, Aitken 2, Lennox | 4000 |
| 1902 | Sheffield United | (a) 1–2 | FA Cup 3rd Round Replay | McColl | 20000 |

The Blades went on to defeat Southampton in a replayed FA Cup final.

1904	Wolves	(a) 2–3	Division One	McColl, Howie	5000
1909	Manchester City	(a) 2–0	Division One	Jobey, Stewart	25000
1911	Liverpool	(a) 0–3	Division One	No Scorer	8000
1915	Sheffield United	(a) 0–1	Division One	No Scorer	15000
1924	Huddersfield Town	(a) 1–1	Division One	Seymour	6000
1926	Sunderland	(a) 2–2	Division One	Mordue, Urwin	36000
1932	Watford	(h) 5–0	FA Cup 6th Round	Allen 3, Boyd, J.R. Richardson	57879

A minute's silence preceded this game in memory of the late Frank Watt, the club's founding secretary.

1933	Death of Billy Lindsay, 60.				
1934	Stan Anderson born, Horden, Durham.				
1954	Wolverhampton Wanderers	(a) 2–3	Division One	Broadis, Milburn	25000
1955	Tony Bell born, North Shields.				
1960	Arsenal	(a) 0–1	Division One	No Scorer	47657
1965	Bury	(h) 2–3	Division Two	Suddick, Anderson	33923

This game eventually lasted for 101 minutes due to the erratic timekeeping of the referee, the visitors' winning goal coming deep in injury time.

1971	Manchester United	(a) 0–1	Division One	No Scorer	41902
1978	Blyth Spartans went down 2–1 in their FA Cup fifth-round replay with Wrexham, conquerors of United in the previous round. The crowd was given as 42,157, but some gates were forced and many people were locked out.				
1982	Derby County	(a) 2–2	Division Two	Waddle, Varadi	12257
1988	Chelsea	(h) 3–1	Division One	Mirandinha 2, Gascoigne	17858
1991	Brighton and Hove Albion	(h) 0–0	Division Two	No Scorer	12692

FEBRUARY 28TH

1903	Wolverhampton Wanderers	(h) 2–4	Division One	Andrew Gardner, Alec Gardner	16000
1914	Manchester United	(a) 2–2	Division One	Hibbert, Shepherd	25000
1920	Bolton Wanderers	(h) 0–1	Division One	No Scorer	40000
1923	Cardiff City	(h) 3–1	Division One	Harris, McDonald, Seymour	11000
1925	Cardiff City	(a) 0–3	Division One	No Scorer	25000

1930	Arthur Bottom born, Sheffield.				
1931	Sheffield United	(h) 1–0	Division One	Hutchinson	30000
1948	West Ham United	(a) 2–0	Division Two	Milburn, Thompson	30000
1951	Bristol Rovers	(a) 3–1	FA Cup 6th Round Replay	Taylor, Crowe, Milburn	30724

Geoff Bradford opened the scoring for the Pirates, but United replied three times in the 30 minutes before half-time.

1953	Wolverhampton Wanderers	(h) 1–1	Division One	G. Robledo	46254
1955	Nottingham Forest	(h) 2–2	FA Cup 5th Round 1st Replay	Keeble, R. Mitchell	38573
1958	Kevin Todd born, Sunderland.				
1959	Leicester City	(a) 1–0	Division One	Eastham	24362
1960	Jamie Scott born, Newcastle.				
1967	Death of Dick Keith, 33. Killed in an accident.				
1970	Tottenham Hotspur	(h) 1–2	Division One	McNamee	34827
1973	Derby County	(h) 2–0	Division One	Tudor, Macdonald	34286
1973	Ray Ellison left Gallowgate, signing for Sunderland at a cost of £10,000.				
1975	West Ham United	(a) 1–0	Division One	Macdonald	33150
	Debut for Micky Barker.				
1976	Manchester City	(w) 1–2	League Cup Final	Gowling	100000

Dennis Tueart's overhead kick dashed United hopes after Gowling had equalised an opener from Peter Barnes.

1981	Oldham Athletic	(a) 0–0	Division Two	No Scorer	5887
1987	Wimbledon	(a) 1–3	Division One	Beardsley	6779

The last goal registered by Peter in his first spell with Newcastle. Such was the poorness of the United midfield, by the end of the season he was attempting to start attacks by collecting the ball from his goalkeeper.

1990	Bournemouth	(h) 3–0	Division Two	Anderson, Quinn 2	15163
1993	Tranmere Rovers	(a) 3–0	Division One	Lee 2, Kelly	13082

After a mini collapse in which United failed to win in six games, normal service was resumed in this televised Sunday fixture at Prenton Park. A pre-match boost was the injury to John Aldridge, and the home side showed little invention up front in his absence.

1995	Ipswich Town	(a) 2–0	Premier League	Fox, Kitson	18639
1998	Everton	(a) 0–0	Premier League	No Scorer	37972

A uniformly miserable encounter with nothing to recommend it. Home fans jeered every time former Evertonian Gary Speed came anywhere near the ball. So that's just the three jeers, then . . .

FEBRUARY 29TH

1876	Willie Stewart born, Glasgow.				
1896	Sunderland	(h) 2–2	Friendly	Lennox, Aitken	5000
1936	Norwich City	(h) 1–1	Division Two	Imrie	4000

The smallness of the crowd can be attributed to ongoing problems between the League and the Pools companies, who refused to pay a levy for using fixtures on their coupons. As a result, the league withheld fixtures until the day of the game, when coupons couldn't be printed. Unfortunately the supporters were similarly in the dark, and crowds fell.

1964	Swindon Town	(h) 4–1	Division Two	Suddick, Cummings, Hilley, Burton	23565
1992	Port Vale	(a) 1–0	Division Two	S. Watson	10321

MARCH 1ST

1893	Bill Bradley born, Wardley.				
1902	Bolton Wanderers	(h) 4–1	Division One	Roberts 2, Rutherford, McColl	12000

Debut goal for 17-year-old Jock Rutherford.

1913	Everton	(h) 2–0	Division One	Shepherd, Stewart	25000
1924	Everton	(a) 2–2	Division One	McDonald, Cowan	30000
1930	Hull City	(h) 1–1	FA Cup 6th Round	Lang	63486
1939	Tottenham Hotspur	(h) 0–1	Division Two	No Scorer	18500
1947	Sheffield United	(a) 2–0	FA Cup 6th Round	Bentley (pen), Milburn	46911
1952	Huddersfield Town	(h) 6–2	Division One	Mitchell 2, G. Robledo, Milburn 3	51394
1958	Aston Villa	(h) 2–4	Division One	Mitchell (pen), Bottom	40135
1967	England Under-23 1, Scotland Under-23 3, at St James' Park. Watched by 22,097.				
1969	West Ham United	(a) 1–3	Division One	Davies	26336
1980	Watford	(h) 0–2	Division Two	No Scorer	23091

The Hornets' goakeeper was Eric Steele, who had a spell at Gallowgate without ever being called into first-team action. ITV's *Shoot* cameras were on hand to preserve a David Barton own goal for future generations to mock.

1986	Arsenal	(h) 1–0	Division One	Roeder	22085
1988	Southampton	(a) 1–1	Division One	O'Neill	13380
1997	Southampton	(h) 0–1	Premier League	No Scorer	36446

MARCH 2ND

1895	East Stirlingshire	(h) 6–1	Friendly	Dickson 2, Thompson 2, Smith, Milne	1000
1897	Jack Hill born, Hetton-Le-Hole.				
1899	Brampton Welfare	(a) 12–2	Friendly	Harvey 2, Stevenson, Higgins, Peddie, Niblo Ghee, Lindsay, Ostler, Stott, Kingsley, MacFarlane	1000

Every member of the team got on the scoresheet!

1901	Notts County	(a) 1–3	Division One	A. Gardner	4000
1901	Jimmy Naylor born, High Crompton, Lancashire.				
1907	Preston North End	(a) 2–2	Division One	Gosnell, Howie	12000
1912	Sheffield Wednesday	(h) 0–2	Division One	No Scorer	22000
1913	John Kelly born, Hetton-le-Hole.				
1932	Blackburn Rovers	(h) 5–3	Division One	Allen 2, Boyd, Lang, J.R. Richardson	20000
1935	Manchester United	(a) 1–0	Division Two	Pearson	16000
1938	Stockport County	(a) 3–1	Division Two	Bowden 2, Park	8000
1945	David Ford born, Sheffield.				
1947	Alex Reid born, Glasgow.				
1955	Nottingham Forest	(h) 2–1	FA Cup 5th Round 2nd Replay	Monkhouse 2	36631
1957	Manchester City	(a) 2–1	Division One	Mitchell, White	25229
1959	All Stars XI	(h) 2–4	Friendly	Allchurch 2	15662
	Testimonial match.				
1963	Sunderland	(a) 0–0	Division Two	No Scorer	62420

A slight improvement in the sub-zero temperatures allowed the first game at Roker Park since Boxing Day to be staged. However, pneumatic drills were used in an attempt to break up the bone-hard pitch. United keeper Dave Hollins saved a Stan Anderson penalty

1968	Sheffield Wednesday	(a) 1–1	Division One	T. Robson	24762
1970	West Ham United	(h) 4–1	Division One	Dyson, Foggon, Davies, Robson	27726
1974	Leeds United	(a) 1–1	Division One	Barrowclough	46611
1977	Leeds United	(h) 3–0	Division One	Burns, Oates, McCaffery	33714
1985	Watford	(h) 3–1	Division One	Cunningham, Reilly, Megson	24875

1991   Leicester City   (h) 2–1   Division Two   McGhee, Sloan   13575
The only goal Scott Sloan managed for United. Two up at half-time, the only interest in the second half was a Leicester goal from winger Tommy Wright, and a large chorus of boos which filled the air when Leicester caretaker manager Gordon Lee left the bench to retrieve the ball.

MARCH 3RD

1900   Wolverhampton   (a) 1–1   Division One   Peddie   8000
        Wanderers
1903   Duncan Hutchison born, Kelty, Scotland.
1906   Middlesbrough   (a) 0–1   Division One   No Scorer   20000
        Debut for James Raine, at outside-right.
1923   Blackburn Rovers   (h) 5–1   Division One   Harris 3, Seymour 2   30000
1933   Stewart Mitchell born, Glasgow.
1934   Sunderland   (a) 0–2   Division One   No Scorer   32358
1951   Derby County   (a) 2–1   Division One   G. Robledo, Walker   25999
1956   Sunderland   (h) 0–2   FA Cup 6th Round   No Scorer   61474
        Bill Holden struck both goals for the visitors, as both teams played in their respective away strips.
1962   Bury   (h) 1–2   Division Two   Thomas   25853
1976   Stoke City   (h) 0–1   Division One   No Scorer   38822
1976   United announced the double signing of Graham Oates and Roger Jones from Gordon Lee's former club Blackburn Rovers.
1979   Charlton Athletic   (h) 5–3   Division Two   Connolly, Shoulder 2   14998
                                                        (1 pen), Martin, Mitchell
1982   Leicester City   (a) 0–3   Division Two   No Scorer   12497
        Two goals from Gary Lineker and one from Alan Young settled it.
1984   Fulham   (a) 2–2   Division Two   Beardsley, Keegan   12290
1990   Barnsley   (h) 4–1   Division Two   Anderson, Scott, Aitken,   18999
                                                McGhee (pen)
In 65 first-team appearances, a well-taken goal at the Leazes end was the only time Roy Aitken netted for United.

MARCH 4TH

1893   Stoke City   (h) 3–4   Friendly   Graham, Reay, Wallace   3000
1899   Liverpool   (h) 1–3   Friendly   Macfarlane   4000
1905   Bolton Wanderers   (a) 2–0   FA Cup 3rd Round   Appleyard, Howie   35574
1908   Bill Imrie born, Methil, Scotland.
1911   Bury   (h) 5–1   Division One   Randall 2, Stewart,   12000
                                            Metcalf, Higgins
1922   Bolton Wanderers   (a) 2–3   Division One   Harris, McDonald   22000
1931   Billy Wright born, Blackpool.
1933   West Bromwich   (a) 2–3   Division One   Bell, Boyd   25000
        Albion
1939   Bradford   (a) 1–0   Division Two   Wright   10148
1944   Len Walker born, Darlington.
1950   Sunderland   (a) 2–2   Division One   Houghton, Taylor   68004
        A record Tyne–Wear derby crowd saw Ivor Broadis score for the Rokermen against his future employers and Len Shackleton prove a point to the club that sold him when he netted the other goal.
1951   Kenny Dalglish born, Dalmarnock, Scotland.
1961   Sheffield United   (h) 1–3   FA Cup 6th Round   McGuigan   54829
1967   Sunderland   (a) 0–3   Division One   No Scorer   50442
        A pair for Bobby Kerr and one for George Mulhall.

| 1972 | Leicester City | (h) 2–0 | Division One | Macdonald, Gibb | 25256 |

1972 Former Magpie 35-year-old George Eastham scored once and inspired Stoke City to a memorable 2–1 victory over Chelsea in the League Cup final at Wembley.

1978	Derby County	(a) 1–1	Division One	Burns	19708
1989	Brondby IF (Denmark)	(h) 2–0	Friendly	O'Brien, Brazil	3338
1995	Liverpool	(a) 0–2	Premier League	No Scorer	39300
1996	Manchester United	(a) 0–1	Premier League	No Scorer	36584

After a run of 14 consecutive away wins at St James' Park, Newcastle pounded their visitors for the first 45 minutes backed by earsplitting support but couldn't conjure up a goal thanks to Schmeichel and the woodwork. A second-half strike from Eric Cantona won it, while David Batty made a steady debut for Newcastle.

| 1997 | Monaco | (h) 0–1 | UEFA Cup 4th Round 1st Leg | No Scorer | 36215 |

MARCH 5TH

1898	Darwen	(a) 3–1	Division Two	Peddie 3	2000
1902	Alnwick St James	(a) 4–0	Friendly	Peddie, Aitken, A. Gardner, Roberts	
1904	St Mirren	(h) 5–2	Friendly	McClarence 4, Rutherford	3000
1910	Leicester Fosse	(h) 3–0	FA Cup 4th Round	Wilson, Shepherd, Howie	52544
1921	Middlesbrough	(a) 0–0	Division One	No Scorer	38000

The debut of Tom McDonald gave little indication of the great career he was to enjoy at Gallowgate, completing 367 games and scoring 113 goals in a decade.

1927	Everton	(h) 7–3	Division One	McDonald, McKay, MacKenzie, Seymour, Gallacher 3	45000
1930	Hull City	(a) 0–1	FA Cup 6th Round Replay	No Scorer	32930
1932	Manchester City	(a) 1–5	Division One	Allen	28000
1938	Bradford	(a) 0–2	Division Two	No Scorer	12000
1949	Sunderland	(h) 2–1	Division One	Milburn, Robledo	58250

A match played in blizzard conditions. Bobby Mitchell made his debut in this Tyne–Wear derby and didn't taste defeat in this fixture until his sixth attempt, when ironically he scored his first goal against Sunderland.

1952	Keith Kennedy born, Sunderland.				
1955	Portsmouth	(a) 1–3	Division One	Keeble	54055
1960	Fulham	(h) 3–1	Division One	Allchurch, Eastham, White	33993
1966	Sunderland	(h) 2–0	Division One	Suddick 2	52051
1973	League of Ireland	(a) 0–0	Friendly	No Scorer	6000
1973	Death of Wilf Feeney, 62.				
1977	Liverpool	(a) 0–1	Division One	No Scorer	45553
1983	Crystal Palace	(a) 2–0	Division Two	Waddle, Varadi	10239
1988	Everton	(a) 0–1	Division One	No Scorer	25674
1994	Sheffield Wednesday	(a) 1–0	Premier League	Cole	33153

It was smash and grab as a last-minute free-kick was awarded to United after Ian Pearce had been sent off. The ball was played in and Cole smacked it home with the referee poised to blow the final whistle.

MARCH 6TH

1897	Walsall	(h) 2–0	Division Two	Connell, Ostler (pen)	6000
1909	Sunderland	(h) 2–2	FA Cup 4th Round	Rutherford, Wilson	53353
1912	Bob Dennison born, Amble.				
1914	Tommy Pearson born, Edinburgh.				

| 1915 | Chelsea | (a) 1–1 | FA Cup 4th Round | Goodwill | 58000 |
| 1920 | Blackburn Rovers | (h) 0–0 | Division One | No Scorer | 35000 |

Debut for Jerry Best.

| 1922 | Blackburn Rovers | (a) 2–0 | Division One | Harris, Seymour | 20000 |
| 1926 | Huddersfield Town | (h) 0–2 | Division One | No Scorer | 57000 |

First of two appearances at left-back for Wearsider Lawrie Crown, who had earlier played league football for South Shields.

1933	Wolverhampton Wanderers	(a) 1–1	Division One	McMenemy	16000
1937	Plymouth Argyle	(a) 1–1	Division Two	Imrie	19000
1948	Bury	(h) 1–0	Division Two	Milburn	56444
1954	Aston Villa	(h) 0–1	Division One	No Scorer	36847
1965	Portsmouth	(a) 2–1	Division Two	Cummings, Robson	19399
1976	Derby County	(a) 2–4	FA Cup 6th Round	Gowling 2	38362

The debut and sole appearance of goalkeeper Eddie Edgar. Unfortunately a patched-up United side caught the Rams on form, and two goals from Bruce Rioch, one a rocket free-kick, and one apiece from Henry Newton and Charlie George settled it. The dream of a second Wembley trip in the season was over.

1982	Barnsley	(h) 1–0	Division Two	Varadi	18784
1991	Newcastle defeated Nottingham Forest 3–2, with Borussia Munchengladbach defender Thomas Huschbeck making his only appearance for the club as a trialist.				
1993	Brentford	(h) 5–1	Division Two	Kelly, Bracewell, Clark 2, Lee	30006

A game remembered more for the goal that was disallowed rather than the six United scored (Kevin Scott putting past his own keeper). Robert Lee 'scored' at the Leazes end from within his own half, only for the referee to rule it out and bring play back for a free-kick to United, awarded for a Brentford offside. Joe Allon and Paul Stephenson made their debuts for Brentford, but would probably rather have been in the stand cheering on the toon.

MARCH 7TH

| 1896 | Loughborough Town | (a) 0–1 | Division Two | No Scorer | 2000 |

Debut for George Adams.

| 1903 | Liverpool | (a) 0–3 | Division One | No Scorer | 15000 |

Only appearance of Bob Benson. Debut for Bobby Templeton, a famed Scottish dribbler, at outside-left.

1908	Grimsby Town	(h) 5–1	FA Cup 4th Round	Appleyard 3, Gardner, OG	44788
1925	Preston North End	(h) 3–1	Division One	Cowan, Harris, Low	20000
1931	Leeds United	(a) 0–1	Division One	No Scorer	10000
1936	Doncaster Rovers	(a) 2–2	Division Two	Pearson, J. Smith	14000
1953	Charlton Athletic	(a) 0–0	Division One	No Scorer	33222
1956	Cardiff City	(a) 1–1	Division One	Curry	42000
1959	Preston North End	(h) 1–2	Division One	White	31962
1962	Middlesbrough	(a) 0–3	Division Two	No Scorer	21023

Not the best of games for Jimmy Fell to make his debut.

| 1963 | Bradford City | (a) 6–1 | FA Cup 3rd Round | McGarry 2, Thomas, Hilley, Hughes 2 | 13605 |
| 1964 | Northampton Town | (a) 2–2 | Division Two | Cummings, Suddick | 11440 |

A draw at the County ground with the Cobblers, who ended the season in second place to United and joined them in the First Division. Hunt and Leck netted for the home side.

| 1979 | Andrew Griffin born, Billinge, Lancashire. | | | | |
| 1981 | West Ham United | (a) 0–1 | Division Two | No Scorer | 26274 |

A late goal preserved the Hammers' 16-game winning streak at Upton Park and left them 20 points ahead of Newcastle, topping the Second Division.

1987	Aston Villa	(h) 2–1	Division One	Cunningham, Beardsley	21224
1990	Hull City	(h) 2–0	Division Two	McGhee 2 (1 pen)	20684
1992	Brighton and Hove Albion	(h) 0–1	Division Two	No Scorer	24597

MARCH 8TH

1884	James Fleming born, Musselburgh, Scotland.				
1897	Jack Wilson born, Leadgate, Durham.				
1902	Manchester City	(a) 0–2	Division One	No Scorer	20000
1913	Sunderland	(a) 0–0	FA Cup 4th Round	No Scorer	28720
1924	Liverpool	(h) 1–0	FA Cup 4th Round	McDonald	56594
1930	Everton	(h) 1–0	Division One	Gallacher	44000
1952	Portsmouth	(a) 4–2	FA Cup 6th Round	Milburn 3, G. Robledo	44699

Jackie Milburn remembered this game as the best performance of his career, witnessed by thousands of United fans who had travelled by train. The home side's Belgian winger Marcel Gaillard opened the scoring, but United hit back twice before Douggie Reid equalised. Milburn then hit a fantastic third to complete his hat-trick before Robledo added the fourth.

1958	Wolverhampton Wanderers	(a) 1–3	Division One	White	34058
1961	Wolverhampton Wanderers	(a) 1–2	Division One	Allchurch	24970
1968	Celtic	(a) 3–2	Friendly	Davies, Scott, T. Robson	42000
1969	Burnley	(h) 1–0	Division One	Horsfield	32460
1972	Giorgos Georgiadas born, Greece.				
1975	SC Internacional (Brazil)	(h) 0–3	Friendly	No Scorer	23475

Top-class Brazilian opposition for this friendly. Internacional were based in the city of Porto Alegre and formed the basis of the national side.

| 1980 | Cambridge United | (a) 0–0 | Division Two | No Scorer | 6908 |

Debut for Bobby Shinton, who enjoyed a love-hate relationship with the St James' crowd, though mostly the latter . . .

| 1995 | West Ham United | (h) 2–0 | Premier League | Clark, Kitson | 34595 |
| 1998 | Barnsley | (h) 3–1 | FA Cup 6th Round | Ketsbaia, Speed, Batty | 36695 |

MARCH 9TH

1894	Jimmy Low born, Kilbirnie, Scotland.				
1895	Crewe Alexandra	(a) 1–2	Division Two	Hedley	2000
1901	Preston North End	(h) 3–5	Division One	Heywood, Peddie, Aitken	17000
1907	Corinthians	(a) 5–2	Friendly	Rutherford, Appleyard, Brown 2, OG	30000

United claimed the Sheriff of London Shield in this forerunner of the Charity Shield held at Craven Cottage. The Corinthians' goalkeeper was Tom Rowlandson, who made one appearance for Newcastle.

1910	Bradford City	(a) 3–3	Division One	Stewart 2, Shepherd	10000
1912	Bury	(a) 1–2	Division One	Stewart	
1929	Sunderland	(h) 4–3	Division One	Gallacher 2 (1 pen), Urwin, OG	66275

An epic derby victory. As the *Sunderland Echo* described, 'The new covered stand at the Leazes end proved a giddy perch for a few zealous followers.'

1935	Port Vale	(h) 1–2	Division Two	Pearson	23000
1957	Bolton Wanderers	(h) 4–0	Division One	Davies, Milburn, Scoular, White	34073
1962	Death of George Jobey, 76.				

1963	Leeds United	(h) 1–1	Division Two	Hilley	29575

1963 United's reserve side went down 3–2 at Anfield to Liverpool, with a young Frank Clark breaking his leg.

1974	Nottingham Forest	(h) 4–3	FA Cup 6th Round	Tudor, Moncur, McDermott (pen), Craig	54500

A pitch invasion was to require a replay of the game. The most remarkable thing about this game is how the Leazes-enders managed to get across the pitch in their sta-press trews and chelsea boots, speed up as they reach the other end and dive headlong into the Forest fans. Memories are made of this . . .

1977	Ipswich Town	(h) 1–1	Division One	Nattrass	33820

1977 A power cut blacked out the floodlights during the game.

1978 Transfer deadline day, and Alan Gowling departed for Bolton Wanderers at a cost of £120,000.

1985	Nottingham Forest	(a) 0–0	Division One	No Scorer	17425
1991	Watford	(a) 2–1	Division Two	Anderson, Quinn	10018

Debuts for Alan Neilson and Andy Hunt, both at substitute. The Rous stand at Watford (similar to the Milburn stand) proved an ideal vantage point to watch the game and had the advantage of not requiring a marathon trek through the allotments to reach the away end. John Anderson hit a memorable opener, and substitute Andy Hunt's first touch in league football set up Quinn to score a second-half winner.

1994 Peter Beardsley belatedly won his 50th England cap three years after his 49th as England defeated Denmark 1–0 at Wembley.

1996 Everton finally completed the £700,000 signing of United defender Marc Hottiger.

MARCH 10TH

1894	Walsall Town Swifts	(h) 2–0	Division Two	Crate, Jeffery (pen)	1000

1894 The second goal was United's first penalty kick.

1900	Aston Villa	(h) 3–2	Division One	Peddie 2, A. Gardner	19549
1902	Wolverhampton Wanderers	(a) 0–3	Division One	No Scorer	2000
1906	Birmingham	(a) 2–2	FA Cup 4th Round	Veitch 2 (1pen)	25000
1909	Sunderland	(a) 3–0	FA Cup 4th Round Replay	Shepherd 2, Wilson	27512

Not for the last time, the Roker administration were criticised for doubling ground admission prices to rip off travelling supporters and locals alike. Happily, they were well beaten.

1915	Middlesbrough	(h) 1–2	Division One	Goodwill	10000

Debut for Richard McGough at centre-half. Unfortunately another victim of the Great War. Fellow newcomer John Soulsby also served in France and returned to play in the Football League for Ashington.

1923	Blackburn Rovers	(a) 1–1	Division One	McDonald	15000
1928	Aston Villa	(h) 7–5	Division One	McCurley 2, McDonald, Seymour, Wilkinson 3	25000

Wildly varying weather (snow, rain, sunshine) and an early 4–0 lead for United. The visitors hit back to make it 4–2 before United hit three more. Even then, Villa hit three late goals to make it 7–5, this after losing their goalkeeper through injury.

1934	Chelsea	(h) 2–2	Division One	McMenemy, Weaver (pen)	14000
1951	Wolverhampton Wanderers	(n) 0–0	FA Cup Semi-Final	No Scorer	62250

Held at Hillsborough.

1956	Aston Villa	(h) 2–3	Division One	Curry, OG	34647
1962	Brighton and Hove Albion	(a) 4–0	Division Two	Allchurch, Thomas, Kerray, Suddick	12286

1968 Pavel Srnicek born, Ostrava, Czechoslovakia.

1973	Stoke City	(h) 1–0	Division One	Macdonald	24020

Debut for Alan Kennedy.

1979	Cardiff City	(a) 1–2	Division Two	Connolly	11368
1984	Chelsea	(h) 1–1	Division Two	McDermott	35544
1988	Morton	(a) 1–0	Friendly	Gascoigne	2000
1990	Watford	(a) 0–0	Division Two	No Scorer	12069

Tony Coton was a controversial figure in this game, seemingly retrieving the ball from a Quinn effort after it had crossed his line. However, the myopic linesman seemed to have failed to keep up with play and refused to grant what looked a legitimate goal.

1992	Cambridge United	(a) 2–0	Division Two	Peacock, Kelly	8254

Third-place Cambridge could have gone top had they won this, but a performance of character saw Newcastle rewarded with three vital points.

1993	Charlton Athletic	(h) 2–2	Division One	Lee, Kelly	29582

Debuts for Keegan's twin signings of Scott Sellars and Mark Robinson, both of whom were to have their Tyneside careers blighted by injury. Things looked promising when Lee netted against his old club within a minute, but Garry Nelson and Carl Leaburn ensured honours ended even.

1997	Liverpool	(a) 3–4	Premier League	Gillespie, Asprilla, Barton	40751

1998 Newcastle signed defender Nicos Dabizas from Greek club Olympiakos.

MARCH 11TH

1893	Annbank	(h) 6–1	Friendly	Reay 5, Thompson	2000

Scottish opposition for this friendly, whom Harry Reay beat almost single-handedly. As well as the five he scored, he had two other efforts disallowed.

1899	Nottingham Forest	(h) 0–1	Division One	No Scorer	18000
1905	Wolverhampton Wanderers	(h) 3–0	Division One	Appleyard, Rutherford, McWilliam	20000
1907	Maidstone	(a) 5–2	Friendly	Appleyard 2, Hardinge, Gosnell, Orr	5000
1908	Preston North End	(h) 0–0	Division One	No Scorer	17000

The one chance to impress that centre-forward Alex McCulloch was given in his year at United went begging.

1922	Bolton Wanderers	(h) 2–1	Division One	Curry, Harris	30000

Debut for Charlie Spencer, at centre-half.

1930	Burnley	(a) 3–0	Division One	Cape, Devine, Lang	10000

1930 Tommy Casey born, Comber, Northern Ireland.

1933	Sheffield Wednesday	(h) 3–1	Division One	Allen 2, McMenemy	33000
1939	Sheffield Wednesday	(h) 2–1	Division Two	Frost, Scott	29000

Successful debut for Arthur Frost, who continued a rich vein of scoring that had seen United vie with many clubs to sign him from then-league club New Brighton. However, after four more games, the imminent war ruined his career.

1950	Derby County	(h) 2–1	Division One	Mitchell, Corbett (pen)	40784

The visitors' goal was scored by Jackie Stamps, who had been signed for the Rams just before the outbreak of war by former United player George Jobey. A bar in Derby now bears his name, in commemoration of his goalscoring achievements. Ironically, football shirts are banned.

1952 John Brownlie born, Caldercruix, Scotland.

1959	Portsmouth	(a) 5–1	Division One	Eastham (pen), Curry 3, Taylor	19404
1961	Manchester United	(h) 1–1	Division One	Scanlon	28867
1967	Manchester United	(h) 0–0	Division One	No Scorer	38203
1970	RSC Anderlecht (Belgium)	(a) 0–2	Fairs Cup 4th Round 1st Leg	No Scorer	30000
1972	Arsenal	(h) 2–0	Division One	Macdonald, Smith	33907
1978	Manchester United	(h) 2–2	Division One	McGhee, Burns (pen)	25825

58 • NEWCASTLE

One of three brief substitute appearances for South African Andy Parkinson, who was allegedly a striker.

| 1989 | Queens Park Rangers | (h) 1–2 | Division One | Ranson | 21665 |

The first goal for Rangers was scored by Colin Clarke on his debut.

MARCH 12TH

1890	Harry Woods born, St Helens, Lancashire.				
1898	Luton	(h) 4–1	Division Two	Wardrope, Harvey 3	15000
1904	Middlesbrough	(a) 3–1	Division One	Appleyard, Howie, Rutherford	15000

Newcastle marked their first visit to Ayresome Park with a victory.

1910	Bury	(h) 2–2	Division One	Wilson, Waugh (pen)	20000
1913	Sunderland	(h) 2–2	FA Cup 4th Round 1st Replay	McTavish, Veitch	56717
1921	Blackburn Rovers	(h) 1–2	Division One	Hudspeth (pen)	44000
1927	Blackburn Rovers	(a) 2–1	Division One	Gallacher 2	40000
1932	Chelsea	(n) 2–1	FA Cup Semi-Final	Allen, Lang	36709

Held at Leeds Road, Huddersfield. Two goals up, the Chelsea reply came from Hughie Gallacher.

1938	West Ham United	(h) 2–2	Division Two	Docking, J.R. Richardson	22000
1949	Wolverhampton Wanderers	(a) 0–3	Division One	No Scorer	40000
1952	Chelsea	(a) 0–1	Division One	No Scorer	42948

Debut for Essex boy Vic Keeble. Although he took seven games to register a goal, he then scored regularly, with 69 goals in 121 senior starts.

1955	Huddersfield Town	(a) 1–1	FA Cup 6th Round	White	55000
1956	Partick Thistle	(h) 1–1	Friendly	Taylor	13735
1960	Bolton Wanderers	(a) 4–1	Division One	Eastham, Mitten 2, White	24648
1966	Burnley	(a) 0–1	Division One	No Scorer	16257
1969	Vitoria Setubal (Portugal)	(h) 5–1	Fairs Cup 4th Round 1st Leg	Davies, Foggon, Gibb, Robson 2	57662

1975 Malcolm Macdonald chose the 100th Wembley international to score his first goal for England, heading in a Colin Bell cross to seal a 2–0 victory over West Germany.

| 1977 | Norwich City | (h) 5–1 | Division One | T. Craig, Gowling, Oates, McCaffery 2 | 27808 |
| 1983 | Leeds United | (h) 2–1 | Division Two | Waddle, Keegan (pen) | 24543 |

The visitors and their supporters left Gallowgate muttering dark threats against referee Neil Midgley, who awarded a penalty against Paul Hart when he tackled Kevin Keegan on the edge of the box. Keegan fell into the area and got up to score the resultant penalty past veteran David Harvey. Terry Connor scored with 20 minutes remaining but Newcastle held out.

| 1991 | Middlesbrough | (a) 0–3 | Division Two | No Scorer | 18250 |

Robbie Elliott crept on as a substitute for his debut in a thoroughly rotten display at Ayresome Park. The only bright spot was a demonstration by Steve Watson of his unique somersault throw-in technique.

| 1994 | Swindon Town | (h) 7–1 | Premier League | Beardsley 2 (1 pen), Lee 2, Watson 2, Fox | 32219 |

A deserved leathering for the Wiltshire side, amazingly achieved without Cole making the scoresheet.

| 1995 | Everton | (a) 0–1 | FA Cup 6th Round | No Scorer | 35203 |

A narrow defeat courtesy of Dave Watson and a bad Fox miss.

MARCH 13TH

| 1897 | Blackpool | (a) 1–4 | Division Two | Smellie | 3000 |
| 1902 | Celtic | (n) 2–4 | Friendly | Rutherford, Heywood | 2000 |

Played at Berwick.

1909	Bury	(a) 1–1	Division One	OG	15000
1911	Derby County	(h) 4–0	FA Cup 4th Round	Shepherd, Stewart, Rutherford, Willis	59700
1915	Chelsea	(h) 0–1	FA Cup 4th Round Replay	No Scorer	49827
1920	Blackburn Rovers	(a) 0–2	Division One	No Scorer	25000
1926	Birmingham	(a) 1–1	Division One	Urwin	30000
1929	Aston Villa	(h) 2–1	Division One	Gallacher 2	35000
1937	Coventry City	(h) 4–2	Division Two	Imrie, Pearson, Smith 2	12000
1948	Southampton	(a) 2–4	Division Two	Milburn, Sibley	28000

Record signing George Lowrie made his debut in the forward line.

| 1954 | Huddersfield Town | (a) 2–3 | Division One | Milburn, Monkhouse | 25710 |

Newcastle arrived late but unscathed after their train had been involved in a derailment en route to the game.

| 1963 | Norwich City | (a) 0–5 | FA Cup 4th Round | No Scorer | 34770 |

The only good thing that came out of this embarrassing defeat was the performance of Canaries centre-half Ollie Burton, who was persuaded to move to St James' Park, joining soon after in an £11,000 transfer.

| 1965 | Norwich City | (h) 2–0 | Division Two | Cummings, Robson | 41441 |
| 1971 | Ipswich Town | (a) 0–1 | Division One | No Scorer | 17060 |

| 1974 | A crowd of 4,511 turned up to watch England Under-23 overcome Scotland Under-23 2–0 at St James' Park. |

| 1976 | West Ham United | (h) 2–1 | Division One | T. Craig (pen), Macdonald | 33866 |

Newly appointed manager Gordon Lee went back to Blackburn for Roger Jones, who made a winning debut in goal. However, his stay at Gallowgate was curtailed by concerns over his fitness, eventually leading to a free transfer.

| 1982 | Rotherham United | (a) 0–0 | Division Two | No Scorer | 16905 |

A last-minute penalty save by Kevin Carr from Tony Towner brought the Millers' charge to a stop. Yorkshire TV later nominated it 'save of the season' and Carr was presented with a dreadful portrait of himself that he probably hid behind a wardrobe.

| 1986 | Injury to Thomas and McKellar forced United to borrow veteran goalkeeper Dave Clarke from Blyth Spartans to play in a Central League match at Aston Villa. Clarke had spent some time at Gallowgate early in his career including being on the bench for some of the Fairs Cup games, and didn't let his old club down, making several good stops as United won 1–0. |

| 1993 | Swindon Town | (a) 1–2 | Division One | Kelly | 17574 |

Another dubious defeat at the County Ground, as a shocking penalty award gave Paul Bodin the chance to equalise against the club that rejected him after taking him on trial. Having made it 1–1, the referee and linesman then missed an outbreak of basketball by Steve White as he controlled a pass and forced a corner. Cue Colin Calderwood, who got the winner. Within ten minutes Andy Cole had made his debut as a substitute, but didn't have an opportunity to make an instant impact.

| 1995 | Newcastle gave a trial to Diego Tur, a central defender from Danish side FC Copenhagen. |

MARCH 14TH

1896	Notts County	(a) 1–0	Division Two	Aitken	5000
1900	Glossop	(h) 1–0	Division One	Peddie	6000
1903	Sheffield United	(h) 0–0	Division One	No Scorer	20000
1906	Birmingham	(h) 3–0	FA Cup 4th Round Replay	Appleyard 2, Howie	39059

All three goals came in the second period of extra time.

| 1908 | Bury | (h) 3–0 | Division One | Appleyard 2, Howie | 25000 |
| 1914 | Preston North End | (a) 1–4 | Division One | Shepherd | 18000 |

1923 West Bromwich (a) 1–2 Division One Harris 5520
Albion
Debut for William Scott, at centre-forward.

1925 Burnley (a) 3–1 Division One Harris 2, McDonald 12000

1931 Blackpool (h) 0–2 Division One No Scorer 20000

1936 Bury (h) 3–0 Division Two Connelly 2, J. Smith 14000

1949 Graham Oates born, Bradford.

1951 Wolverhampton (n) 2–1 FA Cup Semi-Final Milburn, Mitchell 47349
Wanderers Replay
At Leeds Road, Huddersfield.

1953 Arsenal (h) 2–2 Division One Mitchell, G. Robledo 51618

1959 Manchester City (a) 1–5 Division One White 25417

1964 Sunderland (h) 1–0 Division Two McGarry (pen) 27341
A low crowd was partly due to signs maliciously posted outside the Central Station which fooled many into believing the match had been called off due to a waterlogged pitch. Those that turned up saw Charlie Hurley handle the ball in the box and give away the match-winning penalty.

1967 Newcastle sold Ron McGarry to Barrow for £6,000.

1970 West Bromwich (a) 2–2 Division Two Dyson, Robson 19641
Albion
Debut for David Young, in midfield.

1973 Ipswich Town (h) 1–1 Texaco Cup Macdonald 22531

1974 An FA Commission met to consider the events of the previous Saturday's FA Cup tie at St James' Park. Their verdict: a replay at a neutral ground.

1975 Stephen Harper born, Easington, Durham. A highly rated keeper who joined United from Seaham Red Star, he has played much of his football out on loan, including an inspirational spell at Huddersfield. Terriers manager Peter Jackson was desperate to sign him but Dalglish persuaded him to sign a new contract at Newcastle, presumably on the strength of the departure of Srnicek and Hislop. However, within days Lionel Perez had joined United, leaving Harper's position uncertain.

1981 Preston North End (h) 2–0 Division Two Harford 2 12015
Newcastle chose this game to introduce ballboys to the ground. Unfortunately this happened to coincide with monsoon-like rainfall which thoroughly soaked the poor little mites in their nylon tracksuits. Harford mastered the conditions with two finely taken goals to overcome a poor Preston side managed by Nobby Stiles.

1992 Swindon Town (h) 3–1 Division One Kelly, Peacock, Quinn 23138
Pantomime time at United. Keegan took his place on the bench well after kick-off and left before the final whistle. Post-match radio reports began to speculate that he had in fact resigned as manager. John Hall was interviewed and feigned ignorance, while callers jammed Radio Five's *606* programme to express their anger and consternation. Having failed to get the promised funds for purchasing the on-loan Brian Kilcline, Keegan had apparently walked out in disgust commenting, 'It's not like it was in the brochure.' However, frantic behind-the-scenes activity secured the required funding and Keegan was persuaded to return.

1994 Another day, another trialist. This time it was Argentinian Jorge Ivanovic.

1998 Coventry City (h) 0–0 Premier League No Scorer 36767
The nearest United came to scoring was a deflection off the head of Dion Dublin that left Ogrizovic scrambling. One of the few bright spots was the form of debutant substitute Nicos Dabizas.

MARCH 15TH

1902 Wolverhampton (h) 3–1 Division One Veitch, Rutherford 2 7000
Wanderers

1913 Blackburn Rovers (h) 0–1 Division One No Scorer 18000
Debut for midlander Edward Cooper, at outside-right.

1924	West Bromwich Albion	(h) 1–1	Division One	Harris	20000
1930	Sheffield Wednesday	(a) 2–4	Division One	Devine, Weaver	10000
1939	Death of Sandy Higgins, 53.				
1952	Portsmouth	(h) 3–3	Division One	Milburn, Mitchell, G. Robledo	62870
1958	Leicester City	(h) 5–3	Division One	Bottom 2, White 3	33840
1975	Ipswich Town	(a) 4–5	Division One	Tudor 2, Macdonald 2	23450
	Debut for Aiden McCaffery, at centre-half.				
1977	Stoke City	(a) 0–0	Division One	No Scorer	12708
1978	Birmingham City	(h) 1–1	Division One	Nattrass	19493

The Blues included former Sunderland keeper Jimmy Montgomery, who was powerless to prevent Nattrass scoring after defender Gary Pendrey underhit a backpass. Future United manager Jim Smith took charge of the visitors for the first time.

1980	West Ham United	(h) 0–0	Division Two	No Scorer	25474

The infamous petrol bomb incident, which, as legend has it, landed at the feet of Tony Cottee and John Cornwell in the visitors' section. Benches were subsequently installed in front of the East Stand.

1986	Ipswich Town	(h) 3–1	Division One	Beardsley, Whitehurst, Gascoigne	19451

Debut for Dave McKellar against the club that had given him his first chance, some 13 years earlier. Trevor Putney was dismissed for the visitors, while Billy Whitehurst scored his first United goal.

1989	Nottingham Forest	(a) 1–1	Division One	Brock	20800

Nigel Clough scored from the spot for Forest, but Brock deservedly levelled.

1997	Coventry City	(h) 4–0	Premier League	Watson, Elliott, Lee, Beardsley (pen)	36571

Asprilla inspired his colleagues to this overwhelming victory, but couldn't score the goal he deserved.

1998 United Directors Freddy Shepherd and Douglas Hall appeared on the front page of the *News of the World* in what media hacks desperately tried to brand 'the Toongate scandal'. Allegations included calling Newcastle women 'dogs' and lambasting fans for buying overpriced Newcastle shirts. And calling Shearer Mary Poppins and claiming Andy Cole was crocked when they sold him. Oh, and getting very drunk and boasting about the number of prostitutes they'd paid for.

MARCH 16TH

1895	Bury	(h) 1–0	Division Two	Thompson	4000
1898	Manchester City	(h) 2–0	Division Two	Peddie, Aitken	17000
1901	Wolverhampton Wanderers	(a) 0–1	Division One	No Scorer	5000
1907	Aston Villa	(h) 3–2	Division One	Appleyard 2, Rutherford	48000
1910	Darlington	(a) 0–1	Friendly	No Scorer	3000
1912	Middlesbrough	(h) 0–1	Division One	No Scorer	35000
	Debut for Jack Peart.				
1922	Bobby Corbett born, Throckley.				
1929	Huddersfield Town	(a) 1–2	Division One	Cunningham (pen)	12000
1935	Barnsley	(a) 1–2	Division Two	Wilson	14500
1939	Norwich City	(a) 1–1	Division Two	Clifton	7700
1943	Billy Wilson born, Peebles, Scotland.				
1949	Alan Gowling born, Stockport.				
1949	Billy Hibbert died, 64.				
1955	Huddersfield Town	(h) 2–0	FA Cup 6th Round Replay	Keeble, Mitchell	52449

| 1957 | Leeds United | (a) 0–0 | Division One | No Scorer | 33000 |
| 1963 | Swansea Town | (a) 0–1 | Division Two | No Scorer | 8000 |

A home debut for Welsh Youth international Derek 'Didi' Draper, who inspired the Swans to victory. The dismissal of Ron McGarry for fighting with a home defender inspired the nickname of 'Cassius', after the heavyweight legend.

1968	Leeds United	(h) 1–1	Division One	T. Robson	46075
1974	Chelsea	(a) 0–1	Division One	No Scorer	24207
1976	Arsenal	(a) 0–0	Division One	No Scorer	18424
1991	Bristol City	(h) 0–0	Division Two	No Scorer	13578

MARCH 17TH

1894	Burslem Port Vale	(h) 6–1	Friendly	Crate, Quinn, Willis 2, Thompson, Wallace	2000
1900	Liverpool	(a) 0–2	Division One	No Scorer	18000
1906	Wolverhampton Wanderers	(a) 2–0	Division One	Gosnell, J. Rutherford	9000

Blaydon-born Bob Liddell made his debut, at right-half.

1906 Jock McCurley born, Kelty, Scotland.

1913	Sunderland	(h) 0–3	FA Cup 4th Round 2nd Replay	No Scorer	49754
1915	Chelsea	(h) 2–0	Division One	Finlay 2	5000
1923	Bolton Wanderers	(a) 0–1	Division One	No Scorer	25000
1928	Sunderland	(a) 1–1	Division One	McDonald	40071
1934	Sheffield United	(a) 0–4	Division One	No Scorer	25000

The slide into Division Two continued and debutant Bill Imrie could do little to prevent it.

| 1937 | Nottingham Forest | (h) 3–2 | Division Two | Smith, Rogers, Imrie (pen) | 4000 |

1948 Death of Jack Carr, 71.

| 1951 | Blackpool | (a) 2–2 | Division One | Milburn, G. Robledo | 30000 |
| 1956 | Blackpool | (a) 1–5 | Division One | Keeble | 23740 |

1960 Pat Heard born, Hull.

| 1962 | Scunthorpe United | (h) 2–1 | Division Two | Thomas, Day | 37931 |

A goalscoring debut for Billy Day, who was never to repeat the feat in his other 13 runouts for the first team.

1964	Swansea Town	(a) 1–0	Division Two	Anderson	9000
1971	Everton	(h) 2–1	Division One	Tudor, Moncur	22874
1973	Manchester United	(a) 1–2	Division One	Nattrass	48426

After signing from Bury, Terry McDermott returned to Manchester for his First Division debut, replacing Jimmy Smith. The home side's goals came from Jim Holton, who later had a trial for Newcastle, and Mick Martin, who had recently arrived at Old Trafford from Bohemians of Dublin.

1981 Lord Westwood and Bob Rutherford resigned from the Board, Stan Seymour becoming chairman.

| 1984 | Middlesbrough | (h) 3–1 | Division Two | McDermott, Beardsley, Keegan | 30421 |

An ultimately convincing win that looked unlikely when Stephen Bell gave the visitors an early lead. Kelham O'Hanlon kept various good shots out until a Beardsley special tied it up at half-time. The second half was similarly frustrating until McDermott found the net with a fine snap shot and Trewick then crossed for Keegan to head home from close in.

| 1990 | Ipswich Town | (h) 2–1 | Division Two | Quinn 2 | 20554 |

1993 Yet another imported trialist made an appearance for the reserves, a central defender named Mtawali who didn't impress in a goalless draw with Aston Villa. This was the final appearance in a Newcastle shirt for Bjorn Kristensen, who went to Portsmouth to link up again with former boss Jim Smith within 48 hours.

MARCH 18TH

Year	Opponent		Score	Competition	Scorers	Attendance
1893	Derby County	(h)	3–1	Friendly	Collins, OG, Unknown Scorer	3000
1899	Bolton Wanderers	(a)	0–0	Division One	No Scorer	5000

1901 England defeated Wales 6–0 in a full international held at St James' Park. A crowd of 11,000 attended and saw four goals from the prolific Derby County forward Steve Bloomer. Newcastle goalkeeper Matt Kingsley also appeared.

Year	Opponent		Score	Competition	Scorers	Attendance
1905	Bury	(a)	4–2	Division One	Appleyard 3, Aitken	18000
1911	Aston Villa	(h)	1–0	Division One	Shepherd	15000
1914	Burnley	(h)	3–1	Division One	Douglas, Goodwill, Hibbert	15000
1922	Oldham Athletic	(h)	1–1	Division One	Harris	30000
1933	Inverness	(a)	5–3	Friendly	Richardson, Lang, McMenemy	4000
1939	Fulham	(a)	1–1	Division Two	Clifton	20000

Debut for Reg Evans.

1941 Charlie Woods born, Whitehaven, Cumbria.

Year	Opponent		Score	Competition	Scorers	Attendance
1950	West Bromwich Albion	(a)	1–1	Division One	Houghton	33469
1967	Blackpool	(h)	2–1	Division One	Robson 2	30568
1970	RSC Anderlecht (Belgium)	(h)	3–1	Fairs Cup 4th Round 2nd Leg	Dyson, Robson	59309

A devastating end to a pulsating game, when Nordahl scored late on to send the Belgians through on away goals. Had the Anderlecht defender Heylens (who wore a wig) not cleared off the line when the score was 2–0, things could have been very different.

Year	Opponent		Score	Competition	Scorers	Attendance
1972	Liverpool	(a)	0–5	Division One	No Scorer	43899
1974	Nottingham Forest	(n)	0–0	FA Cup 6th Round	No Scorer	40685

This restaged tie was held at Goodison Park.

Year	Opponent		Score	Competition	Scorers	Attendance
1975	Arsenal	(a)	0–3	Division One	No Scorer	16540

Debut for Ray Blackhall and a final appearance at right-back for David Crosson. In his six first-team displays, United unfortunately won none. The Gunners' goals came from Brian Kidd, Alan Ball and Wearsider Wilf Rostron on his debut.

Year	Opponent		Score	Competition	Scorers	Attendance
1978	Chelsea	(a)	2–2	Division One	McGhee, Burns (pen)	22777

Debut for Jamie Scott.

1991 The endless search for new faces during the Jim Smith era included USA World Cup defender John Doyle, who played in a 3–1 reserve-team victory at Roker Park. However, Doyle's chief contribution was to concede two penalties with reckless challenges. The scorers for the reserves were Lee Clark, Billy Askew and Scott Sloan. Doyle did get another chance a few days later at Huddersfield but wasn't retained.

Year	Opponent		Score	Competition	Scorers	Attendance
1996	West Ham United	(h)	3–0	Premier League	Albert, Asprilla, Ferdinand	36331

Keeper Les Sealey kept the score to a respectable level as Newcastle took out their frustrations on the Hammers. The dismissal of Steve Potts wasn't a turning point.

Year	Opponent		Score	Competition	Scorers	Attendance
1997	Monaco	(a)	0–3	UEFA Cup 4th Round 2nd Leg	No Scorer	18500

The Newcastle team took to the field with 'Center Parcs' emblazoned on their shirts rather than the usual brown ale advert due to the French TV ban on alcohol advertising. The fact that pitchside hording advertised Vaux products simply backed up what many have said for years. The game itself was crap; United played without any recognised strikers and were well beaten. The away fans' turnout was tremendous, as was the support, and the locals seemed completely bemused by the black-and-white invasion. As the team were trudging from the field to an undeservedly great reception, the crowd struck up a chorus of 'In your Monaco Slums . . .'

Year	Opponent		Score	Competition	Scorers	Attendance
1998	Crystal Palace	(h)	1–2	Premier League	Shearer	36565

Lombardo and United reject Jansen scored two early goals as the team seemed affected by the Hall/Shepherd fiasco and tabloid hacks interrogated fans outside the ground. A number of reporters and cameramen were attacked after the game and had to seek sanctuary in a police van. Strangely, this wasn't reported.

MARCH 19TH

1878	Jimmy Howie born, Galston, Scotland.				
1896	Joe Harris born, Glasgow.				
1898	Sunderland	(h) 1–1	Friendly	Wardrope	14000
1902	Nottingham Forest	(a) 2–0	Division One	Pattinson, Aitken	21000

Daniel Pattinson was an ouside-left who took his only chance well, with a goal on his debut. However, he returned to the reserve team without ever being called upon again.

1904	Liverpool	(h) 1–1	Division One	Howie	20000
1910	Tottenham Hotspur	(a) 4–0	Division One	Stewart 2, Howie, Rutherford	30000
1921	Blackburn Rovers	(a) 3–3	Division One	McDonald, Smailes, Harris	25000
1924	Notts County	(h) 1–2	Division One	McDonald	10000
1927	Sunderland	(h) 1–0	Division One	Gallacher	67211
1932	Arsenal	(a) 0–1	Division One	No Scorer	62665
1936	Leicester City	(a) 0–1	Division Two	No Scorer	10000
1938	Southampton	(a) 0–1	Division Two	No Scorer	20000
1955	Wolverhampton Wanderers	(a) 2–2	Division One	Milburn 2	36614
1958	Preston North End	(a) 1–2	Division One	White	24793
1960	Luton Town	(h) 3–2	Division One	Eastham, White 2	29269
1966	Chelsea	(h) 0–1	Division One	No Scorer	35118
1967	Darren Bradshaw born, Sheffield.				
1969	Warren Barton born, Islington.				
1977	West Bromwich Albion	(a) 1–1	Division One	Barrowclough	23780
1983	Burnley	(a) 0–1	Division Two	No Scorer	13900
1986	Oxford United	(a) 2–1	Division One	Gascoigne, Beardsley	10052
1988	Arsenal	(a) 1–1	Division One	Goddard	25889

Gazza missed a penalty.

1994	West Ham United	(a) 4–2	Premier League	Lee 2, Cole, Mathie	23132
1995	Arsenal	(h) 1–0	Premier League	Beardsley	35611

The Gunners paid the price of allowing Beardsley to run with the ball at his feet towards goal as he scored with another classic strike in the final seconds of the game.

MARCH 20TH

1897	Gainsborough Trinity	(h) 1–2	Division Two	Lennox	6000
1907	Sunderland	(a) 0–2	Division One	No Scorer	32000

A Tyne–Wear derby may not be the best time to make a Newcastle debut, especially if you hail from Bolton. Such a fate befell goalkeeper Billy Kelsey, who didn't disgrace himself. However, in his next game he conceded four first-half goals at Liverpool and soon returned to non-league football.

1909	Sheffield United	(h)4–0	Division One	Duncan, Shepherd, Stewart, Willis	31000
1915	Bradford	(h) 1–1	Division One	Higgins	10000
1920	Notts County	(h) 2–1	Division One	Smailes 2	30000
1926	Bury	(h) 4–0	Division One	Clark, Gallacher 2, McDonald	30000
1937	Doncaster Rovers	(a) 2–1	Division Two	Imrie, McMenemy	12000
1942	Wyn Davies born, Caenarfon, Wales.				
1948	Doncaster Rovers	(h) 2–0	Division Two	Lowrie, Thompson	48724
1954	Sheffield United	(h) 4–1	Division One	Milburn, Monkhouse 3	36668

1959	Dave Beasant born, Willesden.				
1964	Cardiff City	(a) 2–2	Division Two	Cummings, McGarry (pen)	9300
1965	Rotherham United	(a) 1–1	Division Two	Penman	9693
1971	Southampton	(h) 2–2	Division One	Dyson 2	15683
1976	Manchester United	(h) 3–4	Division One	Gowling, Macdonald, Burns	45043

Substitute Graham Oates made his first-team debut as Newcastle managed to gift the visitors the victory when Bird and Howard both scored own goals.

1982	Oldham Athletic	(h) 2–0	Division Two	Mills, Brownlie	18531
1985	Leicester City	(h) 1–4	Division One	Beardsley	21764

1991 Newcastle's home game with Oxford United was abandoned due to incessant rain which flooded the pitch and made play impossible, with the score 1–0 to United, Mick Quinn having got the goal. A total of 9,658 poor souls had turned out.

1993	Notts County	(h) 4–0	Division One	Lee, Kelly 2, Cole	30029

MARCH 21ST

1877	Jock Peddie born, Glasgow.				
1896	Manchester City	(h) 4–1	Division Two	Wardrope, Thompson, Collins, Lennox	12000
1903	Grimsby Town	(a) 0–1	Division One	No Scorer	4000
1908	Birmingham	(a) 1–1	Division One	Howie	20000
1914	Tottenham Hotspur	(a) 0–0	Division One	No Scorer	20000
1925	Leeds United	(h) 4–1	Division One	Harris 2, McDonald 2	19000
1931	Portsmouth	(a) 2–1	Division One	Bedford, Lang	17000
1934	Manchester City	(a) 1–1	Division One	Leighton	14000
1936	West Ham United	(a) 1–4	Division Two	Wilson	40000
1953	Derby County	(a) 2–0	Division One	G. Robledo 2	19741
1959	Arsenal	(h) 1–0	Division One	Curry	32774
1967	Malcolm Allen born, Deiniolen, Wales.				
1970	Stoke City	(h) 3–1	Division One	Davies, Robson 2 (1 pen)	28485

After the exertions of the Fairs Cup campaign, a below-strength Newcastle without Moncur, Clark, Craig, Smith, McNamee, Guthrie and Craggs overcame Stoke to consolidate sixth place in the league.

1973	Bologna (Italy)	(h) 1–0	Anglo-Italian Cup	Gibb	15220
1974	Nottingham Forest	(n) 1–0	FA Cup 6th Round Replay	Macdonald	31373

Another trek to neutral Goodison Park.

1981	Shrewsbury Town	(a) 0–1	Division Two	No Scorer	4975
1987	Manchester City	(a) 0–0	Division One	No Scorer	23060
1990	Bradford City	(a) 2–3	Division Two	McGhee (pen), OG	10364
1992	Grimsby Town	(a) 1–1	Division Two	Sheedy	11613

Debut for Darren McDonough.

MARCH 22ND

1897	Peter Mooney born, Walker.				
1902	Liverpool	(a) 1–0	Division One	Orr	12000
1913	Derby County	(a) 1–2	Division One	Hudspeth (pen)	9000
1920	Sheffield Wednesday	(a) 1–0	Division One	Smailes	15000
1924	West Bromwich Albion	(a) 0–0	Division One	No Scorer	16000
1925	Andy Donaldson born, Newcastle.				
1930	Manchester City	(h) 2–2	Division One	Devine, Gallacher	30000
1947	Fulham	(h) 1–3	Division Two	Shackleton	43647
1952	Liverpool	(a) 0–3	Division One	No Scorer	48996
1961	Tottenham Hotspur	(a) 2–1	Division One	Allchurch, Scanlon	46470

Debut for Jimmy Harrower, overshadowed by the penalty save pulled off by fellow newcomer Dave Hollins. A rare home defeat for Spurs, who recovered to claim a League and Cup double. United fared less well, being relegated, partly due to the injury inflicted on Len White by Dave Mackay.

1969	Sunderland	(h) 1–1	Division One	Sinclair	48588

Future Newcastle player, coach and manager Colin Suggett netted for the visitors.

1975	Derby County	(h) 0–2	Division One	No Scorer	32201

Damage inflicted by David Nish and Bruce Rioch.

1980	Cardiff City	(a) 1–1	Division Two	Shinton	9304
1986	Tottenham Hotspur	(h) 2–2	Division One	Whitehurst, Anderson	31028

Chris Waddle made his first return to Tyneside and put the visitors 2–1 ahead, Hoddle having hit a third-minute free-kick.

1989	Everton	(h) 2–0	Division One	Mirandinha, O'Brien	21012

On a snowy and blustery night at St James', the visitors never looked likely to go home with anything other than a cold.

1991 Death of Jimmy Boyd, 83.

1995	Southampton	(a) 1–3	Premier League	Kitson	14666

1–0 up with three minutes left, the roof fell in as Heaney, Watson and Shipperley all waltzed through to score.

MARCH 23RD

1894	Crewe Alexandra	(h) 2–1	Division Two	Jeffery, Unknown Scorer	10000
1895	Notts County	(a) 1–2	Division Two	Thompson	5000
1901	Everton	(h) 2–1	Friendly	Heywood, Peddie	4000
1907	Liverpool	(a) 1–4	Division One	Brown	20000
1908	Blackburn Rovers	(a) 1–1	Division One	Appleyard	15000
1909	Bradford City	(a) 2–1	Division One	Allan, Stewart	15000

Debut for Charles Randall, at inside-left.

1911 Joe Wilson born, High Spen, Durham.

1912	Notts County	(a) 4–1	Division One	Finlay 2, Peart, Wilson	6000
1929	Manchester City	(h) 4–0	Division One	Lang, Gallacher 2 (2 pens), Urwin	25000

1930 Len White born, Skellow, Yorkshire.

1935	Sheffield United	(h) 4–1	Division Two	Weaver 2 (1 pen), McMenemy, Bott	19000
1951	Sunderland	(h) 2–2	Division One	Harvey, Milburn	62173

An estimated 20,000 supporters were locked out and kept informed by a match commentary given via the public address system. United Director William McKeag was the man behind the microphone. Ford and Bingham scored for the visitors.

1957	Tottenham Hotspur	(h) 2–2	Division One	Davies, Milburn	37955
1963	Chelsea	(h) 2–0	Division One	Fell, Thomas	39418
1968	Everton	(a) 0–1	Division One	No Scorer	43519
1974	Leicester City	(h) 1–1	Division One	McDermott (pen)	32116
1977	Coventry City	(h) 1–0	Division One	Burns	25332
1985	Ipswich Town	(a) 1–1	Division One	McDonald	14366
1991	Portsmouth	(a) 1–0	Division Two	Brock	9607

Two poor teams met at Fratton Park and the much-maligned Kevin Brock scooped in the only goal. When he was substituted late in the game, as the *Pink* reported, 'Some United fans sitting in the stands passed comments to Brock and the visiting player shouted back at them.' Thankfully the paper failed to record what was shouted at Brock, but it wasn't very complimentary . . .

1993	Watford	(a) 0–1	Division One	No Scorer	11634

The only goal of the game was a scrappy effort from the ungainly Paul Furlong as Andy Cole had a frustrating night.

| 1994 | Ipswich Town | (h) 2–0 | Premier League | Sellars, Cole | 32234 |

Debut for Chris Holland, who set up both goals with crosses from the right flank. Meanwhile at Roker Park, 16-year-old goalkeeper Adam Wheeler had a baptism of fire as United's reserves went down 3–0. Sheffield-born Wheeler was on trial, having been released by Manchester United.

1995 Jimmy Crawford signed from Irish club Bohemians, at a cost of £75,000. Crawford had been voted FAI Young Player of the Year in the previous season. It was one in, one out, as the hugely disappointing Jason Drysdale signed for Swindon Town on transfer deadline day.

| 1996 | Arsenal | (a) 0–2 | Premier League | No Scorer | 38271 |
| 1997 | Wimbledon | (a) 1–1 | Premier League | Asprilla | 23175 |

1998 In the wake of a second Sunday of *News of the World* allegations about them, Freddy Shepherd resigned as chairman and Douglas Hall resigned as a director of the football club, while still maintaining their shareholding.

MARCH 24TH

1894	Burton Swifts	(h) 4–1	Division Two	Law, Wallace, Willis 2	3000
1900	Burnley	(h) 2–0	Division One	Fraser, Rogers	12000
1906	Aston Villa	(h) 3–1	Division One	Gosnell, Orr, J. Rutherford	16000

Debuts for Sandy Higgins and James Kirkcaldy.

1923	Hull City	(h) 3–2	Friendly	Scott 2, McDonald	5000
1928	Bury	(h) 2–3	Division One	Gallacher, McDonald	30000
1934	Tottenham Hotspur	(h) 1–3	Division One	Imrie (pen)	30000
1951	Liverpool	(h) 1–1	Division One	Mitchell	45535

1953 Jim Pearson born, Falkirk, Scotland.
1955 Rocky Hudson born, Dunston.

1956	Huddersfield Town	(h) 1–1	Division One	Davies	20008
1962	Norwich City	(a) 0–0	Division Two	No Scorer	18022
1967	Stoke City	(h) 3–1	Division One	McNamee, Noble 2	39408
1973	Chelsea	(h) 1–1	Division One	Barrowclough (pen)	24663

Debut for striker Keith Robson, who after 14 appearances followed his namesake Pop to West Ham.

| 1978 | Everton | (h) 0–2 | Division One | No Scorer | 28933 |
| 1979 | West Ham United | (a) 0–5 | Division Two | No Scorer | 24651 |

Debut for Kenny Wharton, on as substitute.

| 1984 | Shrewsbury Town | (a) 2–2 | Division Two | Keegan, OG | 8313 |

The equaliser via Johnson of Shrewsbury.

| 1990 | Blackburn Rovers | (a) 0–2 | Division Two | No Scorer | 13285 |

Debut for Billy Askew.

1994 Transfer deadline day, and Darren Peacock joined Newcastle in a £2.7 million move, a British record fee for a defender at the time.

1996 Newcastle Striker Les Ferdinand was voted Player of the Year by the Professional Footballers Association.

MARCH 25TH

1890 Bob Hewison born, Backworth.

| 1893 | Nottingham Forest | (h) 4–1 | Friendly | Sorley 2 (1 pen), Reay 2 | 3000 |
| 1899 | Derby County | (h) 2–0 | Division One | Stevenson, Reid | 14000 |

Goal on his debut for Billy Reid, who didn't add to his tally during a four-match loan period and returned to Scotland.

| 1905 | Sheffield Wednesday | (n) 1–0 | FA Cup Semi-Final | Howie | 40000 |

Played at Hyde Road, Manchester.

| 1910 | Woolwich Arsenal | (h) 1–1 | Division One | Finlay | 30000 |
| 1911 | Chelsea | (n) 3–0 | FA Cup Semi-Final | Wilson, Shepherd, Stewart | 40000 |

Played at St Andrews, Birmingham.

1921	Oldham Athletic	(h) 1–2	Division One	Curry	32000
1922	Oldham Athletic	(a) 0–0	Division One	No Scorer	15600
1926	Tottenham Hotspur	(a) 0–1	Division One	No Scorer	26000
1932	Leicester City	(h) 3–2	Division One	Starling, Allen, Boyd	35000
1933	Arsenal	(h) 2–1	Division One	Boyd, Weaver (pen)	50000
1939	Blackburn Rovers	(h) 2–2	Division Two	Scott, Clifton	42000
1950	Bolton Wanderers	(h) 3–1	Division One	Houghton, Mitchell, Taylor	33752
1953	Airdrie	(h) 5–1	Friendly	Foulkes, Davies 2, Hannah, G. Robledo	38800
1960	Everton	(a) 2–1	Division One	Allchurch, White	54868
1961	Chelsea	(h) 1–6	Division One	Neale	28975

Dave Hollins made his home debut, in goal apparently. Jimmy Greaves was tormentor-in-chief, scoring four.

1967	Chelsea	(a) 1–2	Division One	Noble	26388
1972	Manchester City	(h) 0–0	Division One	No Scorer	37506
1975	Liverpool	(a) 0–4	Division One	No Scorer	41147
1978	Nottingham Forest	(a) 0–2	Division One	No Scorer	35552
1987	Tottenham Hotspur	(h) 1–1	Division One	Goddard	30782
1989	Norwich City	(a) 2–0	Division One	Mirandinha, O'Brien	22440

Title-chasing Norwich suffered as Mirandinha found some form on the ground where he had made his United debut.

1992   Newcastle reserves overcame Manchester United 2–0. Both goals were scored by Andy Hunt, and the Magpies included Ivory Coast defender Diaby Sekana, on a brief trial at Gallowgate.

MARCH 26TH

1894	Leicester Fosse	(a) 0–2	Friendly	No Scorer	3000
1898	Grimsby Town	(h) 4–0	Division Two	Campbell, Smith, Peddie 2	4000
1900	Sheffield United	(a) 1–3	Division One	A. Gardner	3000
1904	Bury	(a) 3–0	Division One	Orr 2, Appleyard	3000
1910	Swindon Town	(n) 2–0	FA Cup Semi-Final	Stewart, Rutherford	33000

Played at White Hart Lane.

1912   Harry McMenemy born, Glasgow.

1921	Derby County	(a) 1–0	Division One	Smailes	18000
1927	West Bromwich Albion	(a) 2–4	Division One	Gallacher, McDonald	22000
1932	Derby County	(h) 3–3	Division One	Boyd, Starling, Weaver	28000
1937	Aston Villa	(h) 0–2	Division Two	No Scorer	46000
1938	Blackburn Rovers	(h) 2–0	Division Two	Cairns, Park	14000
1948	Barnsley	(h) 1–0	Division Two	McCall	64757
1949	Huddersfield Town	(a) 2–0	Division One	OG 2	24000
1951	Sunderland	(a) 1–2	Division One	Mitchell	55150
1955	York City	(n) 1–1	FA Cup Semi-Final	Keeble	65000

'United Fight Again' was the headline in the *Evening Chronicle Football Edition* (later the *Pink*). Arthur Bottom (later to join United) equalised for Division Three (North) side York in this game at Hillsborough, Vic Keeble having put the Magpies ahead. The second half saw no further scoring as York completely overwhelmed their more illustrious opponents but couldn't find a winner. Even the presence of the 80-year-old Archbishop of York, at his first game for 50 years, couldn't invoke divine intervention.

1955   While York sent Newcastle to a replay at Roker Park, Sunderland had been eliminated by Manchester City in the other semi-final at Villa Park, the only goal coming from Clarke.

1955   With the first team battling in the FA Cup, the reserves drew 0–0 at Blackpool and the third team beat Alnwick Town 7–2 in the Northern Alliance. The Juniors won 2–1 away at Sheffield United.

1958 A Football League XI defeated its Scottish counterparts as the new floodlights were inaugurated at St James' Park.

1966 Arsenal (a) 3–1 Division One Suddick, Robson 2 13979
All four goals were credited to United players, as Peter Noble put one past his own keeper for the visitors' consolation.

1969 Vitoria Setubal (a) 1–3 Fairs Cup 4th Davies 34000
(Portugal) Round 2nd Leg
Back to the Jose Alvalade Stadium in Lisbon, scene of United's previous victory over Sporting, and a bruising encounter with Setubal. Even the presence of pitchside clowns and brass bands, who erupted into song each time Setubal scored, failed to keep United out of the semi-final.

1977 Middlesbrough (h) 1–0 Division One Kennedy 33643
Alan Kennedy gave United a third-minute lead and there was no further scoring. However, Terry Cooper was dismissed for the visitors. Among the 'Boro ranks were David Mills, John Craggs and Stuart Boam, all of whom subsequently moved to Gallowgate.

1983 Leicester City (h) 2–2 Division Two McDermott, Keegan 22692

1985 Bobby Robson turned to Newcastle's Chris Waddle and handed him an international debut at Wembley as England defeated the Republic of Ireland 2–1.

1988 Coventry City (h) 2–2 Division One O'Neill 2 19050

MARCH 27TH

1897 Burton Swifts (h) 2–1 Division Two Blyth, Lennox 4000
Goalscoring debut for Tosh Hope, who never had another senior appearance due to the form of Richard Smellie. Tosh later became a referee.

1901 Bolton Wanderers (h) 3–0 Division One Heywood, MacFarlane, 16000
A. Gardner

1909 Manchester United (n) 0–1 FA Cup Semi-Final No Scorer 40118
Newcastle lost this FA Cup semi-final held at Bramall Lane, Sheffield, to the eventual cup winners. Harold Halse scored the all-important goal.

1915 Oldham Athletic (a) 0–1 Division One No Scorer 7836
1920 Notts County (a) 0–0 Division One No Scorer 15000
1920 Eric Garbutt born, Scarborough.
1937 Fulham (h) 1–1 Division Two Smith 10000
1948 Nottingham Forest (a) 0–0 Division Two No Scorer 30000
1954 Cardiff City (a) 1–2 Division One Monkhouse 20000
1959 West Ham United (a) 0–3 Division One No Scorer 35000
Debut at outside-right for Terry Marshall.
1960 Death of Matt Kingsley, 84.
1963 Grimsby Town (h) 0–0 Division Two No Scorer 27884
The nearest anyone came to breaking the deadlock was Jimmy Fell, who missed a penalty.
1964 Leeds United (h) 0–1 Division Two No Scorer 55039
1965 Swansea Town (h) 3–1 Division Two Penman 3 28634
1967 Stoke City (a) 1–0 Division One Robson 17802
1970 Sunderland (a) 1–1 Division One Smith 51950
Bobby Park saved a point for Sunderland.
1971 Derby County (h) 3–1 Division One Dyson, Foggon 2 26502
Debut for Irving Nattrass, as a substitute for John Craggs.
1974 Manchester City (a) 1–2 Division One Cassidy 21590
1976 Coventry City (a) 1–1 Division One Bird 14144
1982 Chelsea (h) 1–0 Division Two Waddle 26994
1989 Sheffield Wednesday (h) 1–3 Division One Mirandinha (pen) 31010

An early goal by the Owls was scored by 19-year-old Dean Barrick with his first touch in senior football.

1992 Death of Colin Gibson, 68.

1996 Les Ferdinand scored the only goal as England defeated Bulgaria 1–0.

1997 Newcastle signed Des Hamilton from Bradford City for a fee of £1.5 million.

MARCH 28TH

1902	Grimsby Town	(a) 0–3	Division One	No Scorer	8000
1903	Aston Villa	(h) 2–0	Division One	McColl 2	20000
1908	Fulham	(n) 6–0	FA Cup Semi-Final	Appleyard, Gardner, Howie 2, Rutherford 2	45571

FA Cup semi-final time at Anfield, and an easy victory for United despite being without Peter McWilliam.

1914	Glasgow Rangers	(h) 1–1	Friendly	Dixon	15000
1921	Oldham Athletic	(a) 0–0	Division One	No Scorer	16801
1925	Birmingham	(a) 1–1	Division One	Harris	36000
1931	Sunderland	(h) 2–0	Division One	Bedford 2	38000

A hat-trick of sorts for Harry Bedford, who netted twice and broke the jaw of opponent Alex Hastings with an accidental kick.

1936	Sheffield United	(h) 3–0	Division Two	Connelly, J. Smith, Weaver	22000
1952	Death of Andy McCombie, 75.				
1953	Blackpool	(h) 0–1	Division One	No Scorer	41205
1959	Luton Town	(a) 2–4	Division One	Allchurch, Hughes	20878
1970	Nottingham Forest	(a) 2–2	Division One	Dyson, Robson	21360
1979	Wrexham	(h) 1–1	Division Two	Cassidy	7152

The match was abandoned after 45 minutes due to torrential rain.

1981	Chelsea	(h) 1–0	Division Two	Halliday	17297

Revenge for Bruce Halliday, who had made his debut in the pasting earlier in the season at Stamford Bridge. His only senior goal was a header at the Gallowgate end.

1984	Leeds United	(h) 1–0	Division Two	OG	31222

Denis Irwin was credited with the only goal.

1987	Southampton	(h) 2–0	Division One	Goddard, Gascoigne	22717
1993	Birmingham City	(h) 2–2	Division One	Cole, Lee	27087

A stormy Sunday afternoon at Gallowgate, as Andy Saville and Ian Rodgerson put the Blues two ahead, much to the delight of their owner David Sullivan in the directors' box. Two quick goals sent the home fans into raptures and one fan in particular confirmed the score to Mr Sullivan in a rather forceful manner, for which he temporarily lost his season ticket.

1994 Newcastle reserves lost 1–0 at home to Leicester City, central defender Brian Reid playing for the opening 45 minutes. Reid joined United on loan until the end of the season, but then returned to Rangers.

1998	Southampton	(a) 1–2	Premier League	Lee	15251

A Pearce own goal and a Le Tissier penalty brought late joy for the Saints, as usual.

MARCH 29TH

1907	Stoke	(h) 1–0	Division One	Rutherford	30000

Debut for Glaswegian goalkeeper Tom Sinclair.

1913	Tottenham Hotspur	(h) 3–0	Division One	Higgins 2, Hibbert	20000
1915	Liverpool	(a) 2–2	Division One	Hall, King	3000
1924	Manchester City	(n) 2–0	FA Cup Semi-Final	Harris 2	50039

Held at St Andrews, Birmingham.

1930	Portsmouth	(a) 0–2	Division One	No Scorer	18000
1932	Leicester City	(a) 2–4	Division One	Allen, Weaver (pen)	25000
1947	Charlton Athletic	(n) 0–4	FA Cup Semi-Final	No Scorer	47821

An FA Cup semi-final at Elland Road, Leeds. Internal divisions within the club wrecked preparations for this game, with Charlie Wayman dropped and Harvey and Shackleton in dispute with the club, although they played.

1948	Barnsley	(a) 1–1	Division Two	McCall	30247
1950	Derby County	(a) 1–1	Division One	Hannah	16029
1952	Blackburn	(n) 0–0	FA Cup Semi-Final	No Scorer	65000

Held at Hillsborough.

1957	Ian Davies born, Bristol.				
1957	Death of Tom Mather, 68. Former manager.				
1958	Luton Town	(h) 3–2	Division One	Bottom, Davies, White	16775
1969	Coventry City	(h) 2–0	Division One	Robson (pen), McNamee	26750
1969	Steve Guppy born, Winchester.				
1975	Leeds United	(a) 1–1	Division One	Nulty	41225
1978	Manchester City	(h) 2–2	Division One	Bird, Kennedy	20256

The end of an era, as the Leazes terrace that had been home to generations of United fans was closed after this game. The financial health of the club was such that the replacement stand never got any further than a few walls in the 15 years before the whole ground was revamped under the Hall regime.

| 1980 | Bristol Rovers | (h) 3–1 | Division Two | Withe 2, Cassidy | 18975 |
| 1986 | Everton | (a) 0–1 | Division One | No Scorer | 41116 |

Geordie Kevin Richardson scored the only goal, with Peter Beardsley missing a late penalty for United.

| 1992 | Sunderland | (h) 1–0 | Division Two | Kelly | 30306 |

What the *Scorer* called 'a spawny goal' settled this derby, played on a Sunday because of the fear of crowd disturbance. Mick Quinn claimed a second goal after Anton Rogan appeared to clear from well behind the goal line, but the referee disagreed.

| 1994 | Norwich City | (h) 3–0 | Premier League | Cole, Lee, Beardsley | 32228 |

MARCH 30TH

| 1895 | Glasgow Rangers | (h) 2–5 | Friendly | Milne 2 | 5000 |

Reserve striker William McKay impressed the United hierarchy in this friendly match, and joined Newcastle shortly afterwards.

| 1901 | Liverpool | (a) 0–3 | Division One | No Scorer | 10000 |

Wilf Innerd made his entrance, at centre-half.

| 1907 | Bristol City | (h) 3–0 | Division One | Howie, Rutherford 2 | 40000 |

This win over newly promoted City, who were United's closest title contenders, virtually wrapped up the First Division championship with four games remaining.

1912	Tottenham Hotspur	(h) 2–0	Division One	Hibbert, Peart	15000
1923	Oldham Athletic	(a) 0–0	Division One	No Scorer	19149
1929	Birmingham	(a) 0–0	Division One	No Scorer	30000
1934	Middlesbrough	(h) 1–1	Division One	Weaver	36000
1935	Bradford City	(a) 3–3	Division Two	McMenemy, Bott, J. Richardson	8000
1937	Aston Villa	(a) 2–0	Division Two	Smith 2	65000
1941	John Mitten born, Manchester.				
1949	John Hope born, Shildon.				
1955	York City	(n) 2–0	FA Cup Semi-Final Replay	Keeble, White	59239

Held at Roker Park.

1956	Manchester United	(a) 2–5	Division One	Keeble, Stokoe	58748
1957	Everton	(a) 1–2	Division One	OG	29775
1959	West Ham United	(h) 3–1	Division One	Allchurch, Keith, Taylor	20911

Jimmy Gibson scored on his debut, but only managed to force his way into the first team once more, despite being recommended by no less an authority on strikers than Jackie Milburn.

1963   Luton Town   (a) 3–2   Division Two   Fell, Thomas, Suddick   7281
Debut for Bobby Moncur. Despite two goals from Ron Davies, later to star for Southampton, United reached fourth place with an outside chance of promotion.

1964   Leeds United   (a) 1–2   Division Two   Iley   40105
The Magpies were reduced to ten men following the departure on a stretcher of George Dalton (fractured leg) after a tackle by Johnny Giles. Dalton never played for United again and his injury gave Frank Clark the chance to establish himself.

1968   Hibernian   (h) 2–1   Friendly   Scott, McNamee   14650
1970   Burnley   (h) 0–1   Division One   No Scorer   33264
1974   Burnley   (n) 2–0   FA Cup Semi-Final   Macdonald 2   55000
The massed ranks of Newcastle fans on the Kop at Hillsborough were 'a sea of black and white going up into the clouds', according to Malcolm Macdonald. The game will be remembered not only for Supermac's two goals but also the most perfect first-time ball from Terry Hibbitt that sent Mac away to score the second and seal a place at Wembley.

1985   Sheffield Wednesday (a) 2–4   Division One   Beardsley (pen), Waddle   26525
Goals from Gary Shelton, Brian Marwood and two from Lee Chapman meant United had failed to record a victory on their travels in 16 attempts.

1987   Death of Ron Williams, 80.
1991   Swindon Town   (a) 2–3   Division Two   Peacock, Quinn   9309
The only game that caretaker manager Bobby Saxton faced was an unlucky defeat when United appeared to be playing the home side and all three officials. An unbelievable penalty was given against John Anderson as a home player blasted the ball at him from point-blank range.

MARCH 31ST

1873   Dave Gardner born, Glasgow.
1893   Blyth   (a) 3–2   Friendly   Reay, Unknown Scorers   3000
1894   Middlesbrough   (h) 3–0   Friendly   Crate, Wallace, Law   3000
        Ironopolis
1897   Sunderland   (h) 5–2   Friendly   Lennox 2, Aitken,   3000
                                                          Thompson 2 (1 pen)
1899   Everton   (h) 2–1   Friendly   Rogers, Aitken (pen)   2000
1900   Preston North End (a) 1–4   Division One   Mole   4000
Debut goal for George Mole on his only appearance.

1902   Sunderland   (a) 0–0   Division One   No Scorer   35000
1906   Woolwich Arsenal   (n) 2–0   FA Cup Semi-Final   Veitch, Howie   19964
Held at the Victoria Ground, Stoke.

1909   Middlesbrough   (h) 1–0   Division One   Allan   45000
1923   Huddersfield Town (a) 0–2   Division One   No Scorer   8000
1928   Burnley   (a)1–5   Division One   Wilkinson   15000
Only appearance of Stan Barber, at left-half.

1928   While United were going down 5–1 at Turf Moor, Hughie Gallacher was part of the Scotland team which inflicted the same score on England at Wembley. Although he failed to score, he played in his part in a wonderful team performance by the team dubbed the 'Wembley Wizards'.

1933   Death of Jock Finlay, 40.
1934   Leicester City   (a) 2–3   Division One   Allen, Pearson   18000
1951   Fulham   (a) 1–1   Division One   Walker   30000
1956   Wolverhampton   (a) 1–2   Division One   Keeble   31940
        Wanderers
1961   Sheffield Wednesday (h) 0–1   Division One   No Scorer   42181
Bobby Craig won it for the Owls as relegation for Newcastle looked a formality.

1962   Rotherham United   (h) 1–0   Division Two   Thomas   21865
1973   Leicester City   (a) 0–0   Division One   No Scorer   18712

1975	Queens Park Rangers	(h) 2–2	Division One	Tudor, Macdonald	29819
1976	Leeds United	(h) 2–3	Division One	T. Craig (pen), Gowling	32685

Graham Oates made his home debut and within five minutes had beaten Newcastle keeper Mick Mahoney with a backpass.

1979	Oldham Athletic	(a) 3–1	Division Two	Withe, Shoulder (pen), Nattrass	6329
1982	Crystal Palace	(h) 0–0	Division Two	No Scorer	22151
1984	Swansea City	(h) 2–0	Division Two	Beardsley, Wharton	27329
1986	Sheffield Wednesday	(h) 4–1	Division One	Stephenson, Gascoigne, Beardsley, Whitehurst	25714
1990	Brighton and Hove Albion	(h) 2–0	Division Two	Quinn, Gallacher	18742
1992	Wolverhampton Wanderers	(a) 2–6	Division Two	Quinn, Peacock	14480

Manager Kevin Keegan showed more fight than his players, being reported to the FA after he berated the linesman for not signalling the fifth Wolves goal offside. Steve Bull only managed to score one.

1993	Death of Tot Smith, 70.				
1998	Wimbledon	(a) 0–0	Premier League	No Scorer	15478

Two nervous sides, the spectre of relegation and a not-unexpected goalless draw.

APRIL 1ST

1893	London Casuals	(h) 5–0	Friendly	Pattinson, Collins 3, Crate	2000
1899	West Bromwich Albion	(a) 0–2	Division One	No Scorer	2304
1903	Everton	(h) 3–0	Division One	Alec Gardner 2, McIntyre	18000

Debut for Teddy McIntyre.

1904	Manchester City	(a) 3–1	Division One	Orr, Appleyard, Howie	25000
1905	Blackburn Rovers	(a) 0–2	Division One	No Scorer	6000
1907	Blackburn Rovers	(h) 3–1	Division One	Duffy, Appleyard, Speedie (pen)	30000
1908	Bolton Wanderers	(a) 0–4	Division One	No Scorer	15000
1911	Woolwich Arsenal	(h) 0–1	Division One	No Scorer	15000

Debut for John Scott, at outside-left.

1914	Liverpool	(h) 1–2	Division One	Hudspeth (pen)	20000

Ed Dixon made his debut after having joined United for the princely sum of £5.

1922	Cardiff City	(h) 0–0	Division One	No Scorer	28000
1933	Manchester City	(a) 2–1	Division One	Allen, J.R. Richardson	30000
1936	Bradford City	(a) 2–3	Division Two	Connelly 2	3901
1939	Millwall	(a) 1–1	Division Two	Cairns	26000
1950	Birmingham City	(a) 2–0	Division One	Taylor, Walker	30000
1957	John Bailey born, Liverpool.				
1961	West Ham United	(a) 1–1	Division One	Scanlon	17103
1964	Ian Baird born, Southampton.				
1967	Leicester City	(h) 1–0	Division One	Hilley	35183
1972	Sheffield United	(a) 0–1	Division One	No Scorer	28103
1974	Steve Watson born, North Shields.				
1978	Bristol City	(a) 1–3	Division One	Barrowclough	17344
1987	Death of Trevor Hockey, 43. Collapsed and died after playing in a five-a-side game.				
1989	Southampton	(a) 0–1	Division One	No Scorer	16175

The Saints had failed to record a victory in any of their previous 17 games, so obviously triumphed against United, for whom Paul Sweeney made his debut as substitute. Within seconds of coming on to the pitch, Sweeney was cautioned for kicking an opponent. Neil

Ruddock scored a last-minute penalty after one of his team-mates theatrically tumbled in the box, and most United fans realised they were doomed to return to Division Two.

1989	Death of George Robledo, 62.				
1991	Bristol Rovers	(h) 0–2	Division Two	No Scorer	17509
1994	Leeds United	(a) 1–1	Premier League	Cole	40005

Cole hit his 50th United goal in the opening minute of this televised game, and despite a miraculous goal-line clearance from Neilson, Leeds eventually levelled it in the last minute through Chris Fairclough.

1995	Chelsea	(a) 1–1	Premier League	Hottiger	22987

Gavin Peacock had given the home side a first-half lead they held until the last minute, when Hottiger was on hand to knock the ball in after Venison had seen his shot parried.

APRIL 2ND

1898	Gainsborough Trinity	(h) 5–2	Division Two	Smith 2, Peddie 3	12000
1904	Blackburn Rovers	(h) 2–1	Division One	Orr, Veitch	20000
1910	Notts County	(a) 2–2	Division One	Shepherd, Liddell	8000
1915	Tottenham Hotspur	(a) 0–0	Division One	No Scorer	18000

An insignificant scoreline, but one which saw inside-forward John King keep a clean sheet after playing in goal for the whole 90 minutes. This followed an injury sustained by keeper Bill Mellor before kickoff.

1920	Burnley	(a) 0–1	Division One	No Scorer	30000

Debut for Chris Swan.

1921	Derby County	(h) 0–1	Division One	No Scorer	35000
1924	Everton	(h) 3–1	Division One	Seymour, Harris, Gibson	12000
1926	Burnley	(a) 0–1	Division One	No Scorer	30000
1927	Bury	(h) 3–1	Division One	Clark, McDonald, McKay	20000
1929	Arsenal	(a) 2–1	Division One	Cunningham, Lang	25000
1930	Bimingham	(h) 1–1	Division One	Devine	30000
1932	West Bromwich Albion	(a) 1–2	Division One	Allen	20000
1934	Middlesbrough	(a) 0–1	Division One	No Scorer	15000
1938	Plymouth Argyle	(a) 1–2	Division Two	Pearson	22000
1949	Blackpool	(h) 3–1	Division One	Milburn 2, Robledo	62672
1952	Blackburn Rovers	(n) 2–1	FA Cup Semi-Final Replay	G. Robledo, Mitchell (pen)	54000

Held at Elland Road. With five minutes of the match left and the scores level at 1–1, United were awarded a penalty following a handball in the area. With penalty-taker Milburn injured and nobody else willing to take responsibility, Mitchell grabbed the ball, put it on the spot and scored the winner.

1955	Charlton Athletic	(a) 1–1	Division One	Hannah	24918
1956	Manchester United	(h) 0–0	Division One	No Scorer	37395
1960	Blackpool	(h) 1–1	Division One	Mitten	32152
1969	Tottenham Hotspur	(a) 1–0	Division One	Horsfield	22528
1977	Birmingham City	(a) 2–1	Division One	T. Craig (pen), Barrowclough	20283
1980	Notts County	(h) 2–2	Division Two	Shoulder, Cassidy	22005
1983	Grimsby Town	(h) 4–0	Division Two	Varadi 2, McDonald, Keegan	20202
1988	Luton Town	(h) 4–0	Division One	O'Neill 3, Goddard	20565
1996	Death of Ian Mitchell, 49.				

APRIL 3RD

1893	Stockton	(a) 3–3	Friendly	Crate, Graham, Collins	
1896	Burslem Port Vale	(h) 4–2	Division Two	McDonald 2, Collins, OG	8000
1897	Walsall	(a) 2–0	Division Two	Aitken, Smellie	4000

1899	Liverpool	(a) 2–3	Division One	Stevenson, Higgins	12000
1906	Tommy Lang born, Larkhall, Scotland.				
1909	Nottingham Forest	(h) 1–1	Division One	Allan	22000
1911	Sheffield United	(a) 0–0	Division One	No Scorer	8000
1915	Manchester United	(h) 2–0	Division One	Hibbert 2	12000
1920	Sheffield Wednesday	(h) 1–1	Division One	Phillipson	20000
1926	Cardiff City	(h) 0–1	Division One	No Scorer	25000
1927	Tom Patterson born, Lochore, Scotland.				
1931	Huddersfield Town	(h) 1–1	Division One	Lindsay	35000
1937	Burnley	(a) 3–0	Division Two	Cairns, Docking 2	9400
1948	Bradford Park Avenue	(h) 2–0	Division Two	Stobbart, Woodburn	50367
1953	Middlesbrough	(h) 1–0	Division One	Hannah	48434
1954	Manchester City	(h) 4–3	Division One	Milburn 2 (2 pens), Monkhouse, Davies	27764

Debut for Bill Punton, at outside-left.

1954	United's Ivor Broadis was on international duty and scored for England as they won 4–2 at Hampden Park.				
1961	Sheffield Wednesday	(a) 1–1	Division One	Woods	35273

Bobby Craig scored his second goal against United in four days to push them nearer to Division Two.

1963	Charlton Athletic	(h) 3–2	Division Two	Penman, Hilley, Suddick	30360

Debut goal for Willie Penman.

1965	Derby County	(a) 3–0	Division Two	Knox, Hilley, Iley	9668
1968	Leicester City	(h) 0–0	Division One	No Scorer	33932
1971	Blackpool	(a) 1–0	Division One	Foggon	14637

This defeat made relegation for Blackpool a certainty.

1972	Derby County	(a) 1–0	Division One	Cassidy	38119
1974	Stoke City	(a) 1–2	Division One	Tudor	16437

The only highlight was a spectacular bicycle kick from John Tudor, which earned him a man-of-the-match award selected by Stoke boss Tony Waddington. His prize? Ten whole pounds.

1974 Newcastle played without Malcolm Macdonald, who had been recalled to the England team and started the 0–0 draw in Lisbon before being replaced by Alan Ball.

1976	Queens Park Rangers	(h) 1–2	Division One	Gowling	30145
1982	Charlton Athletic	(a) 1–0	Division Two	Waddle	6357
1984	Death of Joe Wilson, 73.				
1989	Kevin Keegan XI	(h) 2–2	Friendly	Pingel, Mirandinha	20899

Kenny Wharton's testimonial match. Chris Waddle scored both goals for Kevin Keegan's XI, which also included Paul Gascoigne and Peter Shilton. Before the main game, a Bobby Moncur XI had drawn 2–2 with a Bobby Kerr XI. Ex-United players Stewart Barrowclough and Pop Robson scored for the home side, which also included Dave Hilley and Tony Green.

1990	Plymouth Argyle	(h) 3–1	Division Two	Quinn, McGhee 2 (1 pen)	16528
1993	Cambridge United	(a) 3–0	Division One	Howey, Kelly, Cole	7925

A record-equalling 11th away win in the league, which hadn't been achieved since 1936–37. Two more victories before the end of the season extended the record further.

1996	Liverpool	(a) 3–4	Premier League	Ferdinand, Ginola, Asprilla	40702

'We saw you cry on the telly' – well, not me, I was straight off to see if the car was still in one piece. Classic football, classic television, heartbreaking result.

1996 Death of Joseph Wilson, 85.

APRIL 4TH

1896	Burton Swifts	(h) 5–0	Division Two	Wardrope 2, Thompson 2, Stott	7000

1903	Nottingham Forest	(a) 2–3	Division One	Alec Gardner 2	
1904	Queens Park	(h) 2–1	Friendly	Orr 2	5000
1906	Sheffield United	(h) 2–1	Division One	Appleyard, Hardinge	20000
1908	Everton	(a) 0–2	Division One	No Scorer	10000

Debut for Archie Duncan, at outside-right; he later managed Manchester United. William Hughes also played for the first and only time, becoming the first Welshman to do so.

1914	Aston Villa	(a) 3–1	Division One	Shepherd 2, G. Wilson	20000

The solitary appearance of Whitley Bay-born Thomas Grey came in a notable victory over the eventual First Division runners-up.

1925	West Bromwich Albion	(h) 0–1	Division One	No Scorer	25000
1925	Death of Archie Turner, 47.				
1931	Blackburn Rovers	(a) 0–1	Division One	No Scorer	12000
1936	Nottingham Forest	(a) 2–1	Division Two	Bott, Ware	5000
1940	Death of Jimmy Hay, 59.				
1947	Birmingham City	(h) 2–2	Division Two	Bentley, Milburn	57259
1951	Aston Villa	(h) 0–1	Division One	No Scorer	38543
1953	Chelsea	(a) 2–1	Division One	Mitchell 2	40218
1954	George Hope born, Haltwhistle.				
1959	Halmstads (Sweden)	(h) 3–1	Friendly	Taylor, Eastham, Gibson	10696
1964	Manchester City	(a) 1–3	Division Two	Thomas	15450
	Debut for Joe Butler, at left-back.				
1969	Chelsea	(a) 1–1	Division One	Robson (pen)	42078
1970	Manchester United	(h) 5–1	Division One	Smith, Davies, Robson 3 (2 pens)	43024

Bobby Charlton hit the visitors' goal.

1973	Como (Italy)	(a) 2–0	Anglo-Italian Cup	Moncur, Tudor	3000
1978	Coventry City	(a) 0–0	Division One	No Scorer	22135
1979	Preston North End	(h) 4–3	Division Two	Connolly, Withe, Shoulder, Barton	12167
1981	Watford	(a) 0–0	Division Two	No Scorer	10986
1983	Derby County	(a) 1–2	Division Two	Waddle	19779
1987	Leicester City	(h) 2–0	Division One	Goddard, Wharton	23360
1988	Derby County	(a) 1–2	Division One	O'Neill	18591
1992	Tranmere Rovers	(h) 2–3	Division Two	Brock 2	21125

A frantic finish to this game, as Newcastle tried desperately to conjure an equaliser against ten-man Rovers, Dave Higgins having been sent off. John Aldridge had earlier struck twice.

1994	Chelsea	(h) 0–0	Premier League	No Scorer	32218

APRIL 5TH

1894	Sunderland	(h) 1–2	Friendly	Graham (pen)	5000
1901	Sunderland	(h) 0–0	Division One	No Scorer	30000

An estimated 70,000 packed St James' Park and rioted after the 25 policemen on duty failed to clear the pitch sufficiently for the match to begin. Once the referee abandoned the game without a ball being kicked, widespread fighting broke out and the goals were torn down.

1902	Aston Villa	(h) 2–1	Division One	Stewart 2	14000
1904	Distillery	(a) 5–4	Friendly	Orr 2, Aitken, Rutherford, Appleyard (pen)	4000
1905	Aston Villa	(h) 2–0	Division One	Veitch, Appleyard	25000
1911	Nottingham Forest	(a) 1–0	Division One	Higgins	2500
1912	Oldham Athletic	(h) 1–1	Division One	Hay	30000
1913	Middlesbrough	(a) 0–0	Division One	No Scorer	10000

1915	West Bromwich Albion	(a) 0–2	Division One	No Scorer	15000
1920	Aston Villa	(a) 0–4	Division One	No Scorer	50000
1924	Birmingham	(a) 1–4	Division One	Aitken	20000

Debut for Frank Thompson, at centre-forward.

1926	Leeds United	(h) 3–0	Division One	Curry, Gallacher, McDonald	18000
1930	Arsenal	(h) 1–1	Division One	Devine	30000
1933	Everton	(a) 0–0	Division One	No Scorer	20000
1947	Luton Town	(h) 7–2	Division Two	Wayman 2, Stobbart 2, Shackleton, Milburn, Harvey	40372
1954	Millwall	(a) 1–4	Friendly	Foulkes	12507
1958	Blackpool	(a) 2–3	Division One	Mitchell (pen), Franks	18719
1972	Ipswich Town	(h) 0–1	Division One	No Scorer	22979
1975	Leicester City	(a) 0–4	Division One	No Scorer	23132
1980	Sunderland	(a) 0–1	Division Two	No Scorer	41752
1986	Watford	(a) 1–4	Division One	OG	14706

United's only goal came courtesy of John McClelland.

1997	Sunderland	(h) 1–1	Premier League	Shearer	36582
1998	Sheffield United	(n) 1–0	FA Cup	Shearer	53452

Played at Old Trafford.

APRIL 6TH

1895	Newton Heath	(a) 1–5	Division Two	Dickson	6000
1896	Woolwich Arsenal	(a) 1–2	Division Two	OG	16000
1901	Sheffield Wednesday	(h) 0–0	Division One	No Scorer	13000

Debut for local player Jim Littlefair, who won honours with the reserves but was only called up to senior action twice in his two years with the club.

1907	Notts County	(a) 0–1	Division One	No Scorer	12000

A depleted Newcastle team went down by a single goal at Trent Bridge Cricket Ground.

1907 While the first team were on duty at Meadow Lane, 35,829 fans saw England draw 1–1 with Scotland in a full international at St James' Park. In the days before postponements of league games for international call-ups, Veitch and Rutherford played for England while McWilliam appeared for the Scots. England's goal came, almost inevitably, from Steve Bloomer, now of Middlesbrough. Scotland were recorded as playing the game in a strip of 'primrose and pink'.

1912	Manchester United	(a) 2–0	Division One	Duncan, Finlay	15000
1927	Arsenal	(h) 6–1	Division One	Gallacher 3, McDonald, McKay 2	33000
1929	Portsmouth	(h) 0–1	Division One	No Scorer	25000
1935	Notts County	(h) 1–1	Division Two	Pearson	12000
1949	Portsmouth	(h) 0–5	Division One	No Scorer	60611

All five goals came from headers and Pompey went on to win the league by five points, the trophy being presented to their president Field-Marshal Montgomery at Fratton Park.

1953	Middlesbrough	(a) 1–2	Division One	Mitchell (pen)	37600

Both 'Boro goals came from Wilf Mannion.

1957	Blackpool	(h) 2–1	Division One	Davies, Milburn	31777

1961 Peter Jackson born, Bradford.

1963	Southampton	(h) 4–1	Division Two	Fell, Penman, Suddick, Dalton	28744

1965 Andy Walker born, Glasgow.

1968	West Ham United	(a) 0–5	Division One	No Scorer	27780

With Wyn Davies in the midst of a 13-match barren run following the injury to his partner Bennett, United were further weakened by the late withdrawal of Dave Elliott. He had collapsed on the morning of the game and was detained in Charing Cross hospital. Trevor

Brooking hit a hat-trick, with two for Johnny Sissons.

1971	Liverpool	(a) 1–1	Division One	Tudor	44289
1974	Everton	(h) 2–1	Division One	Macdonald 2 (1 pen)	45497
1982	Wrexham	(a) 2–4	Division Two	Varadi 2	4517
1985	West Bromwich Albion	(h) 1–0	Division One	Beardsley	22694
1991	Notts County	(a) 0–3	Division Two	No Scorer	7806
1996	Queens Park Rangers	(h) 2–1	Premier League	Beardsley 2	36583

APRIL 7TH

1878	Sam Graham born, Galston, Scotland.				
1894	Dundee	(a) 2–8	Friendly	MacFarlane, Willis	1000
1896	Leicester Fosse	(a) 0–2	Division Two	No Scorer	5000
1900	Nottingham Forest	(h) 3–1	Division One	MacFarlane, Peddie, D. Gardner (pen)	14224

1902 The first Ibrox disaster, 26 supporters being killed when a section of wooden terracing gave way during a Scotland *v* England international. United's Andy Aitken was in the home line-up.

1903 Tom Evans born, Maerdy, Wales.

1923	Huddersfield Town	(h) 1–0	Division One	R. Clark	20000

Match winner from debutant forward Bob Clark. Right-half Roddie MacKenzie also made the first of his 256 senior appearances for United.

1928	Leicester City	(h) 1–5	Division One	Chalmers	30000

An inauspicious debut for Robert Bradley, at right-back; he was never selected again. The consolation goal was scored by Scot William Chalmers, also on his debut.

1931	Aston Villa	(a) 3–4	Division One	Hutchinson, Bedford (pen), Boyd	35000
1934	Aston Villa	(h) 1–1	Division One	Dennison	30000
1939	Chesterfield	(a) 0–2	Division Two	No Scorer	30968

Record attendance at Saltergate.

1947	Birmingham City	(a) 0–2	Division Two	No Scorer	43000
1950	Huddersfield Town	(h) 0–0	Division One	No Scorer	46886
1951	Tottenham Hotspur	(h) 0–1	Division One	No Scorer	41241
1952	Blackpool	(h) 1–3	Division One	Foulkes	47316
1956	Manchester City	(h) 3–1	Division One	Keeble, Milburn, White	26181

Debut for Bobby Ferguson.

1958	Manchester City	(a) 1–2	Division One	White	36995
1959	Nigel Walker born, Gateshead.				
1962	Bristol Rovers	(a) 1–2	Division Two	Thomas	10770
1967	Liverpool	(a) 1–3	Division One	Davies	44824
1973	West Ham United	(h) 1–2	Division One	Tudor	24075
1976	Birmingham City	(h) 4–0	Division One	Gowling, Macdonald 2, Burns	18893

Newcastle were without Tommy Craig as they cruised to victory over Birmingham. Craig was making his full Scotland debut in an international against Switzerland at Hampden Park, which the Scots won 1–0.

1979	Crystal Palace	(h) 1–0	Division Two	Shoulder	18862

The deadlock was finally broken with eight minutes to go, Palace defender Kenny Sansom bungling a clearance from a Peter Withe header and Alan Shoulder nipping in to beat John Burridge. The result was cheered all over the north-east, as Sunderland were vying with Palace for a promotion spot. The Wearsiders did themselves no good, though, future United defender Jeff Clarke being sent off at Bristol Rovers, and Palace and Brighton claiming the promotion spots.

1980	Burnley	(h) 1–1	Division Two	Davies	18863

Midfielder Brian Ferguson made his debut as a substitute and did enough to start the final four games of the season. However, he was never selected again and went to Hull on a free transfer shortly after John Trewick joined United.

1984	Charlton Athletic	(a) 3–1	Division Two	McDermott, Waddle, Beardsley	15289
1990	Port Vale	(a) 2–1	Division Two	Quinn, McGhee	10290
1993	Barnsley	(h) 6–0	Division One	Cole 3, Clark, Beresford, Sellars	29460

Tykes boss Mel Machin admitted afterwards, 'We got off lightly with six.' Sellars and Beresford scored their first goals for United as they struck their first six-goal haul in a league game since 1964.

APRIL 8TH

1889	Arthur Metcalfe born, Seaham.				
1893	Liverpool	(h) 0–0	Friendly	No Scorer	2500
1899	Blackburn Rovers	(h) 1–0	Division One	MacFarlane	12000
1901	Everton	(a) 1–0	Division One	A. Gardner	20000
1905	Nottingham Forest	(h) 5–1	Division One	Gosnell, McClarence, Howie 2, Aitken	22000
1908	Aston Villa	(h) 2–5	Division One	Wilson, Soye	15000

Only appearance of Noel Brown in the first team, at outside-right.

1911	Bradford City	(a) 0–1	Division One	No Scorer	30000
1922	Cardiff City	(a) 0–1	Division One	No Scorer	25000
1933	Sunderland	(h) 0–1	Division One	No Scorer	36000
1939	Manchester City	(h) 0–2	Division Two	No Scorer	23000
1950	Liverpool	(h) 5–1	Division One	Hannah, Mitchell 2, Taylor, Walker	48639
1955	Everton	(a) 2–1	Division One	Hannah, Keeble	60080
1961	Everton	(h) 0–4	Division One	No Scorer	30342
1964	Rotherham United	(h) 5–2	Division Two	McGarry, Thomas 3, Anderson	18308
1966	Everton	(h) 0–0	Division One	No Scorer	30731
1972	Nottingham Forest	(a) 0–1	Division One	No Scorer	12470

Debuts for Gordon Hodgson and Keith Kennedy, who beat younger brother Alan into the first team by a year but made only this one appearance.

| 1977 | Sunderland | (a) 2–2 | Division One | T. Craig, Cannell | 50048 |

Kevin Arnott and Bob Lee scored for the home side.

1978	Aston Villa	(h) 1–1	Division One	Burns (pen)	19330
1985	Sunderland	(a) 0–0	Division One	No Scorer	28246
1987	Norwich City	(h) 4–1	Division One	Goddard, Gascoigne, McDonald (pen), D. Jackson	24534

Kevin Drinkell gave the Canaries the lead but United then hit back before half-time to equalise through Goddard. The second half was all one-way traffic, with Steve Bruce in the visitors' defence failing to stem the tide of goals.

| 1989 | Aston Villa | (h) 1–2 | Division One | O'Brien | 20464 |

Debut for Benny Kristensen. The crucial goal was a fine individual effort by David Platt.

| 1993 | Death of Bobby Mitchell, 68. | | | | |
| 1995 | Norwich City | (h) 3–0 | Premier League | Beardsley 2 (1 pen), Kitson | 35518 |

Among the appreciative home crowd was future prime minister and alleged Newcastle fan Tony Blair.

| 1996 | Blackburn Rovers | (a) 1–2 | Premier League | Batty | 30717 |

David Batty appeared to have won it against his old club, before a certain Graham Fenton appeared . . .

APRIL 9TH

1898	Leicester Fosse	(a) 1–1	Division Two	Peddie	6000
1901	Distillery	(a) 4–1	Friendly	Peddie 3, Aitken	5000
1904	Nottingham Forest	(a) 0–1	Division One	No Scorer	10000

Debut for George Thompson, at outside-right.

1906	Liverpool	(a) 0–3	Division One	No Scorer	18000
1910	Middlesbrough	(a) 1–1	Division One	Duncan	10000

The referee's report from this match suggested collusion over the result, but a subsequent inquiry found no proof.

1912	Bradford City	(a) 1–1	Division One	Hibbert	18000
1913	West Bromwich Albion	(a) 0–1	Division One	No Scorer	10000
1921	Bolton Wanderers	(a) 1–3	Division One	McDonald	25000
1924	Birmingham	(h) 2–1	Division One	Mitchell, Thompson	8000

Second and final appearance of Birtley-born forward Frank Thompson, who scored the winner.

1927	Birmingham	(a) 0–2	Division One	No Scorer	30000
1930	Bolton Wanderers	(a) 1–1	Division One	Gallacher	6000
1932	Sunderland	(h) 1–2	Division One	Lang	45000
1938	Fulham	(h) 1–2	Division Two	Pearson	12000
1949	Derby County	(a) 4–2	Division One	Harvey, Robledo 2, Sibley	24076
1949	Jackie Milburn was at Wembley on international duty, and although he scored for England, their 3–1 defeat by Scotland gave the visitors the Home International Championship.				
1955	Sheffield Wednesday (h) 5–0		Division One	Davies 2, Hannah, R. Mitchell, White	40883
1956	Partick Thistle	(a) 1–1	Friendly	Milburn	18000
1960	Blackburn Rovers	(a) 1–1	Division One	Eastham	22100
1966	Blackburn Rovers	(h) 2–1	Division One	Hilley, Robson	21607
1969	Sheffield Wednesday (h) 3–2		Division One	Arentoft, Dyson, Horsfield	25973

The end of Geoff Allen's playing career. His return from injury lasted five minutes before he was stretchered off, to be replaced by Arthur Horsfield, who later scored. Pop Robson missed a penalty.

1977	Leicester City	(h) 0–0	Division One	No Scorer	32300
1983	Blackburn Rovers	(h) 3–2	Division Two	Waddle, Varadi, OG	17839

Stuart Metcalfe netted a fantastic own goal.

1985	Death of Ernie Taylor, 59.				
1986	Aston Villa	(h) 2–2	Division One	Whitehurst, Gascoigne	20435

Ten-man Villa had Tony Dorigo sent off but goals from Tony Daley and Steve Hunt gave them a point.

1988	Queens Park Rangers	(h) 1–1	Division One	O'Neill	18403
1994	Manchester City	(a) 1–2	Premier League	Sellars	33774

After Jeffrey had crossed for Sellars to poke an opening goal, United missed a succession of chances and were punished by a debut goal from Paul Walsh and a second-half winner from Ian Brightwell.

APRIL 10TH

1897	Burton Wanderers	(h) 3–0	Division Two	Aitken, Smellie 2	6000
1903	Derby County	(h) 2–1	Division One	Templeton, Roberts	25000
1909	Sunderland	(a) 1–3	Division One	Shepherd	30000
1914	Blackburn Rovers	(h) 0–0	Division One	No Scorer	40000

This point confirmed Rovers as League champions.

1915	Bolton Wanderers	(a) 0–0	Division One	No Scorer	15000

1920	Edinburgh	(n) 5–0	Friendly	Pyke 4, Dark	4000
1922	Newport County	(h) 5–1	Friendly	Smailes 2, McDonald 3	10000
1926	Sheffield United	(a) 3–4	Division One	McDonald, Hudspeth 2 (2 pens)	25000
1928	Birmingham	(a) 2–0	Division One	Wilkinson 2	25000
1936	Hull City	(h) 4–1	Division Two	Pearson, Connelly 2, Weaver (pen)	16000
1937	Southampton	(h) 3–0	Division Two	Cairns, Livingstone, Pearson	12000
1948	Cardiff City	(a) 1–1	Division Two	Stobbart	50000
1954	Portsmouth	(a) 0–2	Division One	No Scorer	26604
1957	Nancy	(h) 2–2	Friendly	White, Hannah	15224
1965	Swindon Town	(h) 1–0	Division Two	Hilley	32503
1971	Leeds United	(h) 1–1	Division One	Tudor	49699
1973	Ipswich Town	(a) 0–1	Texaco Cup	No Scorer	18627

United lost to a goal scored late in extra time.

1974	Burnley	(h) 1–2	Division One	Macdonald	30168

1974 Andreas Andersson born, Sweden.

1976	Wolverhampton Wanderers	(a) 0–5	Division One	No Scorer	20083
1979	Burnley	(a) 0–1	Division Two	No Scorer	7851
1982	Leicester City	(h) 0–0	Division Two	No Scorer	25777
1991	Oxford United	(h) 2–2	Division Two	Hunt, OG	10004

Although claimed by Quinn, the second goal was credited to Oxford's Andy Melville.

1993	Wolverhampton Wanderers	(a) 0–1	Division One	No Scorer	17244

Andy Mutch won it for the home side, who were without his partner Steve Bull.

APRIL 11TH

1896	Clyde	(h) 0–0	Friendly	No Scorer	2000
1898	Loughborough Town	(a) 1–0	Division Two	Campbell	2000

Debut for Tom Niblo.

1903	Bury	(h) 1–0	Division One	Turner	18000
1908	Liverpool	(h) 3–1	Division One	Howie, Jobey, Wilson	30000
1914	Middlesbrough	(h) 1–0	Division One	Shepherd	30000
1925	Tottenham Hotspur	(a) 0–3	Division One	No Scorer	23144
1931	Manchester City	(h) 0–1	Division One	No Scorer	20000
1936	Swansea Town	(h) 2–0	Division Two	Connelly, J. Smith	12000
1950	Huddersfield Town	(n) 2–1	Division One	Houghton, G. Robledo	37700

A debut for Jerry Lowery in goal as United faced the Terriers at Elland Road, Leeds Road having being damaged in a fire.

1951	Portsmouth	(h) 0–0	Division One	No Scorer	32222
1952	Middlesbrough	(h) 0–2	Division One	No Scorer	59364

Debut for Ken Prior, at outside-left.

1953	Manchester United	(h) 1–2	Division One	Mitchell	39078
1955	Everton	(h) 4–0	Division One	R. Mitchell 2, Milburn 2	45329

Debut for Alex Tait, at centre-forward.

1956 Wales drew 1–1 with Northern Ireland at Ninian Park, United players Alf McMichael and Tommy Casey appearing for the visitors alongside the Blanchflower brothers and Billy Bingham of Sunderland.

1959	West Bromwich Albion	(a) 2–2	Division One	Curry 2	22000
1964	Bury	(h) 0–4	Division Two	No Scorer	20001
1966	Everton	(a) 0–1	Division One	No Scorer	32598

1981   Cambridge United   (h) 2–1   Division Two   OG, Shoulder   11013
A helpful Cambridge side did their best to ingratiate themselves with the Geordie public, Chris Turner nodding into his own net for the first and keeper Richard Key hitting his clearance to Shoulder, who passed it back into the empty net. In between, Cambridge debutant Martin Goldsmith had equalised.

1987   Oxford United   (a) 1–1   Division One   Goddard   10526

1990   West Bromwich Albion   (h) 2–1   Division Two   Quinn, Anderson   19471

1992   Ipswich Town   (a) 2–3   Division Two   Peacock 2   20673

1998   Arsenal   (a) 1–3   Premier League   Barton   38102
Two goals from Anelka and one from Vieira, but United probably got off lightly.

APRIL 12TH

1893   Sunderland   (h) 0–4   Friendly   No Scorer

1895   Burslem Port Vale   (h) 1–2   Division Two   McNee   3000

1897   Burton Swifts   (a) 0–3   Division Two   No Scorer

1898   Small Heath   (a) 0–1   Division Two   No Scorer   5000

1902   Sheffield United   (a) 0–1   Division One   No Scorer

1909   Everton   (h) 3–0   Division One   Stewart 2, McCracken (pen)   30000

1913   Notts County   (h) 0–0   Division One   No Scorer   12000

1923   Death of Billy Reid, 47.

1924   Chelsea   (h) 2–1   Division One   Seymour, Keating   20000

1930   Aston Villa   (a) 0–2   Division One   No Scorer   35000

1947   Plymouth Argyle   (a) 1–0   Division Two   Shackleton   32500

1952   Manchester City   (h) 1–0   Division One   G. Robledo   46645

1958   Arsenal   (h) 3–3   Division One   Curry, White, Stokoe   43221

1963   Huddersfield Town   (h) 1–1   Division Two   McGarry   49672

1968   West Bromwich Albion   (h) 2–2   Division One   Iley, T. Robson   40308

1969   Manchester United   (h) 2–0   Division One   Foggon, Robson (pen)   46379

1971   Manchester City   (h) 0–0   Division One   No Scorer   29148

1975   Everton   (h) 0–1   Division One   No Scorer   29585
Debut for Mick Mahoney (super goalie).

1978   West Bromwich Albion   (a) 0–2   Division One   No Scorer   17053

1980   Fulham   (a) 0–1   Division Two   No Scorer   7152

1982   Sheffield Wednesday   (a) 1–2   Division Two   Barton   29917

1986   Birmingham City   (h) 4–1   Division One   Beardsley 2, Anderson, Whitehurst   20334
Paul Gascoigne was sent off after punching Robert Hopkin of City, who had continually fouled and blocked him all afternoon.

1988   Watford   (h) 3–0   Division One   O'Neill, Wharton, Tinnion   16318

1993   Heavy rain washed out the home game against Oxford United. Had this game gone ahead with the same result as in the rearranged fixture, the championship could have been secured at home to Sunderland.

APRIL 13TH

1876   Bob McColl born, Glasgow.

1895   Newton Heath   (h) 3–0   Division Two   McNee, Thompson, Milne   4000

1900   Manchester City   (h) 0–0   Division One   No Scorer   16000

1901   Sheffield United   (h) 3–0   Division One   MacFarlane, Carr, Ghee   16000

1903   Bolton Wanderers   (h) 2–0   Division One   McColl 2   15000

1906   Bury   (a) 4–1   Division One   Gosnell, Veitch (pen), Howie, J. Rutherford   18000

1907	Sheffield United	(h) 0–0	Division One	No Scorer	30000

The only home point that Newcastle dropped in this championship season came in their 19th and final game at Gallowgate. However, non-league Crystal Palace had travelled north and won in the cup.

1910	Sunderland	(h) 1–0	Division One	Higgins	40000
1912	Liverpool	(h) 1–1	Division One	Hibbert	15000
1914	Manchester City	(a) 1–0	Division One	Shepherd	30000
1920	Partick Thistle	(a) 2–3	Friendly	Smailes, Curry	7000
1925	Sheffield United	(a) 2–1	Division One	McDonald 2	20000
1929	Bolton Wanderers	(a) 0–1	Division One	No Scorer	10000

1929 Tom Mulgrew born, Motherwell, Scotland.

1935	Southampton	(a) 0–2	Division Two	No Scorer	9000
1936	Hull City	(a) 3–2	Division Two	Pearson, J. Smith, Imrie (pen)	6000

Debut for Harry Johnson, at left-back.

1936 Albert Franks born, Boldon.

1957	Wolverhampton Wanderers	(a) 0–2	Division One	No Scorer	22335

The opening goal was scored by Bobby Thomson on his Wolves debut.

1964 Stan Anderson held his testimonial at Roker Park.

1968	Burnley	(h) 1–0	Division One	Sinclair	27229
1974	Manchester United	(a) 0–1	Division One	No Scorer	44751

Debut for David Crosson, in place of David Craig at right-back.

1985	Queens Park Rangers	(h) 1–0	Division One	Reilly	21733

The Newcastle substitute, who got a runout, was Paul Gascoigne.

1991	Oldham Athletic	(h) 3–2	Division Two	Peacock, Hunt, Brock	16615
1997	Sheffield Wednesday	(a) 1–1	Premier League	Elliott	33798
1998	Barnsley	(h) 2–1	Premier League	Andersson, Shearer	36534

Moses was dismissed for Barnsley after tangling with Shearer.

APRIL 14TH

1885 Jimmy Soye born, Govan, Scotland.

1894	Grimsby Town	(a) 0–0	Division Two	No Scorer	2000
1900	Glossop	(a) 0–0	Division One	No Scorer	2000

Debut for Jimmy Lindsay, at right-back.

1904	Shaddongate United	(a) 4–1	Friendly	Fraser 3, Finlay	3000

One of the last games Shaddongate played before changing their name to Carlisle United, this match was played at Milholme Bank, Carlisle.

1906	Notts County	(a) 0–1	Division One	No Scorer	18000

Debutant at left-back was Sid Blake, who subsequently converted to a goalkeeper for the rest of his career!

1911	Sheffield Wednesday	(h) 0–2	Division One	No Scorer	30000
1913	Sheffield Wednesday	(a) 2–1	Division One	Hibbert, Cooper	14000
1915	Burnley	(h) 1–2	Division One	Hibbert	6000
1922	Bradford City	(h) 1–2	Division One	Harris	20000
1923	Stoke	(a) 0–1	Division One	No Scorer	20000
1926	Manchester United	(h) 4–1	Division One	McDonald, Clark, Urwin, Hudspeth (pen)	15000

1926 George Robledo born, Iquique, Chile.

1928	Liverpool	(a) 0–0	Division One	No Scorer	25000
1932	Chelsea	(a) 1–4	Division One	McKenzie	20000
1934	Huddersfield Town	(a) 1–4	Division One	Williams	10413

1944 George Watkin born, Chopwell.

1948	Fulham	(h) 1–0	Division Two	Stobbart (pen)	54061

1951	Charlton Athletic	(a) 3–1	Division One	G. Robledo, Taylor, OG	25798
1952	Middlesbrough	(a) 1–2	Division One	Keeble	40000
1956	Bolton Wanderers	(a) 2–3	Division One	Keeble, White	17173
1958	Manchester City	(h) 4–1	Division One	Davies, Franks, White 2	53326
1962	Stoke City	(h) 2–0	Division Two	Thomas, OG	20593
1969	Everton	(a) 1–1	Division One	Davies	36335
1970	Coventry City	(h) 4–0	Division One	Foggon, Dyson, Robson, Gibb	32858
1973	Southampton	(a) 1–1	Division One	Barrowclough	14785

Newcastle goalkeeper Martin Burleigh fractured a finger after tangling with Mick Channon.

1974	John Watson born, South Shields.				
1976	Manchester City	(h) 2–1	Division One	Mcdonald, Cassidy	21095
1979	Sheffield United	(h) 1–3	Division Two	Shoulder	19126
1984	Sheffield Wednesday	(h) 0–1	Division Two	No Scorer	36288
1987	Arsenal	(a) 1–0	Division One	Goddard	17353
1990	Wolverhampton Wanderers	(a) 1–0	Division Two	Scott	19507
1995	Everton	(a) 0–2	Premier League	No scorer	34628

A rotten night as Daniel Amokachi struck twice and Robert Lee was sent off.

1996	Aston Villa	(h) 1–0	Premier League	Ferdinand	36510

The pressure was mounting on United and Kevin Keegan in particular, who took left-back Beresford off after 25 minutes following an argument between player and home bench. Ferdinand scored with a wonderful header to grab three vital points against a Villa side who seemed almost as pleased as the Gallowgate crowd.

APRIL 15TH

1893	West Bromwich Albion	(h) 7–2	Friendly	Sorley 3, Crate, Collins, Wallace, Reay	2000
1895	Burton Wanderers	(a) 0–9	Division Two	No Scorer	3000
1896	Newcastle East End	(h) 3–3	Friendly	Lennox 2, Wardope	200
1899	Sheffield Wednesday	(a) 3–1	Division One	Aitken, Stevenson 2	4000

This was the last match played at Wednesday's old ground of Olive Grove, and the meagre attendance and poor score did little to cheer up Wednesdayites. Worse was to come, however, when news broke that their rivals United had won the FA Cup that afternoon.

1905	Aston Villa	(n) 0–2	FA Cup Final	No Scorer	101117

Held at the Crystal Palace, London.

1911	Blackburn Rovers	(h) 2–2	Division One	Higgins, Stewart	25000

United's star striker Albert Shepherd, who had hit eight goals in the cup run, was stretchered from the field following a collision with the Rovers goalkeeper. Not only did he miss the following week's final and subsequent replay, but he also missed the whole of the following season.

1912	Hibernian	(a) 4–2	Friendly	Fleming 2, Wilson, Hibbert	8000
1922	West Bromwich Albion	(h) 3–0	Division One	Harris 2, Mitchell	28000
1927	Huddersfield Town	(h) 1–0	Division One	Gallacher	62500
1933	Leeds United	(a) 1–6	Division One	Allen	15000
1938	Norwich City	(h) 0–1	Division Two	No Scorer	20000
1939	Bury	(a) 1–1	Division Two	Ancell	6000

Billy Pears made his debut at right-half and managed only one more appearance before the outbreak of hostilities curtailed his promising career.

1949	Middlesbrough	(h) 1–0	Division One	Milburn	64381
1950	Arsenal	(a) 2–4	Division One	Hannah, G. Robledo	55000
1953	East Fife	(h) 4–1	Friendly	Mitchell 2, Mulgrew, Hannah	18600
1960	Sheffield Wednesday	(h) 3–3	Division One	Bell, White 2	39942

1961	Blackpool	(a) 1–2	Division One	Woods	19381
1968	West Bromwich Albion	(a) 0–2	Division One	No Scorer	22367
1974	Norwich City	(h) 0–0	Division One	No Scorer	31132
1978	Arsenal	(a) 1–2	Division One	Burns	33353
1981	Blackburn Rovers	(h) 0–0	Division Two	No Scorer	13128

Newcastle thought they'd got a late winner through Harford, only for referee Michael Lowe to invoke a new rule of 'standing in the goalkeeper's ground', Barton being penalised.

1985	Death of Sammy Weaver, 76.

1989	Arsenal	(a) 0–1	Division One	No Scorer	38023

Debut for David Roche, as substitute. As this match unfolded, it ceased to be important as news spread of the terrible events and loss of life at Hillsborough at the FA Cup semi-final match between Liverpool and Nottingham Forest.

APRIL 16TH

1895	Bolton Wanderers	(h) 1–6	Friendly	McNee	4000
1897	Woolwich Arsenal	(a) 1–5	Division Two	Adams	7000
1898	West Bromwich Albion	(h) 1–1	Friendly	Blyth	10000
1900	Notts County	(a) 0–0	Division One	No Scorer	10000
1904	Sheffield Wednesday	(h) 4–0	Division One	Orr 2, Appleyard 2	26000
1906	Woolwich Arsenal	(h) 1–1	Division One	Orr	20000

Debut for John Dodds.

1910	Liverpool	(h) 1–3	Division One	Rutherford	22000
1921	Bolton Wanderers	(h) 1–0	Division One	Smailes	15000
1923	Bolton Wanderers	(h) 1–0	Division One	McDonald	22000
1927	Tottenham Hotspur	(h) 3–2	Division One	Seymour 2, Urwin	33000
1932	Portsmouth	(a) 0–6	Division One	No Scorer	12000

Centre-forward Tom McBain made one appearance for United, and unfortunately this was it.

1938	Sheffield Wednesday	(a) 0–3	Division Two	No Scorer	30000
1949	Bolton Wanderers	(h) 1–1	Division One	Robledo	39999
1952	Arsenal	(a) 1–1	Division One	Keeble	50000
1954	Sheffield Wednesday	(h) 3–0	Division One	Mitchell 2, Monkhouse	43945
1955	Huddersfield Town	(a) 0–2	Division One	No Scorer	29913
1956	All Star XI	(h) 5–0	Friendly	White 2, Curry, Keeble, Milburn	36240

Testimonial for Bobby Cowell.

1960	Wolverhampton Wanderers	(h) 1–0	Division One	White	47409
1963	Huddersfield Town	(a) 1–2	Division Two	Penman	22022
1965	Bolton Wanderers	(h) 2–0	Division Two	Penman, Iley	59960
1966	Leicester City	(a) 2–1	Division One	Bennett, Robson (pen)	18535
1972	Matty Appleby born, Middlesbrough.
1975	Malcolm Macdonald 5, Cyprus 0, at Wembley.
1977	West Ham United	(h) 3–0	Division One	Gowling, Cannell, Nulty	30967
1979	Preston North End	(a) 0–0	Division Two	No Scorer	12960
1983	Chelsea	(a) 2–0	Division Two	Varadi, Keegan (pen)	13446
1986	Manchester United	(h) 2–4	Division One	Stewart, Cunningham	32183
1988	Liverpool	(n) 1–0	Mercantile Tournament	McDonald	30000

Day one of the Football League's centenary tournament at Wembley, and a victory on sudden-death penalties.

1988	Tranmere Rovers	(n) 0–2	Mercantile Tournament	No Scorer	15000

After overcoming Liverpool in the first round, United deservedly lost to their Merseyside neighbours. The eventual winners of the competition were Nottingham Forest.

1990 Stoke City (h) 3–0 Division Two Kristensen 2, Quinn 26179
Benny Kristensen had made 38 first-team appearances without even the hint of a goal. After grabbing one against Stoke in the first half, he promptly got another in the second.

1994 Liverpool (a) 2–0 Premier League Lee, Cole 44601
A game which United deservedly won, although the game was almost incidental to a unique atmosphere created by both sets of fans. In the penultimate game for the standing Kop, Keegan substituted Venison and Beardsley for the home fans to show their appreciation, and United fans laid a wreath on the pitch in memory of the Hillsborough dead.

1997 Chelsea (h) 3–1 Premier League Shearer 2, Asprilla 36320

APRIL 17TH

1893 Everton (a) 2–5 Friendly Collins, Crate
1897 Hearts (h) 3–0 Friendly Blyth, Aitken 2 4000
1899 Hibernian (a) 0–2 Friendly No Scorer 3000
1900 Coventry City (a) 5–1 Friendly Peddie 2, Rogers 2, 1000
Kingsley (pen)
1901 Aston Villa (h) 3–0 Division One Heywood, MacFarlane, 12000
A. Gardner
1908 Woolwich Arsenal (h) 2–1 Division One Speedie 2 35000
1909 Chelsea (h) 1–3 Division One Wilson 25000
1915 Blackburn Rovers (h) 2–1 Division One Higgins, Hibbert 14000
1920 Manchester City (h) 3–0 Division One Phillipson 2, OG 25000
Debuts for Willie Bertram and Harry Wake.
1922 Bradford City (a) 3–2 Division One Harris, J. Low, Smailes 25000
1926 West Bromwich (h) 3–0 Division One Loughlin, Urwin, 12500
Albion Hudspeth (pen)
1933 Aston Villa (h) 3–1 Division One J.R. Richardson 2, 22000
Weaver (pen)
1937 Swansea Town (a) 2–1 Division Two Rogers, Smith 10000
1948 Sheffield Wednesday (h) 4–2 Division Two Harvey, Stobbart, Houghton 2 66483
Promotion was virtually assured with this victory thanks to two late goals from Frank Houghton, who was injured in the process. Wednesday's scorers were Jack Marriott and Doug Witcomb.
1954 Arsenal (h) 5–2 Division One Davies 3, Hannah, White 48243
1962 After defeating Manchester United, North Shields and Portsmouth, the youth team had reached the final of the FA Youth Cup and played the first leg of the final at Molineux in front of 14,000. Clive Chapman equalised to level the scores at 1–1 and set up a decisive second leg at Gallowgate. Among the young Wolves players were Peter Knowles and future Sunderland manager Ken Knighton.
1965 Crystal Palace (a) 1–1 Division Two Cummings 21756
1971 Arsenal (a) 0–1 Division One No Scorer 48106
Charlie George kept the Gunners on course for a League and Cup double.
1974 Norwich City (a) 1–1 Division One Cassidy 18408
1976 Burnley (h) 0–1 Division One No Scorer 24897
The final appearance of Malcolm Macdonald at St James' for Newcastle was not a memorable one. Old warhorse Peter Noble returned and scored the only goal with a header.
1978 Aston Villa (a) 0–2 Division One No Scorer 25495
Thirty years to the day since promotion was gained, this defeat ensured United would be returning to Division Two.
1982 Luton Town (a) 2–3 Division Two Mills, Trewick (pen) 13041

1985	Coventry City	(h) 0–1	Division One	No Scorer	19577
1991	Sheffield Wednesday	(h) 1–0	Division Two	Brock	18330

An Owls team with their minds firmly set on wearing in new boots for their imminent Wembley appearance. Debut in goal for the popular Pavel Srnicek.

1993	Millwall	(a) 2–1	Division One	Clark, Cole	14262

Pre-match crowd trouble outside the ground and an uneasy atmosphere throughout; the travelling fans were locked in the terrace at half-time for their own safety, without access to any facilities. Just like the old days on the Gallowgate end, then . . .

1995	Leeds United	(h) 1–2	Premier League	Elliott	35626

Within moments of Robbie Elliott scoring with a great shot at the Leazes end he had departed on a stretcher. Leeds won the game thanks to a penalty from McAllister and an unchallenged run from Tony Yeboah.

1996	Southampton	(h) 1–0	Premier League	Lee	36554

The normally reliable Beardsley missed a penalty when faced with the sight of Dave Beasant, but a nervous United held on for the victory. The returning Barry Venison led the Saints and was warmly welcomed.

APRIL 18TH

1896	Sheffield United	(h) 3–1	Friendly	Wardrope 2, Lennox	5000
1903	Blackburn Rovers	(a) 1–3	Division One	McColl	8000

Debut for Bill Appleyard.

1903	While the first team were on duty at Ewood Park, Middlesbrough and Sunderland drew

1–1 in a First Division match held at St James' Park in front of 26,000. Roker Park had been closed due to crowd trouble.

1908	Sunderland	(h) 1–3	Division One	Howie	50000
1914	Sheffield United	(a) 0–2	Division One	No Scorer	17000
1923	South Shields	(a) 1–0	Friendly One	McDonald	

An Ingham Cup tie.

1924	Bolton Wanderers	(a) 1–0	Division One	J. Low	20000
1925	Bolton Wanderers	(h) 0–1	Division One	No Scorer	8000
1928	Everton	(h) 0–3	Division One	No Scorer	
1930	Liverpool	(h) 3–1	Division One	Gallacher, Hill, Weaver	40000
1931	Leicester City	(a) 1–3	Division One	Bedford	12000
1933	Aston Villa	(a) 0–3	Division One	No Scorer	25000
1936	Southampton	(a) 3–1	Division Two	J. Smith 2, Ware	9000
1938	Norwich City	(a) 1–1	Division Two	Imrie (pen)	22500
1949	Middlesbrough	(a) 2–3	Division One	Milburn, Mitchell	43000
1951	Bolton Wanderers	(h) 0–1	Division One	No Scorer	39099
1953	Portsmouth	(a) 1–5	Division One	Keeble	27835

Debut for Arnold Woollard, at right-back.

1955	Manchester United	(h) 2–0	Division One	Hannah, White	35569
1959	Leeds United	(h) 2–2	Division One	Allchurch, Curry	19321
1960	Sheffield Wednesday	(a) 0–2	Division One	No Scorer	33332

The damage was done by John Fantham and Redfern Froggatt, who had scored for Wednesday at St James' Park some 13 years previously!

1964	Scunthorpe United	(a) 0–2	Division Two	No Scorer	6433

Debut for Frank Clark, who inherited the number 3 shirt from George Dalton and settled to such an extent that he was ever-present until September 1965.

1973	Manchester City	(a) 0–2	Division One	No Scorer	25156
1979	Notts County	(h) 1–2	Division Two	Withe	12017
1981	Derby County	(a) 0–2	Division Two	No Scorer	14139

Roy McFarland netted the first for the Rams and another own goal from David Barton left United still searching for their first goal away from home since January.

1984	Death of Stan Barber, 75.

1987   Manchester United (h) 2–1   Division One   Goddard, Roeder   32706
Beardsley made his farewell appearance before leaving for Liverpool and lasted only 35 minutes before departing through injury. An estimated 6,000 fans were locked out and missed a gritty performance by ten-man Newcastle. John Anderson limped off after clashing with Norman Whiteside, but the home side took the points.

1988   John Robertson signed from Hearts in a £750,000 deal but would have to wait until the following season to make his debut, as United's remaining matches could affect promotion and relegation issues.

1990   After many months of disagreement, fan boycotts and newspaper editorials, John Hall was co-opted onto the Newcastle Board by a clearly reluctant Gordon McKeag and his dwindling band of supportive shareholders.

1992   Millwall   (h) 0–1   Division Two   No Scorer   23821
Debut as substitute for Peter Garland.

1998   Manchester United (a) 1–1   Premier League   Andersson   55194
England folk hero David Beckham equalised, but following the dismissal of Solskjaer, Newcastle should have claimed a second victory at Old Trafford within weeks.

APRIL 19TH

1902   Nottingham Forest   (h) 3–0   Division One   Roberts, Rutherford 2 12000
1913   Manchester United   (a) 0–3   Division One   No Scorer   17000
1924   Chelsea   (a) 0–1   Division One   No Scorer   30000
1927   Huddersfield Town   (a) 0–1   Division One   No Scorer   45049
1930   Leeds United   (h) 2–1   Division One   Gallacher 2   30000
1935   Bury   (a) 2–0   Division Two   Bott, Murray   17000
1937   Ipswich Town   (a) 4–1   Friendly   Smith 2, Docking, Pearson 10500
1944   Ron Guthrie born, Burradon.
1947   Leicester City   (h) 1–1   Division Two   Wayman   36739
The only senior appearance of Ron Anderson, in goal. Fellow debutant Andy Donaldson replaced Stobbart in the forward line.
1952   Derby County   (a) 3–1   Division One   Harvey, Keeble, Prior 18940
1954   An amazing crowd of 56,008 packed St James' Park to witness Bishop Auckland and Crook Town contest a replay of the FA Amateur Cup final. The game ended 2–2.
1956   Barrow   (a) 4–3   Friendly   White 3, Curry   7098
1957   Chelsea   (h) 1–2   Division One   White   30708
1958   Bolton Wanderers   (a) 1–1   Division One   White   19284
1965   Bolton Wanderers   (a) 1–1   Division Two   Cummings   15762
1969   West Bromwich   (a) 1–5   Division One   Robson   23087
        Albion
1972   Leeds United   (h) 1–0   Division One   Macdonald   42164
1975   Stoke City   (a) 0–0   Division One   No Scorer   32302
1976   Sheffield United   (a) 0–1   Division One   No Scorer   18906
David McLean made his debut, in midfield.
1980   Swansea City   (h) 1–3   Division Two   Shoulder (pen)   14314
1986   Chelsea   (a) 1–1   Division One   Anderson   18970
1988   Watford   (a) 1–1   Division One   Anderson   12075
1989   Death of George Mathison, 79.
1996   A lorry carrying 4,000 new United away shirts was hijacked by three men, who were apprehended soon after.
1997   Derby County   (h) 3–1   Premier League   Elliott, Ferdinand, Shearer 36553

APRIL 20TH

1890   Frank Hudspeth born, Percy Main.
1896   Burslem Port Vale   (a) 0–2   Division Two   No Scorer   2000
1897   St Mirren   (h) 3–0   Friendly   Stewart, Smellie, Aitken 2000

1898	Stoke	(h) 2–1	Test Match	Smith, Harvey	17000
1901	Manchester City	(a) 1–2	Division One	Peddie	18000
1907	Bolton Wanderers	(a) 2–4	Division One	Orr, Veitch	5000

Debut for George Jobey, signed from Morpeth Harriers for the princely sum of £10.

1908	Middlesbrough	(a) 1–2	Division One	Higgins	20000
1912	Aston Villa	(a) 0–2	Division One	No Scorer	20000
1921	Middlesbrough	(a) 1–2	Friendly	King	12000
1929	Sheffield Wednesday	(h) 2–1	Division One	Gallacher 2 (1 pen)	20000
1935	Bolton Wanderers	(h) 1–3	Division Two	Leach	28000

1942 Jimmy Wilson born, Newmilns, Scotland.

| 1955 | Preston North End | (h) 3–3 | Division One | Davies, Hannah, Milburn | 38681 |

On the same day, Newcastle's Alf McMichael and Tommy Casey appeared for Northern Ireland as a John Charles hat-trick gave Wales a 3–2 victory at Windsor Park, Belfast. In the Wales team that day was future Magpie Ivor Allchurch, who played alongside his brother Len.

1957	Aston Villa	(h) 1–2	Division One	Mitchell	28453
1962	Derby County	(h) 3–0	Division Two	Fell (pen), Hale, Thomas	33138
1963	Bury	(h) 1–3	Division Two	McGarry	25017
1966	Blackpool	(a) 1–1	Division One	Suddick	12446
1968	Fulham	(a) 0–2	Division One	No Scorer	21612
1974	Birmingham City	(h) 1–1	Division One	Robson	34066

1976 Shay Given born, Lifford, Ireland.

1981	Grimsby Town	(h) 1–1	Division Two	Shoulder	13170
1983	Rotherham United	(h) 4–0	Division Two	McDermott, Varadi, Keegan, Wharton	18523
1985	Liverpool	(a) 1–3	Division One	McDonald	34733
1987	Everton	(a) 0–3	Division One	No Scorer	43576

Debut for Brian Tinnion, at left-back, as Neil McDonald was sent off for moaning to the referee. Wayne Clark scored a hat-trick for Everton, who were well on their way to becoming champions.

| 1991 | Ipswich Town | (h) 2–2 | Division Two | Stimson, Quinn | 17638 |
| 1992 | Derby County | (a) 1–4 | Division Two | Peacock | 21363 |

Referee Brian Coddington sent off Brock, Scott and O'Brien and banished McDermott from the bench as United were in a relegation position with only two games left.

1994 After finally becoming a first choice for United, Alan Neilson made his senior Welsh debut against Sweden.

APRIL 21ST

1894	Sunderland	(h) 4–1	Friendly	Quinn, Crate, Cambell, Willis	8000
1900	Stoke	(h) 2–2	Division One	Peddie, Alec Gardner	12000
1905	Stoke	(h) 4–1	Division One	Orr 2, McClarence, Howie	25000
1906	Everton	(n) 0–1	FA Cup Final	No Scorer	75609

A second successive defeat at the Crystal Palace.

1920	Middlesbrough	(a) 1–2	Friendly	Smailes	10000
1923	Stoke	(h) 1–0	Division One	Spencer	15000
1924	Aston Villa	(a) 1–6	Division One	J. Clark	40000

This was a dress rehearsal for the following week's FA Cup final between the two clubs, and while Villa were at full strength, United fielded nine reserves. They were subsequently fined for fielding a weakened team. Ironically, first-choice goalkeeper Sandy Mutch was injured in this match and missed the final.

1928	Arsenal	(h) 1–1	Division One	Seymour	25000
1930	Liverpool	(a) 0–0	Division One	No Scorer	40000
1934	Wolverhampton Wanderers	(h) 5–1	Division One	Williams, J.R. Richardson, Imrie 3 (1 pen)	26000

1951	Manchester United	(h) 0–2	Division One	No Scorer	45209
1956	Chelsea	(h) 1–1	Division One	Milburn (pen)	24322
1962	Sunderland	(a) 0–3	Division Two	No Scorer	57666
1963	Death of Jock Rutherford, 78.				
1969	Wolverhampton Wanderers	(h) 4–1	Division One	Davies, Robson 2, Sinclair	24986
1973	Liverpool	(h) 2–1	Division One	Tudor 2	36810

A rare dent in Liverpool's championship season, as United hit back after going behind to a Keegan header. Tudor nodded an equaliser, and then capitalised on a Tommy Smith mistake in the box to hit the winner.

| 1977 | Future Newcastle manager Jackie Charlton quit as Middlesbrough boss. | | | | |
| 1979 | Fulham | (h) 0–0 | Division Two | No Scorer | 11924 |

The unlucky John Brownlie broke his collarbone.

1984	Blackburn Rovers	(a) 1–1	Division Two	Trewick	19196
1986	West Ham United	(a) 1–8	Division One	Whitehurst	24735
1990	Plymouth Argyle	(a) 1–1	Division Two	McGhee	11702

APRIL 22ND

1893	Accrington	(h) 5–0	Friendly	Crate, Pattinson, Collins 3	
1895	Sunderland	(h) 1–0	Friendly	Thompson	5000
1896	Aston Villa	(h) 1–1	Friendly	Lennox	6000
1899	Sunderland	(h) 0–1	Division One	No Scorer	22000
1905	Sunderland	(h) 1–3	Division One	Veitch	30000
1911	Bradford City	(n) 0–0	FA Cup Final	No Scorer	69800

Deadlock at the Crystal Palace.

| 1912 | Norwich City | (a) 0–0 | Friendly | No Scorer | 12000 |

A Hospital Cup match which took place at the Canaries' former ground of The Nest, a cramped enclosure built on a former chalk pit. A then-record crowd of 12,000 squeezed into the ground but, unbelievably, before the FA petitioned Norwich to close the ground in 1935, over 25,000 somehow witnessed a cup-tie against Sheffield Wednesday.

| 1922 | West Bromwich Albion | (a) 2–1 | Division One | Curry, Harris | 25000 |
| 1933 | Blackburn Rovers | (h) 2–1 | Division One | Allen, Dryden | 12500 |

A winning goal from Johnny Dryden, his only one for the club. Dryden was a distant relative of the Charltons and Milburns, and joined United from Ashington.

1936	Blackpool	(a) 0–6	Division Two	No Scorer	8000
1939	Swansea Town	(h) 1–2	Division Two	Clifton	14000
1950	Manchester United	(h) 2–1	Division One	Milburn, Walker	52203
1957	Chelsea	(a) 2–6	Division One	Milburn, White	20795
1959	Bolton Wanderers	(h) 2–0	Division One	Curry, Taylor	17451
1961	Bolton Wanderers	(h) 4–1	Division One	Tuohy, McGuigan, Keith, McKinney (pen)	18820
1967	Sheffield Wednesday	(a) 0–0	Division One	No Scorer	25007
1972	Chelsea	(a) 3–3	Division One	Tudor 2, Macdonald	33000
1978	Queens Park Rangers	(h) 0–3	Division One	No Scorer	13463
1989	Luton Town	(h) 0–0	Division One	No Scorer	18636

A suitably sombre game which virtually sealed relegation kicked off at 3.06 p.m. as a tribute to the victims of the Hillsborough tragedy the previous week.

| 1991 | Death of Jackie Bell, 51. | | | | |
| 1998 | Promotion from the Pontins League Third Division was secured with a 1–0 victory for the reserves at Scunthorpe. Ralf Keidel netted and Shaka Hislop saved a penalty on his farewell appearance for United. Newcastle took the opportunity to check on two young trialists from Ajax of Amsterdam, Jimmy Guy and Luciano Van Callen, but they failed to impress. | | | | |

APRIL 23RD

1894	Willington	(a) 2–0	Friendly	Unknown Scorers	
1898	Stoke	(a) 0–1	Test Match	No Scorer	20000

Debut for James Lockey at right-back in this test match to decide promotion and relegation issues.

1901	Albert McInroy born, Walton-le-Dale, Lancashire.				
1902	Middlesbrough	(h) 2–1	Friendly	Rutherford, Orr	2000

The first of a number of matches United took part in to raise funds for the Ibrox Disaster Fund.

1904	Sunderland	(a) 0–3	Friendly	No Scorer	3000
1907	Leith	(a) 0–1	Friendly	No Scorer	6000
1910	Barnsley	(n) 1–1	FA Cup Final	Rutherford	76980

The fourth trip to the Crystal Palace and at last the jinx was cracked, if not broken entirely.

1921	Arsenal	(w) 1–1	Division One	King	30000
1924	Frank Brennan born, Annathill, Scotland.				
1927	West Ham United	(a) 1–1	Division One	Seymour	30000

This point confirmed that the League championship was on its way to Tyneside for the fourth time, even though two games still remained to be played.

1928	Sheffield United	(a) 1–1	Division One	Gallacher	16000
1932	Arsenal	(w) 2–1	FA Cup Final	Allen 2	92298

Wembley success again, in what became known as the 'over the line' final.

1938	Chesterfield	(h) 3–1	Division Two	Mooney 2, Park	16000
1949	Liverpool	(a) 1–1	Division One	Mitchell	43488
1952	West Bromwich Albion	(h) 1–4	Division One	Prior	31188
1955	Bolton Wanderers	(h) 0–0	Division One	No Scorer	48194
1958	Manchester United	(a) 1–1	Division One	White	28393
1960	Nottingham Forest	(a) 0–3	Division One	No Scorer	28066

Debut for Brian Wright, at right-half.

1962	Derby County	(a) 2–1	Division Two	Allchurch, Thomas	10745
1963	Charlton Athletic	(a) 2–1	Division Two	Suddick, McKinney	12341
1966	Sheffield United	(h) 0–2	Division One	No Scorer	25733
1975	Arsenal	(h) 3–1	Division One	Bruce, Macdonald, T. Craig	21895
1976	Darren Huckerby born, Nottingham.				
1977	Queens Park Rangers	(a) 2–1	Division One	Barrowclough, Nattrass	20544
1977	Death of Matthew McNeil, 49.				
1983	Charlton Athletic	(h) 4–2	Division Two	McDermott, Varadi 2, Wharton	20567
1984	Carlisle United	(h) 5–1	Division Two	Waddle, Beardsley 2, Keegan 2	33458

Vandals broke into the ground before this bank holiday fixture and sprayed slogans on the pitch related to an ongoing criminal trial. A claim of broken glass having being scattered was found to be false, and after the slogans had been painted out the match went ahead as scheduled. Kevin Carr saved a penalty.

1988	Charlton Athletic	(a) 0–2	Division One	No Scorer	7482
1994	Oldham Athletic	(h) 3–2	Premier League	Fox, Beardsley, Lee	32214

APRIL 24TH

1897	Glasgow Rangers	(h) 3–1	Friendly	Connell, Lennox, Smellie	7000
1899	Hibernian	(h) 2–2	Friendly	Aitken, Macfarlane	2000
1901	Sunderland	(h) 0–2	Division One	No Scorer	20000

1906	Stoke	(h) 5–0	Division One	Orr, Howie, J. Rutherford 2, Veitch	12000

150 officers and crew from the Japanese warship Kashima, which was docked on the Tyne, were guests of the club and watched the game from the Centre Paddock. They returned for the next home game, and saw United score another three goals.

1907	Glasgow Rangers	(a) 0–3	Friendly	No Scorer	10000
1909	Blackburn Rangers	(a) 4–2	Division One	Allan, Rutherford 3	7000
1915	Notts County	(a) 0–1	Division One	No Scorer	10000
1920	Manchester City	(a) 0–0	Division One	No Scorer	25000
1926	Everton	(a) 0–3	Division One	No Scorer	15000
1937	Bradford City	(h) 2–0	Division Two	Rogers, Smith	10000

Seventeen-year-old Arnold Grundy got one of only two starts in this win, at left-half.

1948	Tottenham Hotspur	(a) 1–1	Division Two	Sibley	44164

This point confirmed United's return to the First Division, in second place behind Birmingham City. A few miles away at Wembley, Manchester United beat Blackpool 4–2 to win the FA Cup final.

1954	Chelsea	(a) 2–1	Division One	Mitchell, White	46991
1962	Stuart Pearce born, Hammersmith, London.				
1962	Bobby Moncur signed full professional forms for Newcastle, during the short managerial reign of Norman Smith.				
1965	Manchester City	(h) 0–0	Division Two	No Scorer	35600
1967	Lionel Perez born, Bagnoles, France.				
1971	West Ham United	(h) 1–1	Division One	Tudor	22790

An equaliser from Geoff Hurst.

1974	Burnley	(h) 2–1	Texaco Cup	Macdonald, Moncur	36076
1976	Tottenham Hotspur	(h) 3–0	Division One	Macdonald 2, Burns	29649
1982	Grimsby Town	(h) 0–1	Division Two	No Scorer	14065
1991	West Ham United	(a) 1–1	Division Two	Peacock	24195

The unbeaten run was extended to five games as the influence of recently appointed boss Ardiles began to be seen. Evenly the staunchly southern *Daily Mail* was moved to comment that the game was a 'classic exposition of footballing skills'.

APRIL 25TH

1894	Shankhouse	(a) 1–1	Friendly	Crate	
1896	Derby County	(h) 4–2	Friendly	Stott 2, Lennox, Collins	8000
1903	Sunderland	(h) 1–0	Division One	McColl	26500
1904	Hearts	(a) 3–2	Friendly	Appleyard 2, Orr	6000
1907	Wilf Bott born, Featherstone, Yorkshire.				
1908	Wolverhampton Wanderers	(n) 1–3	FA Cup Final	Howie	65000

The Crystal Palace jinx struck for a third time, although Jimmy Howie scored the first Newcastle goal in an FA Cup final.

1910	Bristol City	(a) 3–0	Division One	Randall, Stewart 2	4000
1914	Derby County	(h) 1–1	Division One	Hibbert	16000
1922	Glasgow Rangers	(a) 1–1	Friendly	Harris	18000
1925	Notts County	(a) 0–2	Division One	No Scorer	8000
1927	Hull City	(a) 0–3	Friendly	No Scorer	6000

Hospital Cup match.

1931	Arsenal	(h) 1–3	Division One	Lang	25000
1936	Blackpool	(h) 1–0	Division Two	Weaver	12000

Debut for Ernie Hall, who also appeared in the following game at centre-half as United finished eighth in Division Two but was never called upon again.

1938	Chesterfield	(a) 0–2	Division Two	No Scorer	
1953	Bolton Wanderers	(h) 2–3	Division One	Hannah, Harvey	34824

1955	Blackpool	(h) 1–1	Division One	Broadis	41380
1956	Hartlepools United	(a) 3–6	Friendly	Keeble, Mitchell (pen), Cummings	7206

Testimonial match.

1959	Burnley	(a) 2–2	Division One	Curry, Allchurch	15430
1964	Norwich City	(h) 2–0	Division Two	Cummings, Iley	12256

Debut for 17-year-old apprentice Geoff Allen in the final game of the season.

1973	Everton	(h) 0–0	Division One	No Scorer	22390
1979	Blackburn Rovers	(a) 3–1	Division Two	Withe 3	4902

The sparse attendance at Ewood Park saw relegation confirmed by this defeat. Future Magpie John Bailey was in the home line-up.

1981	Blackburn Rovers	(a) 0–3	Division Two	No Scorer	10609

Well beaten. Scorers included Lowey from the spot.

1987	Chelsea	(h) 1–0	Division One	Goddard	21962
1990	Swindon Town	(h) 0–0	Division Two	No Scorer	26548
1992	Portsmouth	(h) 1–0	Division Two	Kelly	25989

Possibly the most important goal ever scored by a Newcastle player.

1993	Sunderland	(h) 1–0	Division One	Sellars	30364

Terry Butcher brought his 'red-and-white commandos' (his words) to a rain-soaked Gallowgate and clumsily gave away a free-kick outside the box at the Leazes end. Up stepped Scott Sellars to crack it in off a post and send United a step closer to the Premier League. The end of the match saw the first unfurling of the 'Champions' flag, paid for by United fans, and a rousing chorus of 'Terry Butcher on the dole'.

1998	Tottenham Hotspur	(a) 0–2	Premier League	No Scorer	35874

Klinsmann and Ferdinand scored for Tottenham.

APRIL 26TH

1893	Middlesbrough Ironopolis	(h) 1–0	Friendly	Unknown Scorer	
1897	Third Lanark	(h) 1–0	Friendly	Aitken	1000

A friendly match in which Newcastle witnessed at first hand the talent of Lanark centre-forward Jock Peddie, even though he failed to score. A trial at United had led to him becoming a permanent signing by November.

1902	Bury	(a) 0–4	Division One	No Scorer	3500
1904	St Mirren	(a) 2–1	Friendly	McClarence, Howie	2500
1905	Sheffield Wednesday	(a) 3–1	Division One	Orr (pen), Howie, McWilliam	12000

Goalkeeping debutant Bob Crumley was to make three more appearances for United, but failed to keep a clean sheet in any of them, before returning to his native Dundee.

1906	Preston North End	(a) 0–0	Division One	No Scorer	5000
1909	Aston Villa	(a) 0–3	Division One	No Scorer	8000
1911	Bradford City	(n) 0–1	FA Cup Final Replay	No Scorer	66646

Held at Old Trafford.

1913	Aston Villa	(h) 2–3	Division One	Higgins, Veitch	20000
1921	Glasgow Rangers	(a) 0–0	Friendly	No Scorer	25000

Testimonial match.

1930	Derby County	(a) 1–3	Division One	Devine	10093
1947	Chesterfield	(a) 0–1	Division Two	No Scorer	14800
1950	Dundee	(h) 2–3	Friendly	G. Robledo, Taylor	16490
1952	Aston Villa	(h) 6–1	Division One	Brennan, Davies 2, Hannah, Milburn, Mitchell	36852
1954	Reading	(a) 2–2	Friendly	Milburn, Davies	8428

Testimonial match.

1958	Leeds United	(h) 1–2	Division One	R. Mitchell	32594
1967	West Ham United	(h) 1–0	Division One	OG	38863

1975	Birmingham City	(h) 1–2	Division One	Macdonald	24787
1978	Norwich City	(h) 2–2	Division One	Burns, Kennedy	7986
1978	Paddy Kelly born, Kirkcaldy, Scotland. He joined up with his former manager Tommy Burns when he became a coach at Newcastle, having played one first-team game for Celtic. Following the departure of Burns to become Reading manager, Paddy spent some time on loan but was allowed to return to Tyneside.				
1980	Queens Park Rangers	(a) 1–2	Division Two	Ferguson	11245
1982	Newcastle reserves recorded a resounding 4–0 victory over Sheffield United, the first goal coming from a powerful free-kick from Graeme Hedley, a midfielder on trial from Middlesbrough. He turned out in a couple of reserve games but failed to impress Arthur Cox.				
1983	England Under-21 1, Hungary Under-21 0 at St James' Park, watched by 7,810.				
1986	Manchester City	(h) 3–1	Division One	Clarke, Roeder, Whitehurst	23479

APRIL 27TH

1877	Andy Aitken born, Ayr, Scotland.				
1895	Preston North End	(h) 5–3	Friendly	Wright 2, Dickson 2, McNee	4000
1896	Sheffield Wednesday	(h) 1–4	Friendly	Aitken (pen)	4000
1901	Bury	(h) 0–0	Division One	No Scorer	
1903	Workington Black Diamond	(a) 2–3	Friendly	Graham, Appleyard	
1904	Glasgow Rangers	(a) 0–2	Friendly	No Scorer	8000
1907	Aberdeen	(a) 2–4	Friendly	Dodds, Court	3000
1910	Aston Villa	(a) 0–4	Division One	No Scorer	12000
1912	Blackburn Rovers	(a) 1–1	Division One	Peat	10000
	Debut for John McTavish, at inside-right.				
1924	Aston Villa	(n) 2–0	FA Cup Final	Seymour, Harris	91695
	United's first appearance at the new Empire Stadium.				
1925	Glasgow Rangers	(a) 0–1	Friendly	No Scorer	15000
1929	Derby County	(a) 2–1	Division One	Chalmers 2	13355
	Debut for Dave Fairhurst, at left-back.				
1932	Blackpool	(h) 2–2	Division One	Boyd, McMenemy	32000
1933	Liam Tuohy born, Dublin.				
1935	Oldham Athletic	(a) 2–3	Division Two	Wilson, Weaver (pen)	3638
	Debut for Jimmy Gordon, at right-half.				
1953	Berwick Rangers	(a) 1–1	Friendly	G. Robledo	3000
1955	Cardiff City	(h) 3–0	Division One	Hannah 2, McMichael	19252
1957	Barrow	(a) 8–0	Friendly	Milburn 4, Franks, Davies, Tait, Hughes	6000
	Testimonial match.				
1963	Rotherham United	(a) 1–3	Division Two	McGrath	9384
1968	Tottenham Hotspur	(h) 1–3	Division One	T. Robson	30281
1974	Burnley	(a) 1–1	Division One	Macdonald	21340
1985	Southampton	(h) 2–1	Division One	Reilly, McDonald	20845
	With time running out and a slender lead, Beardsley and Waddle frustrated the opposition by interpassing their way down the wing, to the delight of the crowd. As the whistle blew, an irate Jack Charlton ran onto the field and started giving Waddle and Beardsley a very public dressing-down for not hoofing the ball into the crowd when they had had the chance.				
1991	Charlton Athletic	(a) 0–1	Division Two	No Scorer	7234
1994	Aston Villa	(h) 5–1	Premier League	Bracewell, Beardsley 2 (1 pen), Cole, Sellars	32217
	Andy Cole hit his 40th league goal of the season to beat the all-time record set by Robledo and Gallacher.				

APRIL 28TH

1893	District XI	(a) 5–3	Friendly	Unknown Scorers	
1894	Middlesbrough	(a) 0–0	Friendly	No Scorer	2000
1897	Sunderland	(h) 3–0	Friendly	Aitken 2, Ostler	4000
1898	Blackburn Rovers	(a) 3–4	Test Match	Wardrope, Smith, Aitken	30000
1900	Sunderland	(a) 2–1	Division One	Fraser, A. Gardner (pen)	22000
1902	Glasgow Rangers	(a) 5–0	Friendly	Peddie 2, McColl 2, Orr	4500
1903	Kilmarnock	(a) 2–0	Friendly	Carr, Appleyard	2000
1904	Kilmarnock	(a) 1–4	Friendly	Aitken	3000
1906	Bolton Wanderers	(a) 1–1	Division One	Appleyard	12000
1909	Northampton	(a) 2–0	Charity Shield	Allan, Rutherford	7000

1909 Newcastle's only Charity Shield victory came in this game at Stamford Bridge between the Football League and Southern League Champions.

1910	Barnsley	(n) 2–0	FA Cup Final Replay	Shepherd 2 (1 pen)	55364

The unlikely surroundings of Goodison Park saw Newcastle lift the FA Cup for the first time.

1915	Aston Villa	(h) 3–0	Division One	Goodwill, Hibbert, Cooper	10000

Single appearance of Tom Cairns for Newcastle; within a year he had been killed in France.

1923	Manchester City	(a) 0–0	Division One	No Scorer	25000

1925 George Hair born, Ryton.

1928	Portsmouth	(a) 1–0	Division One	Seymour	30000
1934	Stoke City	(a) 1–2	Division One	Murray	10000
1937	Third Lanark	(h) 1–3	Friendly	Smith	4000
1937	Queen of the South	(a) 4–2	Friendly	Cairns 2, McMenemy, Ware	2500
1951	Blackpool	(n) 2–0	FA Cup Final	Milburn 2	100000

Two superb Milburn strikes took the trophy back to Tyneside, despite the pre-match presence on the Wembley turf of Donald, the Seasiders' lucky mascot – a white duck. The trophy was presented to Joe Harvey by King George VI.

1954	Hartlepools United	(a) 1–1	Friendly	OG	9635

Testimonial match.

1958	Burnley	(h) 1–3	Division One	Bottom	21610

The sole appearance between the posts for Chris Harker, whose career on Tyneside was curtailed by National Service and injuries sustained in a road accident.

1962	Leeds United	(h) 0–3	Division Two	No Scorer	21708

Debut for Dave Turner. A vital win for the visitors, who still had the threat of relegation to Division Three hanging over them going into this final game of the season.

1971	West Bromwich Albion	(h) 3–0	Division One	Young, Smith, Tudor	18444

Three goals in the last 15 minutes were enough to do the double over the Albion.

1973	Tottenham Hotspur	(a) 2–3	Division One	Tudor, McDermott	21721
1975	Sunderland	(a) 2–3	Friendly	Gibb, Burns	13654

A testimonial match for Martin Harvey.

1976	Sunderland	(h) 6–3	Friendly	Kennedy 2, Burns 2, Macdonald, Guy	19974
1979	Stoke City	(a) 0–0	Division Two	No Scorer	23217
1984	Cambridge United	(a) 0–1	Division Two	No Scorer	7720
1986	Middlesbrough	(a) 1–2	Friendly	Cunningham	3500

A testimonial match for David Mills, who served both sides well.

1990	West Ham United	(h) 2–1	Division Two	Kristensen, Quinn	31461
1992	Ando's All Stars	(h) 3–2	Friendly	Clark 2, Watson	13780

A deserved testimonial match for John Anderson saw a host of former Magpies return to Gallowgate, including Roy Aitken, Chris Waddle (and Marseille team-mate Basile Boli),

Peter Jackson, Darren Jackson, John Burridge, Andy Thorn, Paul Stephenson, Ian Bogie, Paul Goddard, Neil McDonald and Mark McGhee. Manager Kevin Keegan also had a runout. The only notable absentee was recovering injury victim Paul Gascoigne, who was banned from turning out by Tottenham. Goddard and Aitken netted for the All Stars.

1994   A crowd of 11,010 were at St James' Park to see England Under-15s retain the International Victory Shield with a 2–1 victory over Scotland. Despite the game being live on Sky, the attendance was a record for a schoolboy game outside Wembley. The England winner came from Michael Owen, a promising young lad . . .

APRIL 29TH

1893	Preston North End	(h) 5–0	Friendly	Sorley 2, Collins 2, Crate	2000
1899	Derby County	(h) 4–1	Friendly	Aitken, Stevenson, Wardrope, Peddic	2000
1902	Glasgow Rangers	(a) 1–3	Friendly	MacFarlane	2000

This match was held to raise money for the families of the 25 victims of the Ibrox Stadium disaster some weeks earlier.

1903	Glasgow Rangers	(n) 2–2	Friendly	Rutherford, Templeton	3000

Another Ibrox Disaster Fund benefit match, held at Cathkin Park, home of Third Lanark.

1905	Middlesbrough	(a) 3–0	Division One	Orr, Appleyard, Rutherford	12000

This victory gave United their first league title, rivals Everton having already finished their programme one point ahead. Ironically, Everton should have clinched it, but were forced to replay their game against Arsenal, which had been abandoned with Everton 3–1 ahead. Arsenal won the restaged game.

1907	Fulham	(h) 1–1	Friendly	Hall	7000
1907	Jimmy Boyd born, Glasgow.				
1908	Manchester United	(a) 1–4	Friendly	Ridley	10000

1910   Twenty-four hours after capturing the FA Cup in a replay at Goodison Park, the victorious United team arrived back on Tyneside and were led from Central Station by the pipe band of the Northumberland Veterinary Association, no less.

1911	Manchester City	(h) 3–3	Division One	Metcalf, Willis, McCracken (pen)	5000
1912	Aberdeen	(a) 1–0	Friendly	Hudspeth (pen)	3000
1917	Duggie Wright born, Rochford, Essex.				
1922	Manchester City	(h) 5–1	Division One	Hagan 2, McDonald 3	34000

The only appearance between the posts for third-choice John Archibald, who subsequently left for Grimsby, to guarantee first-team football, before returning to his native Scotland.

1925	Hibernian	(a) 1–3	Friendly	Low	10000
1929	Hearts	(a) 3–3	Friendly	Chalmers 2, Boyd	15000
1932	Death of John Auld, 70.				
1933	Derby County	(a) 2–3	Division One	Allen, J.R. Richardson	6528
1939	Luton Town	(h) 2–0	Division Two	Pearson (pen), Clifton	10341
1950	Chelsea	(a) 3–1	Division One	Milburn, Walker 2	24667
1955	Ralph Callachan born, Edinburgh.				
1956	Atletico Madrid (Spain)	(a) 1–4	Friendly	Curry	60000
1959	Birmingham City	(h) 1–1	Division One	Allchurch	19776
1961	Blackburn Rovers	(a) 4–2	Division One	Allchurch, McGuigan 2, Neale	12700
1967	Southampton	(h) 3–1	Division One	Davies, Noble, Robson	42426
1978	Leicester City	(a) 0–3	Division One	No Scorer	11530

Farewell to Division One for a dispirited United, already relegated along with their hosts.

1989	Wimbledon	(a) 0–4	Division One	No Scorer	5206

Vinnie Jones and Dennis Wise were among the scorers in a one-sided encounter at Plough Lane.

Kevin Keegan is welcomed on to the field before his Newcastle debut against Queens Park Rangers. Steve Hardwick looks slightly less eager to start the new season

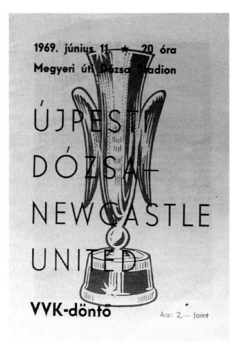

Programme from the second leg of the Fairs Cup final of 1969 which United won 3–2, a 6–2 aggregate win

Programme from Frank Clark's testimonial match v. Sunderland

A pensive Paul Gascoigne pictured just before the first leg of the Youth Cup final against Watford at St James' Park. The Watford player is Malcolm Allen, who joined United nearly a decade later

Promotion celebrations immediately after the 4–0 demolition of Derby County at St James' Park. The whole team is pictured, minus Glenn Roeder, but including substitute David Mills

Neil McDonald jumps for joy after scoring in a 4–1 victory over West Bromwich Albion at St James' Park. Ian Stewart has his back to the camera, while Chris Hedworth and Alan Davies can also be seen

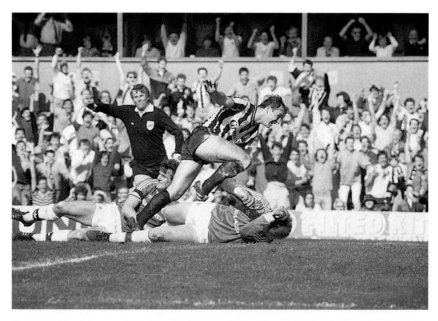

Paul Goddard leaves Walsh and Moran of Manchester United floundering as he scores, much to the delight of supporters in the benches. Portly referee Keith Hackett signals the goal

Newcastle have just drawn 2–2 with Tottenham Hotspur at St James' Park and on-loan keeper Dave McKellar is followed off the field by Chris Waddle, making his first appearance at the ground since joining Spurs

A delighted Peter Beardsley celebrates Newcastle's opening goal against Sheffield Wednesday. The short-lived grey away strip and open standing kop at Hillsborough are now no more than memories

A year after joining United from Huddersfield, Malcolm Brown finally made his first appearance at St James' Park in this friendly match against Middlesbrough. A training injury had ruled him out of the previous promotion season

Two Newcastle legends together, as Jackie Milburn presents
an award to Peter Beardsley

An anxious Willie McFaul introduces his new signing Mirandinha
to the St James' faithful, including those housed on the temporary Leazes
stand, shown behind

Michael O'Neill has just completed the only hat-trick of his Newcastle career, as Luton are crushed 4–0 at St James' Park

United manager Willie McFaul proudly perches on the groundsman's tractor along with new signings John Hendrie, John Robertson, Dave Beasant and Andy Thorn

1994   Another of Keegan's less successful signings, Peter Cormack, son of the former Liverpool star, went to Brighton on trial with a view to a permanent transfer.

1995   Manchester City   (a) 0–0   Premier League   No Scorer   27389
Newcastle fans were seated in a section of the new Kippax Stand which was only in a partially finished state due to non-payment of bills by City, according to local gossip. United goalkeeping coach John Burridge played for City in the second half after Tony Coton had gone off at half-time.

1996   Leeds United   (a) 1–0   Premier League   Gillespie   38862
A header from Gillespie settled this nervous encounter, but the real headlines were made in the post-match interview by Kevin Keegan, which culminated in the infamous 'love it, just love it' comment, directed at Alex Ferguson.

1998   Leicester City   (a) 0–0   Premier League   No Scorer   21699
Neil Lennon, who had been fined for making obscene gestures at United fans in the corresponding fixture the previous season, was accidentally kicked in the face by Alan Shearer. How unfortunate. Steve Guppy played for Leicester and justified Keegan's decision to sell him by being constantly outwitted by his marker, Barton.

APRIL 30TH

1894	Sunderland	(a) 1–3	Friendly	Crate	4000
1895	Jarrow	(a) 1–0	Friendly	Wallace	2500
1896	Sunderland	(h) 3–3	Friendly	Thompson, Aitken, Collins	5000
1897	Hibernian	(h) 0–3	Friendly	No Scorer	3000
1898	Blackburn Rovers	(h) 4–0	Test Match	Campbell, Harvey, Ghee, Jackson	13324
1901	Hearts	(a) 0–2	Friendly	No Scorer	
1902	St Mirren	(a) 2–1	Friendly	Stewart, Harvey	4000

Another fundraising game for the Ibrox Disaster Fund.

1903	St Mirren	(a) 0–1	Friendly	No Scorer	3000
1904	Aberdeen	(a) 7–1	Friendly	McClarence 2, Templeton, Orr 2, McColl, Howie	5000
1906	Blackburn Rovers	(h) 3–0	Division One	Gosnell, Higgins, Raine	
1909	Liverpool	(h) 0–1	Division One	No Scorer	1000
1910	Sheffield United	(h) 0–0	Division One	No Scorer	40000
1912	Inverness	(a) 3–3	Friendly	Peart, Duncan, Hudspeth (pen)	5000
1921	Arsenal	(h) 1–0	Division One	Smailes	40000

Winning debut for right-back Robert Roxburgh, signed from Morpeth Comrades for £50.

1927	Sheffield Wednesday	(h) 2–1	Division One	Gallacher 2	30000
1931	Yeovil	(a) 3–2	Friendly	Boyd, Starling 2	2000
1932	Sheffield United	(a) 3–0	Division One	Boyd, McMenemy, J.R. Richardson	12000

1933   Death of Wilf Lawson, 48. Former player turned trainer Wilf died in a road accident.

1934	Bohemians	(a) 3–1	Friendly	Williams, Richardson 2	5000
1938	Swansea Town	(a) 0–2	Division Two	No Scorer	11000
1949	Manchester United	(h) 0–1	Division One	No Scorer	38266
1955	Tottenham Hotspur	(a) 1–2	Division One	Mitchell	37262
1960	Manchester City	(h) 0–1	Division One	No Scorer	27812

1963   Glyn Hodges born, Streatham.

1966	Leeds United	(a) 0–3	Division One	No Scorer	29531
1969	Stoke City	(h) 5–0	Division One	Arentoft, Davies, Robson, Scott 2	28015
1975	Sunderland	(h) 5–3	Friendly	Macdonald 2, Tudor, Burns, Kennedy	21280

A testimonial match for David Craig.

| 1977 | Arsenal | (h) 0–2 | Division One | No Scorer | 44677 |
| 1983 | Cambridge United | (a) 0–1 | Division Two | No Scorer | 7591 |

1985 The FA Youth Cup final 1st leg at St James' Park finished 0–0 in front of a crowd of nearly 7,000.

| 1988 | Oxford United | (h) 3–1 | Division One | Lormor, O'Neill, Goddard | 16617 |
| 1994 | Sheffield United | (a) 0–2 | Premier League | No Scorer | 29013 |

Two goals from Blake were loudly celebrated by the home fans, but their team were still to be relegated. The away fans celebrated European qualification after hearing the results from other games.

1996 Tino Asprilla was fined and banned by an FA Commission following his entanglements with Keith Curle at Maine Road.

MAY 1ST

| 1902 | Kilmarnock | (a) 0–2 | Friendly | No Scorer | 3000 |

Third benefit match in three days for the victims of the Ibrox Stadium disaster.

| 1920 | Derby County | (a) 0–1 | Division One | No Scorer | 21366 |
| 1926 | Manchester City | (h) 3–2 | Division One | Gallacher 3 | 20000 |

A missed penalty by City sealed their relegation from Division One, as they finished a point short of safety.

| 1939 | York City | (a) 3–1 | Friendly | Cairns, Isaac, OG | 5000 |

Testimonial match.

1943 Trevor Hockey born, Keighley, Yorkshire.

1948	Millwall	(h) 1–0	Division Two	Harvey	43328
1953	Aston Villa	(a) 1–0	Division One	Milburn	20000
1957	Lincoln City	(a) 2–2	Friendly	Hannah, Hale	5600

Testimonial match.

1959	Brighton and Hove Albion	(a) 1–1	Friendly	Hughes	6682
1963	Stoke City	(h) 5–2	Division Two	Hilley, McGarry, Suddick, McKinney 2 (1 pen)	26781
1971	Coventry City	(a) 0–2	Division One	No Scorer	20596

1973 Jimmy Crawford born, Chicago, USA.

| 1982 | Blackburn Rovers | (a) 1–4 | Division Two | Varadi | 5207 |

Derek Bell made his debut and Paul Ferris came on as substitute for his only league appearance. The misery was completed when John Brownlie was dismissed.

MAY 2ND

| 1921 | Manchester City | (a) 1–3 | Division One | Smailes | 25000 |

Debut for Sam Russell.

| 1923 | South Shields | (h) 0–0 | Friendly | No Scorer | 4000 |

United clinched the Ingham Cup 1–0 on aggregate after this goalless draw.

| 1931 | Chelsea | (a) 1–1 | Division One | MacKenzie | 30000 |
| 1936 | Plymouth Argyle | (a) 0–1 | Division Two | No Scorer | |

1944 Alan Suddick born, Chester-le-Street.

| 1951 | Wolves | (a) 1–0 | Division One | G. Robledo | 40000 |

1959 Gary Megson born, Manchester.

1962 Mickey Quinn born, Liverpool.

1962 Newcastle won the FA Youth Cup for the first time, defeating Wolves 1–0 in front of 20,000 at St James'. A Moncur header clinched a 2–1 aggregate victory for a side also including David Craig, Alan Suddick and Colin Clish.

1970	Aberdeen	(h) 0–1	Friendly	No Scorer	10300
1973	Torino (Italy)	(h) 5–1	Anglo-Italian Cup	Tudor, Macdonald, Smith, Hibbitt, OG	9580
1978	Chelmsford City	(a) 2–1	Friendly	Larnach 2	1500

A week after ending a miserable relegation campaign, United turned out at New Writtle Street in a fundraiser for the cash-strapped Clarets. The fact that Chelmsford's secretary was former Newcastle favourite Vic Keeble may explain how Newcastle got involved. Continuing financial problems caused Chelmsford to be wound up in 1980, but they subsequently reformed.

1979	Bristol Rovers	(h) 3–0	Division Two	Withe, Shoulder, Bird	9627

Debut for Peter Manners, in midfield.

1981	Orient	(h) 3–1	Division Two	Walker, Harford, Trewick	11639
1987	West Ham United	(a) 1–1	Division One	McDonald (pen)	17844

John Anderson was sent off but another point ensured First Division survival.

1988	Portsmouth	(a) 2–1	Division One	Lormor, Scott	12468

A sunny day to end the away programme for the season, and a good crowd of well-oiled away fans conga'd across the Milton End as Portsmouth were relegated, despite the considerable presence of Mickey Quinn in their side.

1992	Leicester City	(a) 2–1	Division Two	Peacock, OG	21861

Steve Walsh scored at both ends within a minute as this tense game ended with United safe from relegation, Leicester in the play-offs, home fans on the pitch and David Kelly sheltering in the away section. Numerous incidents throughout the whole day resulted in a multitude of injuries and arrests, and seats were used as weapons inside the ground as riot police struggled to keep the two sets of fans apart.

1996	Nottingham Forest	(a) 1–1	Premier League	Beardsley	28280

A slip from Batty and a shot from Woan that was a goal as soon as it left his foot dashed all realistic hopes of the Premiership title going anywhere but Old Trafford.

1998	Chelsea	(h) 3–1	Premier League	Dabizas, Lee, Speed	36710

An unexpected flourish to end the home season, as the goals flowed. Chelsea, for whom player-manager Vialli seemed to be in particularly bad fettle, looked uninterested, and few observers apart from Kenny Dalglish picked out the figure of Charvet, who moved to United within weeks. One Chelsea fan was content to amuse himself by sliding down a banister in the away section, to great applause from all sides. A post-match lap of the pitch by the players was followed by a tannoy announcement from Kenny Dalglish that I thought mentioned bringing the FA Cup back to Newcastle, but obviously his accent fooled me.

MAY 3RD

1922	Rest of League XI	(h) 2–3	Friendly	Hagan, Smailes	8000

Testimonial match for Jack Carr.

1922	Len Shackleton born, Bradford.	

1924	West Stanley	(a) 2–1	Friendly	Seymour 2	15000

A week after their Wembley triumph, the whole cup-winning side turned out in this North-Eastern League game.

1930	West Ham United	(h) 1–0	Division One	Devine	50000

A match which Newcastle had to win to avoid relegation to Division Two. It was to be the last game Hughie Gallacher played for the club.

1947	Manchester City	(a) 2–0	Division Two	Walker, Wayman	46492
1951	The Thursday after the cup final, and at last the homecoming to Newcastle with the trophy.				

An estimated quarter of a million lined the streets from the Central Station to cheer the lads. The homecoming had been delayed because United had played a league match at Wolverhampton the previous evening and had returned to their Brighton cup base on the Sunday.

1952	Arsenal	(w) 1–0	FA Cup Final	G. Robledo	100000

To Wembley again, and a successful defence thanks to a late goal from the Chilean George Robledo, who played in every round alongside his brother Ted. The referee was Arthur Ellis – later to be known as 'Uncle Arthur' on TV's *It's a Knockout*. Again Joe Harvey received the trophy, this time from Sir Winston Churchill.

| 1956 | Altona and St Pauli (Hamburg) | (a) 1–1 | Friendly | Keeble | 18000 |

The end-of-season tour moved to Germany after a brief visit to Spain.

| 1960 | Shamrock Rovers | (a) 3–0 | Friendly | White 2, Eastham | 20000 |

Testimonial match held at the Royal Showgrounds, Dublin.

| 1972 | West Bromwich Albion | (h) 4–2 | Division One | Macdonald 2 (1 pen), Green, OG | 18927 |
| 1976 | Leeds United | (a) 5–4 | Friendly | Macdonald 2, Gowling, Kennedy, Burns | 16000 |

Testimonial match for Paul Reaney, who made over 700 appearances for Leeds.

1977	Leicester City	(a) 0–1	Division One	No Scorer	14289
1980	Luton Town	(h) 2–2	Division Two	Shoulder, Rafferty	13765
1986	Leicester City	(a) 0–2	Division One	No Scorer	13171
1989	West Ham United	(h) 1–2	Division One	Lormor	14445

Relegation was confirmed by this defeat, the fateful goal being scored by Mark Ward.

| 1989 | Death of George Lowrie, 69. |

| 1995 | Tottenham Hotspur | (h) 3–3 | Premier League | Gillespie, Peacock, Beardsley | 35603 |

An enthralling game, as Spurs netted through Barmby, Anderton and Klinsmann after Peacock and Gillespie had both scored their first league goals. Srnicek was then sent off for upending Barmby in the area and Hooper earned the cheers of the crowd by saving Klinsmann's penalty with his first touch. Beardsley then hit a great equaliser and both teams were applauded from the field.

| 1997 | Arsenal | (a) 1–0 | Premier League | Elliott | 38179 |

Gillespie was sent off for two bookable offences after coming on as a substitute.

| 1998 | Death of Justin Fashanu, 37, apparently having taken his own life. |

MAY 4TH

| 1919 | Death of Stanley Allan, 31. |
| 1927 | Middlesbrough | (a) 0–0 | Friendly | No Scorer | 21000 |

Testimonial match for 'Boro's Charlie Cole.

1929	Everton	(h) 2–0	Division One	Gallacher 2	20000
1932	Everton	(h) 0–0	Division One	No Scorer	40000
1935	Burnley	(h) 2–0	Division Two	McMenemy, Pearson	7000
1959	Peterborough United	(a) 5–3	Friendly	Eastham 2, Curry 2, Mitchell	11000

A benefit match held to raise funds for the Professional Footballers (Peterborough) Testimonial Fund, which dispensed funds to many ex-footballers. The first to benefit was ex-Magpie Andy Donaldson.

| 1963 | Norwich City | (a) 2–1 | Division Two | McGarry, McKinney | 16665 |
| 1968 | Manchester United | (a) 0–6 | Division One | No Scorer | 59697 |

A hat-trick from George Best, two goals from Kidd and one from Sadler as Alex Stepney was hardly called into action. This was in stark contrast to his previous game, when he had conceded six to West Bromwich Albion.

| 1974 | Liverpool | (w) 0–3 | FA Cup Final | No Scorer | 100000 |

There are so many stories from this day. From overnight bus trips from Northumberland to post-match brown-ale drinking in a graveyard, Brendan Foster winning a race round the ground in a black-and-white vest, United fans drowning out the cheers that greeted the presentation of the cup and emotional scenes in Trafalagar Square. Everything, in fact, bar actually winning the cup or looking anything but second best in a one-sided second half.

| 1983 | Barnsley | (a) 5–0 | Division Two | Varadi 2, McDonald 2, Keegan | 10958 |

Debut for Martin Thomas in goal, who was somewhat underemployed.

| 1985 | Stoke City | (a) 1–0 | Division One | OG | 7088 |

The first away league victory since the opening day of the season, some 19 games.

| 1987 | Charlton Athletic | (h) 0–3 | Division One | No Scorer | 26950 |

1988 Malcolm Macdonald resigned as Huddersfield manager, his side having been relegated to Division Three.

| 1991 | West Bromwich Albion | (a) 1–1 | Division Two | Quinn | 16706 |

Relegation-haunted Albion went ahead through future Sunderland striker Don Goodman, but Quinn equalised. Lee Makel made his senior debut as a substitute and did enough to earn a place in the starting line-up at Barnsley the following Tuesday.

1991 United youngster Alun Armstrong had a Wembley debut to remember as he netted four in Durham Boys Club's 6–1 victory over Middlesex.

| 1993 | Grimsby Town | (a) 2–0 | Division One | Cole, Kelly | 14402 |

Promotion party.

MAY 5TH

1907	Frankfurt (Germany)	(a) 6–2	Friendly	Hall 3, Blackburn, McWilliam, Brown	
1923	Manchester City	(h) 3–1	Division One	Aitken, McDonald 2	12000
1928	West Ham United	(h) 3–1	Division One	McDonald (pen), Gallacher, Boyd	20000
1948	Linfield (Northern Ireland)	(a) 6–0	Friendly	Milburn 4, Stobbart, Taylor	

Alf McMichael was in the Linfield side and subsequently moved to St James' Park, while Woodburn and Thompson of United guested for the home side at Windsor Park.

| 1951 | Middlesbrough | (h) 1–0 | Division One | Walker | 35935 |

1952 Another homecoming as United brought the FA Cup back to Newcastle for the second year in succession.

1959 Andy Parkinson born, Johannesburg, South Africa.

| 1965 | Horsens (Denmark) | (a) 5–3 | Friendly | Hilley, Penman, Anderson, Cummings 2 | 3300 |
| 1969 | Manchester City | (a) 0–1 | Division One | No Scorer | 20108 |

John Hope made his only appearance in goal, replacing McFaul. Although he never played at St James' Park for the first team, he was named as a substitute for a number of Fairs Cup matches.

| 1971 | All Star XI | (h) 6–5 | Friendly | McNamee 2, Craggs 2, Dyson, Craig | 10000 |

Geoff Allen testimonial match.

1976	IK Start (Norway)	(a) 3–1	Friendly	Macdonald, Burns, Kennedy	3000
1979	Brighton and Hove Albion	(h) 1–3	Division Two	Shoulder	28434
1982	Queens Park Rangers	(h) 0–4	Division Two	No Scorer	10748

Four defeats in a row had seen Newcastle drop out of the top ten in Division Two, and promotion-chasing QPR strolled to an easy victory – in borrowed yellow Newcastle away kit! An early headed goal from Mick Martin was disallowed, but after that it was a case of how many for the visitors. Things were to be slightly improved when Rangers returned the following season . . .

| 1984 | Derby County | (h) 4–0 | Division Two | Keegan, Waddle, Beardsley 2 | 35866 |

Promotion was achieved with this fine victory over the Rams, although Keegan missed the next game at Huddersfield, where a point meant United were mathematically safe, after sustaining a bang in the face when scoring the opener. The post-match victory parade will live long in the memory, as the players, draped in scarves, bowed down before the Gallowgate corner and saluted delirious fans on all four sides of the ground.

| 1990 | Middlesbrough | (a) 1–4 | Division Two | OG | 18484 |

Owen McGee was credited with an OG, but two goals apiece from Bernie Slaven and Ian

Baird made it meaningless. Middlesbrough avoided relegation and United were condemned to play-off torture. Around 14,000 United fans watched the match live on a big screen erected on the St James' pitch.

1990 Death of George Hannah, 61.

1996 Tottenham Hotspur (h) 1–1 Premier League Ferdinand 36589
A victory for Newcastle combined with a crushing 'Boro victory at the Riverside over Alex Ferguson's men would have taken the title to Tyneside, but neither part came to pass thanks to Bryan Robson and his generous Teessiders and a drained performance from Keegan's men.

MAY 6TH

Year	Opponent		Score	Competition	Scorer	Att
1922	Manchester City	(a)	0–1	Division One	No Scorer	15000
1933	Blackpool	(h)	1–2	Division One	McMenemy	11000
1939	Barnsley	(a)	1–4	Friendly	Clifton	7500
1950	Blackpool	(h)	3–0	Division One	Milburn 2, Taylor	35274
1956	Frankfurt C XI (Germany)	(a)	2–1	Friendly	Keeble, Davies	16000
1959	Drumcondra	(a)	6–3	Friendly	White 4, Allchurch, Mitten	7000

United manager Mitten on the scoresheet.

| 1960 | Southend United | (a) | 6–3 | Friendly | Unknown Scorers | 10000 |

Testimonial match.

| 1967 | Leicester City | (a) | 2–4 | Division One | Davies, Noble | 13951 |
| 1976 | Fredrikstad (Norway) | (a) | 4–2 | Friendly | Burns, Gowling, Nattrass, Kennedy | 2000 |

1977 On a whirlwind visit to the north-east of England, US President Jimmy Carter greeted an audience in Newcastle with a jolly 'Howay the lads', to great applause.

| 1985 | Tottenham Hotspur | (h) | 2–3 | Division One | Beardsley 2 (2 pens) | 29652 |
| 1989 | Millwall | (h) | 1–1 | Division One | Anderson | 14731 |

An already-relegated Newcastle entertained Millwall on a sunny day and the sparse crowd saw two cracking goals. Firstly Teddy Sheringham swivelled and volleyed a piledriver past Tommy Wright, while many United fans missed Anderson's raker as it coincided with the appearance of Mirandinha in the Milburn stand, to loud cheers.

1990 Newcastle sent a team to play a non-league select XI at Evenwood Town. The game was a fundraiser for former Magpie Jackie Bell, who had been forced to lose a leg through amputation.

| 1993 | Oxford United | (h) | 2–1 | Division Two | Clark, Cole | 29438 |

A rearranged game at St James' which the new North-East Player of the Year Lee Clark marked with a goal.

| 1997 | West Ham United | (a) | 0–0 | Premier League | No Scorer | 24617 |

MAY 7TH

| 1904 | Copenhagen XI (Denmark) | (a) | 6–1 | Friendly | Unknown Scorers | |

All but the score has been forgotten from the first game United played outside the British Isles.

1907	Mannheim (Germany)	(a)	5–0	Friendly	Howie 2, Hall 2, McWilliam	
1911	Koln 1899 (Germany)	(a)	5–0	Friendly	Fleming 4, Kelly	
1921	Manchester City	(h)	1–1	Division One	Pyke	35000
1927	Leicester City	(a)	1–2	Division One	Low	25000
1932	Birmingham	(h)	0–3	Division One	No Scorer	10000
1938	Luton Town	(a)	1–4	Division Two	Park	15000

Debut for Albert Stubbins, at centre-forward. Despite losing this final game of a desperate season, United stayed in Division Two by one tenth of a goal, at the expense of Barnsley.

The Yorkshire side actually beat United home and away.

1949	Sheffield United	(a) 0–0	Division One	No Scorer	20000
1955	Manchester City	(w) 3–1	FA Cup Final	Milburn, Mitchell, Hannah	100000

Forty-five seconds from kick-off and the cup was already inching its way towards Tyneside, thanks to Milburn's head. This time Jimmy Scoular collected the cup from Prince Philip. Tyneside streets were deserted as the game was televised, and those who owned televisions became very popular.

1962   Brian Kilcline born, Nottingham.

| 1966 | Fulham | (h) 1–1 | Division One | McGrath | 18818 |

1968   Death of Tom Urwin, 72.

1971   Newcastle beat off late interest from Chelsea to sign Luton centre-forward Malcolm Macdonald for a fee of £180,000. Macdonald had ended his Kenilworth Road career by scoring a hat-trick in his final match against Cardiff City.

1973   Ayresome Park hosted a testimonial for Harold Shepherdson in which a 'Boro side beat an England XI 7–5. Newcastle's Terry Hibbitt guested for 'Boro.

| 1977 | Ipswich Town | (a) 0–2 | Division One | No Scorer | 24760 |
| 1983 | Sheffield Wednesday (h) 2–1 | | Division Two | Varadi, OG | 29874 |

The second goal was credited to Mel Sterland, while future United flop Pat Heard netted for the Owls. Midway through the second half, a rumour spread round the ground that all of the other promotion candidates were losing by improbable results and United were in a promotion place. The rumour was, of course, false, but a pitch invasion at the final whistle ended with the team saluting the fans from the directors' box, an echo of 1965 when promotion actually had been achieved. Unfortunately it also prompted the United Board to adopt pitchside fencing.

| 1984 | Huddersfield Town | (a) 2–2 | Division Two | Mills, Beardsley | 25101 |

Promotion assured.

| 1988 | West Ham United | (h) 2–1 | Division One | O'Neill, Gascoigne | 23731 |
| 1991 | Barnsley | (a) 1–1 | Division Two | Peacock | 9534 |

1991   While the first team were away at Oakwell, United's reserves travelled to Coventry, having escaped relegation after beating Derby County the previous week. A measure of the turnover at the club was that the 50th player of the season played for the reserves. This was coach Derek Fazackerley, who had named himself as emergency substitute to make up the numbers. He played for the last ten minutes, by which time Coventry were already 4–0 ahead.

| 1994 | Arsenal | (h) 2–0 | Premier League | Cole, Beardsley (pen) | 32216 |

The Newcastle team formed a guard of honour to welcome Arsenal, who had captured the Cup-Winners' Cup during the week, Cole extended the goalscoring record to 41 and Newcastle fans held a post-match party all over the city.

MAY 8TH

| 1904 | Copenhagen XI (Denmark) | (a) 6–2 | Friendly | Unknown Scorers | |

The second game of Newcastle's first continental tour.

1935   Jackie Charlton born, Ashington.

1936   Malcolm Scott born, South Shields.

| 1939 | Grimsby Town | (a) 2–3 | Friendly | Clifton, Cairns | 10000 |

Hospital Cup match.

1940   Carl Wilson born, Lanchester, Durham.

| 1948 | Ballymena United | (a) 3–2 | Friendly | Sibley, Stobbart 2 | |

This match at The Showgrounds was arranged as part of the transfer of Frank Houghton to Tyneside some months before. Houghton was unable to take part due to the injuries suffered in scoring a vital goal against Sheffield Wednesday, but got the game under way by kicking off before returning to his seat.

1955   Twenty-four hours after the FA Cup final, the victorious Newcastle team attended 'Sunday

Night at the London Palladium' and, unlike the Rolling Stones some years later, were persuaded to join the cast on the revolving stage for the finale.

1959	Evergreen United	(a) 4–2	Friendly	Allchurch 2, White, Eastham	5000
1963	Walsall	(h) 0–2	Division Two	No Scorer	21797

The penultimate home game of the season, and Newcastle, with nothing to play for, slipped to a Walsall side still engaged in a vain attempt to escape relegation to Division Three. Despite goals from Newton and O'Neill, they were relegated along with Luton Town. The outside-left for the Saddlers, Colin 'Cannonball' Taylor, signed for United within days of the game. Three days later United ended the season with a draw against Preston in front of fewer than 14,000 bored souls.

1965	SV Gottingen (Germany)	(a) 3–0	Friendly	Cummings 2, Penman	5000

1965 Death of Harry Hardinge, who represented England at football and cricket after leaving St James' Park.

1970	Chicago (USA)	(a) 5–0	Friendly	Guthrie, Robson 2, Dyson 2	3000

Newcastle's North American tour got under way without Wyn Davies, Frank Clark and David Ford, all injury victims who stayed at home. The first game was held at Soldiers' Field, and Ron Guthrie opened the scoring within 15 seconds.

1972	Stoke City	(h) 0–0	Division One	No Scorer	21264

1973 Death of Andy Cunningham, 83.

1973 Laurent Charvet born, France.

1978	Jim Smith XI	(h) 3–6	Friendly	McGhee, Burns, Barton	17428

Testimonial match for Jinky.

1979	Wrexham	(h) 2–0	Division Two	Pearson, Shoulder	7134
1982	Wrexham	(h) 4–2	Division Two	Waddle, Varadi, Trewick (pen), Brownlie	9419
1990	Derry City	(a) 1–1	Friendly	O'Brien	2000

Played at the Brandywell.

1995	Blackburn Rovers	(a) 0–1	Premier League	No Scorer	30545

Rovers took a massive step towards the Premiership thanks to a Shearer effort, but their hero was Tim Flowers, who defied United with a series of fine saves.

1997	Manchester United	(a) 0–0	Premier League	No Scorer	55236

The home side were presented with the Premiership trophy but couldn't break through Newcastle's confident defence, as another point towards second place was collected.

MAY 9TH

1907	Freiburg (Germany)	(a) 8–1	Friendly	Hall 5, Dodds, Higgins	
1911	Dusseldorf (Germany)	(a) 7–0	Friendly	Unknown Scorers	
1924	Real Sociedad (Spain)	(a) 3–0	Friendly	Keating 2, Cowan	

1934 Bill Punton born, Glenkinchie, Scotland.

1946 Ian Mitchell born, Falkirk, Scotland.

1951	Stade Rennais (France)	(h) 1–1	Friendly	G. Robledo	12222

A match which celebrated the Festival of Britain.

1951 Just days after his match-winning performance in the FA Cup final, Milburn returned to Wembley and was on target again, scoring the winner for England in a 2–1 defeat of Argentina.

1956	Ausberg C XI (Germany)	(a) 4–2	Friendly	Hannah, Keeble, White 2	26000

1959 David Barton born, Bishop Auckland.

1964 Frank Pingel born, Resskov, Denmark.

1977	International XI	(h) 2–5	Friendly	Burns, T. Craig (pen)	14000

Joe Harvey testimonial match. The International XI goals came from David Mills with a hat-trick and Kenny Dalglish with two.

1979	Cognac (France)	(a) 2–1	Friendly	Withe, Shoulder	1500

1980 Death of Joe Cassidy, 74.

1983	Hull City	(a) 2–3	Friendly	Varadi 2	5431
1987	Nottingham Forest	(a) 1–2	Division One	Gascoigne	17788
1993	Leicester City	(h) 7–1	Division One	Cole 3, Lee, Kelly 3	30129

1995 Goals from Jimmy Crawford and Malcolm Allen gave Newcastle reserves a 2–0 victory over Oldham to clinch promotion to the First Division as champions. Due to building work at Boundary Park, the game was played at Bower Fold, home of Stalybridge Celtic.

MAY 10TH

1904	Southampton	(n) 4–0	Friendly	Unknown Scorers	

The two touring sides met in Copenhagen for this friendly.

1922	South Shields	(h) 3–2	Friendly	Hudspeth (pen), Aitken, Swan	12000

Ingham Cup match.

1936 Wilf Humble born, Ashington. Wilf joined United as a left-back but was converted to a left winger at Gallowgate. In his two seasons of playing for the reserves he failed to make the breakthrough from amateur status, and he returned to Ashington, then managed by former Magpie Dave Davidson. He then reverted to left-back and a string of good performances saw him sign for Mansfield Town.

1947	Bradford	(h) 5–0	Division Two	Bentley 3, Walker, Wayman	33131
1948	Shelbourne	(n) 6–0	Friendly	Sibley, Stobbart, Milburn 3, Taylor	

Played at Tolka Park, Dublin.

1950	Ayr United	(n) 2–1	Friendly	Mitchell 2	10000

Played at Portland Park, Ashington.

1961 Northern Ireland suffered their tenth consecutive international defeat, at the hands of West Germany in Berlin, going down 2–1. Dick Keith of Newcastle played in defence.

1967	International XI	(h) 1–3	Friendly	Milburn	45404

Jackie Milburn's testimonial match.

1970	Victoria Royals (Canada)	(a) 3–0	Friendly	Gibb, Robson, Smith	1800

The North American tour continued with the first of two games against Victoria, this one taking place on Nanaimo Island.

1974	Middlesbrough	(h) 5–3	Friendly	Tudor 3, Bruce, OG	28000

A deserved testimonial match for Tony Green was well supported. Alan Foggon scored for the visitors.

1975	Hearts	(a) 2–2	Friendly	Tudor, Burns	8500

1985 The FA Youth Cup final second leg saw United lift the trophy for the first time since 1962 with a fine 4–1 victory at Vicarage Road. After going a goal down, two each from Paul Gascoigne and Joe clinched the trophy 4–1 on aggregate.

1988 Paul Gascoigne agreed to leave United and join Tottenham in a £2 million deal. News of his departure not having yet broken, Gazza played in a friendly at Whitley Bay in front of 1,200. A mixed Newcastle reserve and senior side won 1–0 with a goal from Anth Lormor.

1996	Nottingham Forest	(a) 5–6	Friendly	Ferdinand 2, Barton, Keegan (pen), Guinan	23818

Stuart Pearce's testimonial match. Kevin Keegan sent a full-strength Newcastle team to the City Ground for Pearce's benefit, and Keegan himself and McDermott made a late appearance for United. The final Newcastle goal came from Steve Guinan, a young Geordie on Forest's books, who was allowed to turn out for United and immediately dubbed 'mystery man' by the travelling support. Former Forest striker Nigel Jemson returned for the evening and scored, as did Pearce, Roy, Colin Cooper and goalkeeper Crossley when playing outfield. Almost inevitably, Ian Woan also got on the scoresheet.

1998 Blackburn Rovers (a) 0–1 Premier League No Scorer 29300
Sutton scored a late goal for Rovers to earn them a place in Europe, while David Batty was sent off after appearing to push the referee.

MAY 11TH

1905 Austria XI (a) 8–0 Friendly Unknown Scorers
Played in Prague.
1911 Pforzheim (a) 5–2 Friendly Unknown Scorers
(Germany)
1924 Jackie Milburn born, Ashington.
1958 Barcelona (Spain) (a) 2–3 Friendly Mitchell (pen), Davies 50000
1959 Glentoran (a) 3–3 Friendly Eastham 2, White 7500
1963 Preston North End (h) 2–2 Division Two Suddick, Hughes 13502
1968 Manchester City (h) 3–4 Division One McNamee, B. Robson, 46492
Sinclair
1973 Crystal Palace (a) 0–0 Anglo-Italian Cup No Scorer 12001
1974 Tottenham Hotspur (h) 0–2 Division One No Scorer 21601
1975 Malcolm Macdonald was unable to repeat his goalscoring feat in the return game against Cyprus, but a Kevin Keegan goal secured an England victory in Limassol.
1985 Norwich City (a) 0–0 Division One No Scorer 18399
1991 Hull City (h) 1–2 Division Two Clark 17940
The end of the season and a strange conclusion: Lee Clark scored his first home goal late in the game when already-relegated Hull were two ahead, most of the away fans turned up in bizarre fancy dress, and by the time John Watson came on for his only senior appearance, the crowd had lost interest in the game. The reason? Sunderland were in the process of relegating themselves from Division One at Maine Road!
1997 Nottingham Forest (h) 5–0 Premier League Asprilla, Ferdinand 2, 36554
Shearer, Elliott
A fitting performance on what would have been Jackie Milburn's 73rd birthday.

MAY 12TH

1904 Danish (a) 3–1 Friendly Unknown Scorers
Representative XI
1913 Danish (a) 4–1 Friendly Unknown Scorers
Representative XI
1924 Bilbao (Spain) (a) 0–12 Friendly No Scorer
1948 John Blackley born, Falkirk, Scotland.
1965 VFL Wolfsberg (a) 3–1 Friendly Cummings 2, Penman 3000
(West Germany)
The touring United party had been given a tour of the neighbouring Volkswagen car factory before this game.
1984 Brighton and Hove (h) 3–1 Division Two Waddle, Beardsley, Keegan 36286
Albion
Keegan's final League game.
1993 Former Magpie defender Frank Clark was appointed as successor to Brian Clough as Nottingham Forest manager.

MAY 13TH

1906 FK Vienna (Austria) (a) 7–1 Friendly Gosnell 2, Orr 3, Aitken, 4000
Higgins
Another end-of-season tour began, as the League champions faced a variety of teams in Austria, Germany and Bohemia.
1907 Karlsruhe (n) 7–0 Friendly Unknown Scorers
(Germany)

1913   Jimmy Denmark born, Glasgow.
1917   Jack Shiel born, Amble.
1953   Aberdeen   (n) 4–0   Friendly   White, Hannah, Milburn, OG 16000
        Coronation Cup match, played at Ibrox.
1967   West Bromwich   (a) 1–6   Division One   Noble   19928
        Albion
1974   Sunderland   (a) 3–2   Friendly   McDermott 2 (1 pen), Bruce 29000
        Jimmy Montgomery's testimonial match.
1976   Bill McGarry's reward for taking Wolves down to the Second Division was the sack,
        confirmed today.
1984   Darlington   (a) 3–0   Friendly   Keegan (pen), Clarke,   5000
                                                         Wharton

        David Barton's testimonial match.
1989   Manchester United   (a) 0–2   Division One   No Scorer   30379
        A debut for Steve Howey as a striker. Newcastle's fans gave the already-relegated team a
        memorable send-off and did their best to antagonise the home fans with frequent
        renditions of 'You'll Never Walk Alone'. After the teams had left the field, an impromptu
        minute's silence was held in memory of Darren, a Newcastle fan who had been killed after
        a London game earlier in the season, allegedly in a fight with rugby league fans.
1990   Sunderland   (a) 0–0   Second Division No Scorer   26641
                                       Play-Off 1st Leg
        Last-minute drama, as Paul Hardyman was dismissed following a penalty which John
        Burridge had managed to stop. Hardyman ran in and attempted to score with Budgie's
        head, and mayhem erupted.

MAY 14TH

1911   Stuttgart (Germany) (a) 6–1   Friendly   Higgins 2, Kelly 2,
                                                         Anderson 2
1950   England continued their World Cup warm-up with a 5–3 defeat of Portugal, with Milburn
        restored to the team but failing to score.
1960   Schalke (Germany)   (a) 3–0   Friendly   White 2, McGuigan
1965   Holstein Keil   (a) 1–1   Friendly   Anderson   4000
        (Germany)
1969   Glasgow Rangers   (a) 0–0   Fairs Cup Semi-Final No Scorer   75580
                                       1st Leg
        The game hinged on a penalty save Willie McFaul made from Andy Penman in front of
        where the 12,000 Newcastle fans were massed. In a fighting performance, Wyn Davies
        broke his nose, but United held out for a draw.
1973   Sunderland   (h) 2–1   Friendly   Cassidy, Tudor   35873
        Ollie Burton's testimonial match.
1977   Aston Villa   (h) 3–2   Division One   Cannell 2, Oates   29873
        Qualification for the following season's UEFA Cup was gained by victory in this eventful
        game. Brian Little struck for the visitors after 50 seconds, but Cannell soon equalised past
        John Burridge in the Villa goal. Two further goals followed before Little pulled one back.
1983   Wolverhampton   (a) 2–2   Division Two   Varadi, McDonald   22446
        Wanderers
1995   Crystal Palace   (h) 3–2   Premier League   Fox, Lee, Gillespie   35626
        Already-relegated Palace bowed out with goals from Chris Armstrong and Ray Houghton.
        This was the last game at St James' where spectators could still stand.

MAY 15TH

1905   Austria XI   (n) 11–0   Friendly   Unknown Scorers
        Played in Prague.
1913   Danish XI   (a) 3–2   Friendly   Unknown Scorers

1921	Barcelona (Spain)	(a) 3–2	Friendly	McDonald 2, Pike	
1922	Frigg (Norway)	(a) 5–0	Friendly	Smailes 2, McDonald, Dixon, OG	
1924	Real Sociedad (Spain)	(a)	Friendly	Unknown Scorers (if any)	
1927	Dutch Olympic XI	(a) 0–4	Friendly	No Scorer	25000

Played in Amsterdam.

1929 Newcastle centre-half Jack Hill was part of the England team who lost 4–3 to Spain in Madrid, the first defeat by an England team on foreign soil.

1933 Dick Keith born, Belfast.

| 1948 | Cork City | (a) 2–2 | Friendly | Stobbart, Milburn | 10000 |

Played at the Turners Cross Ground.

| 1982 | Crystal Palace | (a) 2–1 | Division Two | Waddle, Mills (pen) | 8453 |

MAY 16TH

1893 Stan Seymour born, Kelloe, Durham.

| 1905 | Austria XI | (n) 4–0 | Friendly | Unknown Scorers | |

Played in Prague.

1906	Austria XI	(a) 7–0	Friendly	Gardner 3, Higgins 3, Orr	4000
1909	Danish XI	(a) 1–1	Friendly	Unknown Scorer	
1911	Furth (Germany)	(a) 2–1	Friendly	Unknown Scorers	

1921 Charlie Wayman born, Bishop Auckland.

| 1953 | Hibernian | (n) 0–4 | Friendly | No Scorer | 48876 |

Coronation Cup match, played at Ibrox Park.

1954 Newcastle's Ivor Broadis was part of the England side that lost 1–0 to Yugoslavia in a friendly held in Belgrade.

1966	Leeds United	(h) 2–0	Division One	Suddick, Robson	21669
1970	Victoria Royals (Canada)	(a) 2–1	Friendly	Robson, Foggon	2335
1990	Sunderland	(h) 0–2	First Division Play-Off 2nd Leg	No Scorer	32216
1998	Arsenal	(n) 2–0	FA Cup Final	No Scorer	79183

Goals from Overmars and Anelka. Insert your own comments here . . .

MAY 17TH

| 1905 | Bohemia Spartans | (a) 3–2 | Friendly | Unknown Scorers | |

Played in Prague.

1921	Barcelona (Spain)	(a) 2–3	Friendly	Unknown Scorers	
1922	Christiana (Norway)	(a) 1–0	Friendly	Smailes	
1924	Madrid XI (Spain)	(a) 2–3	Friendly	Unknown Scorers	

1924 Roy Bentley born, Shirehampton, Bristol. He was one of United's post-war striking heroes, who hit 25 goals in 54 first-team games. Despite the fact that he was sold midway through season 1947–48, promotion was still achieved back to Division One.

| 1947 | Bury | (a) 2–2 | Division Two | Bentley, Wayman | 17298 |

Goal for Bentley on his 23rd birthday; by his 24th he was a Chelsea player.

| 1952 | Southern Transvaal (South Africa) | (a) 3–2 | Friendly | G. Robledo 2, Hannah | 25000 |

The first match of United's South African tour, held in Johannesburg.

| 1960 | Dinamo Zagreb (Yugoslavia) | (a) 3–1 | Friendly | McGuigan, Allchurch, Hughes | |

1963 The Newcastle Supporters Club held their end-of-season dance at the Mayfair. Members were enticed by the prospect of 'dancing to Jimmy Bence and his orchestra'.

| 1965 | Aalborg (Denmark) | (a) 2–1 | Friendly | Cummings, Robson | 3000 |
| 1967 | Bournemouth | (a) 4–1 | Friendly | Bennett 2, Davies, Robson | 4039 |

Testimonial match.

1969	Liverpool	(h) 1–1	Division One	Davies	34927

1975   Frustration for Malcolm Macdonald again as Pat Jennings defied England in a 0–0 draw in Belfast.

| 1976 | North Shields | (a) 4–2 | Friendly | Unknown Scorers | 2000 |
| 1984 | Liverpool | (h) 2–2 | Friendly | Keegan (pen), McDermott | 36722 |

Billed as 'Keegan's Farewell', it was actually a benefit match for the club, not for him.

1986   Peter Beardsley scored his first goal for England as they overcame Mexico 3–0 in a friendly staged in Los Angeles.

| 1988 | Trinidad & Tobago | (a) 0–1 | Friendly | No Scorer | 8000 |

Played at the Queen's Park Oval, Port of Spain.

MAY 18TH

1909	West Bromwich Albion	(a) 3–0	Friendly	Shepherd 2, Anderson	5000
1913	Danish XI	(a) 1–1	Friendly	Unknown Scorers	
1924	Real Sociedad (Spain)	(a)	Friendly	Unknown Scorers (if any)	
1927	Dutch Olympic XI	(a) 2–0	Friendly	Gallacher, McDonald	16000

Played in Rotterdam.

1943   Roker Park was hit during a bombing raid, presumably by the Germans . . .

1950   Jackie Milburn became the first England player to be substituted when he went off injured in a 4–1 victory over Belgium in Brussels. Former Magpie Roy Bentley scored once.

1958   Howard Gayle born, Liverpool.

1961   Only a win would have retained Wales's interest in World Cup qualification, but a 1–1 draw against the Spaniards in Madrid was still a creditable result. United's Ivor Allchurch scored the Welsh goal.

1968   Jeff Wrightson born, Walker.

| 1970 | Vancouver Spartans (Canada) | (a) 4–3 | Friendly | Robson 2, Dyson, Young | 6000 |

1974   Newcastle striker Malcolm Macdonald replaced the ineffective Frank Worthington as England crashed 2–0 at Hampden to a Scotland side which included the outstanding Kenny Dalglish.

1978   Death of Norman Smith, 80. Former manager Smith collapsed after visiting St James' Park.

| 1982 | Hartlepool United | (a) 6–2 | Friendly | Varadi 5, Wharton | 1037 |
| 1983 | Select XI Malaya | (a) 5–2 | Friendly | Keegan 3, Carney, Varadi | |

Played in Kuala Lumpur.

| 1985 | New Zealand FA | (a) 2–1 | Friendly | Anderson, McDonald | 5000 |

Newcastle's Pacific tour started in Christchurch, against the 'All Whites'.

MAY 19TH

| 1929 | Ambrosiana Milan (Italy) | (a) 1–0 | Friendly | Chalmers | 30000 |

1937   Barrie Thomas born, Measham, Leicestershire.

| 1949 | Montreal XI (Canada) | (a) 4–1 | Friendly | Milburn 2, G. Robledo, Taylor | 15000 |
| 1951 | Cumberland XI | (a) 6–5 | Friendly | Stokoe 2, Hannah 2, Cameron, OG | 10000 |

1951   Jackie Milburn scored the final two goals of his England career as Portugal succumbed 5–1 at Goodison Park. Tom Finney captured the headlines after an inspirational display.

| 1967 | Chelmsford City | (a) 2–0 | Friendly | Allen, Bennett | 2210 |
| 1985 | New Zealand FA | (a) 2–2 | Friendly | Beardsley 2 | 4000 |

A second meeting with the 'All Whites', this time in Wellington.

1987   Wembley hosted a Rous Cup game between England and Brazil which finished 1–1, future

United striker Mirandinha scoring for the visitors. Peter Beardsley was joined by debutant and future United colleague (briefly) Stuart Pearce.

MAY 20TH

| 1906 | Vienna XI | (a) 4–0 | Friendly | Higgins 4 | |
| 1909 | Danish XI | (a) 2–1 | Friendly | Unknown Scorers | |

1947 Newcastle announced the appointment of George Martin as first-team manager.

1957 Mark McGhee born, Glasgow.

1972 Malcolm Macdonald made his full England debut in a friendly at Ninian Park, Cardiff, as Wales were easily beaten 3–0.

| 1983 | Select XI Malaya | (a) 1–0 | Friendly | Varadi | |

1994 Newcastle made the first of numerous applications to the Department of Employment for a work permit as they attempted to secure the services of US goalkeeper Brad Friedel. Eventually they gave up, although Friedel continued his quest to play in English football and eventually joined Liverpool, who managed to acquire the necessary paperwork.

MAY 21ST

1895 Andy Smailes born, Radcliffe, Northumberland.

| 1905 | Berlin British | (a) 10–1 | Friendly | Unknown Scorers | |

United's ten-day stay in Prague ended with them having scored 36 goals in the five games they played.

1911	Basle (Switzerland)	(a) 7–1	Friendly	Unknown Scorers	
1922	Gais (Sweden)	(a) 3–1	Friendly	Smailes, McDonald, Dixon	6000
1924	Everton	(n) 2–3	Friendly	Unknown Scorers	

Played in Barcelona.

| 1947 | Blackburn Rovers | (a) 1–0 | Friendly | Hair | 9000 |

Cumberland Cup match at Workington.

1952	Natal	(a) 6–2	Friendly	G. Robledo 4, Harvey, Davies	8000
	(South Africa)				
1969	Glasgow Rangers	(h) 2–0	Fairs Cup Semi-Final 2nd Leg	Scott, Sinclair	59303

Rioting Rangers hooligans invaded the pitch after the second goal and fought with police as the players were withdrawn by the referee.

| 1973 | Crystal Palace | (h) 5–1 | Anglo-Italian Cup | Macdonald 3, Barrowclough, Gibb | 12510 |

MAY 22ND

1881 Colin Veitch born, Heaton.

1901 Roddie MacKenzie born, Inverness.

| 1924 | Real Madrid (Spain) | (a) 1–2 | Friendly | Unknown Scorer | |
| 1927 | Dutch Olympic XI | (a) 4–1 | Friendly | McDonald, Clark, MacKenzie, Harris | 12000 |

Played in Deventer, Holland.

1931 George Lackenby born, Newcastle.

| 1932 | Racing Club Paris/ Red Star XI | (a) 1–3 | Friendly | Weaver (pen) | |

Cup winners United embarked upon a brief tour of France and Germany, but left behind goalscoring hero Jack Allen in hospital for a double hernia operation. Racing Club Paris derived their name from a student athletics club who began to play football.

1956 Dave McKellar born, Ardrossan, Scotland.

| 1958 | Progresul Bucharest (Romania) | (a) 1–1 | Friendly | Mitchell | 40000 |

1959 Alan Brown born, Easington.

1960	Hadjuk Split (Yugoslavia)	(a) 2–3	Friendly	White, Stokoe (pen)	
1968	Paul Moran born, Enfield.				
1983	Select XI Thailand Played in Bangkok.	(a) 1–0	Friendly	McDermott	25000
1985	New Zealand FA	(a) 4–0	Friendly	Reilly 2, Beardsley, Gascoigne	6500

Game three of the series against the 'All Whites', this time in Napier.

| 1988 | Jamaica Played in Kingston. | (a) 1–1 | Friendly | OG | 1000 |

MAY 23RD

1906	Vienna AS (Austria)	(a) 4–0	Friendly	Veitch, Gosnell, Orr, Gardner	
1909	Danish XI	(a) 3–1	Friendly	Unknown Scorers	
1922	Gothenberg (Sweden)	(a) 4–0	Friendly	McDonald 2, OG 2	6000
1929	WAC Vienna (Austria)	(a) 0–2	Friendly	No Scorer	

1954 A humiliation for England, as a Puskas-inspired Hungary won 7–1 in a friendly held in Budapest. Ivor Broadis of Newcastle was in the England side.

1957 Death of Jimmy Stewart, 73.

1972 A second cap for Malcolm Macdonald and a first appearance at Wembley, but he failed to impress and was substituted by Martin Chivers.

MAY 24TH

1924	Barcelona (Spain)	(a) 2–0	Friendly	Unknown Scorers	
1927	Ajax Amsterdam (Holland)	(a) 3–0	Friendly	McDonald 2, Seymour	10000
1947	Sheffield Wednesday	(a) 1–1	Division Two	Hair	25000

Tommy Ward put Wednesday in front, but George Hair's first league goal meant the points were shared.

1949	Ontario AS (Canada)	(a) 8–2	Friendly	Milburn 4, Mitchell 2, G. Robledo, Taylor	17000
1952	Natal (South Africa)	(a) 4–0	Friendly	Davies 3, Mitchell (pen)	
1958	Dinamo Bucharest (Romania)	(a) 2–3	Friendly	Eastham, Scoular	
1970	Seattle Seatacs (USA)	(a) 2–1	Friendly	Young, Craig	3000

The only time that Newcastle have ever won on an artificial pitch, despite Seattle making innumerable substitutions and using upwards of 20 players. Their goalkeeper also wore glasses on the field.

| 1977 | Everton | (a) 0–2 | Division One | No Scorer | 25208 |

1997 Robert Lee netted for England as South Africa were defeated 2–1 in an international held in the unfamiliar surroundings of Old Trafford.

MAY 25TH

1896 Death of James Logan, 25. Logan contracted pneumonia after playing for his club Loughborough Town in a game against Newton Heath (later Manchester United). On a rainy day, he was forced to complete 90 minutes in his own clothes, his kit not having arrived.

1909	Prossen (Denmark)	(a) 2–1	Friendly	Unknown Scorers	
1924	Barcelona (Spain)	(a) 1–0	Friendly	Unknown Scorer	
1955	Wacker and Hertha (Germany)	(a) 3–2	Friendly	Milburn 2, Keeble	15000

| 1960 | Espanol (Spain) | (a) 5–2 | Friendly | White 2, Allchurch 2, Eastham | |
| 1983 | Select XI Thailand | (a) 3–0 | Friendly | McDermott 2, Keegan | |

Played in Lopburi.

| 1985 | New Zealand FA | (a) 3–2 | Friendly | Reilly, McDonald 2 | 4400 |

The last of four meetings with the 'All Whites' took place in Auckland.

MAY 26TH

| 1894 | Ed Dixon born, Choppington. | | | | |
| 1906 | German Sport XI | (n) 4–1 | Friendly | Orr, Carr, Gardner 2 | 4000 |

Played in Prague.

| 1927 | Dutch Olympic XI | (a) 4–2 | Friendly | Unknown Scorers | |

Played in Eindhoven.

| 1929 | Slovak | (a) 1–8 | Friendly | Unknown Scorer | |

(Czechoslovakia)

1947	West Ham United	(h) 2–3	Division Two	Milburn, Shackleton	30112
1949	Death of Dave Willis, 67.				
1951	RSC Anderlecht	(a) 6–0	Friendly	Milburn 2, Taylor 2,	

(Belgium)   G. Robledo, OG

A challenge match between the cup holders and Belgian champions at the Heysel Stadium, Brussels.

1957	Kenny Mitchell born, Sunderland.				
1977	Bradford City	(a) 4–3	Friendly	Burns 2, Callachan,	3292
				Barrowclough	

Testimonial match.

| 1985 | Fiji FA | (a) 0–3 | Friendly | No Scorer | 4800 |

Played in Nadi.

MAY 27TH

| 1929 | Reg Davies born, Cymmer, Wales. |

1940   Death of Stan Docking, 25. Tragically, Stan succumbed to a heart attack while on leave from the RAF at his home in Whitley Bay.

| 1967 | Gazza born, Dunston. | | | | |
| 1970 | Vancouver Spartans | (a) 3–0 | Friendly | Robson, Dyson, McGovern | 4000 |

(Canada)

1972   Team-mates Bobby Moncur and Malcolm Macdonald were on opposite sides as England met Scotland at Hampden Park. Little Alan Ball scored the only goal of a rough match.

MAY 28TH

1908	Stan Barber born, Wallsend.				
1909	William Forster born, Walker.				
1914	Harry Clifton born, Newburn.				
1921	Gallia (France)	(a) 4–1	Friendly	Aitken 3, McDonald	

Played in Paris.

| 1922 | Copenhagen XI | (a) 2–1 | Friendly | Dixon, McDonald | 15000 |

(Denmark)

| 1929 | Slavia Prague | (a) 1–1 | Friendly | Chalmers | 12000 |

(Czechoslovakia)

| 1949 | Saskatchewan | (a) 13–2 | Friendly | G. Robledo 4, | 5000 |

(Canada)   Thompson 2, Walker 2
                                                               Milburn, Dodgin,
                                                               Houghton, Mitchell, OG

| 1955 | Nuremberg | (a) 0–1 | Friendly | No Scorer | |

(West Germany)

A friendly victory at a cost, as Bobby Cowell's career in football was ended by a calf injury inflicted by a German tackle.

1961   A gallant Wales performance saw them narrowly defeated 3–2 by Hungary in Budapest, thanks to a debatable late penalty. Newcastle's Ivor Allchurch netted the second goal for Wales.

1985   Fiji FA   (a) 2–0   Friendly   Gascoigne, Anderson   12000
The final match of the Pacific tour was played in Suva, the capital of Fiji.

MAY 29TH

1906	Prague	(a) 9–1	Friendly	Gardner 2, Higgins, Veitch 3, Orr 3	
1921	Celtic	(n) 0–3	Friendly	No Scorer	
	Played in Paris.				
1926	Billy Foulkes born, Merthyr Tydfil, Wales.				
1927	Dutch Olympic XI	(a) 5–0	Friendly	Unknown Scorers	
	Played in Groningen.				
1932	Frankfurt XI	(a) 6–3	Friendly	Richardson 2, McMenemy,	15000
	(Germany)			Lang, Boyd, Cape	
1960	Sevilla Coruna	(a) 1–2	Friendly	Eastham	
	(Spain)				
1969	Ujpesti Dozsa	(h) 3–0	Fairs Cup Final	Moncur 2, Scott	59234
(Hungary)			1st Leg		
1983	Japan XI	(a) 4–0	Friendly	Waddle 2, Keegan, Clarke	

United recorded a resounding victory in their first Japan Cup game, played at the Olympic Stadium in Tokyo.

MAY 30TH

1895	Dick Little born, Ryton.				
1922	Copenhagen XI	(a) 1–0	Friendly	Mitchell	10000
	(Denmark)				
1929	Hungarian XI	(a) 1–4	Friendly	Gallacher (pen)	4000
1970	Eintracht Frankfurt	(a) 4–0	Friendly	Robson 2, Foggon, D. Craig	6000
	(West Germany)				
1977	Sliema Wanderers	(a) 4–0	Friendly	Cannell, Kennedy,	2000
				Barrowclough, Nulty	

1996   Tino Asprilla scored the only goal of the game as Colombia defeated Scotland in a friendly, played in Miami.

1997   Shay Given signed from Blackburn Rovers, with a fee of £1.5 million being fixed by a tribunal after the two clubs failed to agree on a price for the out-of-contract goalkeeper. Neighbours Sunderland were apparently also interested in signing the goalkeeper, who had previously appeared for them while on loan, but seemed to have difficulty in raising the fee . . .

MAY 31ST

1952	West Province	(a) 8–0	Friendly	Davies 3, Milburn 3,	13000
	(South Africa)			G. Robledo, Mitchell	
	Played in Cape Town.				
1958	Petrolul Ploiesti	(a) 2–3	Friendly	White 2	
	(Romania)				

Centre-half John Nesbitt played the whole of this game as an emergency goalkeeper, usual custodian Ronnie Simpson having already being injured.

1972	Rajpracha Nukrow	(a) 3–1	Friendly	Tudor 3	
	(Thailand)				
1983	Syria XI	(n) 1–1	Friendly	McCreery	

The Japan Cup campaign continued with a match in Okayana.

1991   Former Magpie Wes Saunders scored for his club Torquay in their Wembley Fourth

Division play-off final against Blackpool. With the scores level at 2–2, Torquay triumphed on penalties. Saunders returned to Torquay, taking over as manager for the 1998–99 season.

1997   England defeated Poland 2–0, both goals coming from Shearer, who also missed a penalty.

JUNE 1ST

1949   Alberta All Stars   (a) 16–2   Friendly   Milburn 6, G. Robledo 5,   5000
(USA)   Walker, Mitchell 2, Harvey 2
Amongst the All Stars was a native American, Charlie Greyeyes, who was renowned for his speed. Fast he was; unfortunately, he had never kicked a ball before . . .

1955   Munich Combined   (a) 1–2   Friendly   Mitchell
XI (West Germany)
Match three of United's end-of-season tour to Germany.

1995   Alan Neilson signed for Southampton, as Keegan continued to trim his squad in preparation for new arrivals.

JUNE 2ND

1908   Hugh Bulloch born, Larkhall, Scotland.
1960   Death of George Wilson, 75.
1972   Select XI (Thailand)(a) 2–2   Friendly   Tudor   28000
1977   Floriana (Malta)   (a) 1–1   Friendly   Gowling   8000
1997   Lee Clark signed for Sunderland at a cost of £2.5 million.

JUNE 3RD

1906   Berlin (Germany)   (a) 6–0   Friendly   Unknown Scorers
1957   John Trewick born, Stakeford.
1973   AC Fiorentina   (a) 2–1   Anglo-Italian Cup   D. Craig, OG   45000
(Italy)   Final
1986   Peter Beardsley made his World Cup debut as a substitute for Chris Waddle, but was unable to prevent England losing 1–0 to Portugal in Monterrey.
1998   Newcastle announced that they intended to sign Sunderland's goalkeeper Lionel Perez, who had turned down a contract offered by Peter Reid. Judging by his performance for the mackems in the play-off final, many thought he had already signed for Charlton.

JUNE 4TH

1905   Dave Davidson born, Aberdeen.
1949   Vancouver All Stars (a) 5–2   Friendly   Milburn 2, Walker, Mitchell   7408
(Canada)
1952   Griqualand West   (a) 3–0   Friendly   G. Robledo, T. Robledo,   8000
(South Africa)   Milburn
The South African tour continued with this match in Kimberley.
1972   Santos (Brazil)   (n) 2–4   Friendly   Green, Tudor
This match in Hong Kong pitted United against the brilliance of Pele, who hit a hat-trick.
1983   Yamaha XI   (a) 1–0   Friendly   Waddle
The Japan Cup continued with United travelling to the city of Nagoya.
1985   Bruce Springsteen and the E Street Band brought their 'Born in the USA' tour to St James' Park. In the first of two nights, a slightly below-capacity 35,000 people attended.

JUNE 5TH

1949   Washington State   (a) 11–1   Friendly   Milburn 4, G. Robledo 4,   8000
(USA)   Taylor 2, Brennan
1955   Karlsruhe   (a) 4–2   Friendly   Hannah, Keeble, Milburn,
(West Germany)   White
The German tour ended with a victory, after two successive defeats.
1974   Supermac was hoping for better things as the Joe Mercer era came to an end and his final

England team drew 2–2 with Yugoslavia in Belgrade. Keegan and Channon scored the goals, while Macdonald came on as a substitute.

1985 Second night of Bruce Springsteen's residency at Gallowgate, and an all-ticket capacity crowd of 38,000 turned up to pay homage to the Boss. No, not Willie McFaul . . .

1995 Warren Barton joined United in a £4 million move from Wimbledon.

JUNE 6TH

1994 Death of Jackie Cape, 82. Remembered as the man who scored the only goal of Hughie Gallacher's emotional homecoming to St James' in the match with Chelsea in 1930.

JUNE 7TH

1885 John McTavish born, Govan, Scotland.

1908 Mick Burns born, Leeholme, Durham. Beginning as a goalkeeper, Mick was at one stage pushed into the forward line due to his inconsistencies between the posts. However, by the time he joined United he had recovered enough of his skill to make over 100 senior appearances.

1910 Bill McPhillips born, Musselburgh, Scotland.

| 1947 | Newport County | (a) 2–4 | Division Two | Pearson, Shackleton | 16000 |
| 1949 | Vancouver All Stars (a) 8–1 (Canada) | | Friendly | Milburn 5, G. Robledo 2, Walker | 8815 |

The second game that United played against the All Stars on the tour, and an even more convincing victory.

| 1952 | Northern Transvaal (a) 2–1 (South Africa) | | Friendly | Milburn, Hannah | |

Game seven of the South African tour, played in Pretoria.

1963 Joe Harvey secured the services of Welsh international Ollie Burton from Norwich City.

1974 Lord Westwood was elected Chairman of the Football League Management Committee.

| 1983 | Botafogo (Brazil) | (n) 0–0 | Friendly | No Scorer | 30000 |

This draw in Toyko's National Stadium meant that United clinched the Japan Cup, which was actually a blue jade vase, provided by the sponsors Kirin Breweries.

1988 Wimbledon keeper Dave Beasant was persuaded to move to Tyneside, less than a month after a decisive penalty save in the FA Cup final. At the time, his £850,000 fee was a British record for a goalkeeper.

1995 Les Ferdinand agreed to join United after Queens Park Rangers reluctantly accepted a slighter lower bid than Aston Villa had made – Les had refused to sign for the Midlands club.

1997 England defeated hosts France 1–0 thanks to a Shearer goal in Le Tournoi.

JUNE 8TH

1906 Death of Johnny Campbell, 36.

1944 David Craig born, Comber, Northern Ireland.

JUNE 9TH

1948 John Bird born, Rossington, Doncaster.

1970 Andy Hunt born, Thurrock.

| 1972 | Javanan (Iran) | (a) 1–1 | Friendly | Tudor | |

The Far East tour moved on to Iran after Thailand and Hong Kong.

1979 Kevin Keegan was at number 31 in the UK chart with a ditty entitled 'Head over Heels in Love'. The nation suffered further punishment when he subsequently 'sang' on BBC's *Little and Large Show*.

JUNE 10TH

1927 Bill McGarry born, Stoke.

| 1952 | Lourenco Marques (a) 5–0 (South Africa) | | Friendly | Mitchell 2 (1 pen), Davies, G. Robledo, Crowe | 9000 |

The South African tour moved on to the colony of Portugese East Africa, watched by a young Eusebio.

1959   Billy Whitehurst born, Thurnscoe, Yorkshire.

1973   Nearly a year after his last call-up, Malcolm Macdonald made an appearance for England as a substitute in their 2–1 victory over Russia in Moscow's Lenin Stadium.

1984   Future United veteran John Barnes scored a Brazilian-type goal in the Maracana Stadium, Rio de Janeiro, as England overcame Brazil 2–0 to record their first defeat of their hosts in that stadium for a quarter of a century.

1996   Euro '96 came to Tyneside as France beat Romania by a single goal, scored by Christophe Dugarry. A crowd of 26,323 attended, mostly Newcastle fans, who jeered the France manager as a result of the non-appearance of David Ginola in the squad.

JUNE 11TH

1918   Joe Harvey born, Edlington, Yorkshire.

1941   John McNamee born, Coatbridge, Scotland.

| 1949 | Winnipeg (Canada) | (a) 7–4 | Friendly | Milburn 2, Taylor 2, G. Robledo 2, Walker | 6000 |

1957   Death of Hughie Gallacher, suicide.

| 1969 | Ujpesti Dozsa (Hungary) | (a) 3–2 | Fairs Cup Final 2nd Leg | Moncur, Arentoft, Foggon | 34000 |

Two-nil down at half-time on a 'balmy night', as Bob Moncur called it, then an inspirational speech from birthday boy Joe Harvey about scoring a goal and 'foreigners folding up like a pack of cards'. Within minutes of the restart Moncur volleyed a goal to make it 4–2 on aggregate, then Dane Benny Arentoft (obviously unaffected by Harvey's theory) grabbed a third. Finally Alan Foggon scored from his own rebounded shot to clinch the trophy. Both goalposts were painted with stripes and Alan Weeks presented highlights on BBC.

1998   Out-of-contract defender Darren Peacock left United to join Blackburn Rovers on a free transfer.

JUNE 12TH

1960   Ray Ranson born, St Helens, Lancashire.

1975   Gordon Lee appointed as Newcastle manager.

1992   Paul Bracewell was persuaded to defect from Roker Park to join Newcastle, for a fee of £250,000.

1997   Kenny Dalglish brought in former Celtic manager Tommy Burns as his new assistant.

1998   As the news broke of the capture of Stephane Guivarc'h, a worldwide television audience and 55,077 fans at the Stade Velodrome in Marseilles saw him play for 20 minutes before being withdrawn through injury. After his early departure, France managed to beat South Africa 3–0.

·JUNE 13TH

1902   Jack Wilkinson born, Wath upon Dearne, Yorkshire.

1950   John Connelly born, Barrhead, Scotland.

1957   Jackie Milburn ended his association with United when he announced he was moving to Northern Ireland to take up the position of player-manager of Linfield.

1962   Dave Mitchell born, Glasgow.

1996   The second match of Euro '96 at St James' Park, where 19,107 saw Bulgaria overcome Romania thanks to a Stoichkov goal.

1998   While the future of John Barnes was still undecided, he continued his World Cup summarising safe in the knowledge that he had been awarded an OBE in the latest honours list.

JUNE 14TH

1931   Tommy Cahill born, Glasgow. There were to be only four outings in four seasons with United for this left-back. Tommy junior also played for the juniors but was unable to emulate his father and graduate to the first team.

1952   Northern Rhodesia   (a) 6–1   Friendly   Walker 2, G. Robledo,   8815
        Crowe, Harvey, Cowell (pen)
        Match played in N'Kana.
1975   Death of Joe Richardson, 66.
1997   Forty-eight hours after the arrival of Tommy Burns, Mark Lawrenson was relieved of his
        duties at St James' Park, whatever they were . . .

JUNE 15TH

1949   Kamaterna   (n) 4–0   Friendly   Milburn 3, Mitchell   22105
        (Sweden)
        United broke from their schedule of North American opponents to play fellow touring side
        Kamaterna in Toronto. Both sides moved on to New York and played a second game four
        days later.
1995   Jim Smith returned to football management and took the vacant manager's job at Derby
        County.
1998   England's World Cup final campaign got under way at the Stade Velodrome in Marseilles
        (although a different sort of campaign had already begun in the streets some hours earlier).
        Alan Shearer opened the scoring with a header on 42 minutes, and a solid David Batty
        performance ensured Tunisia deservedly lost 2–0.

JUNE 16TH

1896   Ted Ward born, Cowpen.
1911   Bobby Ancell born, Dumfries, Scotland.
1963   Wayne Fereday born, Warley, West Midlands.
1995   Peter Beardsley awarded the MBE.

JUNE 17TH

1954   Ivor Broadis became the third Newcastle player to compete in the World Cup finals when
        he took to the field in Basle and scored twice in England's 4–4 draw with Belgium.
1974   The end of a distinguished career on Tyneside for Bobby Moncur, who signed for the
        mackems at a cost of £30,000.
1994   Death of Len White, 64.

JUNE 18TH

1952   Southern Rhodesia   (a) 4–2   Friendly   G. Robledo 3, Harvey
        Game nine of their gruelling schedule saw United in Salisbury (now Harare, Zimbabwe).
1986   Peter Beardsley scored England's second goal against Paraguay in the World Cup match
        in Mexico City. The match finished 3–0.
1996   The third and final match of Euro '96 hosted by Newcastle and a convincing win for the
        French which saw them qualify for the second stage of the tournament. Goals from Blanc
        and Loko and a Penev own goal sealed a 3–1 victory over Romania, for whom Stoichkov
        scored again. Sadly, most of 'Les Bleus' who travelled from France came for the day and
        spent little time in the north-east. Due to the farcical nature of the ticketing arrangements,
        many of the empty seats were in fact sold to French travel companies, who simply threw
        them in the bin once they had acquired the second-stage allocation, only available when
        bought with first-round games.
1998   Without the absent Guivarc'h, France eventually overcame Saudi Arabia 4–0 in the new Stade
        de France, Paris.

JUNE 19TH

1936   Gordon Hughes born, Washington, Tyne and Wear.
1949   Kamaterna   (n) 3–0   Friendly   Milburn, Mitchell   18000
        (Sweden)
        Second match of the North American tour against the Swedish side, this time in New York.

1949   Viv Busby born, Slough. Viv managed four games in his three-month loan spell with United from Luton Town in December 1971. Unfortunately the last of his five appearances was in the Hereford Disaster, which didn't enhance his prospects of a permanent move.

1996   Death of Bob Dennison, 84.

1998   John Dahl Tomasson returned to Holland, signing for Feyenoord. At least United recouped their £2.5 million transfer outlay on a player who looked a world-beater in pre-season games but lacked a good first touch, seeming to need too long to settle on the ball. While he was played out of position for much of the season, few tears were shed on his departure.

1998   Newcastle completed the signing of Stephane Guivarc'h from Auxerre at a cost of £3.5 million.

JUNE 20TH

1987   Death of Andy Donaldson, 62. A talented striker who was forced to leave the area to further his career following the emergence of Milburn.

JUNE 21ST

1936   Alan Kirkman born, Bolton.

1952   East Transvaal   (a) 2–0   Friendly   Mitchell, Brennan   13000
(South Africa)
Match held in Benoni.

1995   Conflicting stories at Gallowgate over the abortive transfer of Crystal Palace winger John Salako. He had allegedly agreed to join United before releasing a statement that Newcastle was 'too far north'. Other sources claimed United had pulled out of the deal over concerns that an old leg injury hadn't healed fully. He eventually signed for Coventry and made his debut for them at . . . St James' Park.

JUNE 22ND

1868   Bob Foyers born, Hamilton, Scotland.

1879   Bobby Templeton born, Coylton, Scotland.

1914   Alf Garnham born, Birtley.

1986   Maradona's 'hand of God' goal put England out of the World Cup at the quarter-final stage. Peter Beardsley lined up alongside future United players Sansom and Barnes, former colleague Waddle and future Sunderland managers Reid and Butcher.

1998   Game two of World Cup '98 for England and a setback as Romania triumphed by two goals to one. A quiet night of few chances for Shearer in Toulouse at the ground nicknamed 'Little Wembley', and another booking-free evening for Batty.

JUNE 23RD

1917   Dominic Kelly born, Sandbach, Cheshire.

1923   Bobby Robinson born, Newbiggin.

1935   Keith Burkinshaw born, Higham, Yorkshire. He was United's coach during the 1974 FA Cup campaign.

1982   St James' Park hosted its first live music venture (apart from numerous brass and military bands and horrible infants with kazoos) when the Rolling Stones came to town. A large stage was set up at the Leazes goalmouth and fans were allowed to stand on the pitch.

1998   Newcastle got the go-ahead to increase the capacity of St James' Park to 51,000, after John Prescott ruled against a public inquiry.

JUNE 24TH

1870   James Logan born, Troon, Scotland.

1946   John Tudor born, Ilkeston, Derbyshire.

1976   Death of Harry Bedford, 76.

1998   Stephane Guivarc'h made a brief appearance as a late substitute for France as they overcame Denmark 2–1 in Lyons.

JUNE 25TH

1930   Vic Keeble born, Colchester.
1950   Newcastle's George Robledo hit the bar as his Chile side faced England in the first game of their World Cup campaign. England won 2–0 in Rio de Janeiro, with Robledo's United colleague Jackie Milburn watching from the sidelines.
1952   Orange Free State   (a) 3–0   Friendly   Foulkes 2, Mitchell
        (South Africa)
        United had reached Bloemfontein in their South African marathon.
1992   Rumours of a return to Gallowgate were dashed as Chris Waddle signed for Sheffield Wednesday in a £1 million deal.

JUNE 26TH

1995   Barry Venison departed from United in a £750,000 deal to join Galatasaray of Turkey. After a brief, eventful stay he returned to English football with Southampton before injury curtailed his career.
1998   England qualified for the second stage of the World Cup with a convincing 2–0 victory over Colombia in Lens. Without Tino Asprilla, the Colombians posed little threat to England and Robert Lee was given a late runout when victory was assured. Alan Shearer was bizarrely booked for taking a free-kick too early, but laughed it off.

JUNE 27TH

1976   United season tickets were selling slowly following the team's poor showing in finishing 15th in the previous campaign. Those who were tempted by prices ranging from £12 for the old stand Centre Paddock to £30 for the Centre Pavilion of the new stand may have regretted their decision within weeks, as it became clear that the only time they would see Malcolm Macdonald was when Arsenal visited in the following December.
1977   Geoff Nulty had his plaster removed and prepared to join his colleagues in pre-season training.

JUNE 28TH

1902   Bert Keating born, Swillington Common, Yorkshire.
1948   Jimmy Thomson born, Glasgow.
1952   South Africa   (a) 3–0   Friendly   Davies 3, Milburn   20000
        First of two matches against the South African national side, this one held at the Kingsmead ground in Durban. Most of the home side had already faced United in the previous regional games.
1998   Stephane Guivarc'h was brought on for France with 77 scoreless minutes gone of their ineffectual performance against Paraguay in Lens. The host nation eventually qualified for the quarter-finals with a golden goal, but wor Stephane did little to aid the victory.

JUNE 29TH

1928   Tommy Cavanagh born, Liverpool. He was assistant to Arthur Cox during the first year of his reign.
1935   Keith Kettleborough born, Rotherham.
1937   Chris Harker born, Shiremoor.
1938   Bobby Gilfillan born, Cowdenbeath, Scotland.
1950   Jackie Milburn watched the infamous 1–0 defeat of England by the USA in Belo Horizonte from the sidelines, not having made the starting team.
1954   Ivor Broadis failed to score for England, who defeated Switzerland 2–0 in Berne thanks partly to future manager Bill McGarry having a sound game in defence.
1969   Archie Gourlay born, Greenock, Scotland.
1976   Sacked Wolves boss Bill McGarry accepted the job of coach to the Saudi Arabian national team. He lasted just over a year and then returned to England to become Newcastle manager.

JUNE 30TH

1876 Andy McCombie born, Inverness.
1998 The World Cup second round presented us with Argentina against England in St Etienne. After Shearer had equalised an early Batistuta effort and Michael Owen scored 'that' goal, extra time came and went and penalties were required. David Batty strode to the spot, Kevin Keegan assured us all he'd score and he promptly missed. Another World Cup dream ended.

JULY 1ST

1916 Death of Tommy Goodwill, 20. Another victim of the Great War.
1940 George Heslop born, Wallsend.
1975 Farewell to Tommy Gibb, who departed on a free transfer to Roker Park, where he spent two unhappy years.
1997 In a controversial move, Robbie Elliott was sold to Bolton Wanderers for £2.5 million. Elliott, who had been instrumental in the team qualifying for the Champions League, was reportedly in tears when told of Newcastle's decision to offload him.

JULY 2ND

1939 Gordon Marshall born, Farnham, Surrey.
1950 Jackie Milburn made his World Cup finals debut for England as Walter Winterbottom reshuffled his team in the wake of the defeat by the USA. Spain won with the only goal in a tight match in Rio de Janeiro, with Milburn unluckily seeing a 'goal' chalked off.
1952 Border Province   (a) 10–0   Friendly   G. Robledo 7, Davies,   4000
(South Africa)   Foulkes, Crowe (pen)
1954 England bowed out at the quarter-final stage of the 1954 World Cup, losing 4–2 to Uruguay in Basle. It was to be the final time Newcastle's Ivor Broadis played for his country.
1959 Mirandinha born, Fortaleza, Brazil.

JULY 3RD

1998 More penalty shootout drama, with France wisely having already substituted Guivarc'h before extra time. Victory over Italy in the Stade de France took the home nation into the semi-finals.

JULY 4TH

1932 John Thompson born, Newcastle.
1981 Stuart Boam left United to manage Mansfield Town, one of his former clubs. United received £20,000.

JULY 5TH

1898 James Hunter born, Balfron, Scotland.
1946 Arthur Horsfield born, Newcastle.
1952 Eastern Province   (a) 5–1   Friendly   Davies 3, G. Robledo,
(South Africa)   Mitchell
1969 Michael O'Neill born, Portadown, Northern Ireland.
1984 It was Bob Dylan's turn to tread the boards as St James' Park hosted another concert.
1987 Death of Bobby Ancell, 76.
1988 Death of Jack Little, 83.

JULY 6TH

1984 Death of Lawrie Crown, 86.
1995 Newcastle announced the signing of David Ginola in a £2.5 million deal from Paris St Germain. Originally the French club had been approached for Liberian striker George Weah, but amid threats of legal action from United he signed for AC Milan at an inflated price. The Ginola deal was then agreed and the legal threat was forgotten.

1988   Paul Gascoigne put pen to paper and became a Tottenham player.
1998   Shaka Hislop returned to London, where he spent the first two years of his life, in a freedom-of-contract move to West Ham United.

JULY 7TH

1887   Bob Pailor born, Stockton-on-Tees.
1907   Jesse Carver born, Aigburth, Liverpool. Jesse coached Lazio, Juventus, Roma and Inter Milan after his playing career was curtailed by the outbreak of World War Two. He also briefly coached the Swedish national team after their losing World Cup final appearance in 1958.
1989   Former Magpie Chris Waddle joined Olympique Marseilles from Tottenham Hotspur in a record transfer of £4.5 million.
1997   Newcastle announced the signing of Temuri Ketsbaia on a free transfer from AEK Athens. He had caught the eye in the previous April when playing for his native Georgia in a World Cup qualifier against England at Wembley.
1997   Chris Waddle entered the world of football management when he joined Burnley as player-manager.
1998   Carl Serrant, a left-sided defender, arrived on Tyneside in a £500,000 deal, with another £100,000 due to his club Oldham Athletic based on appearances. Serrant had reputedly been watched by up to 30 clubs in the previous season, but only West Bromwich Albion made a bid, which was rejected. United also signed out-of-contract Spurs youngster Garry Brady on a free transfer. Midfielder Brady had made a handful of appearances for the London club.

JULY 8TH

1959   Imre Varadi born, Paddington.
1980   United completed the signing of Ray Clarke from Brighton at a cost of £180,000.
1993   Nearly a double transfer swoop by Kevin Keegan. Firstly he frightened John Hall into agreeing to pay £1.5 million for Peter Beardsley after inventing phoney Sunderland interest, and then he flew to Heathrow to meet Soviet striker Sergei Yuran and his battalion of advisors. After hearing the outrageous wage demands, Keegan chose not to do business, being proved right when Yuran later appeared for Millwall looking overweight and ineffective in a lower-league team.
1994   Full-back Mark Robinson moved to Swindon Town, having failed to secure a first-team spot following injury.
1998   A better performance by Guivarc'h for France, as Croatia were defeated 2–1 at St Denis, but he still failed to score and was replaced after 69 minutes.

JULY 9TH

1951   Mick Martin born, Dublin.
1986   Queen and Status Quo upset the Gallowgate pigeons when they appeared on a double bill at St James' Park.
1997   Death of Ivor Allchurch, 67.

JULY 10TH

1965   Paul Ferris born, Belfast.
1978   Future United manager Ossie Ardiles was unveiled by Tottenham as their new signing, along with fellow countryman Ricky Villa.
1980   The departure of Tommy Cassidy from Gallowgate after virtually a decade. He signed for Burnley in a £30,000 deal.
1995   Glasgow Rangers paid Italian club Lazio £4.3 million for the 'individual' talents of Paul Gascoigne.
1997   Slapstick time as horseracing pundit and self-proclaimed 'Newcastle Nut' John McCririck had an icecream shoved in his face by a punter during a live broadcast. Odds on this happening were apparently 3–1 'on the nose' . . .

JULY 11TH

1872 Matt Scott born, Airdrie, Scotland. Scottish international left-back, whom United recruited from his hometown club.

JULY 12TH

1952 South Africa (a) 3–5 Friendly Milburn, Mitchell, Davies 25000
Penultimate game of the South African tour and the only defeat, in Johannesburg.
1956 Tony Galvin born, Huddersfield. Assistant to Ossie Ardiles during his time as United manager.
1998 The World Cup final between Brazil and France, and Stephane Guivarc'h started the game in St Denis, almost scoring in the opening seconds. Further chances came and went and he was replaced after 66 minutes, having failed to break his World Cup duck, but he got a winners' medal nonetheless.

JULY 13TH

1919 Albert Stubbins born, Wallsend.
1934 Gordon Lee born, Pye Green, Staffordshire.
1987 Peter Beardsley joined Liverpool for a fee of £1.9 million, claiming later that Newcastle had made no attempt to keep him by offering an improved contract.
1997 Former Newcastle striker Darren Jackson moved from Hibernian to Celtic, a transfer which caused some discontent in Edinburgh. Ironically, his first game for Celtic was against his old club. In a strange season for Jackson, he won a championship medal and was drafted into the Scotland World Cup squad, but also survived brain surgery which threatened to wreck his career.

JULY 14TH

1899 George Martin born, Bothwell, Scotland.
1944 Colin Clish born, Hetton-le-Hole.
1975 Newcastle announced they had signed full-back Peter Kelly as a professional, having taken him on as an apprentice in the previous season and seen him play well for the reserves. Unfortunately Kelly was to spend a large part of his career sidelined by injury.
1982 Arthur Cox took central defender Jeff Clarke on a free transfer from Sunderland, an astute signing, while media attention centred on the arriving Kevin Keegan. Injury prevented Clark from playing a greater role in the club returning to the First Division, but he gave valuable service once the club were back in the top flight.

JULY 15TH

1908 William Carlton born, Washington, Tyne and Wear.
1921 Doug Graham born, Ashington.
1997 PSV Eindhoven (n) 3–2 Friendly Gillespie, Tomasson 2 18000
(Holland)
Match played at Lansdowne Road, Dublin.
1997 David Ginola concluded his £2 million move to Tottenham Hotspur, after having refused to take part in pre-season training at Newcastle and seemingly spending the summer growing his hair and losing whatever fitness he had.

JULY 16TH

1944 Albert Bennett born, Chester Moor.
1952 Southern Transvaal (a) 6–4 Friendly Foulkes 2, Crowe, Walker, 10000
(South Africa) Mitchell, Davies
A floodlit encounter in Johannesburg to end the South African tour which, unbelievably, had begun two months earlier with the same fixture. The sheer scale and length of the tour was blamed by the players for their below-par start to the following season, and future tours were drastically reduced in length.

1988   Neil McDonald left United to join Everton, at a cost of £525,000. The transfer was prompted by his frustration at being continually played in midfield rather than his preferred right-back position.

1997   Derry City   (a) 2–0   Friendly   Crawford, Beardsley   14500
United easily won the Irish International Club Soccer tournament at Lansdowne Road, Dublin.

1998   United announced the signing of French utility player Laurent Charvet from Cannes at a cost of £520,000. Charvet had spent the latter part of the previous season on loan to Chelsea and had actually appeared for them in the final game of the season at St James' Park.

JULY 17TH

1997   Leeds United left for a pre-season tour of Sweden with their contract rebels staying behind. Among these was Ian Rush, who had been linked with a move to Swindon Town. In the event the move broke down.

1998   United took an Argentinian midfielder on trial, Luciano Filomeno, who had been playing junior football in his home country.

JULY 18TH

1908   Monte Wilkinson born, Esh Winning, Durham.

1990   The sixth and final live act (to date) to appear at Gallowgate saw the return of the Rolling Stones.

1997   Stuart Pearce signed for United on a free transfer, following the demotion of Nottingham Forest to the Nationwide League.

JULY 19TH

1902   Blackburn Rovers   (h) 0–3   Division One   No Scorer   12000
1962   Paul Bracewell born, Heswall, Cheshire.
1978   Death of Harry Wake, 77.
1980   Newcastle announced they had beaten off competition from Sunderland to sign teenage winger Chris Waddle from local non-league side Tow Law Town.

1997   Birmingham City   (a) 3–2   Friendly   OG, Tomasson, Beardsley   13799
Newcastle's first goal was credited to Ian Bennett, their former keeper. Brian Pinas was introduced as a second-half substitute hours after arriving from Holland, too late to be included in the programme or the announcer's notes. Cue the United fans, who dubbed him 'Watsie', i.e. 'What's he called?'

JULY 20TH

1906   Dave Fairhurst born, Blyth.
1936   Bill McKinney born, Newcastle.
1980   Solvesborgs   (a) 0–0   Friendly   No Scorer   1500
        (Sweden)
An uneventful start to a five-match pre-season tour of Sweden.

JULY 21ST

1888   Willie Gibson born, Larkhall, Scotland.
1943   Jackie Sinclair born, Culross, Scotland.

JULY 22ND

1905   Tom Mordue born, Horden, Durham.
1980   Oskarashams ATK   (a) 3–0   Friendly   Clark, Rafferty, Davies   2000
        (Sweden)
1991   Mjolby Sodra   (a) 7–0   Friendly   Hunt 2, Robinson, O'Brien, 1000
        (Sweden)   Clark, Makel, Quinn

1995 Hartlepool United (a) 4–0 Friendly Allen 2, Kitson, Brayson 7000
A testimonial game for Hartlepool's Brian Honour, a lifelong Newcastle supporter.

1997 Newcastle completed the signing of Alessandro Pistone from Inter Milan for a fee of £4.5 million.

JULY 23RD

1978 Trollhattan (a) 2–1 Friendly Kennedy, Bird
(Sweden)

1991 Orebro SK (a) 8–2 Friendly Quinn 4, Elliot, Clark,
(Sweden) Robinson, Peacock
The second match of Newcastle's Swedish tour saw them in the town of Orebro (to the west of Stockholm) at the Eyravellen Stadium, one of the venues for the 1958 World Cup.

1995 Douglas Hall, Freddie Shepherd and an unnamed Tyneside restaurant owner flew to Turin with the aim of returning with unsettled Juventus star Roberto Baggio. Amid farcical scenes, they were shunned by the club and player, who ultimately signed for AC Milan.

1997 A Newcastle reserve team travelled to Croft Park, Blyth, and beat Spartans 1–0 thanks to a Stuart Elliott penalty. A crowd of 2,200 attended.

JULY 24TH

1921 Albert Clark born, Ashington.

1975 Jersey Select XI (a) 6–0 Friendly Burns 2, Bruce, Nulty, 2000
Macdonald, Keeley

1980 Trelleborgs FF (a) 1–1 Friendly Shinton 1000
(Sweden)

1993 Hartlepool United (a) 2–0 Friendly Sellars, Beardsley 5033
Mark Robinson joined the injured list after three minutes of this game, following a scything tackle. Former Sunderland goalkeeper Tim Carter conceded both goals in the first half, to the great amusement of the travelling support, and failed to reappear for the second period.

1996 Newcastle faced two teams in one friendly match at St James', Gateshead playing the first half and Blyth Spartans the second. It was a benefit match for drug charities in the Blyth area, but the original venue of Croft Park had been ruled out due to fears of congestion caused by the large numbers attending. The final score was 6–0, with two goals each from Ferdinand, Lee and Kitson.

1998 In a statement to the London Stock Exchange, it was announced that Freddy Shepherd and Douglas Hall had returned to the board of Newcastle United, with Shepherd resuming as chairman.

JULY 25TH

1966 Darren Jackson born, Edinburgh.

1978 Tidaholm (Sweden) (a) 2–1 Friendly McGhee, Mitchell

1988 Hestra (Sweden) (a) 6–0 Friendly Stephenson 2, Robertson, 1000
Mirandinha, Robinson 2

1991 IF Sylvia (Sweden) (a) 3–0 Friendly Peacock 2, Scott 2000
The Swedish pre-season tour continued in the city of Norrkoping, not against the well-known club but against a suburban minor-league outfit who played in a black-and-white striped kit.

1997 On the eve of the Goodison tournament, Les Ferdinand was sold to Tottenham for £6 million and accusations of asset-stripping by the club filled the media. However, when the dust settled, it became apparent that Dalglish had his eyes on a different team formation which didn't include Les.

1998 Newcastle announced they had reached agreement with Bayern Munich and Dietmar Hamann to buy the German international midfielder for a fee of £5 million. Freddie Shepherd had flown to Munich for final talks and the player was expected on Tyneside within days for a medical. On the same day, a Newcastle reserve team was in action in a pre-season game against Whitley Bay at Hillheads. The final score was 4–1 to United, with a hat-trick from Paddy Kelly and a goal from Argentinian trialist Luciano Filomeno. Carl Serrant made his first appearance for the club at centre-back, switching to left wing-back in the second half.

JULY 26TH

1919	South Shields	(h) 0–1	Friendly	No Scorer	15000

1928 Ted Robledo born, Iquique, Chile.

1935 Ken Leek born, Pontypridd, Wales.

1978	Gislaved (Sweden)	(a) 0–0	Friendly	No Scorer	
1979	Bath City	(a) 1–1	Friendly	Shoulder	2146
1980	Hoor IS (Sweden)	(a) 1–0	Friendly	Brownlie	1000

1988 With the first-team squad off on a tour of Sweden, another Womble was persuaded to come north, Andy Thorn following Beasant to St James' Park at a cost of £850,000.

1989	Nybro LF (Sweden)	(a) 2–1	Friendly	Brazil, McGhee	1000

1992 Southampton sold their star striker Alan Shearer to Blackburn Rovers for a fee of £3.6 million.

1993 A mixed junior and reserve side including Kilcline and O'Brien travelled to Borough Park and went down 2–1 to home side Workington.

1995	Rushden and Diamonds	(a) 3–1	Friendly	Ferdinand 2, Brayson	4600
1997	Chelsea	(a) 1–1	Friendly	Tomasson	15264

As the sale of Ferdinand was being concluded, Alan Shearer contrived to twist and fall awkwardly in the closing moments of this match and was stretchered off in obvious agony. He was later diagnosed as having a broken leg and severely damaged ankle ligaments. In the penalty shootout, Chelsea triumphed 3–0 as Pearce, Tomasson and Asprilla all missed.

JULY 27TH

1964 Newcastle schoolboy Tot Winstanley signed apprentice professional forms for United.

1975 Alessandro Pistone born, Milan, Italy.

1986	Blackburn Rovers	(a) 2–2	Friendly	Gascoigne, McDonald	3000

Part of the Isle of Man Cup competition.

1988	Oskarshamn (Sweden)	(a) 6–2	Friendly	Roeder, Mirandinha 3, Robinson 2	1500
1991	IF Hille (Sweden)	(a) 11–1	Friendly	Robinson 4, Quinn 2, Clark 2, Makel, Hunt, O'Brien	

Match four of the Swedish pre-season tour saw United in the east-coast town of Gavle. In a rural setting, fourth division Hille provided no serious competition, a fact underlined when one of United's second-half substitutes was assistant boss Tony Galvin, at left-back.

1992	Hearts	(a) 0–1	Friendly	No Scorer	11105

A former Magpie scored the only goal as a home side featuring John Robertson defeated a United line-up which included the talents of Kevin Keegan.

1994	Mypa (Finland)	(a) 1–2	Friendly	Cole	

In a match played in Anjalan Koski, the home side's second goal was scored by defender Sam Hyypia, who later came to United on trial but didn't impress.

1994 Newcastle announced the signing of Swiss international right-back Marc Hottiger from Sion at a cost of £520,000.

1997	Ajax (Holland)	(a) 0–3	Friendly	No Scorer	10289

Day two of the Umbro tournament at Goodison Park and late goals from McCarthy (2) and Oliseh sealed a miserable weekend for United. Behind the scenes, frantic attempts continued to try and stop Les Ferdinand's move to Tottenham, but he refused to return and signed for the London club officially in the early evening.

1998 Another day, another nationality, as United were set to pay £2.5 million for 23-year-old Peruvian winger Nolbert Solano, from Boca Juniors.

JULY 28TH

1906   Isaac Tate born, Gateshead.
1927   Matthew McNeil born, Glasgow.
1952   Derek Craig born, Ryton.

| 1979 | Plymouth Argyle | (a) 3–0 | Friendly | Martin, Shoulder, Withe | 2397 |
| 1980 | Tormelilla (Sweden) | (a) 3–0 | Friendly | Cartwright, Rafferty, Montgomerie | 2000 |

A goal for Ray Montgomerie, a young Scot who spent a couple of years playing for the reserves without making the step up to senior grade.

| 1985 | Leicester City | (a) 2–3 | Friendly | Beardsley, Reilly | 3000 |

Isle of Man Cup match, held in Douglas.

1988	Nykvarn (Sweden)	(a) 4–0	Friendly	Robinson 2, D. Jackson, Mirandinha	1000
1992	Hearts	(a) 0–1	Friendly	No Scorer	
1994	Visan Pallo (Finland)	(n) 2–0	Friendly	Lee, Mathie	

Played in the town of Kemi.

1997   A Newcastle reserve side drew 1–1 with Gateshead in front of 3,918 at the International Stadium. Paul Brayson scored for United.

JULY 29TH

| 1972 | St Johnstone | (a) 7–3 | Friendly | Macdonald 3, Tudor 3, Hibbitt | 4600 |

Macdonald's first goal was timed at four seconds, a shot direct from the kick-off that caught keeper Derek Robertson off his line. Saints, managed by Willie Ormond, included future Magpie Jim Pearson, who netted once.

| 1974 | Queen of the South | (a) 2–0 | Friendly | Macdonald, McDermott | 3411 |

1976   Malcolm Macdonald left United bound for Arsenal, a victim of Gordon Lee's 'no stars' policy.

| 1978 | Oeckeroa (Sweden) | (a) 2–0 | Friendly | Parkinson, McGhee | |
| 1986 | Portsmouth | (a) 2–2 | Friendly | McDonald, Allon | 2500 |

Isle of Man Cup match.

| 1989 | Askeroda (Sweden) | (a) 0–0 | Friendly | No Scorer | 1000 |
| 1991 | Nykoping (Sweden) | (a) 0–1 | Friendly | No Scorer | |

JULY 30TH

1932   Alex Gaskell born, Leigh, Manchester.

1969	Hearts	(h) 1–0	Friendly	Robson	21000
1971	St Etienne (France)	(a) 1–2	Friendly	Macdonald	8000
1978	Saetila (Sweden)	(a) 3–2	Friendly	Connolly, Kennedy, Walker	
1985	Blackburn Rovers	(a) 1–2	Friendly	Gascoigne	5000

Isle of Man Cup match, held in Ramsey.

| 1986 | Isle of Man XI | (a) 5–1 | Friendly | Stewart, Beardsley, Allon 2, Ferris | 3000 |
| 1989 | Rydobruk (Sweden) | (a) 1–0 | Friendly | McGhee | 1000 |

1991   With the first team away on another tour of Swedish clubs nobody had ever heard of, those first-teamers left at home and some juniors beat Alnwick Town 7–2 at one of the other St James' Parks. Roy Aitken was on the scoresheet, while Stimpson, Simpson and Askew also turned out. All four players had been told that their first-team careers at United were over and were all keeping fit while searching for new employers.

| 1996 | Thailand | (a) 2–1 | Friendly | Asprilla, Lee | |
| 1997 | Bradford City | (a) 3–0 | Friendly | Asprilla, Beardsley, Watson | 8470 |

JULY 31ST

1944	Tommy Robson born, Gateshead.				
1959	Peter Manners born, Sunderland.				
1966	Rob McKinnon born, Glasgow.				
1972	Partick Thistle	(a) 2–2	Friendly	Macdonald, Gibb	7012
1991	IF Rimbo (Sweden)	(a) 6–2	Friendly	Quinn 3, Hunt 3	
1993	Berwick Rangers	(a) 3–0	Friendly	Cole, Papavasiliou (pen), Mathie	2000

An easy victory over the part-timers of Berwick. The biggest hazard was the wind that blew across Shielfield Park and scattered sand and cinders from the surrounding speedway track in spectators' eyes.

AUGUST 1ST

1892	Robert McIntosh born, Dundee.				
1959	Edinburgh Select XI	(a) 3–4	Friendly	McGuigan, White, Eastham	30000
1970	Dundee United	(a) 2–1	Friendly	Smith, Davies	7000
1977	SC Telstar (Holland)	(a) 1–2	Friendly	Burns	
1979	Torquay United	(a) 3–2	Friendly	Shoulder, Walker, Mitchell	2450
1985	Wigan Athletic	(a) 4–1	Friendly	McDonald 2, Beardsley, Roeder	3000

Third and final match United played in the Isle of Man Cup, held in Castletown.

1987	Brondby IF (Denmark)	(a) 1–2	Friendly	Goddard	1452
1988	Katrineholm (Sweden)	(a) 4–0	Friendly	Mirandinha, Hendrie, Robertson, O'Neill	1000
1989	Mjallby AIF (Sweden)	(a) 3–0	Friendly	Quinn, McGhee, Brazil	1000
1990	Oadby Town	(a) 3–0	Friendly	OG, Gallacher, O'Brien	980

The new black-and-white 'bar code' strip made its debut in a match arranged by Newcastle director and Oadby president Peter Mallinger. After the match, boss Jim Smith performed the opening ceremony on a new clubhouse for the Leicester Senior League club.

1992	York City	(a) 3–1	Friendly	Sheedy, Peacock, Carr	3424

A mildly entertaining afternoon, the home side's goal coming from Darren Tilley.

1994	Wrexham	(a) 3–4	Friendly	Beardsley, Mathie 2	5842

1995 Former Sunderland player David Rush was fined £500 and ordered to pay another £250 compensation by Oxford magistrates. Rush was found guilty of headbutting a Newcastle fan who had called him a mackem while they were queueing at a kebab van.

1996	S League All Stars (Singapore)	(a) 5–0	Friendly	Kitson 2, Ginola, Ferdinand	

Held in the National Stadium, Singapore.

AUGUST 2ND

1969	Hull City	(a) 0–1	Friendly	No Scorer	8559
1975	Carlisle United	(a) 0–2	Friendly	No Scorer	9209
1988	Gullringen (Sweden)	(a) 0–0	Friendly	No Scorer	1000
1989	Falkenberg (Sweden)	(a) 1–1	Friendly	Kristensen	1500

1994 A double signing for United, as left-back Jason Drysdale joined from Watford and Steve Guppy came from Wycombe Wanderers. However, neither managed to establish himself on Tyneside and both were soon to leave.

AUGUST 3RD

1952	Ossie Ardiles born, Cordoba, Argentina.

1966 Gary Kelly born, Fulwood, Lancashire.

1968	Hibernian	(a) 2–1	Friendly	Davies, OG	14737

Bobby Moncur injured a cartilage and missed the first 13 games of the season.

1971 The 'Mighty Wyn' Davies left United, joining Manchester City for a fee of £60,000.

1973 Nicos Dabizas born, Greece.

1974	Sunderland	(a) 1–2	Texaco Cup	Tudor	28738
1977	Sparta Rotterdam (Holland)	(a) 2–2	Friendly	Burns 2	
1979	Exeter City	(a) 2–3	Friendly	Withe, Brownlie	1829
1987	Hearts	(a) 1–0	Friendly	Gascoigne	10113
1991	Morton	(a) 4–1	Friendly	Quinn 2, Peacock 2	3000
1993	Rangers	(a) 2–1	Friendly	Cole, Sellars	42000

Ally McCoist's testimonial. A full-blooded game which was nothing like the usual sterile friendly fare and played in a cracking atmosphere. Hateley scored for Rangers.

1997	Juventus (Italy)	(a) 2–3	Friendly	Asprilla 2	22511

A friendly match held in Cesena as part of the centenary celebrations for the Turin club, who wore their original colours of pink while United played in traditional black and white. Goals from Ferrara and Inzaghi (2) could have been many more, but Juve dropped the pace and allowed United to give the score a respectable look. Des Hamilton left the field on a stretcher with a leg injury.

AUGUST 4TH

1973 David Terrier born, Verdun, France. This reputedly talented Metz defender sought refuge at West Ham following a knee injury, and failed to make an appearance at Upton Park. His next destination was St James', where a similar fate befell him, a few shaky reserve outings convincing Kenny to say 'au revoir' at the end of season 1997–98.

1976	Southend United	(a) 2–0	Friendly	Nattrass, Gowling	5000
1980	Hearts	(a) 1–1	Friendly	Shinton	3334

An unlucky return to Edinburgh for John Brownlie, who damaged knee ligaments and had to be hospitalised. Bobby Moncur was the Hearts manager.

1984	Queen of the South	(a) 1–1	Friendly	Beardsley	2000

An early-evening (6.30 p.m. kick-off) pre-season stroll at Palmerston Park.

1988	Trollhattan (Sweden)	(a) 2–1	Friendly	Mirandinha, D. Jackson	1500
1990	Yeovil Town	(a) 2–1	Friendly	McGhee, Anderson	5093

Newcastle continued their pre-season tour with a game to mark the opening of the New Huish Stadium of Yeovil Town. The ceremony was carried out by Bert Millichip and Gordon McKeag on the pitch before kick-off, who were joined by a priest, and subsequently a parachute display team. Most of the 250 travelling United fans barracked McKeag throughout the ceremony over the club's lack of investment in talented players.

1992	Doncaster Rovers	(a) 1–1	Friendly	O'Brien	3951

Oh dear. An unenergetic Newcastle were almost shamed by their enthusiastic lower-league opponents, Mike Jeffrey making an impression on Kevin Keegan when scoring for the home side and eventually joining United.

1996	Gamba Osaka (Japan)	(a) 1–3	Friendly	Ferdinand	6949

Hans Gillhaus, once of Aberdeen, hit two goals as United went down in the Expo '70 Commemorative Stadium.

AUGUST 5TH

1950	Edinburgh Select XI	(a) 1–1	Friendly	Milburn	50000

A charity match played at Tynecastle.

1968	Aberdeen	(h) 1–0	Friendly	Bennett	16000
1969	Hibernian	(a) 0–0	Friendly	No Scorer	15309

Marshalled by Glenn Roeder, the Newcastle team manage to get the letters in the right order to wish supporters well for 1986. The game against Everton ended 2–2

A pensive look from debutant Kenny Sansom, who has just realised what a relegation struggle is all about

Relief for Rob McDonald as he celebrates scoring his first goal for United in a 2–1 victory at Hillsborough

One fan makes his 'Sack the Board' protest during the home match with Millwall, when United had already been relegated

Kenny Wharton lines up with Paul Gascoigne and Kevin Keegan, both members of his testimonial team, while Glenn Roeder keeps a watchful eye on proceedings

Mick Quinn strikes home his first Newcastle goal from the penalty spot, watched by the envious Wayne Fereday. Quinn scored another three goals as Leeds perished 5–2

On-loan Leicester striker Kevin Campbell foxes debutant Roy Aitken at St James' Park. United eventually won a seesaw game 5–4

Laura Milburn, widow of Jackie, is welcomed on to the St James' Park pitch by the Newcastle and Ipswich teams. A presentation was made to her by Gordon McKeag to mark the opening of the stand named after her late husband

A line-up of former team-mates joins Laura Milburn on the St James' Park pitch as she takes the applause of the crowd. Among the faces are Frank Brennan, Ivor Broadis, Bobby Cowell, Charlie Crowe, Bobby Mitchell, Bob Stokoe, Albert Stubbins, Charlie Wayman and Len White

A youthful Steve Watson receives his second successive Barclays Young Eagle of the Month award. Newcastle Chairman George Forbes is on the left

An airborne David Mitchell scores the only goal of his short United career as
Blackburn are beaten 1–0 at St James' Park

A rare shot of Paul Moran touching the ball in his only appearance for Newcastle. Those who witnessed it would agree that the scoreboard advert was definitely not referring to his playing prowess

A typical pose from Faustino Asprilla, as he crosses the ball for Ferdinand to equalise against Tottenham Hotspur on the last day of a memorable season, when Newcastle could still have won the Premiership

Gavin Peacock scores against Sporting Lisbon in the final of a pre-season
tournament held at St James' Park. Despite going 3–0 up, United
contrived to lose 5–3

1970	Dundee United	(h) 1–0	Friendly	Davies	15000
1972	Morton	(a) 1–1	Friendly	Howard	4061
1984	Hibernian	(a) 3–0	Friendly	Beardsley, Wharton 2	6000
1986	Linfield	(a) 3–2	Friendly	Whitehurst, Allon	5000

Newcastle took part in this game at Windsor Park, which was part of the Linfield centenary celebrations.

| 1987 | | | | | |

Newcastle announced that they had reached agreement with Brazilian striker Mirandinha, and he would be flying in to join his new team-mates within a few weeks.

| 1987 | | | | | |

In a private friendly played at Benfield Road, Newcastle, Newcastle drew 1–1 with Middlesbrough.

| 1993 | Gateshead | (a) 3–0 | Friendly | Mathie 2, O'Brien | 4500 |

Derek Bell's testimonial.

| 1994 | Manchester United | (n) 1–1 | Friendly | Fox | 27282 |
| | | | Ibrox tournament | | |

Newcastle fans were accused of displaying anti-Munich sentiments by throwing paper aeroplanes at the few Manchester United fans who bothered to turn up. Fox hit a rasping drive to put Newcastle ahead, but Cantona equalised to send the game to penalties. The shootout ended 6–5 to the Magpies, with Hottiger hitting the winner after Beardsley, Watson, Beresford, Peacock and Cole had netted and Drysdale and Fox had missed. Srnicek saved an effort from future team-mate Keith Gillespie.

| 1994 | Death of Terry Hibbitt, 47. | | | | |
| 1995 | Celtic | (a) 1–1 | Friendly | Ferdinand | 31000 |

Rod Stewart performed the opening ceremony for the new North Stand at Parkhead in a tropical heatwave but thankfully refrained from singing.

AUGUST 6TH

1880	Ronald Orr born, Bartonholm, Scotland.				
1916	Ernie Hall born, Crawcrook.				
1933	Ken Waugh born, Newcastle.				
1955	Edinburgh Select XI	(a) 1–1	Friendly	Keeble	50000
1966	Aalborg (Denmark)	(h) 1–1	Friendly	Suddick	7754
1974	Carlisle United	(a) 2–2	Texaco Cup	Burns 2	13560
1975	Sunderland	(h) 0–2	Friendly	No Scorer	20088
1977	FC Volendam	(a) 1–2	Friendly	Callachan	
	(Holland)				
1981	Ray Clarke announced his retirement from the game, forced by a persistent hip injury.				
1987	Scarborough	(a) 2–2	Friendly	Gascoigne, McDonald	3000
1994	Sampdoria (Italy)	(n) 1–3	Friendly	Cole	31362
			Ibrox tournament		

United fans paid tribute to the recently departed midfield maestro with a rousing chorus of 'Terry Hibbitt on the wing'. Balding Attilio Lombardo showed many of Terry's passing skills as he prompted the Italians to an easy victory, despite having being a goal down.

| 1996 | | | | | |

Alan Shearer was officially unveiled as a Newcastle player in front of a delirious crowd in the Leazes car park and a slightly more restrained invited audience in the Leazes stand. The crowd outside 'made some noise' and thankfully managed to drown out the embarrassment that is MC Alan Robson.

AUGUST 7TH

| 1939 | Willie Penman born, Coaltown of Wemyss, Scotland. | | | | |
| 1971 | Benfica (Portugal) | (h) 1–0 | Friendly | Gibb | 27630 |

The famous visitors included Eusebio in their line-up.

1976	Sheffield United	(a) 1–0	Friendly	Gowling	7933
1978	Hull City	(a) 0–0	Friendly	No Scorer	2960
1982	Morton	(a) 3–1	Friendly	Todd, Doyle, Varadi	2000

1984	Berwick Rangers	(a) 3–1	Friendly	Beardsley, Wharton, Waddle	2000
1985	Carlisle United	(a) 0–0	Friendly	No Scorer	2297
1986	Coleraine	(a) 0–0	Friendly	No Scorer	2000
1990	Gloucester City	(a) 2–0	Friendly	Quinn, Robinson	500

The pre-season warm-up continued at Meadow Park, as only Gloucester keeper David Mogg kept the score to a reasonable level, restricting twin strikers Mickey Quinn and David Robinson to a single goal each.

1991	Darlington	(a) 2–1	Friendly	Bradshaw, O'Brien	3027
1993	Scunthorpe United	(a) 1–1	Friendly	Watson	3975
1995	Gateshead	(a) 4–0	Friendly	Ferdinand 2, Beardsley, Gillespie	11750

AUGUST 8TH

1913 Harry Johnson born, Walker.

| 1964 | Burnley | (h) 1–1 | Friendly | McGrath | 14800 |

Newcastle arranged this friendly with the intention of testing out a 4–2–4 team formation, and sent the reserves to Turf Moor on the same day to try the same tactic. Unfortunately the reserves were rather less adept than the seniors and went down 6–0.

1967	Middlesbrough	(a) 2–3	Friendly	Hilley, Robson	15008
1970	Bolton Wanderers	(h) 3–0	Friendly	Gibb, Moncur, Foggon	9900
1977	Chesterfield	(a) 4–2	Friendly	Gowling 2, T. Craig, D. Craig	2201
1988	Dundee	(a) 0–2	Friendly	No Scorer	3000

The teams competed for the Dunclare Dispensers Challenge Trophy, no less. Wes Saunders played for the home side, who were managed by former United coach Dave Smith, he of the wild hair.

| 1989 | Raith Rovers | (a) 4–0 | Friendly | Quinn 2 (1 pen), OG, Brazil (pen) | 1959 |
| 1992 | Middlesbrough | (h) 1–0 | Friendly | Peacock (pen) | 8548 |

Day one of the Exhibition Super Challenge tournament at St James', and while Sporting Lisbon and Real Sociedad battled it out, Newcastle faced somewhat less exotic opponents. John Hendrie played for the 'Boro, while Michael O'Neill made a second-half appearance but looked a shadow of his former self.

AUGUST 9TH

1896 William Cowan born, Edinburgh.

1915 Tom Swinburne born, East Rainton, Durham.

| 1961 | Aarhus (Denmark) | (h) 6–0 | Friendly | Leek 3, Neale, Allchurch, Tuohy | 13667 |

Instant hero status for Ken Leek on his first appearance for his new club.

| 1969 | West Ham United | (a) 0–1 | Division One | No Scorer | 33323 |

1973 Death of William Aitken, 79.

| 1975 | Middlesbrough | (h) 2–2 | Friendly | Hibbitt, Gowling | 11624 |
| 1979 | Blyth Spartans | (a) 1–1 | Friendly | Shoulder | 2398 |

A testimonial game for Blyth stalwarts Eddie Alder and Ronnie Scott. Shoulder scored on his return to Croft Park, but Les Mutrie equalised. Local youngster Robin Armstrong played the full game as a centre-back, but failed to make the breakthrough to the senior team.

1980	Leeds United	(h) 2–2	Friendly	Davies (pen), Rafferty	7448
1982	Kilmarnock	(a) 0–0	Friendly	No Scorer	1500
1992	Sporting Lisbon (Portugal)	(h) 3–5	Friendly	Clark, Peacock 2	7642

When Gavin Peacock scored twice in the minute before half-time to make it 3–0, the Exhibition Super Challenge Trophy looked to be won, but a whirlwind second half from the visitors saw two goals each from Balakov and Filipe and one from Celtic-bound Jorge Cadete.

1993 Liverpool (a) 0–1 Friendly No Scorer 21757

Yet again Newcastle were victims of their own generosity, sending a team to Anfield for Ronnie Whelan's benefit match on the eve of the season opener and losing a crucial player. Peter Beardsley was disgracefully assaulted by Ruddock and fractured a cheekbone. The injury was such that for a time it was rumoured Beardsley was considering legal action against his assailant. To complete a poor night, Beresford missed a penalty when confronted with the might of Mike Hooper.

1995 Hearts (a) 1–0 Friendly Beardsley 13337

A rare headed goal from Peter won it for United on a glorious sunny evening at Tynecastle. Among the interested spectators was Shaka Hislop, who had signed for United earlier that day and journeyed north to meet his new colleagues for the first time.

1996 Lincoln City (a) 2–0 Friendly Shearer, Albert 10069

A match arranged as part of the deal which took Darren Huckerby to United. Unfortunately, injury prevented him from playing.

1997 Sheffield Wednesday (h) 2–1 Premier League Asprilla 2 36711

The opening day of the season, and while United welcomed Given, Pistone, Tomasson, Pearce and Ketsbaia, comparatively old stagers Albert and Asprilla combined for the latter to score in the first 90 seconds. After Carbone had acrobatically equalised, Tomasson missed the first of many chances, but thankfully Tino was on hand to poke the ball home.

AUGUST 10TH

1908 Jimmy Murray born, Saltcoats, Scotland.

1960 Racing Paris (a) 3–2 Friendly White, Stokoe (pen), 3000
(France) Allchurch

1965 Middlesbrough (a) 0–2 Friendly No Scorer 13500

1966 Carlisle United (h) 2–2 Friendly Robson (pen), Suddick 6007

1967 Philippe Albert born, Bouillon, Belgium.

1968 West Ham United (h) 1–1 Division One Robson 37307

The first game of a momentous season, and the return from injury of Albert Bennett. Unfortunately, he lasted less than 40 minutes and twisted the same knee he had damaged the previous January.

1971 Aberdeen (a) 2–3 Friendly Tudor, Cassidy 17000

1974 Middlesbrough (h) 4–0 Texaco Cup Macdonald, Cassidy, 11571
Tudor, Burns

Featuring a memorable solo strike from Mickey Burns, making his first appearance at St James'.

1976 Hull City (a) 0–0 Friendly No Scorer 4715

1977 Carlisle United (a) 1–1 Friendly OG 5413
Testimonial match.

1978 Gateshead (a) 1–0 Friendly Callachan 3000

1981 Reserve striker Gary Nicholson left United in a £25,000 move to Mansfield Town.

1983 Hamburg Altona (a) 6–1 Friendly Anderson 3, Ryan, 4500
(Germany) Keegan, Wharton

1985 Sheffield United (h) 1–1 Friendly Cunningham 4952

1989 Carlisle United (a) 1–2 Friendly Brazil (pen) 2994

1990 Videoton (Hungary) (a) 1–2 Friendly McGhee 5000

Defying the UEFA ban, United travelled to Budapest and took part in a four-team tournament with local sides Ferencvaros and Videoton, and Belgians Cercle Bruges. Videoton were United's first opponents in the Ulloi Uit stadium, and were two up within 30 minutes. The second half was a little better, as O'Brien was felled in the box and McGhee slotted home the resultant penalty. The secretive nature of the match meant that only five United fans were present. For the record, these were S. Harrison, S. Phillips, G. McDougall, P. Lewis and the author. This select band were allocated a terrace with a capacity of some 7,000.

| 1991 | Ujpest Dosza (Hungary) | (h) 3–0 | Friendly | Quinn 3 | 10000 |

1994 A reserve team travelled to the Victoria Pleasure Grounds at Goole for a friendly and triumphed 10–0, Alex Mathie scoring five.

1994 Philippe Albert signed for United in a £2.65 million deal from Anderlecht on his 27th birthday.

AUGUST 11TH

1971 Mike Jeffrey born, Liverpool.

| 1973 | Middlesbrough | (a) 3–1 | Friendly | Cassidy 2, Howard | 12272 |
| 1979 | Sparta Rotterdam (Holland) | (h) 0–1 | Friendly | No Scorer | 7596 |

A debut for Keith Armstrong, a midfield player who joined United from Sunderland on a non-contract basis but who wasn't retained. Among the Rotterdam players who travelled to Tyneside was Louis Van Gaal, who as a manager almost two decades later brought his Barcelona side to St James'.

| 1982 | Partick Thistle | (a) 2–0 | Friendly | Varadi 2 | 1500 |
| 1983 | SC Drochtersen (Germany) | (a) 5–0 | Friendly | Varadi, Waddle, Trewick, Wharton, Ferris | 3000 |

1984 Newcastle sent a reserve team to Portland Park, Ashington, as part of the Colliers' centenary celebrations.

| 1986 | Carlisle | (a) 2–3 | Friendly | Allon 2 | 3500 |
| 1990 | Cercle Bruges (Belgium) | (a) 2–0 | Friendly | Stimpson, O'Brien | 6000 |

A much-improved Newcastle performance secured third place in the four-team tournament held in Budapest. Bruges were reduced to ten men when Iovino was dismissed for whacking Neil Simpson. Mark Stimpson opened the scoring on the hour with a header which went in via both posts, and O'Brien rounded the keeper with eight minutes left to seal the victory. The tournament was won by hosts Ferencvaros, who beat Videoton 4–3 on penalties after playing a 1–1 draw in the final.

1991 A Newcastle reserve team defeated Coldstream 3–0, Archie Gourlay getting two and Cole the other. The game was to officially open the new changing-room block at Coldstream, and United agreed to play a game after a request was made to George Forbes, the then chairman, who lives in the Borders town.

| 1996 | Manchester United | (a) 0–4 | Friendly | No Scorer | 73214 |

The Charity Shield, although there wasn't much bloody charity about it. As the dispirited Newcastle supporters left the stadium, a cloudburst gave them a good soaking, and roadworks all along the A1 completed the misery, causing hours of delays.

AUGUST 12TH

1961	Odense (Denmark)	(h) 2–0	Friendly	Allchurch 2	9869
1967	Middlesbrough	(h) 2–2	Friendly	Hilley, Davies	13850
1972	Wolverhampton Wanderers	(h) 2–1	Division One	Tudor, Green	33790

The Wolves goal came from Steve Kindon on his debut.

| 1993 | Annfield Plain | (a) 1–1 | Friendly | Costa | 3000 |

Cypriot trialist Costas Costa scored a memorable goal from just over the halfway line past former United keeper Kevin Carr. Proceeds from the game at Derwent Park went to the West Stanley Colliery Disaster Memorial Fund.

| 1994 | Northern Ireland XI | (a) 5–2 | Friendly | Cole, Fox, Lee, Mathie, Elliott | 7000 |

A testimonial game for former Sunderland player and Northern Ireland manager Billy Bingham. Included in the select XI were many former heroes from Bingham's teams including Gerry Armstrong, responsible for Bingham's finest moments, in the 1982 World

Cup. The game ended with Kevin Keegan playing for Newcastle and George Best for the Irish. Keith Rowland and Keith Gillespie scored for Ireland, while Jason Drysdale made a rare appearance for United, coming on as a substitute.

1995 Tottenham Hotspur (a) 2–0   Friendly   Sellars, Ferdinand   17388
Testimonial match for the long-serving Gary Mabbutt. He's a diabetic, you know . . .

AUGUST 13TH

1969 Sheffield Wednesday (h) 3–1   Division One   Foggon, Robson 2   41341
1970 Alan Shearer born, Gosforth.
1978 Alan Kennedy left United, signing for Liverpool in a £330,000 transfer.
1979 Death of Ed Dixon, 85.
1985 Scarborough   (a) 5–4   Friendly   Gascoigne, Scott,   681
                                                   Dunn, OG, Allon
The third goal was scored by 'Boro player-manager Harry Dunn, while United were managed by Willie McFaul following the departure of Jack Charlton three days previously.
1988 Whitby Town   (a) 5–1   Friendly   Robertson, OG, Mirandinha, 1500
                                                   O'Neill, Thorn
Onlookers at the Turnbull Ground were treated to the rare sight of John Robertson scoring in England.
1996 Anderlecht   (a) 2–1   Friendly   Asprilla, Ginola   18000
     (Belgium)
1997 Croatia Zagreb   (h) 2–1   Champions League Beresford 2   34465
                                 Qualifier 1st Leg
1997 John Barnes signed for Newcastle in a free-transfer move from Liverpool, after having apparently agreed to join West Ham. This was the second time within days that Harry Redknapp had been gazumped by United, Stuart Pearce having made a late choice to move north.

AUGUST 14TH

1959 Mallorca Deportivo (a) 1–1 Friendly   White
     (Spain)
1965 Middlesbrough   (h) 3–2   Friendly   Hockey, Cummings, OG   13534
1968 Sheffield Wednesday (a) 1–1 Division One   Robson   27258
Tommy Gibb made his debut in the absence of more established midfielders and held down a first-team place for over 150 consecutive games.
1971 Crystal Palace   (a) 0–2   Division One   No Scorer   25281
Quiet debuts for Hibbitt and Macdonald.
1973 Workington   (a) 4–1   Friendly   Hodgson 2, Gibb,   1000
                                                   McDermott
1976 Middlesbrough   (h) 3–0   Friendly   Gowling 2, Barrowclough   15703
1981 West Bromwich   (h) 0–1   Friendly   No Scorer   6843
     Albion
1984 Hartlepool United (a) 4–2   Friendly   Wharton 3, Roeder   2084
The monkey hangers were 'celebrating' a 14th re-election to the Fourth Division and included former Magpies John Brownlie and John Bird in their ranks.
1989 Scarborough   (a) 1–0   Friendly   McGhee   3000
1989 Michael O'Neill joined up with former United colleague Darren Jackson, after completing a move to Dundee United for a fee of £350,000. He was in good company on Tayside, with neighbouring Dundee having Albert Craig and Wes Saunders on their books, as well as assistant manager John Blackley – all former Magpies.
1990 St Johnstone   (a) 3–1   Friendly   Quinn, O'Brien, McGhee   5000
1993 Tottenham Hotspur (h) 0–1   Premier League   No Scorer   34565
A tough baptism in the Premier League, Teddy Sheringham giving former manager Ossie Ardiles a successful return to St James' Park. The Leazes Stand was open for the first time

and United gave debuts to Nicky Papavasiliou and Malcolm Allen, an eve-of-season signing from Millwall, after Ruddock's pre-season thuggery had robbed United of the services of Beardsley. O'Brien hit the post with a last-minute free-kick.

AUGUST 15TH

1924	Ray King born, Amble.				
1948	Stuart Alderson born, Bishop Auckland.				
1964	Burnley	(a) 1–0	Friendly	Iley	6070
1966	Carlisle United	(a) 2–4	Friendly	Robson 2	10000
1970	Wolverhampton Wanderers	(h) 3–2	Division One	Foggon, Smith, Gibb	38346
1972	Birmingham City	(a) 2–3	Division One	Macdonald, Barrowclough	35831
1976	Des Hamilton born, Bradford.				
1978	Arbroath	(a) 0–0	Friendly	No Scorer	1736
1986	Durham City	(a) 8–0	Friendly	Allon 2, Davies, Bogie, McDonald (pen), Anderson, Whitehurst, McCreery	1000

A pre-season runout at the former home of Durham, Ferens Park.

1989   A transfer tribunal fixed the transfer of Portsmouth striker Mick Quinn to United at £680,000.

1992	Southend United	(h) 3–2	Division One	Bracewell, OG, Clark	28545

Debuts for John Beresford, Paul Bracewell and Barry Venison. The largest crowd of the day in England saw a ten-minute piledriver from Bracewell open the scoring on a damp day. Spencer Prior increased the lead with an own goal and Clark sealed it. Former Magpie John Cornwell was almost unnoticed at right-back for the visitors.

1997   Ian Rush signed for Newcastle, two months short of his 36th birthday.

AUGUST 16TH

1917	Jack Fairbrother born, Burton upon Trent.				
1924	Bobby Mitchell born, Glasgow.				
1942	Death of Bob Foyers, 74.				
1959	Charleroi (Belgium) (a) 5–1		Friendly	White 3, Allchurch, Eastham	
1961	Death of Archie Livingstone.				
1964	Barry Venison born, Consett, Durham.				
1969	Manchester City	(h) 1–0	Division One	Robson (pen)	46860
1975	Ipswich Town	(a) 3–0	Division One	T. Craig (pen), Macdonald 2	27680

First appearance for Alan Gowling.

1980	Sheffield Wednesday (a) 0–2		Division Two	No Scorer	26164

Ray Clarke and Frans Koenen made their Newcastle debuts, in a match blighted by the sending-off of Steve Carney and crowd trouble throughout the day. A number of policemen were injured and the Wednesday club shop was wrecked by drunken fans from Tyneside.

1988	Peterborough United	(a) 7–0	Friendly	Mirandinha 4, O'Neill, Robertson, Wharton	4000

AUGUST 17TH

1963	Huddersfield Town	(h) 5–1	Friendly	Taylor 3, Hilley, McGarry	12622
1968	Burnley	(a) 0–1	Division One	No Scorer	13500
1974	Coventry City	(h) 3–2	Division One	Macdonald, Howard, Kennedy	35950

A debut win for Micky Burns and Glenn Keeley.

1983	AEK Athens (Greece)	(a) 0–0	Friendly	No Scorer	15000
1985	Southampton	(a) 1–1	Division One	Beardsley (pen)	16401

The opening day of the season brought a debut for Alan Davies, while Paul Gascoigne was given his first senior start.

1990 Dunfermline   (a) 0–0   Friendly   No Scorer   3500
Athletic
A testimonial match for Norrie McCathy (I don't know either).

1996 Everton   (a) 0–2   Premier League   No Scorer   40117
League debut for Alan Shearer, who 'scored' with a header, unfortunately disallowed.

AUGUST 18TH

1880 Finlay Speedie born, Dumbarton, Scotland.
1917 Death of James Fleming, killed in action, 33.
1935 Jimmy Harrower born, Alva, Scotland.
1951 Stoke City   (h) 6–0   Division One   Crowe, Milburn 3,   47047
Mitchell, G. Robledo
1956 Portsmouth   (h) 2–1   Division One   Crowe, Taylor   30191
1962 Cardiff City   (a) 4–4   Division Two   Fell (pen), Kerray,   26800
Hilley, OG
Joe Harvey's Tyneside managerial reign began with this eventful draw, Hilley netting on his League debut.

1971 Tottenham Hotspur (a) 0–0   Division One   No Scorer   42715
Willie McFaul was struck by a missile thrown from the crowd, but recovered after treatment, to keep a clean sheet.

1973 Blackpool   (a) 1–0   Friendly   Hibbitt   6297
1979 Oldham Athletic   (h) 3–2   Division Two   Withe, Shoulder 2 (2 pens)   19099
Winning debut for Ian Davies, at left-back, and a 97th-minute winner for United from the penalty spot after the referee's watch appeared to have stopped.

1981 Sunderland   (h) 1–1   Friendly   Shinton   9982
1984 Middlesbrough   (h) 2–2   Friendly   Waddle 2   6800
Irving Nattrass played his final game at St James', for the visitors.

1986 Monterrey   (h) 1–1   Friendly   OG   8417
1991 Charlton Athletic   (a) 1–2   Division Two   Carr   9322
In a match played at Upton Park, Franz Carr scored a late consolation on his debut.

1993 Coventry City   (a) 1–2   Premier League   OG   15763
Peter Atherton had the dubious distinction of scoring Newcastle's first Premiership goal as he diverted an O'Brien free-kick past his own keeper. Pavel Srnicek was dismissed for a foul; former Magpie Mick Quinn took the resultant penalty and blasted it into the building site that had been the away end. However, another man from the past appeared off the bench for Coventry and Mick Harford headed a late winner, with his first touch. The biggest cheer of the night was reserved for the recently departed David Kelly, who sat in the away section to great applause.

AUGUST 19TH

1898 Loughborough Town   (h) 3–1   Division Two   Peddie, Ostler, OG   4000
1908   Joe Richardson born, Bedlington.
1944 Peter Noble born, Sunderland.
1950 Stoke City   (a) 2–1   Division One   Milburn 2 (1 pen)   22000
1961 Leyton Orient   (h) 0–0   Division One   No Scorer   26638
1967 Southampton   (h) 3–0   Division One   Bennett, T. Robson, Scott   33709
Goalscoring debut for Jimmy Scott.

1970 Stoke City   (a) 0–3   Division One   No Scorer   15197
1972 Sheffield United   (a) 2–1   Division One   Tudor, Macdonald   23078
BBC *Match of the Day* cameras were on hand to record an away win, United in their change strip of all blue.

1978 Millwall (a) 1–2 Division Two Barton 12105
Debuts for John Connolly and Jim Pearson as the newly relegated United struggled to adjust to the rigours of Second Division life.

1981 Mick Harford signed for Bristol City, eight months after joining United. The fee was the same, £150,000.

1982 Nacional (Madeira) (a) 0–0 Friendly No Scorer 1000
Played in Madeira.

1987 Tottenham Hotspur (a) 1–3 Division One McCreery 26261
A debut for the hugely underwhelming Glyn Hodges, who was packed off to Watford following seven forgettable performances and training-ground squabbles with boss Willie McFaul.

1988 Blackburn Rovers (a) 2–2 Friendly Mirandinha, Hendrie 9000
1989 Leeds United (h) 5–2 Division Two Quinn 4, Gallacher 24396
Former United players John Hendrie, Peter Haddock and Ian Baird returned to St James', while David Batty eventually came to United via Blackburn. For the home side Kevin Dillon, Wayne Fereday, John Gallacher and Mark McGhee (for the second time) made their entrance. However, the day belonged to four-goal debutant Mickey Quinn, who emulated Malcolm McDonald by opening his United account with a penalty at the Gallowgate end but then went on to better his three-goal haul. The small attendance was due to an organised boycott by the 'Supporters for Change' group, who were protesting at the mismanagement of the club by the United directors. They gathered in various pubs and clubs and watched reruns of old United games on video.

1990 Scarborough (a) 1–1 Friendly Brazil (pen) 2000
A rare Sunday friendly, and a lucky draw for a lacklustre United gained through the award of an unexplained penalty by the oddly coiffured Steven Lodge of Barnsley, who was probably as bored as the rest of the spectators.

1992 Mansfield Town (h) 2–1 League Cup 1st Peacock 2 14083
Round 1st Leg
A brief trial for Steve Howey in midfield was not a great success. A Phil Stant goal gave the Stags some hope for the second leg, and former Magpie Chris Withe filled their left-back berth.

1994 Death of Frank Houghton, 68.

1995 Coventry City (h) 3–0 Premier League Lee, Beardsley, Ferdinand 36485
Debuts for Shaka Hislop, Warren Barton, David Ginola and Les Ferdinand, who netted a fine debut goal.

AUGUST 20TH

1920 Ray Robinson left United to join rivals Sunderland, after losing his place in the first team.
1936 Death of William Agnew, 55.
1938 Gateshead (h) 2–1 Friendly Cairns, Birkett 30000
1949 Portsmouth (h) 1–3 Division One G. Robledo 54258
1955 Sheffield United (h) 4–2 Division One Davies 2, Hannah, Keeble 42559
1960 Preston North End (a) 3–2 Division One White 3 17363
Debut for Liam Tuohy, at outside-left.
1966 Aston Villa (a) 1–1 Division One McGarry 17673
Debut for Ron Guthrie.
1969 Sheffield Wednesday (a) 0–1 Division One No Scorer 19121
A debut for Jimmy Smith as substitute. Peter Eustace got the only goal for the Owls.
1975 Middlesbrough (h) 1–1 Division One Macdonald 41417
The visitors enjoyed a half-time lead thanks to an Alan Gowling own goal, but total domination from United in the second half could only produce an equaliser when Macdonald's shot went in off 'Boro's John Craggs.
1977 Leeds United (h) 3–2 Division One Burns 2, Kennedy 36700
1980 Notts County (h) 1–1 Division Two Shoulder 17272

1983 League of Ireland (h) 3–0 Friendly Waddle 2, Keegan 7739
This first home game of the season gave supporters a chance to watch football through a security fence for the first time, this measure having been implemented in the summer.

1984 Gateshead (a) 7–1 Friendly Wharton 4, Ryan, 5000
Waddle, Beardsley

1990 Death of Bill Curry, 54.

1991 United midfielder Billy Askew appeared before magistrates, charged with a public order offence after police had been called to a disturbance in Chester-le-Street town centre. He was fined.

1994 Sixteen-year-old Paul Brayson scored eight goals as the juniors overcame their Hartlepool counterparts 10–1 at Durham University. Hartlepool had been 1–0 ahead.

AUGUST 21ST

1908 Johnny Dryden born, Broomhill.

1940 Jimmy Scott born, Falkirk, Scotland.

1948 Everton (a) 3–3 Division One Walker, Lowrie 2 57279
Debut for Colin Gibson, at outside-right.

1954 Arsenal (a) 3–1 Division One Davies, R. Mitchell 2 65334

1959 Keith Mulgrove born, Haltwhistle.

1965 Nottingham Forest (h) 2–2 Division Two Suddick, McGarry 37230
Newcastle named their first substitute for a league game, but Albert Bennett wasn't called on. Elsewhere in the league, the first substitute to be used was Keith Peacock (Gavin's dad) for his club Charlton, away at Bolton Wanderers.

1968 Chelsea (h) 3–2 Division One Gibb, Robson 2 39048
Those United fans who hadn't journeyed to Hillsborough or Turf Moor got their chance to assess Joe Harvey's latest purchase on his home debut. Tommy Gibb didn't let them down with a 25-yard drive which began a fightback from a 2–0 deficit, caused by Bobby Tambling and Alan Birchenall.

1971 Liverpool (h) 3–2 Division One Macdonald 3 (1 pen) 39736

1974 Sheffield United (h) 2–2 Division One Macdonald, Burns 34283

1976 Derby County (h) 2–2 Division One T. Craig (pen), Hudson 35927
Fun and games on the opening day of a new season, as the Rams raced to a 2–0 lead through David Nish and Charlie George. George was then sent off, and United clawed back a point.

1978 Peter Withe arrived on Tyneside in a £200,000 transfer from Nottingham Forest.

1979 Preston North End (a) 0–1 Division Two No Scorer 12707
The opening away game of the season, and scouser Eric Potts made sure United left Lancashire pointless. The brief trend for producing tabloid newspapers instead of a programme resulted in a rather raggy effort for this game.

1982 Maritimo (Madeira) (a) 1–0 Friendly Waddle 1500
Played in Madeira.

1985 Luton Town (h) 2–2 Division One Roeder, Beardsley 21933
Debut for Ian Stewart and a penalty save by Martin Thomas from Gary Parker which would have put the visitors 3–0 ahead.

1993 Manchester United (a) 1–1 Premier League Cole 41829
After Giggs had scored for the home side, a point was secured by a neat finish from Cole at the Stretford End.

1994 Leicester City (a) 3–1 Premier League Cole, Beardsley, Elliott 20048
Debuts for Philippe Albert and Marc Hottiger live on Sky. Pavel Srnicek was sent off after tripping Joachim and was replaced by the lumbering Hooper. Peter Beardsley was led from the field after smashing his cheekbone.

1996 Wimbledon (h) 2–0 Premier League Batty, Shearer 36385
A wonderful lofted shot from Batty and a trademark free-kick from Shearer.

AUGUST 22ND

1951	Bolton Wanderers	(a) 0–0	Division One	No Scorer	40000
1953	Sunderland	(h) 2–1	Division One	Mitchell (pen), Keeble	58516

Debut for Jimmy Scoular, at right-half.

1956	Cardiff City	(a) 2–5	Division One	Davies 2	42000
1959	Tottenham Hotspur	(h) 1–5	Division One	Eastham	40782
1962	Middlesbrough	(a) 2–4	Division Two	Fell, Thomas	30611
1970	Crystal Palace	(a) 0–1	Division One	No Scorer	27287
1981	Sunderland	(a) 1–2	Friendly	Shoulder	10032

A shadow was cast over this pre-season derby when a young Newcastle supporter was accidentally killed at Roker.

1987	Sheffield Wednesday	(a) 1–0	Division One	D. Jackson	22031
1992	Derby County	(a) 2–1	Division One	Peacock, Clark	17522

Revenge for the previous season's Baseball Ground humiliation.

1995	Bolton Wanderers	(a) 3–1	Premier League	Ferdinand 2, Lee	20243

A victory in United's final trip to Burnden Park.

AUGUST 23RD

1938	John McGrath born, Manchester.				
1947	Plymouth Argyle	(h) 6–1	Division Two	Bentley, Pearson, Shackleton 2, Walker, Wayman	52642

Jack Fairbrother made his first-team debut at the age of 30.

1950	West Bromwich Albion	(h) 1–1	Division One	Brennan	48720
1952	Sheffield Wednesday	(a) 2–2	Division One	Hannah, G. Robledo	55000

The opening day of the season, and United frittered away a 2–0 half-time lead at Hillsborough, the Owls drawing level through Redfern Froggatt and Jackie Sewell.

1957	Peter Cartwright born, North Shields.				
1958	Blackburn Rovers	(h) 1–5	Division One	OG	52497
1961	Walsall	(h) 1–0	Division Two	Tuohy	33821

Debut for Ken Leek.

1966	Sheffield United	(a) 1–0	Division One	McGarry (pen)	15188
1967	Chelsea	(a) 1–1	Division One	Bennett	32677
1969	Leeds United	(a) 1–1	Division One	Scott	40403
1972	West Bromwich Albion	(h) 1–1	Division One	Macdonald	29695
1975	Leicester City	(h) 3–0	Division One	Macdonald 2, Burns	36084

Probably the best goal Macdonald scored in his Newcastle career was the opener, as he ran on to a ball played infield at the Leazes end and smashed it past goalkeeper Mark Wallington in one movement.

1977	Liverpool	(a) 0–2	Division One	No Scorer	48267

Kenny Dalglish marked his first game at Anfield with a goal at the Kop to banish memories of the departed Kevin Keegan. Debutant United keeper 20-year-old Steve Hardwick couldn't be blamed for this defeat. If only the same could have been said for some of the other 91 appearances he made . . .

1978	West Ham United	(h) 0–3	Division Two	No Scorer	27167

Debut for Colin Suggett.

1980	Bolton Wanderers	(a) 0–4	Division Two	No Scorer	11835

A good stuffing at a sunny Burnden Park spelt doom for boss McGarry. Alan Gowling played for the home side, for whom Brian Kidd claimed a hat-trick, while United wore their sickly all-yellow away strip.

1986	Liverpool	(h) 0–2	Division One	No Scorer	33306

The programme for this match included an article entitled 'Can Kenny [Dalglish] be as great as a manager?'. Some 12 years later, many Newcastle fans would prefer not to answer the question.

1992   Kevin Keegan and Terry McDermott got their boots out and played in a charity match at Silksworth Sports Centre in aid of cancer research. Keegan turned out for Mick Horswills XI, who unfortunately played in red and white stripes.

1997   Aston Villa   (h) 1–0   Premier League   Beresford   36783
Batty was sent off but United held on for the win following another early goal from John Beresford. Veteran Ian Rush made his Newcastle debut.

AUGUST 24TH

1931   Arnold Woollard born, Pembroke, Bermuda.
1940   Colin Taylor born, Stourbridge.
1949   Everton   (a) 1–2   Division One   Lowrie   49504
1955   Birmingham City   (h) 2–2   Division One   Davies, Keeble   34473
1957   West Bromwich   (a) 1–2   Division One   White   31410
        Albion
1960   Fulham   (h) 7–2   Division One   Gilfillan 2, Neale 2   23498
                                                          Tuohy 2, White
        A pair for Duncan Neale on his debut and also for Liam Tuohy, playing at home for the first time.
1963   Derby County   (h) 3–1   Division Two   Taylor, Penman, McGarry   35269
        Successful debuts for Ollie Burton, goalkeeper Gordon Marshall and goalscorer Colin Taylor on his 23rd birthday. McCann netted for the Rams.
1964   Charlton Athletic   (h) 1–1   Division Two   Hilley   32805
1968   Everton   (h) 0–0   Division One   No Scorer   38851
1974   Wolverhampton   (a) 2–4   Division One   Tudor 2   23526
        Wanderers
        Kenny Hibbitt hit all four goals for Wolves.
1985   Liverpool   (h) 1–0   Division One   Reilly   29941
1991   Watford   (h) 2–2   Division Two   Hunt, Clark   22440
        The first home game of the season saw Andy Hunt grab an early lead, quickly cancelled out by Peter Nicholas as Srnicek dropped the ball under pressure from Butler. Thirty-three-year-old Luther Blissett then headed Watford into the lead before United swept upfield and Clark beat the keeper at the second attempt. Franz Carr was given a warm reception on his debut, but failed to provide decent service to Quinn and Hunt up front.
1993   Newcastle were entertained by Everton reserves and defeated them 1–0 with an Alun Armstrong goal. Man of the match was United's Dutch trialist Gustaff Uhlenbeek.
1994   Coventry City   (h) 4–0   Premier League   Lee 2, Watson, Cole   34163
1996   Sheffield Wednesday (h) 1–2   Premier League   Shearer (pen)   36452

AUGUST 25TH

1878   Ted Birnie born, Sunderland.
1923   Arsenal   (a) 4–1   Division One   Seymour, McDonald,   25000
                                                          Harris 2
1923   Jimmy Greenhalgh born, Manchester. Assistant to manager Joe Harvey.
1928   Cardiff City   (h) 1–1   Division One   Gallacher
1934   Nottingham Forest (a) 1–5   Division Two   Lang   22000
        The first game of a new season, with United having dropped into Division Two and being soundly beaten. New captain Tony Leach made his debut, as did Bob Shankley at inside-forward.
1948   Chelsea   (h) 2–2   Division One   Lowrie, Milburn   59020
1951   Manchester United (a) 1–2   Division One   G. Robledo   48000
1952   Newcastle signed reserve goalkeeper Bob Robinson from Sunderland.

1954	West Bromwich Albion	(h) 3–0	Division One	Milburn, White 2	58548
1956	Sunderland	(a) 2–1	Division One	Davies, Milburn	51032
1958	Blackpool	(a) 0–3	Division One	No Scorer	25531

Solitary appearance of forward Carl Wilson, son of former Magpie Joe Wilson. Also making his debut was Billy Wright, a native of Blackpool who had begun his career at Bloomfield Road.

1962	Portsmouth	(h) 1–1	Division Two	Thomas	35214
1965	West Bromwich Albion	(h) 0–1	Division One	No Scorer	43901
1971	Huddersfield Town	(h) 0–0	Division One	No Scorer	40989
1973	West Ham United	(a) 2–1	Division One	Macdonald 2	28169
1976	Tottenham Hotspur	(a) 2–0	Division One	Burns, Barrowclough	24022
1979	Charlton Athletic	(a) 1–1	Division Two	Cassidy	6849

United boss Bill McGarry gave Peter Cartwright a 22nd birthday present (two days late) – his debut as a substitute, replacing Gary Nicholson.

1980   United signed Imre Varadi, a striker who had been on trial from Everton, for a fee of £125,000.

| 1984 | Leicester City | (a) 3–2 | Division One | McCreery, Waddle, Carney | 18636 |

Malcolm Brown's much-delayed debut, injury having ruled him out since he signed from Huddersfield over a year earlier.

| 1986 | Tottenham Hotspur | (a) 1–1 | Division One | Beardsley | 25381 |
| 1990 | Plymouth Argyle | (h) 2–0 | Division Two | Kristensen, Quinn | 23984 |

A winning start to the new season, as Benny Kristensen calmed any nerves with a fine strike in the first few minutes and Mickey Quinn claimed a second, all in bright sunshine.

| 1992 | Mansfield Town | (a) 0–0 | League Cup 1st Round 2nd Leg | No Scorer | 6725 |

Gavin Peacock missed a last-minute penalty, saved by Stags keeper Jason Pearcey.

| 1993 | Everton | (h) 1–0 | Premier League | Allen | 34490 |

AUGUST 26TH

1884	Billy Hampson born, Radcliffe, Manchester.
1893	George Pyke born, Gateshead.
1910	Wilf Feeney born, Grangetown, Middlesbrough.

| 1922 | Everton | (h) 2–0 | Division One | McDonald 2 | 50000 |

Thirty-nine-year-old Sandy Mutch made his debut on the first day of the season and shared goalkeeping duties with Bill Bradley as United eventually finished fourth in Division One.

1933	Portsmouth	(h) 2–2	Division One	Allen, Lang	30000
1938	Bryan Harvey born, Stepney.				
1939	Millwall	(a) 0–3	Division Two	No Scorer	30000

This was the first of only three games played in the 1939–40 season, after which League football was cancelled due to a rather bigger European fixture.

1950	Everton	(h) 1–1	Division One	Taylor	49096
1953	Liverpool	(a) 2–2	Division One	Davies, Hannah	47263
1959	Birmingham City	(a) 3–4	Division One	White, Eastham 2 (2 pens)	26981
1961	Preston North End	(a) 1–0	Division Two	Woods	14122
1963	Middlesbrough	(a) 0–3	Division Two	No Scorer	37803
1967	Liverpool	(a) 0–6	Division One	No Scorer	51829

Liverpool scorers included a Tony Hateley hat-trick.

1970	Nottingham Forest	(h) 1–1	Division One	McNamee	35132
1972	Ipswich Town	(h) 1–2	Division One	Macdonald	24601
1978	Luton Town	(h) 1–0	Division Two	Pearson	24112

Debut for Peter Withe.

| 1985 | Coventry City | (a) 2–1 | Division One | Reilly, Stewart | 12097 |

After 80 scoreless minutes, the game exploded into life when Terry Gibson scored for the Sky Blues. George Reilly snatched an equaliser with three minutes remaining and Stewart won it in the last seconds. The West Midlands Constabulary were also in fine form, ejecting numerous travelling supporters for the heinous crime of not wearing shirts.

| 1989 | Leicester City | (a) 2–2 | Division Two | Quinn, Gallacher | 13384 |

Debut for Mark Stimson.

AUGUST 27TH

| 1895 | John Archibald born. | | | | |
| 1921 | Huddersfield Town | (a) 2–1 | Division One | McDonald 2 | 25000 |

Start of a brief run in the team for Harry Paton, an inside-right acquired from Clydebank.

1927	Huddersfield Town	(a) 3–1	Division One	Gallacher 3	24500
1932	Bolton Wanderers	(a) 2–2	Division One	Allen, J.R. Richardson	15000
1934	Blackpool	(a) 1–4	Division Two	J.R. Richardson	25000
1938	Plymouth Argyle	(h) 2–1	Division Two	Birkett, Clifton	38000

Scoring debuts for Ralph Birkett and Harry Clifton and first appearance for Duggie Wright.

1938	Death of Colin Veitch, 57.				
1947	Chesterfield	(a) 1–0	Division Two	Wayman	15000
1949	Wolverhampton Wanderers	(a) 1–2	Division One	Milburn	50922
1952	West Bromwich Albion	(a) 0–1	Division One	No Scorer	46206
1955	Preston North End	(a) 3–4	Division One	Hannah, White 2	39583
1960	Burnley	(h) 0–1	Division One	No Scorer	35485
1966	Tottenham Hotspur	(h) 0–2	Division One	No Scorer	35780
1969	Manchester United	(a) 0–0	Division One	No Scorer	53267
1974	Sheffield United	(a) 1–2	Division One	Keeley	17650
1975	Derby County	(a) 2–3	Division One	Macdonald, Bruce	27585

Tempers flared at the Baseball Ground, where Mickey Burns was sent off for arguing with the referee. Francis Lee and Kevin Hector scored for Derby, whose winner came courtesy of an own goal from Tommy Craig.

1977	Middlesbrough	(a) 0–2	Division One	No Scorer	26712
1977	Stuart Elliott born, London.				
1980	Bury	(h) 3–2	League Cup 2nd Round 1st Leg	Rafferty 2, Shoulder	9073

The only appearance of Phil Leaver, in front of one of the smallest crowds St James' Park has seen for a first-team game. Returning Magpies included Shakers boss Jim Iley and players Pat Howard and Keith Kennedy.

| 1983 | Leeds United | (a) 1–0 | Division Two | Anderson | 30806 |

Debut at left-back for John Ryan.

1984	Sheffield Wednesday	(h) 2–1	Division One	Beardsley (pen), Wharton	29673
1987	Mirandinha arrived in England, having agreed to join United in a £570,000 deal from Palmeiras.				
1988	Everton	(a) 0–4	Division One	No Scorer	41560

Beasant, Thorn, Hendrie and Robertson made their debuts. Tony Cottee took precisely 34 seconds to score the first of his three goals, and it was downhill to Division Two from then on . . .

| 1991 | Middlesbrough | (a) 0–3 | Division Two | No Scorer | 16970 |
| 1994 | Southampton | (h) 5–1 | Premier League | Watson 2, Cole 2, Lee | 34182 |

Saints keeper Grobbelaar was powerless to stop any of the goals.

| 1995 | Sheffield Wednesday | (a) 2–0 | Premier League | Beardsley, Ginola | 24815 |

Two classic goals beat the Owls again, Ginola's first for the club and Beardsley from an impossible angle. Sky broadcast this comprehensive victory by United, who wore their new blue-and-red hooped away strip.

1997   Croatia Zagreb   (a) 2–2   Champions League   Asprilla (pen), Ketsbaia   34000
                                 Qualifier 2nd Leg

A remarkable game. United led 2–1 from the first game in England and a Tino penalty extended their advantage. However, a late fightback from Zagreb led to them levelling the tie in the last seconds of normal time. Just as penalties seemed inevitable, the deadlock was broken by Ketsbaia.

AUGUST 28TH

1880   Jimmy Lindsay born, Stockton.
1920   West Bromwich   (h) 1–1   Division One   Seymour   61080
       Albion
       Debuts for William Aitken, Neil Harris, Ted Ward and the legendary Stan Seymour.
1922   Birmingham   (a) 2–0   Division One   Harris 2   35000
1926   Aston Villa   (h) 4–0   Division One   Gallacher 4   36000
1937   Manchester United   (a) 0–3   Division Two   No Scorer   30000
1948   Preston North End   (h) 2–5   Division One   Donaldson, Stobbart   63549
1954   Sheffield United   (h) 1–2   Division One   R. Mitchell   52341
1964   Death of Jimmy Richardson, 53.
1965   Sheffield Wednesday (a) 0–1   Division One   No Scorer   23391
       Albert Bennett's debut. A goal from Colin Dobson left newly promoted Newcastle still searching for their first win in Division One since April 1961.
1968   Nottingham Forest   (h) 1–1   Division One   Robson   34613
       Scorer for Forest was Ian Story-Moore from the penalty spot.
1971   Coventry City   (a) 0–1   Division One   No Scorer   22638
1975   Another departure from United caused by friction between boss Gordon Lee and a player, as Terry Hibbitt moved to Birmingham City. The transfer was concluded within minutes of the previous day's game at Derby County.
1976   Bristol City   (h) 0–0   Division One   No Scorer   31775
1980   Following disagreements with boss McGarry, John Connolly was awarded a free transfer and returned to Scotland with Hibernian.
1982   Queens Park   (h) 1–0   Division Two   Keegan   36185
       Rangers
       A perfect day in the sun, with the centre of attention grabbing a second-half winner, which he later claimed the crowd had sucked in. Debuts also for Jeff Clarke and the returning John Craggs. Keegan was presented with a Newcastle scarf on the pitch by a gentleman clad in only a pair of fluorescent yellow socks. Referee Trelford Mills did nothing to provoke the home crowd on this visit, while England boss Bobby Robson was full of post-match platitudes when asked about the player whose England career he was about to curtail.

AUGUST 29TH

1923   Blackburn Rovers   (h) 2–1   Division One   Seymour, Harris   11000
1925   Bolton Wanderers   (a) 2–2   Division One   Cowan 2   28675
       Debuts at right-back for Bert Chandler and centre-half for Ossie Park.
1927   South Shields   (a) 4–2   Friendly   McDonald, Lang, McKay   2500
       At Wallsend.
1928   Burnley   (h) 2–7   Division One   Chalmers 2   35000
       A traumatic debut for centre-half Ed Wood, as Burnley centre-forward George Beel escaped from him three times to score.
1931   Liverpool   (h) 0–1   Division One   No Scorer   30000
       Debut for Gallacher's striking replacement Jack Allen, who missed a penalty.
1936   Barnsley   (h) 0–1   Division Two   No Scorer   35000
       Debuts for Bobby Ancell, Jesse Carver and Ehud Rogers, better known as 'Tim'.

1951	Bolton Wanderers	(h) 0–1	Division One	No Scorer	49587

Debut for Ronnie Simpson, in goal.

1953	Manchester United	(a) 1–1	Division One	Hannah	25000
1956	Cardiff City	(h) 1–0	Division One	Keeble	34859
1959	Manchester United	(a) 2–3	Division One	Allchurch, White	53257
1960	Barcelona	(h) 3–4	Friendly	Tuohy, Allchurch, Woods	31361

A game of two distinct parts, as United raced to a 3–0 lead, only for Barcelona to up the pace and score four, three from the Hungarian Kocsis.

1961	Walsall	(a) 0–1	Division Two	No Scorer	25453
1962	Middlesbrough	(h) 6–1	Division Two	Thomas 3, Hilley, Hale 2	41550

Making his debut for the Teesiders was goalkeeper Arthur Lightening.

1963	Tommy Wright born, Belfast.				
1964	Southampton	(h) 2–1	Division Two	Thomas, Hilley	24531
1970	Blackpool	(h) 1–2	Division One	Hindson	34041

Debut for Stewart Barrowclough and the only goal Hindson scored in his short first-team career at Gallowgate.

1973	Southampton	(h) 0–1	Division One	No Scorer	25531

A penalty scored by Mick Channon was the difference between the two sides.

1976	Jon Dahl Tomasson born, Copenhagen, Denmark.				
1978	Watford	(a) 1–2	League Cup 2nd Round	Pearson	15346

Two goals from Luther Blissett.

1979	Sunderland	(a) 2–2	League Cup 2nd Round 1st Leg	Davies, Cartwright	27746
1980	It's goodbye to Bill McGarry as he is dismissed, victim of a dismal run that saw United bottom of Division Two and knocked out of the League Cup by lower-league opposition.				
1981	Watford	(h) 0–1	Division Two	No Scorer	19244

This game saw the introduction of three points for a win, which even new signing Imre Varadi couldn't prevent from returning to Watford. Watford were ultimately promoted as runners-up to local rivals Luton.

1983	Shrewsbury Town	(h) 0–1	Division Two	No Scorer	29140

Goalscorer for the visitors was Alan Brown, briefly a Newcastle player when on loan from Sunderland.

1987	Nottingham Forest	(h) 0–1	Division One	No Scorer	20111
1988	Wimbledon	(h) 1–0	Mercantile Credit Trophy	O'Neill	17904
1992	West Ham United	(h) 2–0	Division One	Peacock, Kelly	29855

Julian Dicks was dismissed after attempting to launch Franz Carr into the benches in front of the East Stand. An interested spectator was striker Kennet Andersson, who had attracted the interest of Keegan. However, the move broke down when his club Mechelen refused to allow him to play for United on a trial basis.

1993	Blackburn Rovers	(h) 1–1	Premier League	Cole	33987

Cole opened the scoring in this Sunday afternoon Sky televised game, but Alan Shearer equalised for Rovers on his return from injury.

1996	Death of Jimmy Gordon, 80.				
1996	In the absence of a reserve team, United played a private friendly in Edinburgh against Hearts. Clark and Beardsley scored in a 2–2 draw.				

AUGUST 30TH

1919	Arsenal	(a) 1–0	Division One	Henderson	55000

Debut for Tom Curry, who went on to represent United in a career spanning 17 years and 248 goals. Fellow debutant James Henderson got the only goal but didn't last the season. The game saw first appearances also for Ray Robinson and Jack Wilson, as league football restarted following the end of hostilities.

1924	Huddersfield Town	(h) 1–3	Division One	Cowan	47000
1930	Sheffield Wednesday	(a) 1–2	Division One	Cape	25000

Debuts for Scottish imports Duncan Lindsay and Jimmy Nelson, Lancastrian Jimmy Naylor, and local lad Ron Starling. Also, outside-left Jack Wilkinson made his first appearance for United, against his former club.

1939	Nottingham Forest	(a) 0–2	Division Two	No Scorer	15000

Debut for Dave Hamilton in this penultimate league match of the season, before the war closed down League football for seven seasons.

1947	Luton Town	(a) 1–2	Division Two	Bentley	26000
1950	West Bromwich Albion	(a) 2–1	Division One	Milburn, Mitchell	29377

1951 Peter Withe born, Liverpool.

1952	Tottenham Hotspur	(h) 1–1	Division One	G. Robledo	59629

1957 Aiden McCaffery born, Jarrow.

1958	Everton	(a) 2–0	Division One	McGuigan, Wright	36602

A goal on his debut for John McGuigan.

1967	Chelsea	(h) 5–1	Division One	Bennett, Davies 2, Elliott, T. Robson	34809
1969	Arsenal	(h) 3–1	Division One	Foggon, Davies, Robson	47208
1972	Tottenham Hotspur	(h) 0–1	Division One	No Scorer	27912
1975	Manchester City	(a) 0–4	Division One	No Scorer	31875

A debut to forget for centre-half John Bird, as Dennis Tueart scored twice from the spot and Joe Royle got the other goals.

1980	Luton Town	(h) 2–1	Division Two	Koenen, Hibbitt	13175

Fighting spirit from United, prompted by the caretaker manager Joe Harvey, overcoming a high-flying Hatters side. Frans Koenen struck the only goal of his short career in England.

1986	Luton Town	(a) 0–0	Division One	No Scorer	9254

First appearance for Ian Bogie, who had to wait a year for his second.

1995	Middlesbrough	(a) 1–0	Premier League	Ferdinand	36483

AUGUST 31ST

1910 Harry Heward born, Hetton-le-Hole.

1921	Everton	(h) 3–0	Division One	Harris, Paton 2	40000
1925	Real Madrid (Spain)	(h) 6–1	Friendly	McDonald, Curry, Urwin, Clark, MacKenzie, Cowan	10000
1929	Manchester United	(h) 4–1	Division One	Gallacher 3, McDonald	45000

Debut for Duncan Hutchison, who had been such a popular figure at his former club Dundee United that a party of supporters travelled to Tyneside to cheer him on in his first game.

1932	Middlesbrough	(h) 5–1	Division One	Lang, McMenemy 2, Allen, Weaver (pen)	35000

Debut for Jimmy Murray.

1935	Bradford	(h) 3–3	Division Two	Cairns, McMenemy, Pearson	28000
1936	West Ham United	(a) 2–0	Division Two	McMenemy, Pearson	23000
1938	Luton Town	(a) 1–2	Division Two	Clifton	17689
1946	Millwall	(a) 4–1	Division Two	Bentley 2, Milburn, Stubbins	39187

Domestic football resumed after the war with the 1939–40 fixture list being used again.

1949	Everton	(h) 4–0	Division One	Milburn, Mitchell, G. Robledo, Walker	42689

1954 Alan Kennedy born, Sunderland.

1955	Birmingham City	(a) 1–3	Division One	White	38690

| 1957 | Tottenham Hotspur (h) 3–1 | Division One | Eastham, Keeble, R. Mitchell | 37742 |

The first home game of a traumatic season when relegation was narrowly avoided. In one of only six league victories at home all season, inside-right Jimmy Hill made his debut.

| 1960 | Fulham | (a) 3–4 | Division One | Allchurch, Hughes, Woods | 21361 |

A goal on his debut for inside-right Charlie Woods.

1963	Plymouth Argyle	(a) 4–3	Division Two	Taylor, Thomas 3	13960
1966	Sheffield United	(h) 1–0	Division One	OG	21876
1968	Sunderland	(a) 1–1	Division One	Robson	49807

United hero was Willie McFaul, who saved a Colin Suggett penalty.

| 1970 | Nicky Papavasiliou born, Limassol, Cyprus. |

| 1974 | West Ham United | (h) 2–0 | Division One | Tudor, Macdonald | 30782 |
| 1977 | Millwall | (h) 0–2 | League Cup 2nd Round | No Scorer | 21861 |

| 1983 | Death of Jimmy Naylor, 81. |

| 1985 | Queens Park Rangers | (h) 3–1 | Division One | Beardsley, Reilly, McDonald | 25219 |
| 1991 | Bristol Rovers | (a) 2–1 | Division Two | O'Brien, Quinn | 6334 |

To Twerton Park in the sun, and just as it seemed an inspired first-half performance from Newcastle would go unrewarded, O'Brien hit a dipping shot from 25 yards that eluded the keeper. Franz Carr was in inspired form on the wing and Rovers were reduced to switching full-backs in an attempt to get anywhere near him. Quinn added a deserved second after the break and more could have followed.

| 1993 | Ipswich Town | (a) 1–1 | Premier League | Cole | 19126 |

Keegan remonstrated with home fans after they banged their fists on the roof of the United dugout following their equaliser scored by Kiwomya.

| 1994 | West Ham United | (a) 3–1 | Premier League | OG, Lee, Mathie | 17375 |

An own goal from Steve Potts at a three-sided Upton Park set United on their way to a comfortable win, despite Tyneside-born Don Hutchison scoring from the penalty spot on his Hammers debut.

SEPTEMBER 1ST

| 1894 | Darwen | (a) 0–5 | Division Two | No Scorer | 5000 |

Undistinguished debuts for T. Cambell, who didn't even stick around long enough to tell anyone his first name, Tom Rendell and Jock Smith.

| 1894 | Tom Curry born, South Shields. |

1896	Hibernian	(h) 1–1	Friendly	Thompson	5000
1897	Sunderland	(h) 1–3	Friendly	Ghee	12000
1898	Sunderland	(h) 1–1	Friendly	Peddie	15000
1900	Nottingham Forest	(h) 0–0	Division One	No Scorer	20000

Debut for Charles Burgess, a Montrose-born right-back who was an early victim of the St James' boo boys during his 31-game tenure on Tyneside. He then signed for Portsmouth, about as far away as he could get from Gallowgate.

| 1902 | Glasgow Rangers | (h) 3–1 | Friendly | Rutherford, Orr, McColl | 6000 |
| 1904 | Paris Athletic (France) | (a) 11–2 | Friendly | Appleyard 5, Howie 2, Orr 2, Templeton, Rutherford | 3000 |

Forty-eight hours before the start of the new league season, United faced continental opposition in the French capital.

| 1906 | Sunderland | (h) 4–2 | Division One | Appleyard, Howie, Rutherford 2 | 56375 |
| 1909 | Bolton Wanderers | (h) 1–0 | Division One | Rutherford | 25000 |

Debut for centre-half Wilfred Lawson.

| 1910 | Sunderland | (a) 1–2 | Division One | Shepherd (pen) | 30000 |
| 1913 | Blackburn Rovers | (a) 0–3 | Division One | No Scorer | 20000 |

John King moved from his native Scotland and played the first of 61 senior games for Newcastle.

1920	Everton	(a) 1–3	Division One	Harris	45000
1923	Arsenal	(h) 1–0	Division One	Aitken	40000
1924	Blackburn Rovers	(a) 1–1	Division One	Seymour	30000
1926	Burnley	(h) 1–5	Division One	Hudspeth (pen)	35000
1928	Sheffield United	(a) 1–3	Division One	Chalmers	30000
1934	Brentford	(h) 2–5	Division Two	Gallantree, Kelly	24000
1937	Barnsley	(h) 0–1	Division Two	No Scorer	19000

The first of Jimmy Denmark's 54 appearances at Gallowgate, following his arrival from Third Lanark.

| 1948 | Chelsea | (a) 3–2 | Division One | Gibson, Milburn, Thompson | 43840 |
| 1951 | Tottenham Hotspur | (h) 7–2 | Division One | Mitchell 2, G. Robledo 3, Taylor, Walker | 52541 |

An amazing demolition of the League champions, achieved without the sidelined Milburn.

1954	West Bromwich Albion	(a) 2–4	Division One	Hannah, Scoular	36414
1954	Glen Keeley born, Basildon.				
1956	Sheffield Wednesday	(a) 0–4	Division One	No Scorer	36270
1962	Preston North End	(a) 1–2	Division Two	Hale	13884
1964	Charlton Athletic	(a) 1–0	Division Two	Robson	22939

Goalscoring debut for Pop Robson, who made sporadic appearances for the first team until establishing himself fully in the 1968–69 season.

| 1965 | West Bromwich Albion | (a) 2–1 | Division One | Hilley, McGarry | 22000 |
| 1971 | Leeds United | (a) 1–5 | Division One | OG | 18623 |

This match was held at Hillsborough, as Elland Road was closed due to the crowd trouble which had enveloped the previous season's home game with West Bromwich Albion. The trouble had resulted from referee Ray Tinkler's refusal to disallow an obviously offside 'goal' from Albion.

| 1973 | Arsenal | (h) 1–1 | Division One | McDermott | 30665 |

An equaliser from Charlie George for the Gunners.

| 1976 | Gillingham | (a) 2–1 | League Cup 2nd Round | Cassidy, Cannell | 11203 |

Debut for reserve striker Alan Guy and a competitive debut for Newcastle at Priestfield.

| 1979 | Chelsea | (h) 2–1 | Division Two | Withe 2 | 25047 |

Winning debut for Stuart Boam, newly arrived from Middlesbrough shortly after the crocked Nattrass had gone the opposite way – one of Bill McGarry's better pieces of business.

| 1982 | Blackburn Rovers | (a) 2–1 | Division Two | Keegan, Martin | 14421 |

Debut for John Anderson, on as substitute.

| 1984 | Aston Villa | (h) 3–0 | Division One | Beardsley, Waddle 2 | 31591 |

Newcastle United stood proudly at the top of Division One for the first time since September 1950 after this fine win.

| 1987 | Norwich City | (a) 1–1 | Division One | P. Jackson | 16636 |

Mirandinha's debut, in doubt up to kick-off, tempted thousands of United fans to Norfolk on a weekday night, complete with Brazilian shirts and – for some never-to-be-explained reason – sombreros.

| 1990 | Blackburn Rovers | (a) 1–0 | Division Two | O'Brien | 11329 |

Last-gasp winner for United, virtually the only chance they created in the whole game. Howard Gayle, once on loan at St James', missed a host of chances, to the great amusement of the travelling supporters.

1993 Red Star Belgrade striker Dragan Lukic was on trial at United, but after injuring himself in training he returned home without ever playing for the club. The friendly arranged for him went ahead regardless, and Alex Mathie scored three goals in a 6–1 beating of Doncaster Rovers at Belle Vue.

1996 Keith Gillespie played for Northern Ireland as they lost 1–0 at home to the Ukraine in match at Windsor Park, Belfast.

1996 Chris Holland appeared for the England Under-21 team as they recorded a 2–0 away win against Moldova.

1996 Tino Asprilla scored three of Columbia's goals as they hammered Chile 4–1.

SEPTEMBER 2ND

Year	Opponent	Venue	Score	Competition	Scorers	Attendance
1893	Woolwich Arsenal	(a)	2–2	Division Two	Sorley, Crate	6000

Only recorded appearances of fellow Scots Bowman and Ramsay for United.

1895	Hibernian	(h)	1–2	Friendly	McKay	8000
1896	Sunderland	(h)	2–2	Friendly	Aitken 2	8000
1899	West Bromwich Albion	(a)	1–1	Division One	Peddie (pen)	4000

Debut for Dave Gardner.

1900 Bob McKay born, Govan, Scotland.

| 1901 | Middlesbrough | (a) | 1–2 | Friendly | Orr | 8000 |
| 1903 | Aston Villa | (h) | 1–1 | Division One | Templeton | 8000 |

Debut for Jimmy Howie.

| 1905 | Sunderland | (a) | 2–3 | Division One | Orr, Howie | 30000 |

First of nine appearances for Harry Hardinge at centre-forward, during which time he only netted once and was subsequently sold to Sheffield United.

| 1908 | Bradford City | (h) | 1–0 | Division One | Veitch | 26000 |

The only appearance of Bob Blanthorne, who sadly broke his leg and never played for United again. Fellow debutant Jimmy Stewart was rather more successful, netting 53 goals in 138 first-team games.

1908 United's reserves were at the Victoria Ground, Hartlepool, to play the first match on what had formerly been a rugby pitch against the newly formed Hartlepools United.

1909 A Newcastle reserve team travelled to Carlisle and played before a crowd of 3,000 to officially open Brunton Park.

| 1911 | Bolton Wanderers | (a) | 2–0 | Division One | Stewart 2 | 30000 |

A debut appearance for Jimmy Hay, the former Celtic and Scotland captain. Also making his entrance was Bill Kelly, who had returned to his native Tyneside after a spell with Watford.

| 1912 | Bolton Wanderers | (a) | 2–1 | Division One | McDonald, Rutherford | 30000 |

Scoring debut for John McDonald, at outside-left, after his move from Liverpool.

1914	West Bromwich Albion	(h)	1–2	Division One	Hibbert	15000
1922	Everton	(a)	2–3	Division One	Harris, McDonald	35000
1925	Glasgow Rangers	(h)	0–2	Friendly	No Scorer	10000

1925 Ernie Taylor born, Sunderland.

1931	Birmingham	(a)	1–4	Division One	Boyd	20000
1933	Leeds United	(a)	0–3	Division One	No Scorer	18000
1939	Swansea Town	(h)	8–1	Division Two	Bowden 3, Pearson 2, Hamilton, Scott, Cairns	14000

The last game of the abortive 1939–40 league season. Bowden never played football again and his hat-trick was expunged from the records.

| 1950 | Portsmouth | (a) | 0–0 | Division One | No Scorer | 43244 |
| 1953 | Liverpool | (h) | 4–0 | Division One | Keeble, Milburn, Mitchell 2 | 48439 |

1953 Paul Cannell born, Newcastle.

| 1959 | Birmingham City | (h) | 1–0 | Division One | White | 35395 |
| 1961 | Plymouth Argyle | (h) | 0–2 | Division Two | No Scorer | 28235 |

1967	Stoke City	(h) 1–1	Division One	Davies	38924
1968	Southport	(a) 2–0	League Cup 2nd Round	Robson (pen), Sinclair	8521
1969	Sheffield United	(a) 0–2	League Cup 2nd Round	No Scorer	22101
1970	West Bromwich Albion	(a) 2–1	Division One	Dyson, OG	25183
1972	Crystal Palace	(a) 1–2	Division One	Tudor	21749
1978	Cambridge United	(a) 0–0	Division Two	No Scorer	8174

Steady debut for the stylish John Brownlie.

| 1980 | Bury | (a) 0–1 | League Cup 2nd Round 2nd Leg | No Scorer | 4348 |

Caretaker manager Joe Harvey had to suffer the indignity of a cup exit to another lower-league team. Former hero Wyn Davies watched from the stand and probably couldn't believe what he was seeing. Darren Bradley scored the only goal.

1981 A goalless draw at Gallowgate against Bury reserves gave Central League watchers an opportunity to see Australian international trialist George Christopoulos in action. He was to return home after a protracted saga failed to secure the necessary work permit.

| 1989 | Oldham Athletic | (h) 2–1 | Division Two | Quinn 2 | 21092 |
| 1992 | Luton Town | (h) 2–0 | Division One | Clark, Kelly | 27054 |

SEPTEMBER 3RD

| 1898 | Wolverhampton Wanderers | (h) 2–4 | Division Two | Peddie 2 | 20000 |

Debuts for William Higgins and Matt Kingsley as United began their Second Division career with a loss. The notorious sloping Gallowgate pitch had been levelled in the summer and United were no longer the invincible force at home they had been.

| 1904 | Arsenal | (h) 3–0 | Division One | Orr 2, Rutherford | 21897 |

Debut of Bill McCracken, prime exponent of the offside law.

| 1906 | Sheffield Wednesday | (a) 2–2 | Division One | Appleyard 2 | 8000 |

Debut at outside-right for Robert Blackburn.

1910	Bristol City	(h) 0–1	Division One	No Scorer	26000
1919	West Bromwich Albion	(h) 0–2	Division One	No Scorer	50000
1921	Huddersfield Town	(h) 1–2	Division One	McDonald	50000
1927	Tottenham Hotspur	(h) 4–1	Division One	Seymour 2, McDonald (pen), Gallacher	40000
1930	Chelsea	(h) 1–0	Division One	Cape	68586
1932	Liverpool	(h) 4–3	Division One	Allen, Lang, McMenemy, OG	28000
1938	Sheffield United	(a) 0–0	Division Two	No Scorer	30000
1947	Chesterfield	(h) 2–3	Division Two	Bentley, Milburn	58334

Belated debut for Norman Dodgin, who had represented United during the hostilities.

1948 Death of Jack Peart, 60.

1949	Aston Villa	(h) 3–2	Division One	Milburn 3 (1 pen)	57669
1955	Burnley	(h) 3–1	Division One	Davies, Mitchell, Scoular	41272
1958	Blackpool	(h) 1–0	Division One	White	44979
1960	Nottingham Forest	(a) 2–0	Division One	Gibson, OG	23806
1966	Manchester United	(a) 2–3	Division One	Craig, McGarry	44448

1975 Another fruitless night for Malcolm Macdonald, who missed two good chances as England won 2–1 against Switzerland in Basle. Keegan and Channon again got the goals, and Keegan also missed a penalty.

| 1977 | West Ham United | (h) 2–3 | Division One | Burns, Cassidy | 26942 |
| 1983 | Oldham Athletic | (h) 3–0 | Division Two | Waddle, McDermott, Mills | 22573 |

1986   Queens Park   (h) 0–2   Division One   No Scorer   23080
Rangers

1988   Tottenham Hotspur (h) 2–2   Division One   Thorn, D. Jackson   33508
A 2–0 half-time lead was wiped out by Chris Waddle, who scored straight from the second-half kick-off, and Wearsider Terry Fenwick, with a header. The returning Paul Gascoigne was pelted with confectionery and abuse and substituted in the second half.

1993   Future Magpie Keith Gillespie was loaned out by Manchester United to neighbours Wigan Athletic. He made eight appearances for the Springfield Park club.

1996   Chris Holland became the latest youngster to be farmed out to another club for match practice, as he went to Birmingham City. The move was eventually made permanent for a fee of £600,000.

1997   The return of reserve-team football tempted 10,110 spectators to a Central League game against Doncaster Rovers. With only a handful of turnstiles open, the kick-off had to be delayed 30 minutes to get everyone in. The game finished 3–0, with Ian Rush hitting two and Paul Arnison the third.

SEPTEMBER 4TH

1893   Trafalgar   (a) 2–0   Friendly   Pattison, Thompson   800
1895   Glasgow Celtic   (h) 3–0   Friendly   Logan 2, Milne   6000
1897   Woolwich Arsenal (h) 4–1   Division Two   Wardrope 2, Campbell, 10000
                                                 Lennox
Debuts for Johnny Harvey, James Jackson, Johnny Campbell (who scored) and Tommy Ghee, who subsequently became a trainer and a member of the backroom staff at United.

1907   Notts County   (h) 1–1   Division One   Rutherford   25000
1909   Blackburn Rovers (a) 0–2   Division One   No Scorer   16000
Debut for 16-year-old Jock Finlay, who served United as player, coach and trainer.

1910   Heworth League XI (a) 3–0   Friendly   Metcalf 3   3000
1910   Ike Keen born, Walker.
1920   West Bromwich   (a) 0–0   Division One   No Scorer   35000
Albion
Debut for Robert McIntosh, at right-half.

1926   Bolton Wanderers (a) 1–2   Division One   Seymour   25000
1928   Death of James Raine, 42.
1929   Blackburn Rovers (h) 5–1   Division One   Gallacher, Lang,   40000
                                                 McDonald, Urwin,
                                             J.R. Richardson
Goalscoring debut for Jimmy Richardson, at inside-right.

1935   Barnsley   (h) 3–0   Division Two   Cairns 2, Pearson   21000
1937   Sheffield United (h) 6–0   Division Two   Pearson 2, Livingstone 2, 22000
                                                 Imrie (pen), Gordon
1940   Jimmy Gibson born, Belfast.
1941   George Dalton born, West Moor.
1948   Burnley   (a) 3–0   Division One   Donaldson 2, Milburn   32947
1954   Preston North End (a) 3–3   Division One   Hannah, Milburn, White 36600
All the threes for goalkeeper Stewart Mitchell, born on 3.3.33 and conceding three on his debut for United.

1957   Sheffield Wednesday (a) 0–1   Division One   No Scorer   23060
1962   Scunthorpe United (a) 1–2   Division Two   Kerray   13953
1963   Middlesbrough   (h) 2–0   Division Two   Penman, McGarry   56918
1964   Jackie Milburn resigned as manager of Ipswich Town.
1965   Northampton Town (h) 2–0   Division One   Suddick, Cummings   28051
Ollie Burton became the first substitute used by Newcastle when he replaced Jim Iley.

1966   John Beresford born, Sheffield.
1971   West Ham United (h) 2–2   Division One   Tudor, Cassidy   31972

1973	Ipswich Town	(a) 3–1	Division One	Robson, Cassidy, Smith	21696

1974 Keith Robson left United for West Ham in a £60,000 transfer.

| 1976 | Middlesbrough | (a) 0–1 | Division One | No Scorer | 26000 |

1980 The United Board announced that the new manager was to be Chesterfield boss and former Sunderland coach Arthur Cox.

1982	Bolton Wanderers	(a) 1–3	Division Two	Keegan (pen)	17707
1984	Arsenal	(a) 0–2	Division One	No Scorer	37078
1985	Manchester United	(a) 0–3	Division One	No Scorer	51102
1991	Plymouth Argyle	(h) 2–2	Division Two	Carr, Quinn	19543

The search for a first home win went on, but it could have been worse, as Plymouth were two ahead after an hour, despite their goalkeeper having been taken off injured and replaced by an outfield player. After the opening goal, a home fan had to be removed from the pitch after remonstrating with the goalscorer. Eventually Newcastle made a fight of it and pulled back to draw with two goals in the last ten minutes.

| 1996 | Sunderland | (a) 2–1 | Premier League | Ferdinand, Beardsley | 22037 |

No away fans at the last Tyne–Wear derby to be held at Roker Park, but about 100 actually got in, many well disguised. The game was screened live at the Newcastle Arena for those who couldn't hide their allegiance or get a ticket.

SEPTEMBER 5TH

1894	Sunderland	(a) 1–4	Friendly	Smith	4000
1896	Small Heath	(a) 1–3	Division Two	Thompson	4000

Debuts for Scotsmen Dick Smellie and John White at the Muntz Street ground of Small Heath. Goalkeeper Charlie Watts also made his first appearance.

1899	Kaffirs (South Africa)	(h) 6–3	Friendly	Ghee, Wardrope, Stevenson, Niblo 2, OG	6000
1900	Middlesbrough	(a) 2–1	Friendly	Gardner, Laidlaw	
1903	West Bromwich Albion	(a) 2–1	Division One	Appleyard, Rutherford	15000
1908	Leicester Fosse	(h) 2–0	Division One	Howie, Veitch	32000

Debut for Stanley Allan.

| 1914 | Everton | (h) 0–1 | Division One | No Scorer | 12000 |
| 1925 | Notts County | (h) 6–3 | Division One | Mitchell, McDonald, N. Harris, Cowan 2, OG | 35000 |

The only appearance of goalkeeper Allan Taylor.

| 1927 | Derby County | (a) 1–1 | Division One | Seymour | 21000 |
| 1931 | Grimsby Town | (a) 2–1 | Division One | Boyd, J.R. Richardson | 12000 |

Debuts for David Bell and Harry McMenemy.

| 1936 | Sheffield United | (a) 1–2 | Division Two | McMenemy | 20000 |

1939 Tommy Knox born, Glasgow.

1946	Nottingham Forest	(a) 2–0	Division Two	Bentley, Harvey	32691
1949	Blackpool	(a) 0–0	Division One	No Scorer	25000
1951	West Bromwich Albion	(a) 3–3	Division One	Hannah, G. Robledo 2	29311

United managed to claim a point despite being behind within a minute, courtesy of an Alf McMichael own goal.

1953	Bolton Wanderers	(h) 2–3	Division One	Hannah, Mitchell	61321
1956	Birmingham City	(a) 1–6	Division One	Keeble	32506
1959	Preston North End	(h) 1–2	Division One	Eastham	37683
1960	West Bromwich Albion	(a) 0–6	Division One	No Scorer	22661
1964	Huddersfield Town	(a) 1–0	Division Two	McGarry	8770

1964 Liam O'Brien born, Dublin.

| 1970 | Derby County | (a) 2–1 | Division One | Young, Dyson | 30466 |

| 1972 | Port Vale | (a) 3–1 | League Cup 2nd Round | Macdonald, Barrowclough, Craig | 10370 |
| 1979 | Sunderland | (h) 2–2 | League Cup 2nd Round 2nd Leg | Shoulder, Boam | 30533 |

Alan Brown hit a dramatic late equaliser to send this game to extra time and ultimately a dreaded shootout. Jim Pearson had the misfortune to see Siddall save his penalty and it was to be the last ball he ever kicked for United's first team, being forced to retire through injury the following February. United's penalty scorers were Shoulder, Withe, Martin, Davies, Brownlie and Barton.

| 1981 | Queens Park Rangers | (a) 0–3 | Division Two | No Scorer | 14176 |

Baptism of fire for debutant Peter Haddock, who had to cope not only with the pressures of being a first-team player but also with the dreadful plastic pitch Rangers had installed.

| 1987 | Wimbledon | (h) 1–2 | Division One | McDonald (pen) | 22734 |
| 1992 | Bristol Rovers | (a) 2–1 | Division One | Sheedy, O'Brien | 7487 |

SEPTEMBER 6TH

1893	Sunderland	(h) 1–3	Friendly	Thompson	3000
1897	Hibernian	(h) 1–1	Friendly	Stott	4000
1902	Stoke	(h) 5–0	Division One	Rutherford, McColl 2, Orr 2	17000

Debut for William Agnew.

1905	Manchester City	(h) 2–2	Division One	Gosnell, Orr	20000
1909	Everton	(a) 4–1	Division One	Wilson, Stewart, Howie, Rutherford	30000
1911	Everton	(h) 2–0	Division One	Low, Stewart	20000
1913	Sunderland	(a) 2–1	Division One	Hall, King	40000

A goal on his debut for Tom Hall against the local rivals he'd just left.

| 1919 | Arsenal | (h) 3–1 | Division One | Wilson 2, Hudspeth (pen) | 45000 |
| 1922 | Birmingham | (h) 0–0 | Division One | No Scorer | 20000 |

First of only two appearances for James Keen.

1924	Aston Villa	(a) 0–0	Division One	No Scorer	40000
1926	Burnley	(a) 3–3	Division One	Gallacher, McDonald, Seymour	28000
1930	Grimsby Town	(h) 1–2	Division One	Lindsay	30000
1933	Blackburn Rovers	(h) 3–1	Division One	Lang 2, McMenemy	18000
1937	Barnsley	(a) 0–3	Division Two	No Scorer	9000

The only first-team appearance of stand-in centre-forward John Sheil for the Magpies.

1943 Bobby Saxton born, Bagby, Yorkshire. Coach and caretaker manager for one game.

1947	Brentford	(h) 1–0	Division Two	Woodburn	56622
1950	Huddersfield Town	(h) 6–0	Division One	Milburn 3, Mitchell, G. Robledo, Taylor	34031
1952	Burnley	(a) 1–2	Division One	G. Robledo	35000

Debuts for Tommy Casey and stand-in goalkeeper Bobby Robinson. Following an injury to first-choice Ronnie Simpson, Robinson was signed from Sunderland as cover.

1956 Steve Hardwick born, Mansfield.

1958	Tottenham Hotspur	(a) 3–1	Division One	McGuigan, White 2	41805
1961	Sunderland	(a) 1–0	Friendly	Leek	18239
1966	West Bromwich Albion	(h) 1–3	Division One	Robson	24748
1967	Manchester City	(a) 0–2	Division One	No Scorer	29978
1969	Ipswich Town	(a) 0–2	Division One	No Scorer	18229

1970 Stephane Guivarc'h born, Concarneau, France.

| 1975 | Aston Villa | (h) 3–0 | Division One | T. Craig, Macdonald 2 | 35604 |
| 1977 | Hibernian | (a) 0–3 | Friendly | No Scorer | 5000 |

1980	Cardiff City	(h) 2–1	Division Two	Clarke, Shoulder (pen)	15787
1983	Middlesbrough	(a) 2–3	Division Two	Mills, Keegan	19648
1986	Sheffield Wednesday	(h) 2–3	Division One	Allon, Scott	22010

Goalscoring debut for central defender Kevin Scott, but two goals from Carl Shutt and one from Mel Sterland gave the Owls, who played in a peculiar lilac kit, the points.

1996 Frustrated at a lack of match practice since the reserves were scrapped, Darren Huckerby went on loan to Millwall, where he was an instant success.

SEPTEMBER 7TH

| 1895 | Loughborough Town | (h) 3–0 | Division Two | Wardrope, Aitken, Logan | 7000 |

A tartan invasion, as no fewer than seven Scots-born players made their debuts: Andy Aitken, James Logan, Bob Foyers, John Henderson, William Miller, William McKay and Willie Wardrope. The rest of the team was composed of local lads Willie Thompson and Jimmy Stott and two more Scotsmen, Willie Graham and Bob McDermid.

| 1896 | Edinburgh St Bernard's | (h) 0–3 | Friendly | No Scorer | 4500 |
| 1898 | Grimsby Town | (h) 6–2 | Friendly | Milne 2, Niblo 2, Peddie, Aitken | 4000 |

1900 Willie Wilson born, Port Seaton, Scotland.

| 1901 | Blackburn Rovers | (a) 0–0 | Division One | No Scorer | 7000 |

Debuts for Bob Bennie, Ronald Orr and Richard Roberts.

| 1904 | Middlesbrough | (a) 1–2 | Friendly | Appleyard | 2000 |
| 1907 | Sheffield Wednesday | (a) 1–3 | Division One | Orr (pen) | 20000 |

Debut for Alex Hall.

1909	Bolton Wanderers	(a) 4–0	Division One	Shepherd 3, Rutherford	18000
1912	Sunderland	(h) 1–1	Division One	Shepherd	54200
1921	Everton	(a) 3–2	Division One	Harris, McDonald 2	30000
1929	Grimsby Town	(a) 0–4	Division One	No Scorer	22000
1935	Tottenham Hotspur	(a) 2–1	Division Two	Cairns 2	48112
1938	West Bromwich Albion	(a) 2–5	Division Two	Mooney, Stubbins	17000

1943 Dave Turner born, Retford, Nottinghamshire.

| 1946 | Swansea Town | (h) 1–1 | Division Two | Woodburn | 54966 |

1953 Chris Guthrie born, Dilston, Northumberland.

1955	West Bromwich Albion	(a) 1–1	Division One	Davies	22000
1957	Birmingham City	(a) 4–1	Division One	R. Mitchell (pen), Curry 2, Hill	29784
1963	Charlton Athletic	(h) 5–0	Division Two	Penman 2, Thomas, Suddick 2	33225

1963 John Barnes born, Kingston, Jamaica.

| 1968 | Coventry City | (a) 1–2 | Division One | Sinclair | 34361 |
| 1974 | Derby County | (a) 2–2 | Division One | Macdonald, Burns | 21197 |

1976 Garry Brady born, Glasgow.

| 1985 | Tottenham Hotspur | (a) 1–5 | Division One | Davies | 23883 |

Sole outing for Rob McKinnon, at left-back, and the only goal Alan Davies scored while at United.

| 1991 | Tranmere Rovers | (a) 2–3 | Division Two | O'Brien, Clark | 11465 |

With the scores level at 2–2, Pavel Srnicek banished the memory of the previous year's penalty misery when he saved John Aldridge's spot kick at the same end of Prenton Park. Unfortunately Rovers won it from a set piece in the last minute. The game had exploded into life just before half-time when, after having gifted Rovers an opener, O'Brien and Clark scored within a minute to give United a completely unexpected half-time advantage.

1994   England defeated the USA (and Brad Friedel) 2–0 at Wembley, with a fine performance from Newcastle's Barry Venison.

1996   Tottenham Hotspur   (a) 2–1   Premier League   Ferdinand 2   32535

SEPTEMBER 8TH

1894   Burton Swifts   (h) 6–3   Division Two   Wallace 2, Smith 2, Willis 2   6000
1900   Blackburn Rovers   (a) 0–0   Division One   No Scorer   10000
1905   Joe Cassidy born, Motherwell, Scotland.
1906   Birmingham   (a) 4–2   Division One   Brown 3, Veitch (pen)   17000
       A hat-trick on his debut for Harry Brown, signed in the close season from Southampton.
1919   West Bromwich   (a) 0–3   Division One   No Scorer   21000
       Albion
1920   Everton   (h) 2–0   Division One   Smailes, Finlay   35000
1923   Sheffield United   (h) 2–2   Division One   Harris, Hudspeth (pen)   40000
1924   West Ham United   (a) 0–0   Division One   No Scorer   23000
1928   Bury   (h) 2–1   Division One   Gallacher 2   20000
1934   Fulham   (a) 2–3   Division Two   J.R. Richardson 2   30000
1948   Aston Villa   (h) 2–1   Division One   Gibson, Milburn   56110
1951   Preston North End   (a) 2–1   Division One   G. Robledo 2   39500
       Debut for John Duncan, who managed three goals in only six appearances for United. A knee injury hampered his progress, and after an unsuccessful attempt to convert into a goalkeeper, he retired from football and returned to his native Scotland. Eddie Quigley blasted a penalty wide for the home team.
1954   Aston Villa   (h) 5–3   Division One   Milburn, White 4   39960
       A rollercoaster afternoon, as Milburn netted within the first 90 seconds and White had a hat-trick by the 31st minute. However, Villa hit back, helped by a Cowell own goal, before a White header ended the scoring.
1956   Manchester United   (h) 1–1   Division One   Milburn   50133
       Gordon Hughes and Dick Keith made their debuts.
1957   Alan Guy born, Jarrow.
1962   Plymouth Argyle   (h) 3–1   Division Two   Fell, Kerray 2   34375
       A debut for the prematurely balding Jim Iley.
1964   Northampton Town   (a) 0–1   Division Two   No Scorer   15365
       A midweek match at the County Ground, rescheduled from the opening Saturday of the season when the adjoining cricket pitch had hosted a Northamptonshire match.
1965   Manchester United   (h) 1–2   Division One   Hockey   57436
       The first time George Best faced Newcastle in a First Division game. He didn't score, but Herd and Law did.
1969   Gary Speed born, Mancot, Wales.
1970   Bristol Rovers   (a) 1–2   League Cup   Dyson   16824
                                    2nd Round
       United's dismal run in the League Cup was extended by two Bobby Jones goals as they were humbled by Third Division opposition.
1971   Halifax Town   (h) 2–1   League Cup   Macdonald, Cassidy   19930
                                  2nd Round
1973   Sheffield United   (a) 1–1   Division One   Robson   26897
1976   Barely a month after the departure of 'Supermac', Pat Howard followed him to Highbury, joining Arsenal in a £50,000 move.
1979   Orient   (a) 4–1   Division Two   Cartwright, Hibbitt,   5700
                                         Withe, Shoulder (pen)
1982   Middlesbrough   (h) 1–1   Division Two   Channon   27984
       On-trial Mick Channon treated St James' Park to his trademark windmill salute after scoring on his debut.
1984   Manchester United   (a) 0–5   Division One   No Scorer   54915

1987   Mirandinha struck his first goal since joining Newcastle; unfortunately it was for a Football League XI, who played a 2–2 draw with their Irish League counterparts at Windsor Park, Belfast.

1990   Millwall   (h) 1–2   Division Two   Quinn   23922
Goals from future Magpie Malcolm Allen and Teddy Sheringham took the points south as Millwall extended their winning start to the season. Winger Jimmy Carter caused United problems all afternoon, and subsequently moved to Arsenal.

1990   Former United and England left-back Alan Kennedy marked his 500th league appearance by scoring an own goal for his current team Wrexham, at home to Aldershot.

SEPTEMBER 9TH

1893   Middlesbrough   (a) 2–2   Friendly   Crielly, Crate   1400
1899   Everton   (h) 2–0   Division One   Peddie, Niblo   25000
Debut for Jack Fraser, at outside-left.

1905   Birmingham   (h) 2–2   Division One   Orr, Howie   23912
First of two appearances in United colours for Joe Donnachie, who subsequently became one of the first Roman Catholics to appear for Glasgow Rangers.

1908   Bristol City   (h) 2–1   Division One   Howie 2   22000
1911   Bradford City   (h) 0–2   Division One   No Scorer   40000
1914   Sheffield Wednesday   (h) 0–0   Division One   No Scorer   8000
Debut for Curtis Booth.

1922   Sheffield United   (h) 3–0   Division One   McDonald, Harris,   35000
                                                            Hudspeth (pen)

1925   Blackburn Rovers   (h) 1–7   Division One   McDonald   22000
The first of 127 appearances for debutant goalkeeper Willie Wilson. Rovers striker Harper netted five.

1929   West Ham United   (a) 1–5   Division One   Gallacher   20000
Albert Fidler made his United debut in goal. In his five games, he watched 17 goals flash past him (although he finished on the winning side twice). He was probably glad to be relieved of his position when Albert McInroy regained fitness. George Nevin made a similarly forgettable debut in the defence.

1931   Stan Keery born, Derby.

1933   Derby County   (h) 1–1   Division One   J.R. Richardson   25000
Debut for John Kelly, at centre-forward.

1935   Barnsley   (a) 2–3   Division Two   Cairns, McMenemy   13000
1936   West Ham United   (h) 5–3   Division Two   Cairns 4, McMenemy   22500
1943   Frank Clark born, Highfield, Gateshead.
1950   Chelsea   (h) 3–1   Division One   Milburn, Walker 2   56903
1953   West Bromwich   (a) 2–2   Division One   Keeble, Mitchell   40220
        Albion
1959   West Bromwich   (a) 2–2   Division One   Eastham, White   28200
        Albion
1961   Huddersfield Town   (a) 1–2   Division Two   White   18087
1962   Kevin Brock born, Middleton Stoney, Oxfordshire.
1967   Nottingham Forest   (a) 0–4   Division One   No Scorer   30155
1967   Bob Stokoe was relieved of his duties as Charlton Athletic manager.
1972   Arsenal   (h) 2–1   Division One   Macdonald, Craig   23878
1978   Blackburn Rovers   (h) 3–1   Division Two   Withe 2, McGhee   23751
1989   Bournemouth   (a) 1–2   Division Two   Quinn   9982
1995   Southampton   (a) 0–1   Premier League   No Scorer   15237
Jim Magilton ensured yet another Dell defeat.

SEPTEMBER 10TH

1885   Albert Shepherd born, Great Lever, Lancashire.

1898	Everton	(a) 0–3	Division Two	No Scorer	16000
1904	Derby County	(a) 1–1	Division One	Appleyard	12000
1910	Oldham Athletic	(a) 2–0	Division One	Shepherd 2	34000
1913	Players' Union XI	(h) 1–3	Friendly	Higgins	8000

Players' Union benefit match, played against the wishes of both the Football League and the Football Association.

1921	Burnley	(a) 0–2	Division One	No Scorer	30000
1924	Blackburn Rovers	(h) 4–0	Division One	Harris 3, Hudspeth (pen)	30000

Debut for Tom Urwin, at outside-right. He also appeared for Middlesbrough and Sunderland.

1927	Manchester United	(a) 7–1	Division One	Seymour 2, McDonald, Gallacher, McKay, Harris, Unwin	50000
1928	Burnley	(a) 3–4	Division One	Lang, Hudspeth 2 (2 pens)	20000
1930	Birmingham	(a) 1–1	Division One	Lindsay	20000
1932	Leicester City	(a) 3–0	Division One	Boyd 2, Lang	20000
1938	Burnley	(h) 3–2	Division Two	Bowden, Cairns, Stubbins	30000
1947	Birmingham City	(a) 0–0	Division Two	No Scorer	51704
1949	Charlton Athletic	(a) 3–6	Division One	Milburn 2, Mitchell	42000
1952	Sunderland	(h) 2–2	Division One	Davies, OG	60727

Newcastle's equaliser was an own goal from Jack Stelling.

1955	Luton Town	(a) 2–4	Division One	Milburn 2	25719
1956	Morton	(a) 3–1	Friendly	Milburn 2, Davies	6000

After making his first-team debut two days previously, Gordon Hughes broke his leg in this testimonial match at Cappielow Park, Greenock.

1958	Chelsea	(a) 5–6	Division One	Wright 2, White, Davies, Franks	46601

An exceptional game, with a 40-yard thunderbolt from Albert Franks giving United a 5–3 advantage, only for Gordon Hughes to sustain an injury and have to leave the field.

1960	Manchester City	(h) 1–3	Division One	Marshall	25904
1961	Ian Stewart born, Belfast.				
1966	Burnley	(h) 1–1	Division One	McGarry	25485

Debut for Stuart Alderson.

1974	Nottingham Forest	(a) 1–1	League Cup 2nd Round	Macdonald	14183
1975	Southport	(h) 6–0	League Cup 2nd Round	Gowling 4, Cannell 2	23352
1977	West Bromwich Albion	(h) 0–3	Division One	No Scorer	22705

United were taken apart by the speed and poise of the Albion, most notably from Cyrille Regis and Laurie Cunningham, no doubt to the disgust of the peddlers of racist literature who blighted the ground at this time.

1983	Grimsby Town	(a) 1–1	Division Two	Keegan	9000
1988	Derby County	(a) 0–2	Division One	No Scorer	16014

The second goal was scored by former Magpie Paul Goddard.

1994	Chelsea	(h) 4–2	Premier League	Cole 2, Fox, Lee	34435

A wonderful day began with physio Derek Wright accepting Keegan's latest manager-of-the-month award. United played Hooper in goal in the absence of suspended Pav, with veteran Burridge on the bench. An early rocket from Cole was equalised by former Magpie Gavin Peacock before Robert Lee saw a penalty saved. Fortunately, Fox was on hand to knock in the rebound. Finally Dennis Wise was sent off for saying nasty things to the referee's assistant.

1996	Halmstads (Sweden)	(h) 4–0	UEFA Cup 1st Round 1st Leg	Albert, Beardsley, Ferdinand, Asprilla	28124

SEPTEMBER 11TH

1895	Sunderland	(a) 3–5	Friendly	McKay, Graham, Unknown Scorer	5000
1897	Walsall	(a) 3–2	Division Two	Wardrope, OG 2	4000

Debut for Richard Allan.

1909	Nottingham Forest	(h) 1–2	Division One	Shepherd	25000
1912	Bolton Wanderers	(h) 2–1	Division One	G. Wilson, McTavish	12000
1920	Preston North End	(h) 4–2	Division One	Hagan 2, Harris, OG	48000
1926	Manchester United	(h) 4–2	Division One	Gallacher, McDonald 2, Seymour	29000
1937	Tottenham Hotspur	(a) 2–2	Division Two	Park, Imrie (pen)	26125
1946	Coventry City	(h) 3–1	Division Two	Wayman, Stobbart 2 (1 pen)	55313

Debuts for Geordie Stobbart, who netted twice, and Tommy Walker.

1948	Stoke City	(h) 2–2	Division One	Walker, Donaldson (pen)	59265
1954	Burnley	(h) 2–1	Division One	Milburn, R. Mitchell	47346
1957	Portsmouth	(h) 2–0	Division One	Davies, R. Mitchell	39027
1963	Southampton	(h) 2–2	Division Two	Thomas, McGarry (pen)	42879
1965	Stoke City	(a) 0–4	Division One	No Scorer	25702
1968	Feyenoord (Holland)	(h) 4–0	Fairs Cup 1st Round 1st Leg	Scott, Robson, Gibb, Davies	46348

A sensational opening to the European adventure, as the Dutch league leaders were swept aside. The third goal was credited to Gibb but deflected by Marinus Israel past his own keeper.

1971	Manchester City	(a) 1–2	Division One	Macdonald	32710
1975	Chris Holland born, Whalley, Lancashire.				
1976	Manchester United	(h) 2–2	Division One	Burns, Cannell	39037
1982	Chelsea	(h) 1–1	Division Two	Clarke	29136
1995	St James' Park welcomed Prime Minister John Major, who stopped off while on a visit to the north-east. He was presented with a home shirt bearing the legend 'Major 10'.				

SEPTEMBER 12TH

1894	Hibernian	(h) 1–3	Friendly	Campbell	1500
1896	Small Heath	(h) 4–3	Division Two	Smellie 3, Lennox	10853
1903	Small Heath	(h) 3–1	Division One	McColl, Appleyard, Howie	17000
1908	Woolwich Arsenal	(a) 2–1	Division One	Rutherford, Stewart	20000

Debut for Andrew Anderson.

1914	Chelsea	(a) 3–0	Division One	Hall 2, Hibbert	20000
1923	Bolton Wanderers	(h) 1–0	Division One	Seymour	25000
1925	Aston Villa	(a) 2–2	Division One	Hudspeth (pen), OG	45000
1927	Andy Graver born, Craghead, Durham.				
1931	Chelsea	(h) 4–1	Division One	Boyd, Lang, J.R. Richardson 2	30000

No place for Hughie Gallacher in the visitors' line-up, left behind in disgrace after having been up in front of west London magistrates on a charge of being drunk and disorderly.

1934	Blackpool	(h) 4–1	Division Two	Boyd, Lang, J.R. Richardson, Weaver	30000

Debut for Tom Swinburne, between the posts.

1936	Tottenham Hotspur	(h) 0–1	Division Two	No Scorer	29000
1951	Celtic	(a) 3–3	Friendly	G. Robledo, Mitchell, Taylor	61300

Upset at not being picked for the starting line-up, Ernie Taylor submitted a transfer request and within weeks had joined Blackpool.

1953	Preston North End	(a) 2–2	Division One	Keeble, Milburn	35000

Debut for Joseph Cooper, who spent seven years at United for six appearances in the first team.

1959	Leicester City	(a) 2–0	Division One	Bell 2	24318
1962	Derby County	(h) 0–0	Division Two	No Scorer	34465
1964	Coventry City	(h) 2–0	Division Two	Taylor, Thomas	37481
1970	Liverpool	(h) 0–0	Division One	No Scorer	35595
1973	Ipswich Town	(h) 3–1	Division One	Macdonald 2, OG	30604
1975	Carl Serrant born, Bradford.				
1981	Cambridge United	(h) 1–0	Division Two	Trewick	14666
1987	Manchester United	(a) 2–2	Division One	Mirandinha 2	45137

1988   Opposing United's reserves in a 1–1 draw at Leicester City was winger Lee Payne, on trial from Barnet. While the Foxes dithered, Newcastle nipped in to secure his services for a fee of £25,000.

1992	Portsmouth	(h) 3–1	Division One	Quinn 2, Kelly	29885

SEPTEMBER 13TH

1902	Everton	(a) 1–0	Division One	Stewart	20000
1905	Sheffield Wednesday	(h) 0–3	Division One	No Scorer	20000
1909	Ray Bowden born, Looe, Cornwall.				
1911	Saltburn	(a) 6–2	Friendly	Kelly 3, Wilson 3	1000
1913	Everton	(h) 0–1	Division One	No Scorer	30000

Debut for Tommy Goodwill, at outside-left.

1919	Chelsea	(a) 0–0	Division One	No Scorer	60000
1924	Arsenal	(h) 2–2	Division One	McDonald, Mooney	22000
1930	Manchester United	(a) 7–4	Division One	Starling 2, Lindsay, J.R. Richardson, Cape 3	7000
1947	Leicester City	(a) 2–2	Division Two	Donaldson, Shackleton	35472
1948	Aston Villa	(a) 4–2	Division One	Donaldson, Gibson, Milburn, Walker	55000
1950	Huddersfield Town	(a) 0–0	Division One	No Scorer	30323
1952	Preston North End	(h) 4–3	Division One	Davies 2, G. Robledo 2	52020
1954	Aston Villa	(a) 2–1	Division One	Milburn, Mitchell	20000
1958	Manchester United	(h) 1–1	Division One	Davies	60670
1961	Scunthorpe United	(h) 2–0	League Cup 1st Round	Hale, Allchurch	14372
1964	Paul Bodin born, Cardiff.				
1966	Leeds United	(a) 0–1	League Cup 2nd Round	No Scorer	18131
1967	Lincoln City	(a) 1–2	League Cup 2nd Round	Burton	15454

A debut for Eric Ross, in midfield.

1969	Derby County	(h) 0–1	Division One	No Scorer	39382

A single Roy McFarland strike was enough to take Derby to the top of Division One.

1972	Ayr United	(a) 0–0	Texaco Cup	No Scorer	8500
1975	Everton	(a) 0–3	Division One	No Scorer	28938
1980	Queens Park Rangers	(a) 2–1	Division Two	Hibbitt, Boam	10865

The first game of Arthur Cox's managerial reign, captured by *Match of the Day* cameras. Boam gave the Magpies an interval lead that Bob Hazell cancelled out. Then Terry Hibbitt, who had been so anonymous that his number was being waved from the touchline to come off, struck after a mix-up in the box to win it. Unfortunately the referee had already noted the substitution, so Hibbitt was forced to leave the pitch and be replaced by Cartwright.

1986	Coventry City	(a) 0–3	Division One	No Scorer	11370
1989	Oxford United	(a) 1–2	Division Two	Quinn	7313
1993	Sheffield Wednesday	(h) 4–2	Premier League	Cole 2, Mathie, Allen	33519

A memorable debut for Alex Mathie, who made a goal and then scored with a superb effort at the Leazes end. Northumberland-born Andy Sinton scored twice for the Owls, but United, playing in their blue away strips, were deserved winners.

1994 Royal Antwerp (a) 5–0 UEFA Cup 1st Lee 3, Sellars, Watson 19700
(Belgium) Round 1st Leg
Fairy-tale stuff, as Robert Lee scored the first of a hat-trick of headers within the first minute to send the travelling Toon fans barmy. Despite scaremongering by the club, tickets were on sale for the away sections right up to kick-off and the official party of 3,500 was matched by the number of independent travellers.

1997 Wimbledon (h) 1–3 Premier League Barton 36526
Goals from Cort, Perry and Ekoku sealed a below-par performance from the whole team. John Barnes made his first appearance.

SEPTEMBER 14TH

1895 Liverpool (a) 1–5 Division Two Logan 10000
1901 Stoke (h) 5–1 Division One Roberts 2, Orr 2, Niblo 20000
Debut for Willie Stewart, at outside-right.
1907 Chelsea (h) 1–0 Division One Orr 35000
1912 Oldham Athletic (a) 0–1 Division One No Scorer 30000
1927 Derby County (h) 4–3 Division One Gallacher, McKay 3 37000
1929 Leicester City (h) 2–1 Division One Gallacher 2 (1 pen) 30000
1932 Glasgow Rangers (a) 1–4 Friendly Weaver 48000
1935 Manchester United (h) 0–2 Division Two No Scorer 28000
1936 Bradford Park (a) 3–0 Division Two Cairns 2, Imrie 10000
Avenue
Debut for John Park, at outside-right, in a match played at Bradford's Park Avenue ground in the Horton area of the city.
1938 West Bromwich (h) 5–1 Division Two Cairns 4, Stubbins 31000
Albion
1946 Tottenham Hotspur (a) 1–1 Division Two Harvey 52213
A debut for striker George King, who was left to rue missed chances after he failed to score in either of his appearances.
1955 Chelsea (a) 0–3 Charity Shield No Scorer 12802
Another Charity Shield loss, before a small crowd at Stamford Bridge.
1957 George Reilly born, Bellshill, Scotland.
1957 Chelsea (h) 1–3 Division One Mitchell (pen) 44560
1960 West Bromwich (h) 3–2 Division One Hughes, Tuohy, White 16107
Albion
1963 Grimsby Town (a) 1–2 Division Two McGarry (pen) 9828
1968 West Bromwich (h) 2–3 Division One Davies, Robson 35128
Albion
1974 Carlisle United (h) 1–0 Division One Tudor 40568
1977 Bohemians (Eire) (a) 0–0 UEFA Cup 1st No Scorer 25000
Round 1st Leg
A memorable debut for Ralph Callachan, as keeper Mick Mahoney was felled by a missile hurled from the crowd during disturbances and the referee was forced to suspend play until order had been restored.
1981 United were forced to pull out of a deal to buy Tommy Booth from Manchester City through lack of funds.
1985 West Bromwich (h) 4–1 Division One Reilly 2, McDonald, Clarke 21902
Albion
1988 Within weeks of joining Tottenham, Paul Gascoigne made his senior international debut, replacing Beardsley for the last five minutes of a 1–0 victory over Denmark at Wembley.

| 1991 | Wolverhampton Wanderers | (h) 1–2 | Division Two | OG | 20195 |

Hopes of a first home win of the season at the third attempt looked bleak when Kevin Scott opened the scoring by blasting past his own keeper and Steve Bull netted yet another goal at Gallowgate. Another own goal by Madden didn't give the home fans much encouragement, and attempts at an equaliser failed.

| 1996 | Blackburn Rovers | (h) 2–1 | Premier League | Shearer, Ferdinand | 36424 |

SEPTEMBER 15TH

| 1875 | James Jackson born, Cambuslang, Scotland. | | | | |
| 1894 | Grimsby Town | (h) 0–3 | Division Two | No Scorer | 4000 |

Debut for goalkeeper W.A. Ward, who managed to concede the grand total of 59 goals in his 21 appearances. Tom Rogers scored an own goal to complete a forgettable day.

| 1898 | Grimsby Town | (a) 4–4 | Friendly | Smith 2, Birnie, Harvey | 3500 |
| 1900 | Stoke | (h) 2–1 | Division One | MacFarlane, Peddie | 18000 |

Debut for fellow Scots Edward Allan and Jimmy Laidlaw. Following a complaint from Laidlaw's former club Burnley over an illegal approach, United were fined one guinea.

| 1906 | Everton | (h) 1–0 | Division One | McWilliam | 38000 |

Debut for inside-left Jimmy Soye, who deputised for Bill Appleyard on this occasion.

| 1916 | Death of Tom Rowlandson, killed while serving in France. | | | | |
| 1920 | South Shields | (h) 1–0 | Friendly | Hudspeth (pen) | 4000 |

Testimonial match for Ghee.

1921	Glasgow Rangers	(h) 2–1	Friendly	Harris 2	15000
1923	Sheffield United	(a) 1–2	Division One	Hudspeth (pen)	25000
1928	Aston Villa	(a) 1–1	Division One	Chalmers	35000

First of three appearances for Glaswegian left-half David Flannigan.

1934	Bradford	(h) 0–1	Division Two	No Scorer	28000
1937	Luton Town	(h) 1–3	Division Two	Livingstone	17000
1951	Burnley	(h) 7–1	Division One	Hannah 2, Mitchell, G. Robledo 4	51278
1956	Arsenal	(a) 1–0	Division One	Hannah	46318
1962	Grimsby Town	(a) 1–0	Division Two	Kerray	12318
1965	Manchester United	(a) 1–1	Division One	McGarry (pen)	30401

Bob Moncur made his First Division debut as Newcastle were five minutes away from victory before a Nobby Stiles shot hit Ollie Burton and went in to equalise.

1969	Dundee United	(a) 2–1	Fairs Cup 1st Round 1st Leg	Davies 2	21000
1971	Hearts	(a) 0–1	Texaco Cup	No Scorer	18000
1973	Wolverhampton Wanderers	(h) 2–0	Division One	Howard, Nattrass	36412

Two second-half goals won it, firstly a Nattrass rocket into the Leazes goal and then a late Pat Howard header.

| 1976 | Ayr United | (a) 0–3 | Friendly | No Scorer | 3600 |

Newcastle were disqualified from the Anglo-Scottish Cup and fined £4,000 after fielding an under-strength team.

| 1979 | Leicester City | (h) 3–2 | Division Two | Shoulder 2 (2 pens), Cartwright | 26443 |

An eventful afternoon, involving three penalties (all converted), six bookings and Tommy Williams being sent off for the visitors.

| 1984 | Everton | (h) 2–3 | Division One | Beardsley (pen), Wharton | 29452 |

Andy Gray scored in the last minute to claim the points for the visitors.

| 1990 | Port Vale | (a) 1–0 | Division Two | Quinn | 10025 |

Newcastle gained a second successive League victory away from home, despite the debut of Neil Simpson, on as a substitute.

| 1992 | Grimsby Town | (a) 2–2 | Anglo-Italian Cup | Quinn, Kelly | 2159 |

After United had gone two up in the first 15 minutes, they allowed the Mariners back in the game and goals from Tony Rees and Paul Groves levelled the scores.

1997   A crowd of over 2,000 were at Craik Park to see Morpeth Town take on a Newcastle reserve side. Trialist Carlos Fumero Sierra (from Real Madrid) scored twice and Bernard Allou (from Paris St Germain) managed one. Kevin Henderson scored for Morpeth.

SEPTEMBER 16TH

1899	Blackburn Rovers	(a) 3–2	Division Two	Fraser, Peddie, Wardrope	8000
1905	Everton	(a) 2–1	Division One	Orr, Howie	16000
1906	Robert Bradley born, Washington, Tyne and Wear.				
1911	Woolwich Arsenal	(a) 0–2	Division One	No Scorer	20000
1912	Albert Harris born, Horden, Durham.				
1922	Sheffield United	(a) 0–2	Division One	No Scorer	20000
1923	Colin Gibson born, Normandy on Tees.				
1925	Leeds United	(a) 0–2	Division One	No Scorer	20000
1929	Blackburn Rovers	(a) 2–4	Division One	Gallacher, OG	29000
1933	West Bromwich Albion	(a) 1–1	Division One	Weaver (pen)	25000
1946	Coventry City	(a) 1–1	Division Two	Milburn	26024
1950	Burnley	(a) 1–1	Division One	Milburn	33373
1953	West Bromwich Albion	(h) 3–7	Division One	Keeble, Mitchell 2	57838
1957	David McCreery born, Belfast.				
1959	West Bromwich Albion	(h) 0–0	Division One	No Scorer	39266
1961	Swansea Town	(h) 2–2	Division Two	Leek, Allchurch	23644
1964	Plymouth Argyle	(h) 2–1	Division Two	Taylor, Thomas	29000
1967	Coventry City	(h) 3–2	Division One	Bennett, Davies, Iley	28892
1967	Death of Sandy Mutch, 82, of which 46 years were spent serving United as player and groundsman.				
1972	Coventry City	(a) 3–0	Division One	Macdonald 3	17592
1975	Death of Johnny Dryden, 67.				
1977	Paul Brayson born, Newcastle.				
1978	Wrexham	(a) 0–0	Division Two	No Scorer	14091
1989	Portsmouth	(h) 1–0	Division One	Thorn	19766
1995	Manchester City	(h) 3–1	Premier League	Ferdinand 2, Beardsley	36501

Beleaguered Manchester City manager Alan Ball handed a debut to striker Gerry Creaney, who scored his side's only goal. City were reduced to ten men after Edgehill was sent off for flattening Ginola.

SEPTEMBER 17TH

1898	Notts County	(h) 1–2	Division Two	Aitken	18000
	Debut for Ted Birnie.				
1904	Everton	(h) 3–2	Division One	Veitch 2, Rutherford	21000
1910	Tottenham Hotspur	(a) 2–1	Division One	Ridley, Rutherford	35000
1921	Burnley	(h) 2–1	Division One	Harris 2	48000
1923	Blackburn Rovers	(a) 1–2	Division One	Seymour	26000
1924	West Ham United	(h) 4–1	Division One	Harris 3, McDonald	30000
	Debut in goal for 18-year-old Isaac Tate.				
1927	Everton	(h) 2–2	Division One	McDonald, McKay	40000
1930	Birmingham	(h) 2–2	Division One	Lindsay, J.R. Richardson	30000
1932	Portsmouth	(h) 1–1	Division One	Allen	40000
1938	Tottenham Hotspur	(a) 0–1	Division Two	No Scorer	40531

1947	Birmingham City	(h) 1–0	Division Two	Hair	51704
1949	Manchester City	(h) 4–2	Division One	Hannah, Milburn, G. Robledo, Walker	58141

An immediate impact for debutant inside-left George Hannah, who scored. Alf McMichael also made his debut, at left-back.

1952	Sunderland	(a) 2–0	Division One	Mitchell, G. Robledo	59665
1955	Charlton Athletic	(h) 4–1	Division One	Keeble, Milburn 3	39040
1958	Chelsea	(h) 1–2	Division One	White	50283
1960	Arsenal	(a) 0–5	Division One	No Scorer	34885

The Gunners blooded free-scoring junior and reserve striker Geoff Strong, who scored. The other goals came from Danny Clapton and a David Herd hat-trick.

1966	Nottingham Forest	(a) 0–3	Division One	No Scorer	21732
1968	Feyenoord (Holland)	(a) 0–2	Fairs Cup 1st Round 2nd Leg	No Scorer	45000

A tougher match than the first leg but United held on to their aggregate lead despite injuries to Clark, Davies and McNamee, who all missed subsequent games.

1969	Everton	(h) 1–2	Division One	Elliott	37094
1977	Birmingham City	(a) 0–3	Division One	No Scorer	18953
1983	Crystal Palace	(h) 3–1	Division Two	Waddle, Keegan, Ryan	22869
1988	Norwich City	(h) 0–2	Division One	No Scorer	22809
1991	Ipswich Town	(h) 1–1	Division Two	Quinn (pen)	16336

Another set-piece disaster for Newcastle, who earned a point when Kevin Brock took a tumble and Quinn converted the resultant spot kick.

1996	Scunthorpe took David Burt and Stuart Elliott on loan.				
1997	Barcelona	(h) 3–2	Champions League	Asprilla 3	35274

To see Gillespie scamper down the touchline and cross perfectly for Tino to head home his third was more than even the most optimistic soul had dared predict before kick-off. Barcelona were simply overwhelmed by a magnificent effort from the team and its delirious supporters. Late goals from Enrique and Figo couldn't wipe the grin off the faces of the home fans present. Unfortunately reality intervened, and by the time of the return game in Spain the attractive football had been replaced by a staggeringly negative approach, due to a team lacking quality attackers, confidence and, seemingly, motivation.

SEPTEMBER 18TH

1897	Burton Swifts	(h) 3–1	Division Two	Wardrope, R. Allen, Stott	12000
1904	Jack Little born, Dunston.				
1905	Edinburgh St Bernard's	(a) 2–2	Friendly	Hardinge 2	20000
1909	Sunderland	(a) 2–0	Division One	Shepherd, Stewart	40000

The actual crowd was far in excess of the 40,000 who paid, and such was the crush that the players couldn't reach the dressing-rooms at half-time and had to remain on the pitch. Police horses were brought in to clear the playing surface while the match was in progress, and one stampeded when hit by the ball, while another was supposedly stabbed by a spectator.

1911	Northampton Town	(a) 2–1	Friendly	Kelly, Stewart	10000
	Hospital Cup match.				
1920	Preston North End	(a) 2–3	Division One	King, Harris	20000
1926	Derby County	(a) 1–1	Division One	OG	30000
1933	Blackburn Rovers	(a) 2–3	Division One	Cape, J.R. Richardson	20000
1937	Burnley	(h) 2–2	Division Two	Smith, Imrie (pen)	14000
1939	Ken Hale born, Blyth.				
1948	Charlton Athletic	(a) 0–0	Division One	No Scorer	56711
1954	Leicester City	(a) 2–3	Division One	Mitchell (pen), White	38038
1957	Portsmouth	(a) 2–2	Division One	Curry, Hill	32093

| 1963 | Southampton | (a) 0–2 | Division Two | No Scorer | 18540 |

Debut for Alan Kirkman, who lasted four months at United before departing for Scunthorpe after five appearances at inside-left. United lost four of the five and Kirkman scored once.

| 1965 | Burnley | (h) 3–2 | Division One | Hilley, Bennett, Anderson | 35883 |
| 1971 | Wolverhampton Wanderers | (h) 2–0 | Division One | Hibbitt, Tudor | 29347 |

Debut for Pat Howard.

1974	Aberdeen	(a) 1–1	Texaco Cup	Macdonald	13500
1976	Leeds United	(a) 2–2	Division One	Cannell, Cassidy	35098
1982	Shrewsbury Town	(a) 1–2	Division Two	Varadi	7907
1990	Sheffield Wednesday	(a) 2–2	Division Two	McGhee 2	30628

A tremendous midweek encounter, featuring two great goals from McGhee and the best performances that Bradshaw and Simpson managed. Even Wayne Fereday was tolerable, setting up one of McGhee's goals. David Hirst and a last-gasp Steve McCall equaliser levelled the scores after the introduction of veteran Trevor Francis.

| 1993 | Swindon Town | (a) 2–2 | Premier League | Clark, Allen (pen) | 15393 |

United welcomed back Peter Beardsley but had to settle for a point after goals from Ling and Mutch.

| 1994 | Arsenal | (a) 3–2 | Premier League | Beardsley (pen), Fox | 36819 |

The first goal was a shot from Beardsley which struck Martin Keown.

SEPTEMBER 19TH

1896	Notts County	(a) 1–3	Division Two	Stott	5000
1903	Everton	(a) 1–4	Division One	Howie	20000
1908	Notts County	(h) 1–0	Division One	Wilson	31000
1910	Norwich City	(a) 1–1	Friendly	Veitch	13473

Hospital Cup match.

1914	Bradford City	(h) 1–0	Division One	Douglas	15000
1919	Arnold Grundy born, Whickham.				
1925	Leicester City	(h) 3–2	Division One	Loughlin 3	31000
1931	West Ham United	(a) 1–2	Division One	Allen	25000
1936	Blackpool	(a) 0–3	Division Two	No Scorer	27000
1939	Brian Wright born, Sunderland.				
1944	Eric Ross born, Belfast.				
1953	Tottenham Hotspur	(h) 1–3	Division One	Milburn	53056
1956	Hearts	(h) 1–2	Friendly	Keeble	23780
1959	Burnley	(h) 1–3	Division One	Tait	38576
1962	Derby County	(a) 1–0	Division Two	Fell	14901
1964	Cardiff City	(a) 1–1	Division Two	Cummings	12016

Former United captain Jimmy Scoular was in his first full season in charge at Ninian Park and was to remain there until 1973.

| 1966 | Linfield | (h) 7–2 | Friendly | McGarry 2 (1 pen), Robson 2, Burton Guthrie, Suddick | 4224 |

Linfield goalkeeper Willie McFaul impressed United officials sufficiently, despite conceding seven, to be invited over to Tyneside.

1967	Gary Brazil born, Tunbridge Wells.				
1970	West Ham United	(a) 2–0	Division One	Robson 2	25841
1973	Morton	(a) 2–1	Texaco Cup	Tudor, Smith	4326
1979	Death of Monte Wilkinson, 71.				
1981	Norwich City	(a) 1–2	Division Two	Waddle	14384

Waddle opened the scoring with Newcastle's 5,000th league goal and McGuire missed a penalty for the home team, and we still lost.

1989	Reading	(a) 1–3	League Cup 2nd Round 1st Leg	Gallacher	7960
1992	Bristol City	(h) 5–0	Division One	O'Brien, Peacock 2 (pens), Carr, Brock	29465
1995	Bristol City	(a) 5–0	League Cup 2nd Round 1st Leg	Peacock, Sellars, Ferdinand, Gillespie, Lee	15952

Scott Sellars scored on his return to first-team duty after an 11-month absence through injury.

SEPTEMBER 20TH

1902	Sheffield Wednesday	(h) 3–0	Division One	Roberts 2, Rutherford	25000
1910	Joe Ford born, Edinburgh.				
1913	West Bromwich Albion	(a) 1–1	Division One	Hudspeth (pen)	30000
1919	Chelsea	(h) 3–0	Division One	Dixon 3	40000
1922	Glasgow Rangers	(h) 4–1	Friendly	Harris 3, McDonald (pen)	10000
1924	Manchester City	(a) 1–3	Division One	McDonald	35000
1926	Cardiff City	(a) 1–1	Division One	Urwin	14000
1927	Ron Anderson born, Ponteland.				
1930	West Ham United	(h) 4–2	Division One	Cape, Starling, Wilkinson, OG	20000
1947	Leeds United	(h) 4–2	Division Two	Hair, Shackleton 2, Stobbart	52275
1948	Jackie Milburn was selected to play for the Football League side against their Irish counterparts and scored a hat-trick. Within a month he had been drafted into the England side.				
1952	Stoke City	(a) 0–1	Division One	No Scorer	30000
1958	Wolverhampton Wanderers	(a) 3–1	Division One	Bottom, White 2	39130

A winning start to a brief Newcastle career for Reg Evans. Goalkeeper Bryan Harvey also made his first appearance in league football, having joined from Wisbech Town.

1961	Liverpool	(h) 1–2	Division Two	Hale	38192
1969	Southampton	(a) 1–1	Division One	Robson	19130
1975	Wolverhampton Wanderers	(h) 5–1	Division One	Gowling 3, Tudor, Cassidy	30876
1980	Oldham Athletic	(h) 0–0	Division Two	No Scorer	19786
1986	Wimbledon	(h) 1–0	Division One	Gascoigne	21545

Ireland international Gary Kelly made his debut in goal and Andy Thomas had his first appearance in midfield.

| 1987 | Liverpool | (h) 1–4 | Division One | McDonald (pen) | 24141 |

A hat-trick for Steve Nicol in this one-sided televised game.

| 1997 | West Ham United | (a) 1–0 | Premier League | Barnes | 25884 |

SEPTEMBER 21ST

1884	Billy Hibbert born, Golborne, Lancashire.				
1895	Notts County	(h) 5–1	Division Two	Aitken 3, Logan, McKay	7000
1901	Everton	(a) 0–0	Division One	No Scorer	20000
1907	Bristol City	(a) 1–1	Division One	Orr	18000
1912	Chelsea	(h) 3–2	Division One	Stewart 2, Peart	38000
1929	Birmingham	(a) 1–5	Division One	Lang	35000
1930	Bob Stokoe born, Mickley.				
1932	Glasgow Rangers	(h) 5–0	Friendly	Murray 2, Allen 2, McMenemy	20000
1935	Port Vale	(a) 0–3	Division Two	No Scorer	9178
1946	Burnley	(h) 1–2	Division Two	Wayman	61255

1955	Hartlepools United	(a) 5–0	Friendly	Mitchell 3 (1 pen), Milburn	5435

Testimonial match.

1957	Sunderland	(a) 0–2	Division One	No Scorer	45218
1963	Preston North End	(h) 2–4	Division One	Kirkman, Burton	29710
1968	Manchester United	(a) 1–3	Division One	Gibb	47262

Alan Duffy made his first-team debut, having graduated from the juniors.

1974	Queens Park Rangers	(a) 2–1	Division One	Tudor, Burns	18594

Even Glen Keeley putting the ball past Willie McFaul couldn't stop United winning in front of the *Match of the Day* cameras.

1985	Oxford United	(h) 3–0	Division One	Gascoigne, Beardsley, McDonald	23642

Returning goalkeeper Steve Hardwick was powerless to stop United going fourth in the table.

1985 Robert Lee, then of Charlton, scored the last goal at The Valley before the ground was closed.

1991	Millwall	(a) 1–2	Division Two	Neilson	9156

A forgettable debut for on-loan striker Andy Walker, whom Ardiles chose to play despite the fact he was obviously unfit. He was eventually substituted.

1994	Barnsley	(h) 2–1	League Cup 2nd Round 1st Leg	Cole, Fox	27208

Neil Redfearn scored the best goal of the night to give the Tykes some hope in the return leg.

1996	Leeds United	(a) 1–0	Premier League	Shearer	36070

To complete the fun, Carlton Palmer received his marching orders.

SEPTEMBER 22ND

1878	Peter McWilliam born, Inveravon, Scotland.				
1894	Notts County	(h) 2–2	Division Two	Thompson, Willis	3000

Local lad Dick Hedley got his first runout, at outside-right.

1900	West Bromwich Albion	(a) 1–0	Division One	Peddie	10000
1906	Woolwich Arsenal	(a) 0–2	Division One	No Scorer	30000
1923	Cardiff City	(h) 1–1	Division One	McDonald	40000
1928	Leicester City	(h) 1–0	Division One	Hudspeth	31000
1933	Dave Smith born, Dundee. He was coach during United's victorious Fairs Cup run.				
1934	Plymouth Argyle	(a) 3–1	Division Two	Boyd, Leach, Smith	12000

A debut goal for centre-forward Jack Smith, whose goalscoring record of 73 goals in 112 senior appearances is often overshadowed by memories of the Gallacher and Milburn eras before and after.

1934 While Jack Smith was beginning his league career for United, a former favourite Hughie Gallacher was appearing at Roker Park for his latest club Derby County. In a stormy game watched by 30,000, Derby triumphed 4–1 thanks to a hat-trick by Jack Bowers. Gallacher was dismissed shortly after half-time.

1936	Bob Whitehead born, Ashington.				
1951	Charlton Athletic	(a) 0–3	Division One	No Scorer	49000
1956	Burnley	(h) 1–1	Division One	Keeble	36790
1957	Steve Carney born, Wallsend.				
1962	Norwich City	(h) 2–1	Division Two	Fell (pen), Thomas	6345
1965	Peterborough United	(h) 3–4	League Cup 2nd Round	Hilley, Bennett, Iley	16132
1973	Coventry City	(a) 2–2	Division One	Tudor, Macdonald	24085
1976	Stoke City	(h) 3–0	League Cup 3rd Round	T. Craig (pen), Burns, Nattrass	27143
1979	Wrexham	(h) 1–0	Division Two	Shoulder (pen)	27904

A push on Brownlie by Joey Jones was punished with a penalty which Shoulder converted, and United went top of Division Two.

| 1984 | Queens Park Rangers | (a) 5–5 | Division One | Waddle 3, Wharton, McDonald | 14144 |

Four-nil up at half-time, Newcastle were lucky to hang on for a point as they capitulated in the last quarter of the match. Wharton scored at both ends, while England manager Bobby Robson was present and noted the form of Waddle.

| 1990 | West Ham United | (h) 1–1 | Division Two | McGhee | 25462 |

1992 Robert Lee signed for a fee of £700,000 from Charlton Athletic, after rejecting overtures from his former manager Lennie Lawrence, then in charge at Middlesbrough.

| 1993 | Notts County | (h) 4–1 | League Cup 2nd Round 1st Leg | Cole 3, Bracewell | 25887 |

The Pies took an early lead when Pav fumbled an indirect free-kick from Mark Draper into his own net, but this inspired United and Cole in particular.

1997 The reserve team triumphed 1–0 away at Wigan, thanks to a late winner from David Eatock. Included in Newcastle's line-up were trialists Massimo Oddo from AC Milan and Spanish-Australian Carlos Gonzales from Sydney United.

SEPTEMBER 23RD

| 1893 | Burton Swifts | (h) 1–3 | Division Two | Unknown Scorer | |

The only appearance of J. Barr for United, at right-half, and one of only two runouts for goalkeeper Joe Ryder.

1896	Sunderland	(a) 1–1	Friendly	Wardrope	6000
1899	Derby County	(h) 2–0	Division One	Peddie, Wardrope	19000
1903	Tony Leach born, Sheffield.				
1905	Derby County	(h) 0–1	Division One	No Scorer	31600
1907	Chelsea	(a) 0–2	Division One	No Scorer	25000
1911	Manchester City	(h) 1–0	Division One	Stewart	11000
1914	Sunderland	(h) 0–1	Friendly	No Scorer	6738

Hospital Cup match.

| 1922 | Preston North End | (h) 3–1 | Division One | Harris 2, McDonald | 35000 |

First of two appearances for perennial reserve winger Eddie Richardson, who joined United from South Shields.

1933	Birmingham	(h) 0–0	Division One	No Scorer	22000
1936	George Eastham born, Blackpool.				
1950	Arsenal	(h) 2–1	Division One	Milburn, Taylor	66926
1953	Sheffield Wednesday	(a) 0–3	Division One	No Scorer	29271

The Newcastle defence continued to concede goals at an alarming rate, as two from Clarrie Jordan and one from Jack Marriott made it 3–0 at half-time and 13 in three games.

1961	Southampton	(a) 0–1	Division Two	No Scorer	20064
1964	Blackpool	(a) 0–3	League Cup 2nd Round	No Scorer	13670
1967	Sheffield United	(a) 1–2	Division One	Robson (pen)	16387
1970	Inter Milan (Italy)	(a) 1–1	Fairs Cup 1st Round 1st Leg	Davies	14460
1972	Leeds United	(h) 3–2	Division One	Smith, Tudor, Macdonald	38964

A seesaw game that BBC's *Match of the Day* covered. After Jimmy Smith had struck first, Allan Clarke equalised. Tudor then restored Newcastle's advantage until David Young played a short backpass that Mick Jones intercepted. Finally, Supermac smashed a winner following a great dummy from Tommy Gibb.

1975	Birmingham City	(a) 2–3	Division One	T. Craig, Nulty	31166
1978	Orient	(h) 0–0	Division Two	No Scorer	26361
1981	Shrewsbury Town	(h) 2–0	Division Two	Wharton, Shinton	13783
1986	Bradford City	(a) 0–2	League Cup 2nd Round 1st Leg	No Scorer	6384

This match was played at Odsal Stadium at Bradford following the tragic events which forced the temporary closure of Valley Parade. The United fans were better behaved than their Leeds counterparts, who had run riot in the previous game at Odsal and set alight a mobile chip van.

1987 Blackpool (a) 0–1 League Cup 2nd No Scorer 7959
Round 1st Leg

The Seasiders took a one-goal lead to Gallowgate after former Magpie Tony Cunningham capitalised on a misjudged backpass from Gascoigne.

1992 Middlesbrough (h) 0–0 League Cup 2nd No Scorer 25814
Round 1st Leg

Debut for Robert Lee, who had wisely turned down a move to his first opponents before joining the Magpies.

SEPTEMBER 24TH

1877 Tom Niblo born, Dunfermline, Scotland.
1898 Stoke (a) 0–0 Division One No Scorer 12000

Debut for Joe Rogers, who went on to play over 50 times for United, at outside-right.

1904 Small Heath (a) 1–2 Division One Veitch 15000
1908 Carlisle United (a) 3–4 Friendly Allan 3 7000
1910 Middlesbrough (h) 0–0 Division One No Scorer 40000
1919 Derby County (h) 0–0 Division One No Scorer 25000
1921 Sheffield United (a) 1–1 Division One Harris 25000
1927 Cardiff City (a) 1–3 Division One Gallacher 30000

Debut for Tommy Lang, at outside-left. He went on to play over 200 times for Newcastle, striking the goal against Chelsea which took the club to Wembley in 1932. Fellow newcomer Jack Little was rather less successful, making three appearances before moving on a free transfer to Southport.

1928 Blackburn Rovers (a) 0–2 Division One No Scorer
1930 Hearts (h) 2–3 Friendly Chalmers, Devine 5000
McCombie Test.
1932 Chelsea (a) 1–0 Division One Boyd 55000
1933 John Nesbitt born, Washington, Tyne and Wear.
1938 Southampton (h) 1–0 Division Two Cairns 35000
1949 Fulham (a) 1–2 Division One Milburn (pen) 40000
1951 Tottenham Hotspur (a) 1–2 Charity Shield Milburn 27760

A defeat at White Hart Lane in the Charity Shield for the Magpies, but later in the season they returned in the FA Cup and won when it really mattered.

1952 Manchester United (a) 2–4 Charity Shield Keeble 2 11381

A miserable attendance at Old Trafford as the Charity Shield was lost again. This match was to be the only senior appearance Neville Black made, a centre-forward from Pegswood who found his way to the first team barred by the abundance of talent at the club.

1955 Tottenham Hotspur (a) 1–3 Division One Milburn 41096
1960 Leicester City (h) 1–3 Division One McGuigan 21161
1966 Fulham (h) 1–1 Division One Noble 20427
1966 Franz Carr born, Preston.
1977 Coventry City (h) 1–2 Division One Gowling 22484
1983 Barnsley (a) 1–1 Division Two Waddle 14085

Beardsley made his United debut as a substitute; Jeff Clarke sustained a leg injury which kept him out for the rest of 1983.

1988 Charlton Athletic (a) 2–2 Division One D. Jackson, Tinnion 6088

With the score at 1–0 to Charlton, they were reduced to ten men after referee Mike Reed dismissed Paul Miller for spitting at an opponent.

1989 Sunderland (a) 0–0 Division Two No Scorer 29499
1991 Crewe Alexandra (a) 4–3 League Cup 2nd Hunt, Peacock 3 4251
Round 1st Leg

The home side motored into a 3–0 lead and also struck the woodwork twice, but eventually United woke up and clawed their way back to an unlikely victory.

1994 Liverpool (h) 1–1 Premier League Lee 34435

Philippe Albert was sent off as Barnes and Rush combined for the latter to score.

1995 Chelsea (h) 2–0 Premier League Ferdinand 2 36225
1996 Halmstads (Sweden) (a) 1–2 UEFA Cup 1st Ferdinand 7847
Round 2nd Leg

A number of United fans were left stranded in England after paying for a non-existent excursion to the game against Halmstads in Sweden. Happily, the perpetrator was later found guilty of deception and was imprisoned. Live TV coverage was provided by an obscure cable company.

1997 Everton (h) 1–0 Premier League Lee 36705

SEPTEMBER 25TH

1895	Tom McDonald born, Inverness.				
1897	Lincoln City	(a) 3–2	Division Two	Wardrope 2, Campbell	3000
1907	Chester le Street	(a) 4–0	Friendly	Appleyard 3 (1 pen), Howie	5000
1909	Everton	(h) 1–2	Division One	Shepherd	35000
1920	Sheffield United	(h) 3–0	Division One	Seymour 2, Harris	40000
1926	Sheffield United	(h) 2–0	Division One	Gallacher 2	30000
1937	Bury	(a) 1–1	Division Two	Imrie	8000
1948	Manchester City	(h) 0–0	Division One	No Scorer	49729
1952	Ray Clarke born, Hackney.				
1954	Chelsea	(h) 1–3	Division One	Milburn	45659

Two goals for former Magpie Roy Bentley on his return to Tyneside.

1957 Sheffield Wednesday (h) 0–0 Division One No Scorer 27651

Debut for John Nesbitt, at centre-half.

1962 Chris Withe born, Speke.
1963 Preston North End (h) 3–0 League Cup 2nd McGarry (pen), Thomas, 14906
Round Burton

Debut for Len Walker, at right-half. This was to be Len's only first-team outing at St James' Park in the year he spent at the club.

1965 Chelsea (a) 1–1 Division One Bennett 30856

Debut for Peter Noble. This game saw the rare sight of a United keeper captaining the side, as Dave Hollins led the side out, alongside his brother John Hollins, Chelsea's captain for that afternoon only.

1968 Southampton (a) 1–4 League Cup 3rd Robson 13840
Round

1971 Ipswich Town (a) 0–0 Division One No Scorer 18724
1974 Nottingham Forest (h) 3–0 League Cup 2nd Macdonald, Burns, Keeley 26228
Round Replay

1976 Liverpool (h) 1–0 Division One Cannell 34813
1976 Stephen Glass born, Dundee.
1982 Barnsley (h) 1–2 Division Two Varadi 24522

Debut for Neil McDonald.

1985 Barnsley (h) 0–0 League Cup 2nd No Scorer 18827
Round 1st Leg

1990 Middlesbrough (a) 0–2 League Cup 2nd No Scorer 15042
Round 1st Leg

1993 West Ham United (h) 2–0 Premier League Cole 2 34179

Mike Hooper made his first-team debut after spending most of the previous eight years playing for Liverpool reserves.

SEPTEMBER 26TH

1877	Andrew Gardner born, Oban, Scotland.				
1896	Newton Heath	(a) 0–4	Division Two	No Scorer	7000
1898	Sheffield United	(a) 2–2	Division One	Peddie, Higgins	4000
1903	Stoke	(h) 1–0	Division One	Rutherford	16000
1908	Sheffield Wednesday	(a) 0–2	Division One	No Scorer	20000
1914	Burnley	(a) 0–2	Division One	No Scorer	15000
1925	West Ham United	(a) 0–1	Division One	No Scorer	30000
1931	Sheffield Wednesday	(h) 4–1	Division One	Bedford (pen), Allen, Boyd	230000
1936	Blackburn Rovers	(h) 2–0	Division Two	Cairns 2	22000
1943	Kit Napier born, Dunblane, Scotland.				
1953	Burnley	(a) 2–1	Division One	Keery, Milburn	33738
1958	Kenny Sansom born, Camberwell, London.				
1959	Leeds United	(a) 3–2	Division One	Allchurch, Scott 2	27000
1962	Leyton Orient	(h) 1–1	League Cup 2nd Round	Fell (pen)	22452

Gordon Bolland gave the visitors a lead they would probably have held on to, had their goalkeeper Frank George not had to leave the field with 20 minutes remaining. Skipper Stan Charlton took over in goal as ten-man Orient hung on until conceding a late penalty which Fell converted.

1964	Preston North End	(h) 5–2	Division Two	McGarry 2, Cummings, Hilley, OG	34219
1966	Hearts	(h) 2–7	Friendly	Robson, Noble	5256
1970	Coventry City	(h) 0–0	Division One	No Scorer	32095
1972	Alan Neilson born, Wegburg, Germany.				
1981	Orient	(h) 1–0	Division Two	Trewick	13737
1984	Bradford City	(h) 3–1	League Cup 2nd Round 1st Leg	McDonald, Wharton, Ferris	18884

Third goal scored by Ferris for his only senior strike.

1987	Southampton	(h) 2–1	Division One	Goddard, Mirandinha	18093

Debut for John Cornwell, following his move from Frank Clark's Leyton Orient.

1992	Peterborough United	(a) 1–0	Division One	Sheedy	14487

SEPTEMBER 27TH

1902	West Bromwich Albion	(a) 1–6	Division One	Rutherford	22160
1904	Sunderland	(h) 1–2	Friendly	Appleyard	20000

This exhibition match was kicked off by Admiral of the Fleet, Lord Charles Beresford, and many of the crowd were seamen allowed ashore from the many naval vessels anchored on the Tyne.

1913	Sheffield Wednesday	(h) 3–1	Division One	Hall, Hibbert, Low	30000
1916	Death of Charles Randall, 34.				
1919	Liverpool	(a) 1–1	Division One	Booth	30000
1922	Glasgow Celtic	(h) 1–1	Friendly	Harris	8000
1924	Bury	(h) 2–2	Division One	Seymour, Urwin	35000
1926	York City	(a) 3–2	Friendly	Mordue 2, Nicholson	2500
1930	Bolton Wanderers	(a) 3–0	Division One	Lindsay 2, J.R. Richardson	20000
1947	Fulham	(a) 0–3	Division Two	No Scorer	41500
1952	Manchester City	(h) 2–0	Division One	Hannah, Milburn (pen)	48961

After scoring from the spot, Jackie Milburn was injured in a tackle and missed the rest of the year while recovering from a cartilage operation. He scored on his return to the team.

1958	Portsmouth	(h) 2–0	Division One	Bottom 2 (1 pen)	42302

1969	Wolverhampton Wanderers	(h) 1–1	Division One	Robson (pen)	38072
1972	Ayr United	(h) 2–0	Texaco Cup	Smith, Tudor	14550
1975	Queens Park Rangers	(a) 0–1	Division One	No Scorer	22981
1980	Bristol Rovers	(a) 0–0	Division Two	No Scorer	5171
1986	Norwich City	(a) 0–2	Division One	No Scorer	15735

1987 The end of a brief and unhappy stay on Tyneside for Glynn Hodges, packed off to Watford for £300,000.

1988	Sheffield United	(a) 0–3	League Cup 2nd Round 1st Leg	No Scorer	17900
1989	Watford	(h) 2–1	Division Two	Quinn, Gallacher	17008
1994	Royal Antwerp (Belgium)	(h) 5–2	UEFA Cup 1st Round 2nd Leg	Cole 3, Lee, Beardsley (pen)	29737

1996 United loaned Jimmy Crawford to struggling Rotherham United, for much-needed match practice. He made 11 appearances for them.

| 1997 | Chelsea | (a) 0–1 | Premier League | No Scorer | 31563 |

Poyet for the Blues.

SEPTEMBER 28TH

| 1895 | Rotherham Town | (a) 1–1 | Division Two | Logan | 2000 |
| 1901 | Sunderland | (h) 0–1 | Division One | No Scorer | 25000 |

Debut for Tom Davidson, at left-back, yet another Scotsman.

| 1907 | Nottingham Forest | (h) 3–0 | Division One | Gardner, Hall, Speedie | 25000 |

Debut for Dave Willis, in defence. Willis joined United from Sunderland.

1912	Woolwich Arsenal	(a) 1–1	Division One	Stewart	16000
1929	Huddersfield Town	(h) 5–2	Division One	Chalmers, Gallacher 2, McCurley, Urwin	30000
1931	Hearts	(a) 2–1	Friendly	Ford 2	3000
1935	Fulham	(h) 6–2	Division Two	Cairns, Harris, Pearson 3, Ware	25000

Goalscoring debuts for outside-right Albert Harris and inside-right Harry Ware.

| 1946 | Barnsley | (a) 1–1 | Division Two | Stobbart | 34192 |
| 1957 | Burnley | (a) 2–0 | Division One | Curry 2 | 18405 |

A belated 21st birthday present for right-back Bob Whitehead, who made his debut.

1959	Aberdeen	(a) 3–3	Friendly	Scott 2, Eastham	10100
1960	Racing Paris (France)	(h) 2–1	Friendly	Mitchell, White	9077
1963	Leyton Orient	(a) 0–1	Division Two	No Scorer	12989
1968	Tottenham Hotspur	(h) 2–2	Division One	Allen, McNamee	30469

Debut for Keith Dyson.

| 1971 | Hearts | (h) 2–1 | Texaco Cup | Macdonald 2 | 24380 |

Almost a repeat of the Rangers Fairs Cup riot, as Scottish fans threw bottles at United players when Macdonald hit a second. With the scores level on aggregate at 2–2, the game was settled on penalties, with Tudor hitting the fifth and decisive one after Hibbitt had earlier missed.

1974	Ipswich Town	(h) 1–0	Division One	Howard	43526
1977	Bohemians (Ireland)	(h) 4–0	UEFA Cup 1st Round 2nd Leg	T. Craig 2, Gowling 2	19046
1985	Arsenal	(a) 0–0	Division One	No Scorer	24104

1988 Newcastle reserves drew 2–2 at home with Manchester City. United's goals came from Ian Bogie and a 15-year-old Lee Clark.

| 1991 | Derby County | (h) 2–2 | Division Two | Hunt, Quinn | 17581 |

The elusive first win at home should have come from the penalty spot, as a Derby hand swiped the ball away near the goal line in a frantic finale. However, the referee waved away furious appeals. Once again a static United defence had conceded a set-piece goal and after an hour the on-loan pairing of Bobby Davison and Ian Ormondroyd had both netted. The second appearance of United's on-loan 'striker' Andy Walker ended when he was replaced by Andy Hunt. The former non-league forward then pulled a goal back and set up Quinn for a late equaliser, as the home crowd at last had something to cheer. The most bizarre incident of the game was missed by the pressmen in the Milburn stand, as a fierce dispute between the home and away dugouts ended with Tony Galvin kicking a bucket of water over Rams boss Arthur Cox and his assistants, and then attempting to attack the visitors with a wooden bench! He was disarmed by his colleagues before he damaged anyone.

1992 Former United centre-half Aidan McCaffery was dismissed from his post as Carlisle United manager.

SEPTEMBER 29TH

1894	Leicester Fosse	(h) 2–0	Division Two	Thompson 2	5000
1900	Everton	(h) 1–0	Division One	D. Gardner (pen)	21448
1906	Sheffield Wednesday	(h) 5–1	Division One	Appleyard, Gosnell, Kirkaldy, Speedie 2	40000

Two goals for debutant Finlay Speedie.

1910	Joseph Wilson born, West Butsfield, Durham.				
1923	Cardiff City	(a) 0–1	Division One	No Scorer	45000
1928	Manchester United	(a) 0–5	Division One	No Scorer	35000
1934	Norwich City	(h) 2–0	Division Two	Lang, OG	20000
1951	Fulham	(h) 0–1	Division One	No Scorer	55531
1956	Preston North End	(a) 0–1	Division One	No Scorer	29189
1962	Walsall	(a) 6–0	Division Two	Fell, Kerray, Thomas 2, Suddick, Hilley	10336

1964 Future United boss Bill McGarry left Watford to become the new Ipswich Town manager, succeeding Jackie Milburn.

1973	Queens Park Rangers	(h) 2–3	Division One	Tudor 2	31402
1979	Birmingham City	(a) 0–0	Division Two	No Scorer	19967

1979 While the first team ground out a point at St Andrews, Steve Carney made his debut for the reserves at home to Coventry. Gary Walton scored the only goal to win it for United. Former Newcastle striker Mick Ferguson was in the visitors' line-up. After completing his three-match trial, Carney was offered a contract, which he accepted.

1981	Bolton Wanderers	(a) 0–1	Division Two	No Scorer	6429
1984	West Ham United	(h) 1–1	Division One	Beardsley	29966

Debut for Pat Heard.

1990	Bristol City	(a) 0–1	Division Two	No Scorer	15858

Debut for Lee Clark as substitute almost from the start, after John Gallacher injured himself in the pre-match warm-up and hobbled around for a few minutes of the game before being replaced. This match marked the only start that Neil Simpson made, and he lasted precisely 36 minutes.

1992 Twenty-four hours after the removal of one former United player from Brunton Park, enter another, as David McCreery replaced Aidan McCaffery as Carlisle United manager.

SEPTEMBER 30TH

1893	Woolwich Arsenal	(h) 6–0	Division Two	Wallace 3, Thompson	32000

Tyneside-born Lowery had a gentle introduction to league football as he stood between the posts and watched his new colleagues power through the Gunners. This match also marked the only first-team appearance of Isaac Ryder, a locally born inside-left who played most of his football in United's Northern Alliance side.

1899	Bury	(a) 1–2	Division One	Niblo	5000
1899	Tom Mitchell born, Spennymoor.				
1905	Sheffield Wednesday	(a) 1–1	Division One	McClarence	16000
1908	Glasgow Rangers	(h) 4–1	Friendly	Higgins 4	8000
1911	Everton	(a) 0–2	Division One	No Scorer	15000
1922	Preston North End	(a) 0–1	Division One	No Scorer	16000
1933	Sheffield Wednesday	(a) 1–3	Division One	Lang	14619
1950	Sheffield Wednesday	(a) 0–0	Division One	No Scorer	40000
1961	Luton Town	(h) 4–1	Division Two	Allchurch, White, Hale, Hughes	22452
1964	Plymouth Argyle	(a) 1–2	Division Two	McGarry	21639
1967	Arsenal	(h) 2–1	Division One	Davies, Robson (pen)	33377
1970	Inter Milan (Italy)	(h) 2–0	Fairs Cup 1st Round 2nd Leg	Davies, Moncur	56495
1972	Everton	(a) 1–3	Division One	Barrowclough	33028
1978	Notts County	(a) 2–1	Division Two	Connolly, Bird	11362
1989	Hull City	(a) 3–1	Division Two	McGhee, Anderson, Brazil	9629

Mark McGhee chalked up the first goal of his second spell at Gallowgate.

| 1992 | Leicester City | (h) 4–0 | Anglo-Italian Cup | Brock, Quinn 2, Sheedy | 14046 |

As a measure of United's strength in depth and lack of interest in this competition, only four of the line-up from the previous Saturday's game started this match.

| 1996 | Aston Villa | (h) 4–3 | Premier League | Ferdinand 2, Shearer, Howey | 36400 |

A Sky Monday evening game where Dwight Yorke managed to score a hat-trick and still finish on the losing side.

OCTOBER 1ST

1898	Aston Villa	(h) 1–1	Division One	Rogers	25000
1904	Manchester City	(h) 2–0	Division One	Veitch, Appleyard	20971

This match saw the debut of Jimmy Lawrence; his goalkeeping skills provided the platform for the most successful period in Newcastle's history. By the time he left to manage South Shields in 1922, he had appeared for United in 496 first-team games (over 500 including wartime matches).

1910	Preston North End	(a) 1–2	Division One	Higgins	18000
1921	Sheffield United	(h) 2–1	Division One	Mooney, Smailes	40000
1927	Blackburn Rovers	(h) 0–1	Division One	No Scorer	31000

Debut in goal for Mick Burns.

1932	Huddersfield Town	(h) 0–4	Division One	No Scorer	26000
1932	Alf McMichael born, Belfast.				
1938	Coventry City	(a) 0–1	Division Two	No Scorer	18774

Debut for Jimmy Woodburn, in defence.

1939	Duncan Neale born, Portslade, Sussex.				
1943	Willie McFaul born, Coleraine, Northern Ireland.				
1945	Death of Bob Bennie, 72.				
1949	Stoke City	(h) 4–1	Division One	Houghton 2, Milburn, Thompson	49903
1951	Death of Peter McWilliam, 73.				
1952	Death of Jack Fraser, 75.				
1955	Everton	(h) 1–2	Division One	Tait	40493
1958	Bela Vista (Brazil)	(h) 12–1	Friendly	White 5, Bottom 5, Evans, Davies	25395

The visit of the supposedly 'crack' Brazilian team turned into a farce as they were revealed to be a minor-league part-time outfit. White and Bottom indulged in a private scoring competition, even going so far as to block each other's shots!

| 1960 | Cardiff City | (h) 5–0 | Division One | Luke 2, Mitchell, White 2 | 17627 |

Debut for Jimmy Wilson, at outside-left.

| 1962 | Leyton Orient | (a) 2–4 | League Cup 2nd Round Replay | OG, Suddick | 8037 |

On an atrocious evening at Brisbane Road, with wind and driving rain throughout, United bowed out of the League Cup in extra time. The visitors were gifted an early lead when Malcolm Lucas put through his own goal, but goals from Bolland and Graham restored the home side's advantage. Alan Suddick forced extra time with a late leveller before the floodlights went out. Once power was restored, goals from Graham again and Deeley settled it in favour of the Os.

| 1966 | Everton | (a) 1–1 | Division One | Bennett | 38364 |

Debut for John Craggs.

| 1969 | Dundee United | (h) 1–0 | Fairs Cup 1st Round 2nd Leg | Dyson | 37470 |

A last-minute goal from Dyson preserved United's run of home victories in the Fairs Cup.

| 1973 | Morton | (h) 1–1 | Texaco Cup | OG | 12158 |

Despite scoring an OG, Dennis Laughton later signed for United.

| 1977 | Ipswich Town | (a) 1–2 | Division One | McCaffery | 21797 |
| 1983 | Portsmouth | (h) 4–2 | Division Two | Wharton, Waddle 2, Keegan (pen) | 25488 |

Classic stuff from Beardsley and the final time John Ryan was ever sighted in the team.

| 1988 | Liverpool | (a) 2–1 | Division One | Hendrie, Mirandinha (pen) | 39139 |

Gary Gillespie gave Liverpool an early lead and most of the crowd sat back and waited for an avalanche of goals, only for Hendrie to score his first goal for Newcastle. Better was to follow, as a long punt from Beasant bounced once and Hendrie fell in the box under challenge from Gillespie. Mirandinha scored the resultant penalty and stood in front of the Kop taunting them before being pulled away by Anderson. United hung on for the last seven minutes to give manager Willie McFaul a wonderful birthday present and the local police a problem as they tried to clear the celebrating United fans from the ground.

| 1991 | Tranmere Rovers | (a) 6–6 | Zenith Data Systems Cup | Clark, Peacock 2, Quinn 3 | 4056 |

United lost on penalties after extra time when Quinn, Clark and O'Brien missed and Rovers scored all theirs.

| 1994 | Aston Villa | (a) 2–0 | Premier League | Lee, Cole | 29960 |

Paul Kitson made his debut, coming on as substitute as United edged Ron Atkinson closer to the sack. Ho ho.

| 1995 | Everton | (a) 3–1 | Premier League | Ferdinand, Lee, Kitson | 33080 |

Another away victory witnessed by Sky cameras. Ferdinand surged forward powerfully to open the scoring, Lee converted a penalty in the absence of Beardsley and substitute Kitson scored with his first touch. Anders Limpar got the home side's goal when looking well offside.

| 1997 | Dynamo Kiev (Russia) | (a) 2–2 | Champions League | Beresford 2 | 100000 |

Two down to early goals from Rebrov and Shevchenko and having seen Tino depart on a stretcher, United improbably clawed their way back into the tie with two fortunate goals from Beresford, much to the delight of the small following of fans, under armed guard.

OCTOBER 2ND

| 1897 | Burnley | (a) 0–3 | Division Two | No Scorer | 8000 |

Thought to be the first instance of a United keeper saving a penalty, as Charlie Watts faced a thrice-taken spot kick successfully.

1909	Manchester United	(a) 1–1	Division One	Rutherford	40000
1912	South Shields	(a) 6–2	Friendly	Lowes 4, Hughes, Duncan	5000
1920	Sheffield United	(a) 3–0	Division One	Pyke 2, Ward	28000
1922	Cardiff City	(a) 0–4	Friendly	No Scorer	15000

1926	Arsenal	(a) 2–2	Division One	Clark, Seymour	45000
1937	Coventry City	(h) 1–2	Division Two	Smith	22000
1948	Portsmouth	(a) 0–1	Division One	No Scorer	44000

Debut for Ron McGarry. Portsmouth scored a late goal from Len Phillips, set up by future United captain Jimmy Scoular, and extended Pompey's unbeaten start to 12 games. They went on to win the First Division championship, thumping United 5–0 at Gallowgate in the return game.

1954	Cardiff City	(a) 2–4	Division One	Milburn, White	36000

1955 Almost four years to the day since his previous outing, Jackie Milburn was recalled to the England side for one more cap. He failed to score in a 5–1 victory over Denmark in Copenhagen, as Don Revie hit a hat-trick. Unusually, the game took place on a Sunday.

1959 Billy Askew born, Great Lumley, Durham.

1961	Sheffield United	(a) 2–2	League Cup 2nd Round	McGuigan, McKinney	12065

Debut for Colin Clish.

1963	Portsmouth	(h) 1–0	Division Two	Dalton	22118

1964 John Robertson born, Edinburgh.

1965	Arsenal	(h) 0–1	Division One	No Scorer	42841
1971	Derby County	(h) 0–1	Division One	No Scorer	31972

Debut for Ray Ellison, at left-back.

1974	Aberdeen	(h) 3–2	Texaco Cup	Macdonald 2, Hibbitt	18838
1976	Norwich City	(a) 2–3	Division One	T. Craig (pen), Gowling	21417
1982	Rotherham United	(a) 5–1	Division Two	Todd, Keegan 4 (1 pen)	12436

The start of Terry McDermott's second spell at Newcastle provided the spur for a four-goal blast from Kevin Keegan, the day before the latest England squad was announced. Millers player-manager Emlyn Hughes saw his penalty saved by Kevin Carr, and as *Match of the Day* beamed the game out, the large travelling support sang, 'Bobby Robson, are you watching on the box?'

1993	Aston Villa	(a) 2–0	Premier League	Allen (pen), Cole	37366

Andy Cole had a field day against the veteran Paul McGrath as United, backed by a large and noisy away support, were hugely impressive.

OCTOBER 3RD

1888 Jack Peart born, South Shields.

1896	Darwen	(h) 5–1	Division Two	Wardrope, Smellie 4	7000
1901	Notts County	(a) 2–0	Division One	Peddie, A. Gardner	10000

Debuts for Scotsman Alex Caie and local lad Tom Bamlett, one of his two appearances before moving to West Ham United.

1903	Derby County	(a) 3–1	Division One	McColl, Howie, Rutherford	10000
1908	Bristol City	(a) 3–3	Division One	Higgins, Veitch 2	18000
1910	Annfield Plain	(a) 0–0	Friendly	No Scorer	1000
1914	Tottenham Hotspur	(h) 4–0	Division One	Booth, Hall 2, Hibbert	22000
1925	Arsenal	(h) 7–0	Division One	Clark 3, Loughlin, Seymour 2, Urwin	35000
1931	Bolton	(a) 1–2	Division One	J.R. Richardson	20000
1936	Bury	(a) 2–1	Division Two	Cairns, Park	18000

1951 A below-par England stuttered to a 2–2 draw with France at Highbury, Milburn having a quiet game.

1953	Charlton Athletic	(h) 0–2	Division One	No Scorer	47516

Centre-half Ron Greener ably deputised for Frank Brennan on this, the first of three appearances. He eventually left for Darlington and completed over 500 games for the Quakers.

1956	Hibernian	(h) 2–1	Friendly	Milburn, Hannah	16668
1959	West Ham United	(h) 0–0	Division One	No Scorer	41924

1964	Ipswich Town	(a) 1–3	Division Two	Burton	14447
1970	Manchester City	(a) 1–1	Division One	Ford	31159
1976	Death of Archie Duncan, 87.				
1981	Cardiff City	(a) 4–0	Division Two	Varadi 3, Davies (pen)	5764
1987	Chelsea	(a) 2–2	Division One	Goddard, Wharton	22071
1990	Middlesbrough	(h) 0–0	Division Two	No Scorer	17023

OCTOBER 4TH

| 1902 | Notts County | (h) 6–1 | Division One | Rutherford 2, McColl, Orr, Stewart, Carr | 17000 |

| 1913 | Bolton Wanderers | (a) 1–3 | Division One | Hall | 32000 |
| 1919 | Liverpool | (h) 3–0 | Division One | Hibbert 3 | 45000 |

Debut for Alex Ramsay, who gave way to Stan Seymour in the outside-left role within a year.

1924	Nottingham Forest	(a) 1–1	Division One	Seymour	15000
1930	Liverpool	(h) 0–4	Division One	No Scorer	37000
1947	Coventry City	(h) 0–0	Division Two	No Scorer	55569
1952	Liverpool	(a) 3–5	Division One	Prior, G. Robledo 2 (1 pen)	48002
1954	Plymouth	(a) 2–3	Friendly	Milburn, White	11679
1958	Aston Villa	(a) 1–2	Division One	White	30000
1961	Liverpool	(a) 0–2	Division Two	No Scorer	52419
1969	Crystal Palace	(a) 3–0	Division One	Davies, Dyson, Robson	28407
1972	Blackpool	(h) 0–3	League Cup 3rd Round	No Scorer	19810
1975	Tottenham Hotspur	(h) 2–2	Division One	Tudor, Barrowclough	33284
1980	West Ham United	(h) 0–0	Division Two	No Scorer	24866
1986	Southampton	(a) 1–4	Division One	A. Thomas	14622
1989	Reading	(h) 4–0	League Cup 2nd Round 2nd Leg	Brazil (pen), Brock, Thorn, McGhee	15211
1992	Brentford	(a) 2–1	Division One	Kelly, Peacock	10131

Sunday afternoon live on ITV. Cheering United on from the standing section behind the goal were Dave Beasant and Joe Allon, complete with black-and-white scarves.

| 1995 | Bristol City | (h) 3–1 | League Cup 2nd Round 2nd Leg | Barton, Ferdinand, Albert | 36357 |

Debuts for Paul Brayson and Jimmy Crawford (on as a substitute). Another long-term injury victim returned as Albert played his first game of the season and scored, while Barton struck his first goal for the club.

1995 Christmas came early as Tottenham paid an almighty £4.2 million to lure Ruel Fox away from Tyneside.

1996 Another unannounced game, this time at Longbenton, where the reserves played a Hearts side and recorded a 4–0 victory, with goals from Clark, Lee and two from Kitson.

| 1997 | Tottenham Hotspur | (h) 1–0 | Premier League | Barton | 36709 |

A late winner for boyhood Gunners fan Barton. Fox and Ferdinand made their returns to Tyneside and managed to lock themselves in the away-team toilet, missing the first few seconds of the second half. The match ended with a clearly overwhelmed Ferdinand standing in the centre circle, half wearing a Newcastle shirt, acknowledging the applause from all four sides of the ground.

OCTOBER 5TH

1895	Liverpool	(h) 1–0	Division Two	Wardrope	10000
1895	Leadgate Exiles	(a) n/a	FA Cup Qualifier	Walkover – Opposition Scratched	None
1901	Small Heath	(a) 1–3	Division One	Roberts	12000
1907	Notts County	(a) 1–0	Division One	Hall	20000
1912	Bradford City	(h) 1–1	Division One	Hudspeth (pen)	35000

| 1925 | Raith Rovers | (a) 6–1 | Friendly | Clark 3, Mitchell, McDonald, Cowan | 3000 |

1925 Ron McGarry born, West Stanley, Durham.

| 1929 | Sheffield United | (a) 0–1 | Division One | No Scorer | 20000 |

Debut for goalkeeper Albert McInroy.

| 1935 | Burnley | (a) 2–1 | Division Two | Cairns, McMenemy | 9000 |
| 1946 | Newport County | (h) 13–0 | Division Two | Bentley, Milburn 2, Shackleton 6, Wayman 4 | 52137 |

Shackleton's debut and a penalty miss for United when the score was 0–0! Legend has it that Shack's sixth was scored via his backside.

| 1957 | Preston North End | (h) 0–2 | Division One | No Scorer | 36131 |

1958 Peter Johnson born, Harrogate.

1959	Dundee United	(a) 9–2	Friendly	White 3, Eastham 2, Scott 2, Hale, Scoular	8500
1963	Swansea Town	(h) 4–1	Division Two	Taylor, Thorn, Hilley 2	23711
1968	Leeds United	(h) 0–1	Division One	No Scorer	41999
1974	Everton	(a) 1–1	Division One	McDermott	40000

The Everton equaliser had more than a touch of fortune surrounding it as Mick Buckley's shot hit Malcolm Macdonald and gave Willie McFaul no chance.

1977	Norwich City	(a) 1–2	Division One	T. Craig	16630
1983	Oxford United	(h) 1–1	League Cup 2nd Round 1st Leg	McDermott	21184
1985	West Ham United	(h) 1–2	Division One	Reilly	26957
1991	Portsmouth	(a) 1–3	Division Two	Quinn	10175

The gods must have got together to conspire against Newcastle before this match, as nothing went right for them. The conditions played a part, driving rain drenching the away fans and saturating the pitch, Darren Bradshaw being sent off for a professional foul, Portsmouth scoring, United conceding a penalty and Portsmouth making it 2–0. After a further Portsmouth goal, Mick Quinn then 'scored' but was adjudged offside, then scored again and crashed into the post in the process, limping off the field. This left Newcastle with ten men, both substitutes having already been used. There was no more scoring, the home players presumably taking pity on their luckless visitors.

| 1993 | Notts County | (a) 7–1 | League Cup 2nd Round 2nd Leg | Allen 2 (1 pen), Cole 3, Lee, Beardsley | 6068 |

Beardsley scored his first goal since returning to United, while Gary McSwegan hit a solitary goal for the humiliated home side.

| 1994 | Barnsley | (a) 1–0 | League Cup 2nd Round 2nd Leg | Cole | 10992 |

OCTOBER 6TH

| 1894 | Burslem Port Vale | (a) 4–4 | Division Two | Dickson, McNee, Thompson, Willis | 2000 |

Charles Dickson and John McNee made goalscoring entrances to the first team. At the time, Vale were based at the Cobridge Athletic Grounds, adjacent to where the National Garden Festival was held almost a century later.

| 1900 | Sunderland | (a) 1–1 | Division One | OG | 28688 |
| 1906 | Bury | (a) 2–3 | Division One | Appleyard, Veitch (pen) | 20000 |

1919 Albert Sibley born, West Thurrock, Essex.

| 1923 | West Ham United | (a) 0–1 | Division One | No Scorer | 30000 |
| 1928 | Leeds United | (h) 3–2 | Division One | Boyd, Lang, McDonald | 39000 |

Debut for Bob Thomson, following his transfer from Sunderland.

| 1934 | Swansea Town | (a) 4–3 | Division Two | Boyd, McMenemy, Murray, Weaver | 8000 |

1935	Harry Taylor born, Crawcrook.				
1951	Wolves	(h) 3–1	Division One	Davies, Milburn 2	57558

Scoring debut for Reg Davies.

1956	Luton Town	(h) 2–2	Division One	Hannah, Milburn	36941

Debut for George Eastham.

1962	Stoke City	(a) 1–3	Division Two	Thomas	26775
1971	Arsenal	(a) 0–4	League Cup 3rd Round	No Scorer	34071

The only League appearance of central defender Derek Craig was not a roaring success.

1973	Liverpool	(a) 1–2	Division One	Nattrass	45612
1976	West Bromwich Albion	(h) 2–0	Division One	Gowling, Cannell	28746

A quite disgraceful display by the visitors, who hacked their way through the whole game and crippled Barrowclough, Cannell and Tommy Craig with wild lunges that went unpunished by the referee.

1979	West Ham United	(a) 1–1	Division Two	Withe	23206

David Cross for the Hammers.

1982	Leeds United	(a) 1–0	League Cup 2nd Round 1st Leg	Varadi	24012

Debut boy David McCreery's battling skills were immediately utilised as Newcastle held out in this League Cup first leg.

1984	Ipswich Town	(h) 3–0	Division One	OG, Waddle, Heard	25677

A Burley own goal in the opening 30 seconds propelled United to a trouble-free victory.

1990	Portsmouth	(h) 2–1	Division Two	Quinn 2	17682

Blustery conditions couldn't prevent Mick Quinn from breaking his five-match lean spell in front of goal as he netted one in each half. Portsmouth were poor throughout, and their only goal came from a John Anderson header which gave Burridge no chance.

OCTOBER 7TH

1881	Jimmy Tildesley born, Halesowen.				
1893	Lincoln City	(a) 1–2	Division Two	Wallace	1000

Debut for Toby Gillespie, a local lad who had a short career as a forward, making four appearances without hitting the net.

1899	Notts County	(h) 6–0	Division One	Fraser 2, MacFarlane, Peddie, Stevenson, Wardrope	20000
1905	Nottingham Forest	(h) 3–2	Division One	Orr, McClarence, Howie	15000
1908	Glasgow Rangers	(a) 4–2	Friendly	Duncan, Veitch, Higgins, Howie	10000
1911	West Bromwich Albion	(h) 0–0	Division One	No Scorer	22000

Debut for local lad Robert Gibson at outside-right.

1912	Billy Cairns born, Newcastle.				
1913	John Park born, Douglas Water, Scotland.				
1922	Burnley	(h) 0–2	Division One	No Scorer	38000
1933	Manchester City	(h) 2–2	Division One	Cape, Weaver	20000
1947	Pat Howard born, Dodworth, Yorkshire.				
1950	Aston Villa	(a) 0–3	Division One	No Scorer	45000
1953	Hearts	(h) 2–2	Friendly	Milburn, Davies	38201
1961	Charlton Athletic	(h) 4–1	Division Two	McGuigan 2, Allchurch, OG	22957

Debut for Alan Suddick, in the number seven shirt.

1967	Wolverhampton Wanderers	(a) 2–2	Division One	B. Robson, T. Robson	32386

United snatched a point after Derek Dougan had departed with a groin strain, following an afternoon of special attention from John McNamee.

1972	Norwich City	(h) 3–1	Division One	Tudor 2, Guthrie	18103
1975	Bristol Rovers	(a) 1–1	League Cup 3rd Round	Gowling	17141
1978	Leicester City	(h) 1–0	Division Two	Walker	25731
1980	Preston North End	(a) 3–2	Division Two	Rafferty, Shinton 2	5301

The three-match goal famine was ended in style at Deepdale in this Tuesday evening fixture. The return of Mick Martin to the midfield after a year on the sidelines through injury provided the required boost, although Preston brought the score back level after being two down. Goals from Gordon Coleman and former Magpie Alex Bruce looked to have earned a point before a late attempt from Billy Rafferty was unwittingly diverted in by Bobby Shinton.

| 1981 | Fulham | (h) 1–2 | League Cup 2nd Round 1st Leg | Barton | 20247 |

Goals from Robert Wilson and Dean Coney gave the Cottagers the edge in the return leg of this tie.

| 1987 | Blackpool | (h) 4–1 | League Cup 2nd Round 2nd Leg | Goddard, Mirandinha, D. Jackson, Gascoigne | 21228 |
| 1989 | Ipswich Town | (a) 1–2 | Division Two | McGhee | 15220 |

Newcastle debut for John Burridge, his 11th club. (He is now over the 30 mark.)

| 1992 | Middlesbrough | (a) 3–1 | League Cup 2nd Round 2nd Leg | Kelly 2, O'Brien | 24390 |

1996   Manchester United launched their 'Red Tribe' lager. A laughable press release revealed the product was aimed at 18- to 45-year-old males and females with an interest in football and lager. Further startling facts included the fact that over 2 million UK residents called themselves Manchester United supporters, and only 16 per cent 'were based in Manchester'. I rest my case . . .

OCTOBER 8TH

1896	Alf Maitland born, Leith, Scotland.				
1898	Burnley	(a) 1–2	Division One	Rogers	6000
1900	Dundee	(a) 3–4	Friendly	MacFarlane 2, Burgess	3000
1904	Notts County	(a) 3–0	Division One	Howie, Rutherford 2	10000
1908	Death of Jimmy Stott, 37.				
1910	Notts County	(h) 2–0	Division One	Shepherd, Higgins	30000

Debut for Bob Hewison, at right-half.

1921	Chelsea	(a) 1–1	Division One	Harris	35000
1927	Bolton Wanderers	(a) 2–1	Division One	Gallacher, McKay	25000
1932	Sheffield United	(a) 1–3	Division One	Allen	10000
1938	Nottingham Forest	(h) 4–0	Division Two	Birkett, Cairns 3	31000
1949	Burnley	(a) 2–1	Division One	Harvey, Walker	37319
1955	Portsmouth	(h) 2–1	Division One	Mitchell 2	42320
1960	Aston Villa	(a) 0–2	Division One	No Scorer	25336
1965	Death of Jimmy Nelson, 64.				
1966	Arsenal	(a) 0–2	Division One	No Scorer	24595

The second goal was an OG by Frank Clark.

| 1968 | Nottingham Forest | (n) 4–2 | Division One | Davies, Dyson, Foggon, Robson | 17651 |

Match played at nearby Meadow Lane due to fire damage at the City Ground. It was a win at great cost to United, as young winger Geoff Allen sustained the cruciate ligament injury that was to cost him a promising playing career and probably a Fairs Cup winners' medal.

| 1969 | Manchester City | (a) 1–2 | Division One | Robson | 32172 |
| 1973 | Doncaster Rovers | (h) 6–0 | League Cup 2nd Round | Robson 2, Macdonald 3, Clark | 15948 |

The meagre crowd went crazy when the flying pig aka. Frank Clark hit a shot which bounced past the despairing grasp of the Rovers goalkeeper. An impromptu pitch invasion to celebrate this unheralded event took place, and the first person to reach Frank was his brother-in-law.

| 1974 | Queens Park Rangers | (a) 4–0 | League Cup 3rd Round | Macdonald 3, Tudor | 15815 |

An easy victory, once Macdonald got the first goal of his hat-trick in the first 13 seconds. Rangers were in some disarray after the departure of manager Gordon Jago, with his assistant, ex-United player Stan Anderson, in temporary charge.

| 1977 | Derby County | (h) 1–2 | Division One | Burns | 26578 |

Debut for John Blackley, who had a reasonable game but still couldn't prevent a win for Tommy Docherty's men, thanks to goals from Billy Hughes and Roy McFarland.

| 1983 | Charlton Athletic | (h) 2–1 | Division Two | Keegan 2 | 23329 |

A wet day on Tyneside captured by *Match of the Day* cameras, as two headers from left-wing crosses won a game United had looked like losing.

| 1985 | Barnsley | (a) 1–1 | League Cup 2nd Round 2nd Leg | Cunningham | 10084 |

United went through on away goals after extra time.

| 1986 | Bradford City | (h) 1–0 | League Cup 2nd Round 2nd Leg | Roeder | 15893 |

A single effort wasn't enough to prevent the Bantams from strutting into the next round on away goals. This game marked the end of Billy Whitehurst's United career as he responded to jeers from the fans when being substituted with a hand gesture to which Willie McFaul took exception. Within days Billy had been shipped out to Oxford United.

| 1988 | Coventry City | (h) 0–3 | Division One | No Scorer | 22890 |

OCTOBER 9TH

1897	Newton Heath	(h) 2–0	Division Two	Aitken, Harvey	14000
1905	Dundee	(a) 1–1	Friendly	Gosnell	6000
1905	Jimmy Loughlin born, Darlington.				
1907	Sunderland	(a) 2–0	Friendly	Soye, Hedley	10000
1909	Bradford City	(h) 1–0	Division One	Wilson	25000
1920	Sunderland	(h) 6–1	Division One	Seymour, Smailes 2, Harris 2, Ward	58016
1926	Liverpool	(h) 1–0	Division One	Gallacher	20000
1937	Nottingham Forest	(a) 0–0	Division Two	No Scorer	28582
1948	A full international debut for Jackie Milburn, who scored with a header as England strode to a 6–2 victory over Northern Ireland at Windsor Park. South Shields-born Stan Mortensen scored a hat-trick.				
1954	Sunderland	(a) 2–4	Division One	Mitchell (pen), Milburn	66654
1961	Bobby Mitchell XI	(h) 2–3	Friendly	Allchurch, Tuohy	40993
1961	Testimonial match for Mitch.				
1963	Sunderland	(a) 1–2	Division Two	Taylor	56980
1965	Aston Villa	(h) 1–0	Division One	McGarry	31382
1971	Arsenal	(a) 2–4	Division One	Macdonald 2	40509
1976	Hibernian	(h) 2–1	Friendly	Cannell, Gowling	10284
1976	Future United signings John Brownlie and John Blackley both played for the visitors.				
1982	Oldham Athletic	(a) 2–2	Division Two	Varadi 2	9000
1988	Death of Jackie Milburn, 64, at home in Ashington.				
1991	Crewe Alexandra	(h) 1–0	League Cup 2nd Round 2nd Leg	Howey	9175

Sixth time lucky, as the home jinx was belatedly broken by substitute striker Steve Howey with just three minutes left. Franz Carr, who had attempted to beat the whole Crewe team for most of the game, at last put over a decent cross and Howey stooped to seal the tie. This game marked the final appearance of on-loan Andy Walker.

1994 Blackburn Rovers (h) 1–1 Premier League OG 34344
Newcastle's late equaliser came from a Howey effort diverted into the goal by the posterior of Tim Flowers. Shearer had earlier given Rovers the lead from the penalty spot.
1996 Two goals for Shearer as England defeated Poland 2–1 at Wembley.

OCTOBER 10TH

1896 Grimsby Town (h) 3–0 Division Two Aitken 2 (1 pen), Stott 5000
1903 Manchester City (h) 1–0 Division One Appleyard 19730
1908 Preston North End (h) 2–0 Division One Higgins, Stewart 26000
1914 Manchester City (a) 1–1 Division One Pailor 25000
1916 Willie Scott born, Bucksburn, Scotland.
1925 Manchester United (a) 1–2 Division One Seymour 40000
1928 Hearts (h) 0–1 Friendly No Scorer 20000
1931 Middlesbrough (h) 3–1 Division One Boyd 2, Lang 45000
1934 Army (a) 5–2 Friendly Kelly 2, Cairns 2, Leighton
Played at Catterick Camp.
1935 Bill Redhead born, Newcastle.
1935 Albert Scanlon born, Manchester.
1936 Leicester City (h) 1–0 Division Two Cairns 35000
Debut for Tom Mooney.
1953 Wolverhampton Wanderers (h) 1–2 Division One Mulgrew 39913
1955 Hearts (h) 2–2 Friendly Keeble, Mitchell 22542
1956 Linfield (n) 4–1 Friendly Milburn, Mitchell, Hannah 2 35000
Played at Windsor Park, Belfast. It was a match which indirectly led to Milburn's appointment as Linfield manager.
1959 Nottingham Forest (h) 2–1 Division One White, OG 33764
The sole appearance of Grant Malcolm for United, at outside-right.
1960 Colchester United (a) 1–4 League Cup 1st Round Neale 9130
Duncan Neale had the dubious distinction of scoring Newcastle's first goal in the League Cup, as they made an unsuccessful debut in the competition.
1963 Benny Kristensen born, Malling, Denmark.
1964 Leyton Orient (h) 5–0 Division Two Iley, Robson 2, Anderson 2 28454
1970 Arsenal (h) 1–1 Division One Robson 38024
1979 Preston North End (h) 0–0 Division Two No Scorer 25154
1981 Derby County (h) 3–0 Division Two Wharton, Varadi 2 17224
On a day when nothing went right for the visitors, Dave Swindlehurst contrived to miss the target from the penalty spot. Varadi got his first goals at St James' following his treble at Ninian Park the previous week. Kevin Todd made his debut, as substitute.
1984 Bradford City (a) 1–0 League Cup 2nd Round 2nd Leg Waddle 10210
1988 The large outlay on players and the poor start to the season resulted in Willie McFaul being sacked by an anxious Newcastle Board. Colin Suggett became caretaker manager, a position he held for some weeks while an embarrassing public search for a new manager continued.
1990 Middlesbrough (h) 1–0 League Cup 2nd Round 2nd Leg Anderson 12778
Mick Quinn sent off.

OCTOBER 11TH

1902 Bolton Wanderers (a) 2–0 Division One Orr, Carr 10000
1909 Ron Starling born, Pelaw.
1910 Hull City (a) 3–1 Friendly Higgins 2, Shepherd 12000
1913 Chelsea (h) 1–0 Division One McDonald 22000

1919	Bradford	(a) 1–0	Division One	Dixon	12000
1924	Liverpool	(h) 0–0	Division One	No Scorer	25000
1930	Middlesbrough	(a) 1–3	Division One	Cape	30000
1930	Ronnie Simpson born, Glasgow.				
1933	Peru/Chile XI	(h) 6–1	Friendly	Cape 2, Murray, Pearson, Richardson, OG	3000
1947	West Ham United	(h) 1–0	Division Two	Milburn	55767
1952	Wolverhampton Wanderers	(a) 0–2	Division One	No Scorer	45000

Wolves' scorers were Broadbent and an OG from Ron Batty.

1958	Leicester City	(h) 3–1	Division One	Allchurch 2, White	46686

A pair for Ivor Allchurch on his debut.

1960	Kevin Pugh born, Corbridge.				
1961	Sheffield United	(h) 0–2	League Cup 2nd Round Replay	No Scorer	12595

This defeat resulted in the dismissal of United manager Charlie Mitten. Unlucky right-half Billy Wilson made his only senior appearance.

1965	Hearts	(a) 1–2	Friendly	Moncur	5000
1969	Liverpool	(h) 1–0	Division One	Foggon	44576
1975	West Ham United	(a) 1–2	Division One	Howard	30400
1980	Bristol City	(a) 0–2	Division Two	No Scorer	10539

City's second was a penalty from Ritchie which beat Carr.

1986	Manchester City	(h) 3–1	Division One	McDonald (pen), Gascoigne, Cunningham	21780

OCTOBER 12TH

1884	Jock Rutherford born, Percy Main.

1891 Curtis Booth born, Gateshead. An unfortunate footballer in many ways, his impact at United was lessened by losing his best years to the Great War. Following his appointment as player-manager of Accrington Stanley, his playing career lasted 20 minutes before injury ended his onfield involvement in the game.

1895	West Hartlepool NER	(a) 8–0	FA Cup Qualifier	Logan 2, Thompson, Collins 2, Stott, Graham, OG	3000
1901	Derby County	(h) 0–1	Division One	No Scorer	15000
1904	Alnwick St James	(a) 6–1	Friendly	Orr 2, Aitken 2, Appleyard 2	1000

Bad light forced a premature end to this game with 15 minutes still remaining.

1907	Manchester United	(h) 1–6	Division One	McWilliam	30000

The only appearance of George Hedley, at outside-left.

1912	Manchester City	(a) 1–0	Division One	Stewart	35000
1915	Dave Smith born, South Shields.				
1925	Blackburn Rovers	(a) 2–1	Division One	N. Harris, McDonald	
1929	Burnley	(h) 2–1	Division One	Chalmers, Gallacher	30000
1932	Everton	(h) 3–5	Charity Shield	Boyd, McMenemy 2	15000

United lost this Charity Shield game to the previous season's League champions, and subsequently lost again to them in the League at Gallowgate three weeks later.

1935	Charlton Athletic	(h) 1–2	Division Two	Harris	28000
1935	Bill Curry born, Walker.				
1938	Gateshead	(a) 2–3	Friendly	Park, Dobson	17000
1946	Southampton	(a) 1–1	Division Two	Shackleton	27000
1957	Everton	(h) 2–3	Division One	Curry, Davies	30472
1959	Paul Goddard born, Harlington, Middlesex.				
1968	Ipswich Town	(a) 4–1	Division One	Foggon, Robson 2 (1 pen), Dyson	20763
1974	Stoke City	(h) 2–2	Division One	Tudor, Keeley	39658

1985	Ipswich Town	(a) 2–2	Division One	Beardsley, McDonald	12536
1988	Sheffield United	(h) 2–0	League Cup 2nd Round 2nd Leg	Hendrie, Mirandinha	14520
1991	Leicester City	(h) 2–0	Division One	Hunt, Clark	16966

On-loan Gavin Maguire made his debut in the centre of defence alongside Kevin Scott. Maximum points were gathered at home for the first time in the season against an unimpressive Leicester side who relied on a forward pairing of David Kelly and Paul Kitson for the final half-hour.

1994	Robert Lee made his England debut and scored in a 1–1 draw with Romania at Wembley.				
1996	Derby County	(a) 1–0	Premier League	Shearer	18092

A winning finale to 98 years of facing the Rams at the Baseball Ground. By the following season Derby had relocated to a new stadium at Pride Park, although reserve matches continue to be played at their former home.

OCTOBER 13TH

1894	Darwen	(h) 3–2	Division Two	Dickson 2, McNee	6000
1900	Derby County	(h) 2–1	Division One	Fraser, Peddie	18000

Only a consolation goal this time for visitors' marksman Steve Bloomer.

1906	Manchester City	(h) 2–0	Division One	Appleyard 2	20000
1923	West Ham United	(h) 0–0	Division One	No Scorer	21000
1928	Liverpool	(a) 1–2	Division One	Boyd	35000
1932	Ken Prior born, Newcastle.				
1934	West Ham United	(a) 2–3	Division Two	Lang, Weaver	29000
1951	Huddersfield Town	(a) 4–2	Division One	Hannah, Milburn 2, G. Robledo	32000

Debut for Billy Foulkes, who lost his place the following Saturday, having being picked to represent Wales for the first time. Newcastle actually scored all six goals, Joe Harvey and Frank Brennan putting past their own keeper.

1952	Gordon Hodgson born, Newcastle.				
1954	Hearts	(h) 2–3	Friendly	Milburn 2 (1 pen)	22594
1956	Aston Villa	(a) 1–3	Division One	Eastham	35000
1962	Sunderland	(h) 1–1	Division Two	Kerray	62262

Brian Clough scored for the mackems, while Newcastle's goal was an own goal from future Magpie Stan Anderson.

1964	John Cornwell born, Bethnal Green.				
1973	Manchester City	(h) 1–0	Division One	Macdonald	35346
1979	Shrewsbury Town	(h) 1–0	Division Two	Shoulder	21603
1984	Coventry City	(a) 1–1	Division One	Beardsley (pen)	14091

1988 Jackie Milburn made his final journey past St James' Park as his funeral cortège passed along Barrack Road. Thousands turned out to pay their last respects to the much-loved Newcastle hero.

1990	Oxford United	(a) 0–0	Division Two	No Scorer	6820

Debut for Scott Sloan, on as a substitute.

1992	Tranmere Rovers	(h) 1–0	Division One	Kelly	30137

1997 Newcastle reserves went to Chesterfield and won 2–1 in front of a good crowd at Saltergate. Trialist Carlos Gonzales continued up front and scored, while Marcus Munch appeared whilst on trial from Bayern Munich. Fellow German Ralf Keidel also played in midfield and was eventually given a permanent deal.

OCTOBER 14TH

1893	Notts County	(a) 1–3	Division Two	Wallace	5000

Highly rated Scottish outside-left John Inglis was brought into the side but failed to make an impact and was discarded after only three games.

1899	Manchester City	(a) 0–1	Division One	No Scorer	25000

1901	Dundee	(a) 2–2	Friendly	Roberts	2000
1905	Distillery	(h) 5–0	Friendly	Orr, Howie, Rutherford, McWilliam, McIntyre	3000
1911	Sunderland	(a) 2–1	Division One	Scott, McCracken (pen)	20000
1922	Burnley	(a) 0–0	Division One	No Scorer	25000
1933	Arsenal	(a) 0–3	Division One	No Scorer	40000

A slow start to an impressive United career at outside-left for Tommy Pearson. Arsenal were already on their way to a second successive First Division title (which became a third the following season). The final goal was given as an own goal by Dave Fairhurst.

| 1950 | Derby County | (h) 3–1 | Division One | Milburn, Mitchell, Walker | 54793 |
| 1959 | All Star XI | (h) 11–4 | Friendly | Eastham 3, White 3, Mitchell 2, Hale 2 | 14467 |

Testimonial match for long-serving United trainer Norman Smith. Included in the All Stars were George Cohen, Jimmy Adamson and future United winger Billy Day, then with Middlesbrough.

1961	Bury	(a) 7–2	Division Two	McGuigan, Leek 2, Hale 2, Suddick, Neale	13809
1964	Manchester City	(a) 0–3	Division Two	No Scorer	10215
1967	Fulham	(h) 2–1	Division One	Bennett 2	27664
1972	Stoke City	(a) 0–2	Division One	No Scorer	16609
1978	Sunderland	(a) 1–1	Division Two	Withe	35405
1989	Bradford City	(h) 1–0	Division Two	McGhee	19879
1995	Queens Park Rangers	(a) 3–1	Premier League	Gillespie 2, Ferdinand	18254

The danger of two-goal Dichio for Rangers was nullified by bungled defending which allowed Gillespie to walk the ball into the net.

OCTOBER 15TH

1898	Sheffield United	(h) 1–2	Division Two	Harvey	6000
1899	Harry Bedford born, Chesterfield.				
1904	Sheffield United	(h) 1–1	Division One	Howie	23263
1909	Tim Rogers born, Chirk, Wales.				
1910	Manchester United	(a) 0–2	Division One	No Scorer	50000
1913	Sunderland	(a) 0–1	Friendly	No Scorer	5000
1921	Chelsea	(h) 1–0	Division One	Harris	40000
1927	Sheffield Wednesday	(h) 4–3	Division One	McDonald 2 (1 pen), Gallacher 2	25000
1932	Wolverhampton Wanderers	(h) 3–2	Division One	Boyd 2, McMenemy	25000
1934	Joseph Cooper born, Gateshead.				
1938	Tranmere Rovers	(h) 5–1	Division Two	Cairns 3, Mooney 2	33000
1949	Sunderland	(h) 2–2	Division One	G. Robledo, Walker	57999

Controversy as Sunderland's equaliser, a backheel by Dickie Davis, was adjudged to have crossed the goal line despite protests from United goalkeeper Garbutt that he had reached it.

1949	Jackie Milburn scored a spectacular hat-trick at Ninian Park as England launched their first World Cup campaign with a 4–1 drubbing of Wales.				
1955	Arsenal	(a) 0–1	Division One	No Scorer	46093
	Debut for Ken Waugh, at right-back.				
1960	Wolverhampton Wanderers	(h) 4–4	Division One	Hughes, Mitchell 2, White	23401
1966	Manchester City	(h) 2–0	Division One	McGarry, Suddick	16523
1971	Andy Cole born, Nottingham.				
1975	Bristol Rovers	(h) 2–0	League Cup 3rd Round	T. Craig (pen), Nattrass	26294

1977	Manchester United	(a) 2–3	Division One	Martin, Burns	55056

Debut goal for Dennis Martin.

1994	Crystal Palace	(a) 1–0	Premier League	Beardsley	17739

A last-minute winner from Beardsley.

1996	Ferencvaros (Hungary)	(a) 2–3	UEFA Cup 2nd Round 1st Leg	Ferdinand, Shearer	18000
1997	Hull City	(h) 2–0	League Cup 3rd Round	Hamilton, Rush	35856

After playing the pre-season games and being stretchered off against Juventus, Des Hamilton marked his first-team debut with a goal, while Rush managed his only goal at St James' Park in a black-and-white shirt.

OCTOBER 16TH

1876	Tosh Hope born, Seaham Harbour.				
1897	Woolwich Arsenal	(a) 0–0	Division Two	No Scorer	12000
1909	Sheffield Wednesday	(a) 1–3	Division One	Shepherd (pen)	15000
1920	Sunderland	(a) 2–0	Division One	Seymour, Harris	35000
1926	Everton	(a) 3–1	Division One	Clark, Gallacher, McDonald	45000
1937	Aston Villa	(a) 0–2	Division Two	No Scorer	50000
1954	Tottenham Hotspur	(h) 4–4	Division One	Broadis 2, Crowe, White	45306

Debut for Bill Patterson, at centre-half.

1961	Middlesbrough	(h) 2–3	Friendly	Leek, Hale	10154
1965	Liverpool	(a) 0–2	Division One	No Scorer	47948
1968	Temuri Ketsbaia born, Gale, Georgia (formerly USSR).				
1971	Crystal Palace	(h) 1–2	Division One	Dyson	20711
1974	Wolverhampton Wanderers	(h) 0–0	Division One	No Scorer	30825
1976	Coventry City	(a) 1–1	Division One	Gowling	18083
1982	Fulham	(h) 1–4	Division Two	Keegan (pen)	29647

Keegan scored one penalty but missed another as United crumbled before the *Match of the Day* cameras.

1983	Swansea City	(a) 2–1	Division Two	Wharton, Mills	9807

Heavy rain caused the postponement of this fixture for 24 hours, and it became United's first-ever Sunday league fixture.

1984 Chris Waddle made an Under-21 debut for England, and scored in a 2–0 victory over Finland at the Dell.

1993	Queens Park Rangers	(h) 1–2	Premier League	Allen	33801

A towering performance from Les Ferdinand, who played most of the match with a leg injury, inspired the visitors to victory. He scored one and made one, while Malcolm Allen hit a memorable volley in between. Allen turned villain, however, when he missed a penalty awarded to United in the last seconds.

OCTOBER 17TH

1896	Manchester City	(a) 2–1	Division Two	Smellie, Auld	7000

Debuts for scorer John Auld and John Connell.

1903	Notts County	(a) 2–3	Division One	Templeton, Howie	9000
1908	Middlesbrough	(a) 0–0	Division One	No Scorer	20000
1914	Middlesbrough	(a) 1–1	Division One	Hall	18000
1925	Sunderland	(h) 0–0	Division One	No Scorer	50000
1931	Blackburn Rovers	(a) 3–0	Division One	Allen, Boyd, Lang	15000
1934	Middlesbrough	(h) 3–2	Friendly	Boyd, Smith, Lang	3200

All proceeds from this game went to the Gresford Colliery Disaster Fund.

1936	Chesterfield	(h) 1–2	Division Two	Cairns	27000

1939	Jackie Bell born, Evenwood, Durham.				
1940	Jim Smith born, Sheffield.				
1943	Death of George Thompson, 65.				
1953	Aston Villa	(a) 2–1	Division One	Davies, Milburn	50000
1956	Partick Thistle	(a) 1–4	Friendly	Milburn	20000
1959	Fulham	(a) 3–4	Division One	Eastham, Hale 2	37200

Debut for George Luke, at outside-left.

1964	Bury	(a) 2–1	Division Two	Cummings, Robson	8950
1970	Wolverhampton Wanderers	(a) 2–3	Division One	Davies, OG	24083
1981	Barnsley	(a) 0–1	Division Two	No Scorer	18477
1987	Everton	(h) 1–1	Division One	Mirandinha	20266

Mirandinha had the ball in the visitors' net inside 15 seconds of this game but play was brought back for an earlier foul, much to his annoyance. Ian Snodin gave Everton the lead, but after the dismissal of Adrian Heath, United should have taken all the points.

1988   Arthur Cox turned down the Newcastle manager's job recently vacated by Willie McFaul, preferring to stay at Derby.

OCTOBER 18TH

1902	Middlesbrough	(h) 0–1	Division One	No Scorer	26000

Debut for Peter McWilliam, at left-half.

1913	Oldham Athletic	(a) 0–3	Division One	No Scorer	8000
1919	Bradford	(h) 4–0	Division One	Dixon, Hibbert 3	44000
1924	Sunderland	(a) 1–1	Division One	Clark	55642
1930	Derby County	(h) 2–5	Division One	Lang 2 (1 pen)	30000

The debut and only appearance for the memorably named Errington Keen, thankfully better known as Ike. He went on to make over 200 appearances for his debut opponents. Derby's fifth goal was scored by George Stephenson, who hailed from Seaton Delaval.

1947	Bury	(a) 5–3	Division Two	Milburn 3, Shackleton, OG	23827

The conversion of Jackie Milburn from right wing to centre of the attack took place in this game at Gigg Lane. After the departure of Charlie Wayman to Southampton, Milburn was handed the number nine shirt and proceeded to score a hat-trick. However, it was against stand-in keeper Harry Catterick, who was filling in for George Bradshaw who had broken his leg early in the game.

1952	Charlton Athletic	(h) 3–2	Division One	G. Robledo, Keeble 2	41532

Robledo opened the scoring for United after 12 seconds.

1954	Doncaster Rovers	(a) 2–7	Friendly	White, Milburn	16479
1958	Preston North End	(a) 4–3	Division One	Franks, White 3	25525
1969	Tottenham Hotspur	(a) 1–2	Division One	Robson	33286
1975	Norwich City	(h) 5–2	Division One	Gowling 2, Macdonald 2, OG	32799

1976   One-time Sunderland messiah Bob Stokoe was forced to resign as manager following abuse from disgruntled fans.

1980	Swansea City	(h) 1–2	Division Two	Rafferty	16278

A poor way to celebrate the centenary of football being played at St James' Park. Alan Waddle, a relative of Chris, scored the winner.

1986	Arsenal	(h) 1–2	Division One	Stewart	22368

Debut for Darren Jackson, as a substitute replacing goalscorer Ian Stewart.

1989	Blackburn Rovers	(h) 2–1	Division Two	Quinn, McGhee	20702
1992	Sunderland	(a) 2–1	Division One	OG, O'Brien	28098

Remember where you were when Kennedy, Lennon, etc. were shot? Well, when O'Brien wrote his name across Geordie hearts, I was right in the middle of an almighty celebration on the Roker End with thousands of other joyous United fans. Gary Owers put through his own goal for the first, Gordon Armstrong equalised. Cue Liam.

| 1994 | Athletic Bilbao (Spain) | (h) 3–2 | UEFA Cup 2nd Round 1st Leg | Fox, Beardsley (pen), Cole | 32140 |

United fans were blamed by the local media for celebrating too much when the side were 3–0 up, a Mexican wave apparently distracting the players. Serves them right for taking part in it.

| 1997 | Leeds United | (a) 1–4 | Premier League | Gillespie | 39834 |

A dreadful performance by United, as goals from Ribeiro, Kewell, Wetherall and a Beresford own goal saw them well beaten. Man of the match for Newcastle was former favourite Robbie Elliott, who limped into the away end on crutches to cheer the lads on.

OCTOBER 19TH

1892	Jock Finlay born, Riccarton, Scotland.				
1895	Newton Heath	(a) 1–2	Division Two	Logan	8000
1901	Sheffield Wednesday	(a) 0–0	Division One	No Scorer	15000
1907	Manchester City	(a) 0–1	Division One	No Scorer	25000
1912	West Bromwich Albion	(h) 1–1	Division One	McTavish	30000
1924	Jerry Lowery born, Newcastle.				
1927	Middlesbrough	(h) 2–5	Friendly	Gallacher, McDonald	3350

McPherson's testimonial match.

1929	Sunderland	(a) 0–1	Division One	No Scorer	58519
1935	Leicester City	(h) 3–1	Division Two	Cairns, Harris, Ware	15000
1946	Bradford Park Avenue	(a) 1–2	Division Two	Pearson	26533

United could have had a point, but just as Shackleton was taking a penalty against his former team-mate Chick Farr, he changed his mind about where to hit it and succeeded only in scuffing it directly at the goalkeeper.

1955	Hibernian	(h) 1–2	Friendly	White	17992
1957	Aston Villa	(a) 3–4	Division One	Curry 2, Eastham	28000
1961	Phil Leaver born, Wirksworth, Derbyshire.				
1963	Portsmouth	(a) 2–5	Division Two	McGarry, Hilley	14996

Solitary appearance of Les O'Neil for United, at inside-left.

| 1968 | Queens Park Rangers | (h) 3–2 | Division One | Burton, Dyson, Gibb | 35503 |

A rare error from Moncur, putting through his own goal, couldn't prevent a first home win in six matches. The game marked the first visit of Rangers to Tyneside.

1971	Coventry City	(a) 1–1	Texaco Cup	Howard	12311
1974	Birmingham City	(a) 0–3	Division One	No Scorer	33339
1974	Former United keeper Martin Burleigh made his debut for Darlington after having signed for them on loan.				
1977	Bastia (Italy)	(a) 1–2	UEFA Cup 2nd Round 1st Leg	Cannell	8500
1983	Cardiff City	(a) 2–0	Division Two	Keegan, Beardsley	9926
1985	Nottingham Forest	(h) 0–3	Division One	No Scorer	23304

Two from Peter Davenport and one from Brian Rice deservedly beat an out-of-sorts United, for whom Beardsley had a penalty saved by Steve Sutton.

1987	Blyth Spartans	(a) 0–3	Friendly	No Scorer	4000
1988	Howard Kendall turned down the Newcastle manager's job recently vacated by Willie McFaul, preferring to stay at Spanish club Bilbao.				
1991	Oxford United	(h) 4–3	Division Two	Hunt, Peacock 3	16454

An eventful game for the returning Tommy Wright after 18 months on the sidelines, who replaced the injured Srnicek.The on-loan Maguire continued in defence and was at least partly responsible for two of the goals, as the score steadily increased at both ends. Eventually it seemed 3–3 was to be the final score, until a ball played into the box was knocked down by Scott into the path of Gavin Peacock, who completed his hat-trick.

OCTOBER 20TH

1894	Leicester Fosse	(a) 4–4	Division Two	Dickson, Thompson, Willis, Smith (pen)	8000
1895	James Clark born, Bensham.				
1900	Bolton Wanderers	(a) 2–3	Division One	Peddie 2	18000
1906	Middlesbrough	(a) 3–0	Division One	Appleyard 3	17000
1923	Middlesbrough	(a) 0–1	Division One	No Scorer	25000
1928	Arsenal	(h) 0–3	Division One	No Scorer	30000
1934	Manchester United	(h) 0–1	Division Two	No Scorer	25000
1951	Chelsea	(h) 3–1	Division One	Milburn 2 (1 pen), G. Robledo	52168
1953	Falkirk	(a) 2–3	Friendly	Milburn, OG	11000

United travelled to Brockville and played a friendly to officially open Falkirk's new floodlights.

1956	Manchester City	(h) 0–3	Division One	No Scorer	34802
1961	Ian Rush born, St Asaph, Wales.				
1962	Leeds United	(a) 0–2	Division Two	No Scorer	23250
1967	Glentoran	(a) 1–2	Friendly	OG	8000
1973	Chelsea	(h) 2–0	Division One	Macdonald 2 (1 pen)	32106
1979	Watford	(a) 0–2	Division Two	No Scorer	17715
1984	Nottingham Forest	(h) 1–1	Division One	Wharton	28328
1990	Ipswich Town	(a) 1–2	Division Two	Quinn (pen)	15567

United seemed to have dug out a point with a late equaliser from Benny Kristensen, but after it was chalked off he was sent off for swearing at the linesman, in Danish. Jim Smith had to be forcibly restrained from throttling the referee as the teams left the field.

| 1996 | Manchester United | (h) 5–0 | Premier League | Peacock, Ginola, Ferdinand, Shearer, Albert | 36579 |

Fantastic. Immortalised by the video 'Howay 5–0', issued by the club within days. To paraphrase the famous Norwegian commentator, 'Alex Ferguson, Zoë Ball, Bobby Charlton, your boys took one hell of a beating.' Of course, they still won the League . . .

OCTOBER 21ST

| 1893 | Ardwick | (a) 3–2 | Division Two | Wallace, Crate, OG | 3000 |

Debut for John Patten, at outside-right.

| 1899 | Sheffield United | (h) 0–0 | Division One | No Scorer | 30000 |
| 1905 | Bury | (h) 3–1 | Division One | Orr, Appleyard, Veitch | 20000 |

The only appearance of Darlington-born keeper Tom Rowlandson.

| 1911 | Blackburn Rovers | (h) 4–2 | Division One | Hay, Stewart 2, Wilson | 30000 |

Debut for Billy Hibbert.

1922	Arsenal	(h) 1–1	Division One	J. Low	30000
1933	Sunderland	(h) 2–1	Division One	Weaver 2	45000
1950	Bolton Wanderers	(a) 2–0	Division One	G. Robledo, Taylor	40000
1958	TSV Munich (Germany)	(h) 3–0	Friendly	Allchurch, Eastham, Hughes	20530
1959	Kevin Sheedy born, Builth Wells, Wales.				
1961	Brighton and Hove Albion	(h) 5–0	Division Two	Tuohy, Leek 3, Hale	24408
1963	Alf McMichael's XI	(h) 4–5	Friendly	Taylor 2, Kirkman, Cummings	24175

A testimonial for McMichael. Former Newcastle junior Bobby Cummings led the United attack and scored twice to clinch a return move to Tyneside from Aberdeen.

| 1970 | Pecsi Dozsa (Hungary) | (h) 2–0 | Fairs Cup 2nd Round 1st Leg | Davies 2 | 50550 |

1972	Manchester United	(h) 2–1	Division One	Hibbitt, Tudor	38214
1975	SK Brann (Norway)	(a) 1–1	Friendly	Macdonald	10000
1978	Charlton Athletic	(a) 1–4	Division Two	Walker	11616

United went ahead and then conceded a penalty which Lawrie Madden sent into space, but Mike Flanagan was more successful when another spot-kick was awarded. Two goals from Martin Robinson and one from Steve Gritt began a sequence of away defeats.

| 1989 | Brighton and Hove Albion | (a) 3–0 | Division Two | Quinn 3 | 10756 |
| 1995 | Wimbledon | (h) 6–1 | Premier League | Ferdinand 3, Clark, Howey, Albert | 36434 |

Les Ferdinand scored for the seventh successive game as the Dons fell apart and goalkeeper Heald was dismissed. To the cheers of the St James' crowd, Vinnie Jones took over in goal and conceded three goals.

| 1996 | | | | Newcastle gave a week's trial to Torquay's young striker Rodney Jack, who eventually moved to Crewe 18 months later after being linked with a host of clubs. | |

OCTOBER 22ND

1898	Bury	(a) 1–1	Division One	Rogers	4000
1904	Stoke	(a) 0–1	Division One	No Scorer	10000
1910	Liverpool	(h) 6–1	Division One	Stewart, Shepherd 4, Higgins	23000
1911	Harry Ware born, Birmingham.				
1921	Preston North End	(a) 0–2	Division One	No Scorer	10000
1924	South Shields	(h) 1–2	Friendly	Mooney	2000
	Ingham Cup final.				
1927	Sheffield United	(h) 1–0	Division One	Gallacher	10000
1932	West Bromwich Albion	(h) 3–0	Division One	Cape, McMenemy, J.R. Richardson	25000
1938	West Ham United	(a) 1–1	Division Two	Cairns	30000
1949	Liverpool	(a) 2–2	Division One	Mitchell, Thompson	48987
1955	Wolverhampton Wanderers	(h) 3–1	Division One	Davies, Keeble, Monkhouse	34575
1956	British Olympic XI	(h) 5–0	Friendly	Curry 5	8860
1960	Manchester United	(a) 2–3	Division One	Hughes, Stokoe (pen)	37516

Scorers for Manchester United were Dawson, Stiles and Setters, the small crowd reflecting the fact that both teams were in the bottom half of the league. Elsewhere, the Second Division match at the Valley finished 6–6, with Brian Clough netting a hat-trick for the visitors Middlesbrough.

1960				A 15-year-old Bob Moncur signed apprentice professional forms with Newcastle.	
1966	Blackpool	(a) 0–6	Division One	No Scorer	21202
1973	Birmingham City	(a) 1–1	Texaco Cup	Maconald (pen)	12429
1977	Chelsea	(h) 1–0	Division One	Burns	23683
1980	Shrewsbury Town	(h) 1–0	Division Two	Shinton	11985

A damp night at St James' Park and nearly 5,000 fans stayed in the house after the previous Saturday's home defeat by Swansea. Arthur Cox introduced Chris Withe at left-back and Chris Waddle to the attack, both having impressed in the reserves. It wasn't pretty, but Waddle showed glimpses of his skills.

| 1988 | West Ham United | (a) 0–2 | Division One | No Scorer | 17765 |
| 1994 | Sheffield Wednesday | (h) 2–1 | Premier League | Watson, Cole | 34369 |

Kitson made his home debut, but had to leave the field after being hit in the face with the ball.

| 1997 | PSV Eindhoven (Holland) | (a) 0–1 | Champions League | No Scorer | 29200 |

Wim Jonk scored the only goal of the game as an inexplicably negative United performance never looked likely to conjure up a goal. The most potent attack of the game came as a group of Ajax fans attempted to infiltrate the home end and were forcibly ejected.

OCTOBER 23RD

1897	Blackpool	(h) 2–0	Division Two	Aitken, Campbell	8000
1901	Middlesbrough	(h) 4–1	Friendly	Roberts 2, A. Gardner, Birnie	3000
1909	Bristol City	(h) 3–1	Division One	Anderson, Shepherd 2	10000
1912	Sunderland	(h) 0–1	Friendly	No Scorer	7000
1915	Jimmy Gordon born, Fauldhouse, Scotland.				
1920	Bradford	(h) 2–1	Division One	Harris, Ward	48000
1926	Blackburn Rovers	(h) 6–1	Division One	Clark, McDonald, MacKenzie, Seymour 3	25000
1930	Alan Monkhouse born, Stockton-on-Tees.				
1937	Bradford	(h) 3–0	Division Two	Imrie, Mooney, J.R. Richardson	21000
1954	Manchester United	(a) 2–2	Division One	Broadis, R. Mitchell	37247

First senior appearance for Bill Curry, who became the first player to be brought through from the club's new youth team, the Ns. Goalkeeper John Thompson also made his debut.

1965	Tottenham Hotspur	(h) 0–0	Division One	No Scorer	42430
1971	Manchester United	(h) 0–1	Division One	No Scorer	55603

Rare outing for reserve striker Chris Guthrie, who returned to United in 1989 in the vital role of kit man.

1974	Birmingham City	(h) 1–1	Texaco Cup	Macdonald	20559
1976	Birmingham City	(h) 3–2	Division One	T. Craig, Burns 2	31711
1982	Crystal Palace	(h) 1–0	Division One	Waddle	22616
1996	Oldham Athletic	(h) 1–0	League Cup 3rd Round	Beardsley (pen)	36314

OCTOBER 24TH

1896	Lincoln City	(a) 2–1	Division Two	Wardrope, Connell	2000
1903	Sheffield United	(h) 0–1	Division One	No Scorer	29000
1905	Bob Thomson born, Falkirk, Scotland.				
1908	Manchester City	(h) 2–0	Division One	Howie 2	33000
1914	Sheffield United	(h) 4–3	Division One	Booth, Hall 2, Hudspeth (pen)	25000
1925	Huddersfield Town	(a) 1–0	Division One	McDonald	16000
1931	Manchester City	(h) 2–1	Division One	Lang, McMenemy	20000
1936	Nottingham Forest	(a) 2–0	Division Two	Cairns, Rogers	20000
1953	Huddersfield Town	(h) 0–2	Division One	No Scorer	46644
1959	Bolton Wanderers	(h) 0–2	Division One	No Scorer	34679

Debut for Bobby Gilfillan.

1963	John Hendrie born, Lennoxtown, Scotland.				
1964	Crystal Palace	(h) 2–0	Division Two	Suddick, McGarry	30050

Alan Suddick claimed a goal in his first game of the season, having been sidelined by cartilage trouble.

1970	Everton	(a) 1–3	Division One	OG	43135
1981	Rotherham United	(h) 1–1	Division Two	Shinton	19052
1984	New Zealand FA	(h) 3–0	Friendly	Wharton, Waddle, Heard	3486

This match was arranged as part of the centenary celebrations of the Northumberland Football Association.

1987	Coventry City	(a) 3–1	Division One	D. Jackson, Goddard, Gascoigne	18585
1990	Charlton Athletic	(h) 1–3	Division Two	Brock	14016
1992	Grimsby Town	(h) 0–1	Division One	No Scorer	30088

The end of the unbeaten run, thanks to a memorable goal from Jim Dobbin and numerous saves by Grimsby's new on-loan goalkeeper Dave Beasant.

1993 Southampton (a) 1–2 Premier League Cole 13804

Two great and oft-repeated strikes from Le Tissier and a tantrum from the substituted Lee Clark provided a decent Sunday afternoon's entertainment for the Sky audience.

1994 Death of George Hair, 69.

OCTOBER 25TH

Year	Opponent	Venue/Score	Competition	Scorers	Att
1893	Everton	(h) 4–2	Friendly	Thompson 2, Sorley, Graham	4000
1902	Derby County	(a) 0–0	Division One	No Scorer	12000
1905	Darlington	(a) 7–2	Friendly	Orr 3, Howie 2, Appleyard, Gosnell	2000
1911	Sunderland	(h) 1–0	Friendly	Stewart	11372

Hospital Cup match.

Year	Opponent	Venue/Score	Competition	Scorers	Att
1913	Manchester United	(h) 0–1	Division One	No Scorer	35000
1919	Preston North End	(a) 3–2	Division One	Hibbert, Ramsay 2	18000
1924	Cardiff City	(h) 1–2	Division One	Cowan	22000
1930	Sheffield United	(a) 1–3	Division One	J.R. Richardson	20000
1940	Grant Malcolm born, Musselburgh, Scotland.				
1947	Southampton	(h) 5–0	Division Two	Milburn, Pearson, Stobbart, Walker 2	57184
1950	Mick Mahoney born, Bristol.				
1952	Arsenal	(a) 0–3	Division One	No Scorer	63744
1958	Manchester City	(h) 4–1	Division One	Eastham, McGuigan, White 2	54837
1961	Sunderland	(h) 2–1	Friendly	White 2	12230
1967	Leeds United	(a) 0–2	Division One	No Scorer	30347
1969	Chelsea	(h) 0–1	Division One	No Scorer	40088
1972	West Bromwich Albion	(a) 1–2	Texaco Cup	Hibbitt	7927
1975	Stoke City	(a) 1–1	Division One	Gowling	24057
1980	Chelsea	(a) 0–6	Division Two	No Scorer	22916

Quite how Bruce Halliday must have felt after this traumatic debut only he will know, but the presence of the BBC cameras to record the slaughter was cruel. Chris Withe and Chris Waddle also played only their second games.

Year	Opponent	Venue/Score	Competition	Scorers	Att
1986	Aston Villa	(a) 0–2	Division One	No Scorer	14614

Debut for Peter Jackson.

Year	Opponent	Venue/Score	Competition	Scorers	Att
1989	West Bromwich Albion	(h) 0–1	League Cup 3rd Round	No Scorer	22619
1995	Stoke City	(a) 4–0	League Cup 3rd Round	Beardsley 2, Ferdinand, Peacock	22992

A final visit to the Victoria Ground before closure, and a century-old record of scoring in eight consecutive games was equalled by Ferdinand. Stoke had Ian Clarkson dismissed for bundling Ginola over, while the locals took defeat badly with serious outbreaks of trouble to follow the pre-match skirmishes.

Year	Opponent	Venue/Score	Competition	Scorers	Att
1997	Blackburn Rovers	(h) 1–1	Premier League	Gillespie	36716

Chris Sutton equalised for Rovers after stand-in striker Gilliespie had spectacularly curled in United's opener.

OCTOBER 26TH

Year	Opponent	Venue/Score	Competition	Scorers	Att
1895	Newton Heath	(h) 2–1	Division Two	Wardrope, OG	7000
1901	Notts County	(h) 8–0	Division One	Roberts, Peddie 3, Orr, 4	12000
1907	Blackburn Rovers	(h) 3–0	Division One	Howie, McClarence, Rutherford	28000

Debut for Dick Pudan, at left-back.

1912	Everton	(a) 6–0	Division One	Stewart 2, McTavish 2, Low 2	10000
1921	George Robey XI	(h) 4–7	Friendly	Harris 2 (1 pen), Smailes, Russell	16000

George Robey was a music-hall comedian who first put together a side to play a benefit match for the widow of Chelsea trainer Jimmy Miller in 1907. The tradition continued, and numerous benefit matches were staged for charitable causes.

1929	Bolton Wanderers	(h) 2–3	Division One	McDonald 2	30000
1935	Swansea Town	(a) 2–1	Division Two	McMenemy, J. Smith	12000
1946	Manchester City	(h) 3–2	Division Two	Wayman 3	65798
1957	Wolverhampton Wanderers	(h) 1–1	Division One	Curry	44361

1960 Dick Keith appeared for Northern Ireland as they went down 3–4 to West Germany in a World Cup qualifier, despite a hat-trick from McAdams of Bolton.

1963	Northampton Town	(h) 2–3	Division Two	Taylor, Iley (pen)	25943

Debuts for Bobby Cummings and John Markie.

1968	Liverpool	(a) 1–2	Division One	Gibb	45323

McFaul took the blame for allowing a late winner to squirm through his hands, but the keeper had previously kept the home side at bay in a brilliant exhibition of shot-stopping. Moncur broke his nose.

1971 Steve Howey born, Sunderland.
1972 Death of Dave Fairhurst, 66.

1974	Leicester City	(h) 0–1	Division One	No Scorer	34988
1983	Oxford United	(a) 1–2	League Cup 2nd Round 2nd Leg	Keegan	13040
1985	Aston Villa	(a) 2–1	Division One	Beardsley, Gascoigne	12633

Winning debut for John Bailey.

1988	Middlesbrough	(h) 3–0	Division One	Mirandinha 2, OG	23845

An enjoyable debut for Lee Payne as United recorded their most comfortable win of a wretched season. Payne was soon to depart, one of a number of fringe players Jim Smith took an immediate dislike to.

1991	Bristol City	(a) 1–1	Division Two	Clark	8613
1994	Manchester United	(h) 2–0	League Cup 3rd Round	Albert, Kitson	34178

Steve Guppy will probably look back at his time at United and wonder why he was never given any more than a substitute appearance in this game to make his mark in a black-and-white shirt. Keith Gillespie made an early appearance at St James' for the visitors.

1996	Leicester City	(a) 0–2	Premier League	No Scorer	21134

OCTOBER 27TH

1894	Manchester City	(h) 5–4	Division Two	Dickson, Thompson 3, Graham	3000
1900	Notts County	(h) 2–0	Division One	MacFarlane, A. Gardner	12000
1906	Preston North End	(h) 2–1	Division One	Brown, Howie	30000
1919	Alnwick Ex-Servicemans XI	(a) 8–1	Friendly	Hall 5, Hibbert 2, Carr	
1923	Middlesbrough	(h) 3–2	Division One	Seymour 2, Hampson (pen)	30000
1928	Sunderland	(a) 2–5	Division One	Boyd, MacKenzie	50519

Jack Hill made his United debut, having turned down a move to his first opponents.

1934	Port Vale	(a) 3–1	Division Two	Murray, Smith 2	10600

1942 Death of Jack Dowsey, 37.
1947 Dennis Martin born, Edinburgh.

1951	Portsmouth	(a) 1–3	Division One	Milburn	39944

1954	Hibernian	(a) 1–1	Friendly	Crowe	21000
1956	Charlton Athletic	(a) 1–1	Division One	Curry	21473

The Londoners gave a debut to 18-year-old Brian Kinsey at outside-left. He struggled initially but went on to become a cornerstone of the Charlton team.

1961	Scunthorpe United	(a) 2–3	Division Two	Allchurch, Suddick	13987
1962	Swansea Town	(h) 6–0	Division Two	Fell 2, Suddick 2, Thomas, OG	24005

Death of Willie Bertram, 64.

1966	Wyn Davies signed for Newcastle in an £80,000 move. Within 48 hours he went straight into the first team for a Tyne–Wear derby.
1972	Lee Clark born, Wallsend.

1973	Tottenham Hotspur	(a) 2–0	Division One	Barrowclough, Gibb	31259
1976	Manchester United	(a) 2–7	League Cup 4th Round	Burns, Nattrass	52002

Gordon Hill scored a hat-trick. According to the song, 'We hate Man U cause they beat us 7–2.' Personally, it's more to do with their pious manager, corporate greed, lack of atmosphere and lemmings who follow them from afar.

1979	Cambridge United	(h) 2–0	Division Two	Withe, Shoulder	24104

Debut for Billy Rafferty.

1982	Leeds United	(h) 1–4	League Cup 2nd Round 2nd Leg	Clarke	24984
1984	Watford	(a) 3–3	Division One	Beardsley, Wharton, McDonald	18753

Another penalty save from Kevin Carr, foiling Nigel Callaghan.

1990	West Bromwich Albion	(h) 1–1	Division Two	O'Brien	14774

Debut for Matty Appleby.

1993	Wimbledon	(a) 1–2	League Cup 3rd Round	Sellars	11531

A match more notable for the non-appearance of Andy Cole than a predictable defeat. Lee Clark also missed out, after being dropped to the reserves. Warren Barton netted for the Dons at Selhurst Park.

OCTOBER 28TH

1893	Small Heath	(h) 0–2	Division Two	No Scorer	3000

A debut for locally born William Simm, at outside-right. This match, against the future Birmingham City, was to be his only senior appearance.

1899	Wolverhampton Wanderers	(h) 0–1	Division One	No Scorer	20000

Debut of Colin Veitch, a versatile player who appeared on 322 occasions for United and was later involved with the club, first as coach to the juniors and subsequently as a journalist covering United.

1905	Middlesbrough	(h) 4–1	Division One	Appleyard 3, McWilliam	35000
1911	Sheffield Wednesday	(a) 2–1	Division One	Hibbert, Higgins	18000
1920	Dick Burke born, Ashton, Manchester.				
1922	Arsenal	(a) 2–1	Division One	Aitken, J. Low	30000
1933	Chelsea	(a) 1–2	Division One	Murray	25000
1950	Blackpool	(h) 4–2	Division One	Milburn, G. Robledo 3	61008
1953	South Africa XI	(h) 3–1	Friendly	Milburn, Hannah, Mitchell	17460
1959	York City	(a) 8–2	Friendly	White 3, Allchurch 2, Eastham, Mitchell, Gilfillan	9414
1967	Everton	(h) 1–0	Division One	Iley (pen)	34030
1970	Death of Harry Ware, 59.				

1971 Joe Harvey bought the special talent of Tony Green from Blackpool, with Keith Dyson going to Bloomfield Road in part exchange.

1972	Chelsea	(a) 1–1	Division One	Smith	35273

1976 Central defender Martin Gorry arrived at Gallowgate in a £50,000 move from Barnsley but failed to make the grade with United.

1978	Cardiff City	(h) 3–0	Division Two	Connolly, Withe, Robinson	23477

1980 Arthur Cox signed Peter Johnson from Middlesbrough for £60,000.

1981	Fulham	(a) 0–2	League Cup 2nd Round 2nd Leg	No Scorer	7210

One for Ray Lewington from the spot.

1987	Wimbledon	(a) 1–2	League Cup 3rd Round	McDonald (pen)	6443

After Newcastle had missed chance after chance, midget Terry Gibson scored in the last minute.

1989	Port Vale	(h) 2–2	Division Two	McGhee, Quinn	17824
1992	Chelsea	(a) 1–2	League Cup 3rd Round	Lee	30193

A first goal for United by Rob Lee was a fine header, but Mick Harford netted the Chelsea winner. Former Magpie Joe Allon was never called upon as a home substitute, while the sidelined David Kelly received a great reception from the large travelling support as he limped past.

OCTOBER 29TH

1898	Preston North End	(a) 0–1	Division Two	No Scorer	3000

Debut for Sandy Macfarlane.

1903 William Gillespie born, Fife, Scotland.

1904	Preston North End	(a) 0–1	Division One	No Scorer	13000
1910	Bury	(a) 1–1	Division One	Shepherd	12000
1921	Preston North End	(h) 3–1	Division One	Curry, McDonald 2	40000
1927	Aston Villa	(a) 0–3	Division One	No Scorer	50000

Debut for Monte Wilkinson, at centre-forward.

1932	Sheffield Wednesday	(a) 0–2	Division One	No Scorer	10000

1932 John McGuigan born, Motherwell, Scotland.

1933 Death of Joe Harris, 37.

1938	Bradford	(h) 1–0	Division Two	Cairns	40000
1949	Arsenal	(h) 0–3	Division One	No Scorer	54670

1949 Death of Curtis Booth, 58.

1951 Stewart Barrowclough born, Barnsley.

1953 A double signing for Newcastle: centre-forward Alan Monkhouse joined from Millwall, and inside-right Ivor Broadis came from Manchester City.

1955	Aston Villa	(a) 0–3	Division One	No Scorer	27000
1956	Reading	(a) 3–2	Friendly	Curry, Eastham, White	7023
1960	Tottenham Hotspur	(h) 3–4	Division One	Hughes, White 2	51369
1966	Sunderland	(h) 0–3	Division One	No Scorer	57643

A not-so-mighty debut for Wyn Davies, but better was to come . . .

1970 Anth Lormor born, Ashington.

1977	Everton	(a) 4–4	Division One	T. Craig, Gowling 2, Cassidy	37574
1983	Manchester City	(h) 5–0	Division Two	Waddle, Beardsley 3, Keegan	33675

Beardsley became the first home player to hit a hat-trick at St James' since Alan Gowling in 1976 as United 'ran riot', according to that evening's *Football Pink*.

1983 The Magpie Club on Barrack Road closed with debts of over £200,000.

1988	Nottingham Forest	(h) 0–1	Division One	No Scorer	24642

Lee Chapman scored the only goal.

1991	Peterborough United	(a) 0–1	League Cup 3rd Round	No Scorer	10382

Sole appearance in a Newcastle shirt for the much-travelled Justin Fashanu. Peter Johnson turned out for the victors. To complete the visitors' misery, their dressing-room was broken into and ransacked while the game was in progress.

1994   Manchester United   (a) 0–2   Premier League   No Scorer   43795
Ten thousand fans watched the game on screens at St James' Park, while those who ventured to Manchester without tickets were confronted by touts charging and getting £150 per ticket. Andy Cole missed the first of four league games as he tried to overcome a shin splints problem.

1995   Tottenham Hotspur   (a) 1–1   Premier League   Ginola   32279
Ruel Fox faced his old club, while Geordie Chris Armstrong struck to give Spurs a half-time lead. Ginola equalised in the second half and Ferdinand saw a 93rd-minute shot blocked on the line as he tried to become the first Newcastle player ever to score in nine consecutive matches.

1996   Ferencvaros   (h) 4–0   UEFA Cup 2nd   Asprilla 2, Ferdinand, Ginola 35740
(Hungary)   Round 2nd Leg
One of the goals of the season from the Frenchman, as he controlled the ball with one foot, knocked it up and sent a scorching volley into the Gallowgate goal with the other.

OCTOBER 30TH

Year	Opponent		Score	Competition	Scorer	Att
1894	Neil Harris born, Glasgow.					
1897	Willington Athletic	(h)	6–0	FA Cup Qualifier	Aitken 4, Campbell, Jackson	6000
1902	Dundee	(a)	2–1	Friendly	Roberts, Carr	9000
1909	Bury	(a)	2–1	Division One	Shepherd 2	14000
1920	Bradford	(a)	2–0	Division One	Harris, Aitken	15000
1924	Charlie Crowe born, Walker.					
1926	Sunderland	(a)	0–2	Division One	No Scorer	30000
1937	West Ham United	(a)	0–1	Division Two	No Scorer	33000
1946	Tony Green born, Kinning Park, Scotland.					
1948	Liverpool	(h)	1–0	Division One	Milburn	67362
1954	Wolverhampton Wanderers	(h)	2–3	Division One	Milburn 2	49279
1957	Middlesbrough	(a)	0–3	Friendly	No Scorer	27000
1965	Fulham	(a)	0–2	Division One	No Scorer	19226
1968	Sporting Lisbon (Portugal)	(a)	1–1	Fairs Cup 2nd Round 1st Leg	Scott	9000

A cloudburst in the Jose Alvalade stadium threatened to bring a premature end to this tie, but United held firm until the last minute, when Morais equalised.

1971	Everton	(a)	0–1	Division One	No Scorer	38811

Joe Harvey gave Tony Green a 25th birthday present, the first of only 38 appearances for Newcastle before injury forced him to quit.

1973	Birmingham City	(a)	2–2	League Cup 3rd Round	Gibb, McDermott	13025

1975   England lost 2–1 in Bratislava to a lively Czechoslovakia side, and Malcolm Macdonald again couldn't hit the target.

1976	Stoke City	(h)	1–5	Division One	Cannell	32339
1982	Leeds United	(a)	1–3	Division Two	Anderson	26570

Chris Hedworth made a debut as substitute in a violent encounter, the referee having to take the teams off the pitch after Keegan was struck by objects thrown from the home fans. Police struggled to restore order as fighting broke out between rival fans, with more trouble outside following the final whistle.

1984	Ipswich Town	(a)	1–1	League Cup 3rd Round 1st Leg	McDonald	15084
1985	Oxford United	(a)	1–3	League Cup 3rd Round	Cunningham	8096

1993 Wimbledon   (h) 4–0   Premier League   Beardsley 3 (1 pen), Cole   33371
Happy families again, as Clark and Cole were restored to the team and Cole celebrated
with a goal.

OCTOBER 31ST

1896 Burnley   (h) 4–1   Friendly   Auld, Wardrope, Smellie 2   5000
1898 Tom Phillipson born, Ryton.
1903 Wolves   (h) 3–0   Division One   Orr, Appleyard, Howie   18000
Debut for Jimmy Tildesley, at right-back.
1907 Berwick Rangers   (a) 5–1   Friendly   Appleyard 3, Howie,   2000
                                                           Hardinge
1908 Liverpool   (a) 1–2   Division One   Wilson   28000
1910 Tom Mooney born, Glasgow.
1914 Aston Villa   (a) 1–2   Division One   Hibbert   15000
1925 Birmingham   (h) 1–3   Division One   Hudspeth (pen)   30000
1931 Everton   (a) 1–8   Division One   J.R. Richardson   32000
1935 Jimmy Hill born (not that one), Carrickfergus, Northern Ireland.
1936 Plymouth Argyle   (h) 1–1   Division Two   Smith   30000
1947 Swansea Town   (a) 2–1   Division Two   Shackleton, Wayman   32000
1948 John Craggs born, Flinthill, Durham.
1953 Sheffield United   (a) 1–3   Division One   Hannah   30412
Broadis' debut.
1956 Eddie Edgar born, Jarrow.
1959 Wolverhampton   (a) 0–2   Division One   No Scorer   33999
      Wanderers
Latecomers to Molineux missed all the fun, both goals being scored in the opening 85
seconds.
1964 Norwich City   (a) 1–1   Division Two   Robson   19380
1970 Manchester United   (h) 1–0   Division One   Davies   45176
The visitors' goalkeeper Jimmy Rimmer dropped the ball in the area and Wyn Davies was
on hand to poke the ball home in front of a joyous Leazes end.
1981 Oldham Athletic   (a) 1–3   Division Two   Davies   9010
1987 Arsenal   (a) 0–1   Division One   No Scorer   23662
1990 Newcastle reserves beat their Blackburn counterparts 3–0, Swedish trialist Jan Eriksson
playing for United.
1992 Leicester City   (a) 1–2   Division One   O'Brien   19687
A bad day at Filbert Street. South Shields-born Bobby Davison got one of the home side's
goals and Sheedy was sent off in the final minute for kicking Simon Grayson. The only
bright spot had been a free-kick of awesome power by O'Brien.

NOVEMBER 1ST

1902 Wolverhampton   (a) 0–3   Division One   No Scorer   8000
      Wanderers
Debuts for Sam Graham and Ord Richardson, the latter never playing for United again.
1913 Burnley   (a) 0–1   Division One   No Scorer   25000
Debut on the right wing for Angus Douglas.
1919 Preston North End   (h) 1–0   Division One   Robinson   48000
Clean sheet on his debut for local keeper Bill Bradley.
1921 Norman Dodgin born, Gateshead.
1924 Preston North End   (a) 1–0   Division One   Harris   12000
1929 George Brander born, Aberdeen.
1930 Leeds United   (h) 4–1   Division One   Devine 2, Lindsay 2   10000
1942 Benny Arentoft born, Copenhagen, Denmark.
1947 Doncaster Rovers   (a) 3–0   Division Two   Harvey, Milburn 2   28340

1952	Derby County	(h) 1–0	Division One	Walker	44571

Debut for George Brander on his 23rd birthday in place of the injured Bobby Mitchell.

1958	Arsenal	(a) 2–3	Division One	McGuigan, Allchurch (pen)	62801
1969	Burnley	(a) 1–0	Division One	Davies	16444

Debuts for John Cowan and Jimmy Thomson, in midfield.

1975	Arsenal	(h) 2–0	Division One	Gowling, Nattrass	34968
1980	Watford	(h) 2–1	Division Two	Hibbitt, Shinton	14590

A winning debut for left-back Peter Johnson, who played his best game for the club. All three goals came before half-time, with Malcolm Poskett netting the last.

1986	Oxford United	(h) 0–0	Division One	No Scorer	19622
1989	West Bromwich Albion	(a) 5–1	Division Two	OG, Brazil, Brock, McGhee, O'Brien	12339
1997	Leicester City	(h) 3–3	Premier League	Barnes, Tomasson, Beresford	36754

Two goals for Ian Marshall and one for Matt Elliott, all due to a statuesque United defence. Beresford saved the blushes with a late equaliser.

NOVEMBER 2ND

1888   Archie Duncan born, Dumbarton, Scotland.

1895	Middlesbrough	(h) 4–1	FA Cup Qualifier	Wardrope, McKay, Unknown Scorers	6000
1901	Bolton Wanderers	(a) 1–3	Division One	A. Gardner	11951
1907	Preston North End	(a) 0–2	Division One	No Scorer	12000
1912	Sheffield Wednesday	(h) 1–0	Division One	Higgins	25000

1919   Death of Bobby Templeton, 40, a victim of the nationwide influenza epidemic.

1929	Everton	(a) 2–5	Division One	Gallacher 2	30000
1935	West Ham United	(h) 3–3	Division Two	Bott, J. Smith, Ware	23000
1946	West Ham United	(a) 2–0	Division Two	Bentley, Shackleton	32000
1957	Leicester City	(a) 1–2	Division One	Batty	31884

1960   England Under-23 1, Italy Under-23 1 at St James' Park, watched by 15,000.

1963	Norwich City	(a) 1–3	Division Two	McGarry	17660

1965   Neil McDonald born, Willington Quay.

1968	Leicester City	(h) 0–0	Division One	No Scorer	20374
1974	Luton Town	(h) 1–0	Division One	Tudor	30141
1977	Bastia (France)	(h) 1–3	UEFA Cup 2nd Round 2nd Leg	Gowling	34560

A memorable performance from Johnny Rep destroyed hopes of European progress.

1982   A United reserve side travelled to Raydale Park, Gretna, to officially open their new floodlights. United won 2–1.

1985	Watford	(h) 1–1	Division One	Gascoigne	20640

Referee Trelford Mills returned to a chorus of boos from the Gallowgate faithful and, as usual, controversy followed close behind. Wearsider Colin West opened the scoring and Mills then gave United a dubious penalty which Peter Beardsley pushed wide. Gazza then hit a curling shot past Tony Coton in the Watford goal with three minutes left. George Reilly headed home in the last minute, but Mills ruled that he had pushed his way to the ball and didn't allow the goal to stand. Cue the final whistle, and another round of booing for the man in black.

1988   Former United favourite Bobby Moncur was confirmed as boss of Hartlepool, having been caretaker manager.

1991	Swindon Town	(a) 1–2	Division Two	Peacock	10731

Debut for Alan Thompson as substitute. Once Calderwood had put Swindon ahead, the result was never in doubt, and Peacock hit an undeserved consolation in the last minute, immediately after Swindon had gone two up. Heavy-handed policing broke up a conga on the away terrace as the travelling fans organised their own entertainment to compensate for the lack of any from the players.

1994	Athletic Bilbao (Spain)	(a) 0–1	UEFA Cup 2nd Round 2nd Leg	No Scorer	47000

Despite the fact that the European adventure had ended, most United fans who journeyed to the Basque region had one of the most enjoyable nights of their lives, thanks to the wonderful hospitality of the locals.

NOVEMBER 3RD

1894	Bury	(a) 1–4	Division Two	Thompson	4000
1900	Preston North End	(a) 1–0	Division One	Laidlaw	7000
1906	Derby County	(a) 0–0	Division One	No Scorer	9000
1923	Manchester City	(a) 1–1	Division One	Mitchell	25000
1928	Huddersfield Town	(h) 4–1	Division One	Boyd, Gallacher 2, Lang	38000
1934	Barnsley	(h) 4–1	Division Two	Boyd, Murray, Smith 2	8000
1951	Liverpool	(h) 1–1	Division One	Foulkes	50132

The first of only two appearances of stand-in striker Hugh Cameron, deputising for the injured Bobby Mitchell.

1956	Leeds United	(h) 2–3	Division One	Davies, Keeble	49034
1962	Chelsea	(a) 2–4	Division Two	Suddick, Fell	34428

Contemporary football magazine *Soccer Star* commented that 'United's singing supporters were reduced to a dry-mouthed crackle' when Bobby Tambling opened the scoring after 35 seconds, closely followed by Barry Bridges hitting a second. A third followed through Albert Murray before Suddick got one back, and Jimmy Fell scored direct from a corner. Just when United looked to force a point, the home side broke away again and Bridges claimed a second with nine minutes remaining.

1971	Coventry City	(h) 5–1	Texaco Cup	Macdonald, Tudor 2, Nattrass, OG	25230
1973	Stoke City	(h) 2–1	Division One	Gibb, McDermott	28135

Debut for Rocky Hudson.

1979	Oldham Athletic	(a) 0–1	Division Two	No Scorer	11486
1981	Berwick Rangers	(a) 3–2	Friendly	Trewick 2, Wharton	1167

Centenary celebration for the Borders club.

1984	Luton Town	(a) 2–2	Division One	Beardsley, Heard	10009
1990	Hull City	(a) 1–2	Division Two	McGhee	8375
1996	Middlesbrough	(h) 3–1	Premier League	Beardsley 2 (1 pen), Lee	36577

A unique goal celebration from Beardsley after converting his penalty: he ran to his son Drew, a ballboy for the day, behind the Gallowgate end goal.

NOVEMBER 4TH

1885	Sandy Higgins born, Kilmarnock, Scotland.				
1893	Liverpool	(a) 1–5	Division Two	Thompson	8000
1899	Aston Villa	(a) 1–2	Division One	Ghee	18000
1905	Preston North End	(h) 1–0	Division One	Howie	28000
1911	Bury	(h) 3–2	Division One	Hibbert, Higgins 2	18000
1922	Sunderland	(h) 2–1	Division One	Aitken, McDonald	60000
1933	Sheffield United	(h) 3–1	Division One	Allen, Dennison, Lang	16000
1950	Liverpool	(a) 4–2	Division One	G. Robledo 3, Taylor	48810
1958	Frans Koenen born, Waalwijk, Netherlands.				
1959	United striker Ivor Allchurch played for Wales as they drew 1–1 with Scotland.				
1960	Gary Nicholson born, Newcastle.				
1961	Norwich City	(h) 0–0	Division Two	No Scorer	25895
1967	Leicester City	(a) 2–2	Division One	Bennett, T. Robson	18001
1970	Pecsi Dozsa (Hungary)	(a) 0–2	Fairs Cup 2nd Round 2nd Leg	No Scorer	25000

An unforgettable place for Ian Mitchell to make his bow, on a bumpy pitch in the

Hungarian town of Pecs. After levelling the tie on aggregate and holding on through extra time, the Hungarians triumphed in a penalty shootout. United missed all three of theirs (Robson, Mitchell, Gibb), while McFaul was helpless to stop any of the three he faced. As the stunned United team reached the sanctuary of the dressing-room, they were forced to send out two more penalty-takers, Fairs Cup rules demanding that all ten penalties be taken. Dozsa scored their last two, and Clark and McFaul did likewise.

| 1972 | West Bromwich Albion | (a) 3–2 | Division One | Tudor 2, Smith | 14379 |

| 1978 | Bristol Rovers | (a) 0–2 | Division Two | No Scorer | 10582 |

| 1989 | Middlesbrough | (h) 2–2 | Division Two | McGhee, O'Brien | 23382 |

The end of Alan Comfort's career, as the former Orient winger sustained a leg injury in a tackle in front of the 'Boro dugout and never played again. To make matters worse, the incident took place yards away from where a group of Orient supporters were sitting, having wisely avoided going to Ayresome Park to see their former hero.

| 1992 | Birmingham City | (a) 3–2 | Division One | Peacock, Scott, OG | 14376 |

All the goals came in the first half of this match, Peacock's being quickly equalised by David Speedie, Scott's by Graeme Potter, then Trevor Matthewson putting one past his own keeper to give United the lead again. Newcastle keeper Wright went off injured at half-time and Kevin Brock took over and held firm, despite being dazed and confused. Stan Seymour died in a local hotel following the match.

| 1995 | Liverpool | (h) 2–1 | Premier League | Ferdinand, Watson | 36547 |

Ian Rush netted for the Reds but Steve Watson scored the winner courtesy of a last-minute fumble from David James in the visitors' goal.

NOVEMBER 5TH

| 1898 | Liverpool | (h) 3–0 | Division One | Peddie 2, MacFarlane | 20000 |

Debut for Scotsman Jimmy Stevenson, at inside-right.

| 1904 | Middlesbrough | (h) 3–0 | Division One | Orr, Howie, Rutherford | 23262 |

Winning debut for outside-left Albert Gosnell.

1910	Sheffield United	(h) 1–1	Division One	Duncan	20000
1921	Tottenham Hotspur	(a) 0–4	Division One	No Scorer	34448
1924	South Shields	(a) 2–2	Friendly	Clark, Keating	3000

Ingham Cup final second leg. South Shields won 4–3 on aggregate.

| 1927 | Sunderland | (h) 3–1 | Division One | McDonald, McKay, Seymour | 45000 |

1931 Death of Dave Gardner, 58.

1932	Everton	(h) 1–2	Division One	J.R. Richardson	30000
1938	Sheffield Wednesday	(a) 2–0	Division Two	Cairns 2	25358
1949	Bolton Wanderers	(a) 2–2	Division One	Milburn, Taylor	35000

1951 Derek Fazackerley born, Preston. A coach under Kevin Keegan, his true worth was only really appreciated after he returned to Blackburn.

1955	Blackpool	(h) 1–2	Division One	Milburn	54557
1956	Hearts	(a) 0–0	Friendly	No Scorer	18000
1960	Chelsea	(a) 2–4	Division One	White 2	30489

Debut at centre-half for Bill Thompson. Legend has it that after the match United directors made Jimmy Greaves a substantial offer to come to St James' Park, but he preferred to try his luck in Italy.

| 1966 | Manchester City | (a) 1–1 | Division One | Robson (pen) | 26137 |
| 1977 | Bristol City | (h) 1–1 | Division One | Martin | 23321 |

Debut in midfield for Nigel Walker.

1983	Fulham	(h) 3–2	Division Two	Wharton, Keegan, Mills	31660
1988	Queens Park Rangers	(a) 0–3	Division One	No Scorer	11013
1994	Queens Park Rangers	(h) 2–1	Premier League	Kitson, Beardsley	34278

| 1997 | PSV Eindhoven (Holland) | (h) 0–2 | Champions League | No Scorer | 35214 |

NOVEMBER 6TH

1897	Grimsby Town	(a) 0–2	Division Two	No Scorer	5000
1909	Tottenham Hotspur	(h) 1–0	Division One	Duncan	26000
1920	Burnley	(h) 1–2	Division One	Harris	50000
1926	West Bromwich Albion	(h) 5–2	Division One	Gallacher 2, McKay 3	30000

One of eight hat-tricks United scored at home in this championship-winning season. The match was most notable for it being Bob McKay's debut in English football following his move from Rangers.

| 1937 | Southampton | (h) 3–0 | Division Two | Park, J.R. Richardson, Smith | 30000 |

Debut for Ray Bowden.

1946	Norrkoping (Sweden)	(h) 2–3	Friendly	Milburn, Pearson (pen)	47124
1948	Blackpool	(a) 3–1	Division One	Hair, Stobbart, OG	30000
1954	Blackpool	(a) 0–2	Division One	No Scorer	20701
1957	Gwardia (Poland)	(h) 1–1	Friendly	Punton	17883
1958	Kevin Carr born, Morpeth.				
1963	Bournemouth	(a) 1–2	League Cup 3rd Round	McGarry (pen)	11735

| 1963 | Newcastle captured Stan Anderson from neighbours Sunderland at a cost of £19,000. |

| 1965 | Blackpool | (h) 2–0 | Division One | Robson 2 | 33853 |

Debut at centre-forward for Kit Napier. As in his other seven appearances for United, he failed to find the net, and departed for Brighton once Wyn Davies had been secured.

1971	Southampton	(h) 3–1	Division One	Macdonald 2, Green	32677
1974	Birmingham City	(a) 4–1	Texaco Cup	Kennedy, Nattrass, Cannell, OG	17754
1976	Manchester City	(a) 0–0	Division One	No Scorer	40049
1982	Burnley	(h) 3–0	Division Two	Waddle, Varadi, Keegan	20961

| 1984 | Blyth Spartans stalwart Tommy Dixon was given a testimonial at Croft Park against a Newcastle side, with former Spartans Steve Carney and Alan Shoulder wearing the green and white. |

| 1991 | Cambridge United | (h) 1–1 | Division Two | Hunt | 13077 |

Heroics from Andy Hunt, introduced as a late substitute against the savage Cambridge, who maimed anything that moved after having taken the lead. Hunt levelled it and was close to a deserved late winner as the referee added on injury time to compensate for the visitors' thuggery.

NOVEMBER 7TH

1896	Darwen	(a) 1–2	Division Two	Miller	
1903	Aston Villa	(a) 1–3	Division One	Templeton	20000
1908	Bury	(h) 3–1	Division One	Ridley, Rutherford, Veitch	30000
1914	Liverpool	(h) 0–0	Division One	No Scorer	24000
1925	Bury	(a) 1–1	Division One	Cowan	6000
1931	Arsenal	(h) 3–2	Division One	Allen, Boyd, McMenemy	25000
1936	Coventry City	(a) 2–2	Division Two	Mooney (pen), Smith	33000
1944	John Pickering born, Stockton-on-Tees. Former apprentice, later coach under Willie McFaul.
1953	Cardiff City	(h) 4–0	Division One	Broadis 2, Hannah, Milburn	42355

Debut for unsung goalscoring hero Alan Monkhouse, who hit 11 goals in 23 appearances.

| 1955 | Hearts | (a) 6–4 | Friendly | Keeble 3, Hannah 2, Davies | 12500 |
| 1959 | Everton | (h) 8–2 | Division One | Luke, Allchurch 2, White 3, Eastham (pen), Hughes | 23727 |

Debut for George Heslop, at centre-half.

1959　John Anderson born, Dublin.

1962　Darren McDonough born, Antwerp, Belgium.

1964　Rotherham United　(h) 3–1　Division Two　Suddick, Iley, McGarry　32870

1967　Marc Hottiger born, Lausanne, Switzerland.

1970　Southampton　　(a) 0–2　Division One　No Scorer　19250
Tommy Cassidy made his debut.

1973　Birmingham City　(h) 0–1　League Cup 3rd　No Scorer　19276
　　　　　　　　　　　　　　Round Replay
United perished in extra time.

1981　Chelsea　　　(a) 1–2　Division Two　Waddle　16509
Debuts for Alan Brown, on loan from Sunderland, Kevin Pugh, who came on as a substitute
for Varadi, and Wes Saunders. Sporting Chelsea fans attacked the four supporters' club
coaches as they left after the match, smashing many windows and injuring some of the
occupants.

1984　Ipswich Town　　(h) 1–2　League Cup 3rd　Waddle　23372
　　　　　　　　　　　　　　Round 2nd Leg

1987　Luton Town　　(a) 0–4　Division One　No Scorer　7638
Michael O'Neill made his debut, as a substitute.

1994　Nottingham Forest　(a) 0–0　Premier League　No Scorer　22102
Sitters missed at each end by Kitson and Collymore made a point a fair result against
Frank Clark's men.

NOVEMBER 8TH

1885　James Kirkcaldy born, Newcastle.

1902　Liverpool　　(h) 1–2　Division One　Roberts　8000
Debut for Andrew Gardner, at outside-left.

1905　Blyth　　　(a) 7–1　Friendly　Howie 3, Carr 2,　1000
　　　　　　　　　　　　　　　　　　Rutherford, Bolton

1913　Preston North End　(h) 2–0　Division One　Hall, G. Wilson　12000

1919　Middlesbrough　(a) 1–0　Division One　Booth　30000

1924　Burnley　　　(h) 3–0　Division One　Clark 2, Cowan　2000

1929　Death of Albert Shepherd, 44.

1930　Blackpool　　(a) 0–0　Division One　No Scorer　20000

1946　Roger Jones born, Upton, Hampshire.

1947　Nottingham Forest　(h) 0–2　Division Two　No Scorer　60244

1952　Blackpool　　(a) 2–0　Division One　Brander, G. Robledo　30000
Successful debut for Tom Mulgrew, who created both goals.

1958　Luton Town　　(h) 1–0　Division One　White　53488

1961　Middlesbrough　(a) 3–4　Friendly　McGuigan, Hughes, Woods　5221

1969　Sunderland　　(h) 3–0　Division One　Davies, Dyson 2　6317

1972　West Bromwich　(h) 3–1　Texaco Cup　Tudor, Gibb, Hibbitt　20420
　　　Albion

1975　Leeds United　(a) 0–3　Division One　No Scorer　39304
Well beaten at Elland Road, thanks to two goals from Duncan McKenzie and one from
Terry Yorath.

1979　Aaron Hughes born, Magherafelt, Northern Ireland.

1980　Cambridge United　(a) 1–2　Division Two　Shinton　5684

1986　Leicester City　(a) 1–1　Division One　McDonald (pen)　9836
Debut for Paul Goddard.

1992　Swindon Town　(h) 0–0　Division One　No Scorer　28091

1993　Oldham Athletic　(a) 3–1　Premier League　Cole 2, Beardsley　13821
Richard Jobson opened the scoring for the home side before United turned on the style and
won their tag of 'the entertainers'. Three times on-loan goalkeeper Lance Key looked

totally bewildered as the ball flashed past him.

1995   Blackburn Rovers (h) 1–0 Premier League Lee 36463
A collector's item, as Alan Shearer played against United and didn't score.

1997   Coventry City (a) 2–2 Premier League Barnes, Lee 22679
Shay Given must have been the only Irishman who didn't know where Dublin was, as he put the ball down in his area. Unfortunately big Dion was lurking behind him and popped the ball into the net. A brave Barnes equaliser looked to have been in vain when Dublin scored again, but with time running out Robert Lee picked the ball up in midfield and sent a long shot zooming into the goal to save a point for the Magpies.

NOVEMBER 9TH

1895	Darwen	(a) 4–4	Division Two	Wardrope, Aitken, Thompson, Collins	2000

Debut for Glaswegian Malcolm Lennox.

1901   Manchester City (h) 3–0 Division One Roberts, McColl (pen), Orr 8000
A goal for Bob McColl on his debut, a highly rated forward who was persuaded to move from amateur Scottish club Queen's Park.

1907   Bolton Wanderers (h) 3–0 Division One Appleyard, Orr, Rutherford 28000
1912   Blackburn Rovers (a) 0–2 Division One No Scorer 35000
1929   Sheffield Wednesday (h) 1–3 Division One McDonald 30000
1935   Bury (a) 4–3 Division Two Bott, J. Smith 3 12000
1938   A crowd of 39,887 watched England defeat Norway 4–0 in a full international at St James' Park, the England team including Newcastle player Duggie Wright.
1946   Sheffield Wednesday (h) 4–0 Division Two Wayman 4 46916
1952   Mike Larnach born, Lybster, Scotland.
1957   Blackpool (h) 1–2 Division One OG 36410
1963   Cardiff City (h) 0–4 Division Two No Scorer 38495
Inauspicious debuts for Stan Anderson and Trevor Hockey.

1968   Arsenal (a) 0–0 Division One No Scorer 34168
1974   Middlesbrough (a) 0–0 Division One No Scorer 39000
1977   Richard Dinnis was sacked as Newcastle manager.
1985   Birmingham City (a) 1–0 Division One Reilly 8162
1991   Grimsby Town (h) 2–0 Division Two Hunt, Howey 16959
A thoroughly mediocre Mariners team were never any threat to a home win, and their line-up included the veteran Gary Birtles. Alan Thompson made his first start in the first team, after fully recovering from the horrific neck injuries he had suffered in a road accident which had put his career in jeopardy.

1996   David Batty was in inspired form as England won 2–0 in Georgia, Ferdinand scoring the first goal.

NOVEMBER 10TH

1876   Jack Fraser born, Dumbarton, Scotland.
1894   Burton Wanderers (h) 3–1 Division Two Thompson, Smith, McDermid 6000
Bob McDermid scored on his Newcastle debut from left-back, repeating the feat only once in his other 63 appearances.

1895   Alf Hagan born, Durham.
1900   Wolverhampton Wanderers (h) 3–1 Division One MacFarlane, Peddie, Niblo 16000
1906   Aston Villa (a) 0–0 Division One No Scorer 18000
1923   Manchester City (h) 4–1 Division One Harris 2, Cowan, Aitken 28000
1928   Manchester City (a) 4–2 Division One Lang, Gallacher 3 15000
1928   Tommy Thompson born, Fencehouses, Durham.
1934   Sheffield United (a) 1–5 Division Two Smith 18000

1946   Geoff Allen born, Walker.
1948   England defeated Wales at Villa Park thanks to a Tom Finney goal, with Jackie Milburn keeping his place in the side.
1951   Blackpool   (a) 3–6   Division One   Milburn, G. Robledo 2   28611
1954   Admira Vienna   (h) 3–1   Friendly   Broadis, Mitchell, Milburn   18834
        (Austria)
1956   Tottenham Hotspur   (a) 1–3   Division One   White   51722
1962   Luton Town   (h) 3–1   Division Two   Fell, Thomas 2   27428
1969   Tino Asprilla born, Tulua, Colombia.
1973   Leicester City   (a) 0–1   Division One   No Scorer   20172
        George Hope made his first appearance for Newcastle, in place of the injured Macdonald. Keith Weller struck the only goal for the Foxes.
1979   Cardiff City   (h) 1–0   Division Two   Shoulder   22867
1982   Former Manchester United and Sunderland centre-half Jim Holton trained with United, but failed to make any favourable impression and was released.
1984   Chelsea   (h) 2–1   Division One   Waddle, McDonald   24542
        Kevin Carr saved a Colin Lee penalty.
1987   Walsall striker and future Magpie David Kelly made his debut for Ireland and netted a hat-trick as Israel were defeated 5–0.
1988   Newcastle attempted to raise funds for further purchases by selling Paul Stephenson to Millwall for £275,000.
1990   Wolverhampton   (a) 1–2   Division Two   Clark   18721
        Wanderers
        Debut of Steve Watson, on as a substitute. United recovered from being 1–0 down in the opening seconds, almost before they had touched the ball, and Quinn 'equalised', only to be flagged offside by a terrible decision. Lee Clark scored his first goal for United to set off wild celebrations on the away terrace, but Wolves sealed it shortly after half-time with a scrambled effort. This was probably Scott Sloane's best game in a black-and-white shirt, as he played a succession of good balls in from the wings and received numerous kicks and elbows for his trouble.
1993   Death of Doug Graham, 72.

NOVEMBER 11TH

1893   Sheffield United   (h) 5–1   Friendly   Crate 2, Thompson 2, Milne   4000
1899   Liverpool   (h) 1–1   Division One   MacFarlane   12000
1905   Wolverhampton   (h) 8–0   Division One   Orr 2, Appleyard 3,   15000
        Wanderers   Howie 2, Veitch (pen)
        The visitors, destined to be relegated, were never in this and had conceded five before the interval. Three more goals followed after Wolves had been reduced to ten men through injury, but United could have scored far more.
1911   Middlesbrough   (a) 1–1   Division One   Stewart   32603
        The point taken by both sides from this match saw the First Division table headed by Middlesbrough, with United in second and Sunderland in third place.
1922   Sunderland   (a) 0–2   Division One   No Scorer   50000
        The home side's second goal was scored by Arthur 'Tricky' Hawes, who reputedly always played with a white hanky clasped in his left hand. For surrendering, presumably . . .
1933   Tottenham Hotspur   (a) 0–4   Division One   No Scorer   42032
1941   Ollie Burton born, Chepstow, Wales.
1945   Pop Robson born, Sunderland.
1950   Fulham   (h) 1–2   Division One   OG   54234
1950   Tommy Cassidy born, Belfast.
1961   Rotherham United   (a) 0–0   Division One   No Scorer   11427
1967   West Ham United   (h) 1–0   Division One   Davies   32869
1972   Birmingham City   (h) 3–0   Division One   Macdonald, Howard, Gibb   26042

1975	Queens Park Rangers	(a) 3–1	League Cup 4th Round	Macdonald, Burns, Nulty	21162
1978	Millwall	(h) 1–0	Division One	Pearson	23087
1980	Notts County	(a) 0–0	Division Two	No Scorer	8093

1988   Liam O'Brien arrived at Newcastle, as the Board released some funds to caretaker manager Colin Suggett. Manchester United banked £350,000 from the transfer.

| 1989 | West Ham United | (a) 0–0 | Division One | No Scorer | 25892 |
| 1992 | Lucchese (Italy) | (a) 1–1 | Anglo-Italian Cup | Kristensen | 744 |

A meagre attendance at the Stadio Porta Elisa to witness Mick Quinn's final appearance for United. He came on as a substitute for the final 30 minutes of this game, just after Kristensen had equalised Russo's first-half effort. The home side played in a strip of white shorts and AC Milan shirts, but there the similarity ended.

NOVEMBER 12TH

1898	Nottingham Forest	(a) 0–2	Division One	No Scorer	8000
1904	Wolverhampton Wanderers	(a) 3–1	Division One	Howie 3	6000
1910	Aston Villa	(a) 2–3	Division One	Stewart 2	40000
1921	Tottenham Hotspur	(h) 0–2	Division One	No Scorer	30000
1927	Bury	(a) 4–1	Division One	Seymour, McDonald (pen), Gallacher, McKay	21408
1932	Arsenal	(a) 0–1	Division One	No Scorer	60000

The Gunners allowed spectators in to their magnificent new West Stand for the first time; it was officially opened a month later by the Prince of Wales.

| 1938 | Fulham | (h) 2–1 | Division Two | Birkett, Bowden | 63962 |

1945   David Young born, Newcastle.

| 1949 | Birmingham City | (h) 3–1 | Division One | G. Robledo 2, Walker | 30113 |
| 1955 | Huddersfield Town | (a) 6–2 | Division One | Crowe, Keeble 4, White | 18664 |

Harry Fearnley made his league debut for Huddersfield in goal and required treatment by the trainer after a crack on the head when the first goal was scored. He later claimed not to have known how many he had conceded! The unlucky Fearnley then sustained a finger injury in his next game against Birmingham City and conceded five goals.

1957   Tony Cunningham born, Kingston, Jamaica.

| 1960 | Blackpool | (h) 4–3 | Division One | Neale 2, White 2 | 26657 |
| 1966 | Liverpool | (h) 0–2 | Division One | No Scorer | 36920 |

Debut for Willie McFaul.

1966   Joe Allon born, Washington, Tyne and Wear.

1966   Andy Thorn born, Carshalton, Surrey.

| 1969 | Sunderland | (a) 2–4 | Friendly | Moncur, Scott | 6470 |

Len Ashurst's testimonial match. Former United star George Eastham turned out in a black-and-white shirt once more.

| 1977 | Wolverhampton Wanderers | (a) 0–1 | Division One | No Scorer | 16964 |

Debut as substitute, for Tony Smith.

| 1983 | Chelsea | (a) 0–4 | Division Two | No Scorer | 30638 |

A rotten day at Stamford Bridge, with goals from Nigel Spackman, Peter Rhodes-Brown and two from David Speedie. David Mcreery was carried off injured.

| 1988 | Arsenal | (h) 0–1 | Division One | No Scorer | 23807 |

The final appearance of John Robertson in a United shirt, who was replaced by debutant David Robinson. Within days he had returned to his former club Hearts, rediscovering his goalscoring touch as he crossed the border back into Scotland.

NOVEMBER 13TH

| 1897 | Newton Heath | (a) 1–0 | Division Two | Wardrope | 6000 |

United debutant Jock Peddie later moved to Newton Heath, in their later guise of Manchester United.

1909	Preston North End	(a) 0–4	Division One	No Scorer	16000
1920	Burnley	(a) 1–3	Division One	Dixon	38860
1926	Bury	(a) 2–3	Division One	Gallacher, Hudspeth (pen)	12000
1937	Blackburn Rovers	(a) 1–2	Division Two	Bowden	18000

1938 Following a successful trial match for United when he netted six goals in the second half, Jackie Milburn signed for Newcastle.

1948	Derby County	(h) 3–0	Division One	Hair, Milburn, Stobbart	64061
1954	Charlton Athletic	(h) 3–1	Division One	Mitchell (pen), Curry 2	35988
1965	Blackburn Rovers	(a) 2–4	Division One	Bennett, OG	12293

Mike Harrison scored an own goal, but two goals from his Rovers team-mate Mike England set them on track for victory.

| 1971 | Leicester City | (a) 0–3 | Division One | No Scorer | 28792 |
| 1974 | Fulham | (h) 3–0 | League Cup 4th Round | Cannell, Macdonald, Cassidy | 23774 |

1974 Terry McDermott was transferred to Liverpool, for a fee of £170,000.

| 1979 | Manchester City | (h) 4–1 | Friendly | Macdonald, Withe, Connolly, McDermott | 14995 |

Willie McFaul's testimonial.

| 1982 | Leicester City | (a) 2–2 | Division Two | Keegan 2 | 15044 |

NOVEMBER 14TH

| 1896 | Leicester Fosse | (h) 3–1 | Division Two | Wardrope 2, Smellie | 6000 |
| 1903 | Middlesbrough | (h) 2–1 | Division One | Rutherford 2 | 28000 |

1906 Billy Halliday born, Dumfries, Scotland.

| 1908 | Sheffield United | (a) 1–1 | Division One | Veitch (pen) | 18000 |
| 1914 | Bradford | (a) 0–1 | Division One | No Scorer | 10000 |

1923 Tommy Walker born, Cramlington.

| 1925 | Tottenham Hotspur | (h) 3–1 | Division One | Gibson, Seymour, OG | 24000 |

Debut for Jack Dowsey.

1931	Derby County	(a) 1–1	Division One	Boyd	12730
1936	Doncaster Rovers	(h) 7–0	Division Two	Leighton 2, Rogers, Smith 4	22000
1953	Manchester City	(a) 0–0	Division One	No Scorer	48830
1956	Partick Thistle	(h) 5–0	Friendly	Keeble 2, Milburn, Keery, Speirs	8880
1959	Blackpool	(a) 0–2	Division One	No Scorer	15667
1964	Swansea Town	(a) 1–3	Division Two	McGarry	10457
1970	Ipswich Town	(h) 0–0	Division One	No Scorer	25657
1981	Charlton Athletic	(h) 4–1	Division Two	Wharton, Varadi 2, Brown	5254

Varadi scored a brilliant individual goal, running the length of the pitch to slot home.

| 1987 | Derby County | (h) 0–0 | Division One | No Scorer | 21698 |

A clean sheet for Rams keeper Peter Shilton, on his 800th league appearance.

| 1992 | Charlton Athletic | (a) 3–1 | Division Two | Peacock 2, Howey | 12945 |

Played at Upton Park. Last game for Charlton on a borrowed ground, as they prepared to return to the Valley. Garry Nelson scored their goal, while the match was sponsored by Reg Lee, father of Robert.

NOVEMBER 15TH

| 1902 | Sheffield United | (a) 1–2 | Division One | Roberts | 14000 |

Debut for Scotsman John Watson, at right-back.

| 1913 | Tottenham Hotspur | (h) 2–0 | Division One | Hall 2 | 25000 |

1915 Archie Livingstone born, Pencaitland, Scotland.
1918 Billy Pears born, Willington, Durham.

| 1924 | Leeds United | (a) 1–1 | Division One | Seymour | 35000 |
| 1930 | Portsmouth | (h) 4–7 | Division One | Devine, Lindsay 2, Wilkinson | 23000 |

1933 Full international at St James' Park, with Wales overcoming England 2–1 in front of 12,000 spectators and clinching the Home International Championship.

| 1947 | Bradford | (a) 3–0 | Division Two | Stobbart, Sibley, OG | 24654 |

1950 A short journey for Jackie Milburn as he was selected to play for England in an international held at Roker Park. He scored one as Wales were defeated 4–2, with another local lad Wilf Mannion also hitting the net.

1952	Chelsea	(h) 2–1	Division One	G. Robledo (pen), Brennan	37178
1953	Keith Robson born, Hetton-le-Hole.				
1958	Birmingham City	(a) 0–1	Division One	No Scorer	28720
1961	Neil Simpson born, London.				
1969	Nottingham Forest	(h) 3–1	Division One	Dyson, Craig, OG	24307
1975	Liverpool	(h) 1–2	Division One	Nulty	41145
1980	Sheffield Wednesday	(h) 1–0	Division Two	Shinton	19145
1986	Watford	(h) 2–2	Division One	McDonald (pen), Anderson	23645

1994 A crowd of 25,863 turned up at St James' to see Steve Watson star for England Under-21s as they defeated Ireland 1–0.

NOVEMBER 16TH

1895	Darwen	(h) 7–2	Division Two	Wardrope 3, Aitken, Collins, Lennox, McDermidd	6000
1896	Darlington	(a) 1–2	Friendly	Wardrope	2000
1907	Bury	(a) 2–1	Division One	Appleyard, Rutherford	18000
1911	Jackie Cape born, Carlisle.				
1912	Derby County	(h) 2–4	Division One	Hibbert, McTavish	25000
1929	Manchester City	(a) 0–3	Division One	No Scorer	30000
1935	Doncaster Rovers	(h) 2–1	Division Two	Pearson, J. Smith	27000
1946	Fulham	(a) 3–0	Division Two	Bentley, Wayman 2	44000
1955	Hibernian	(a) 0–2	Friendly	No Scorer	20000

This match was abandoned with 20 minutes remaining when fog descended.

| 1957 | Luton Town | (a) 3–0 | Division One | Bell, White 2 | 19670 |

A goal on his debut for Jackie Bell, with virtually his first touch.

1963	Swindon Town	(a) 0–0	Division Two	No Scorer	20699
1968	Manchester City	(h) 1–0	Division One	Davies	36420
1974	Chelsea	(h) 5–0	Division One	Cannell, Macdonald 2, Kennedy, Barrowclough	35236
1985	Chelsea	(h) 1–3	Division One	Roeder	22394

A Glenn Roeder header gave United the best possible start, but Chelsea recovered to equalise through Speedie and win it with late goals from Nigel Spackman and Kerry Dixon.

1988 Newcastle reserves lost 1–0 to Barnsley at St James' Park. In the United team was full-back Andy Fensome, who spent a short period on loan from Norwich while Anth Lormor temporarily went to Carrow Road.

1994 England faced Nigeria at Wembley and started the game with Beardsley, Cole and Howey in the side.

| 1996 | West Ham United | (h) 1–1 | Premier League | Beardsley | 36552 |

NOVEMBER 17TH

1894	Lincoln City	(a) 1–3	Division Two	Wallace	2000
1900	Aston Villa	(a) 2–2	Division One	Peddie, A. Gardner	20000
1906	Liverpool	(h) 2–0	Division One	Gardner, Speedie	36000
1920	Willie McCall born, Glasgow.				

1923	Preston North End	(a) 2–1	Division One	Harris 2	12500

Debut for Willie Gibson, at left-half.

1928	Birmingham	(h) 1–0	Division One	Wilkinson	30000
1934	Bradford City	(h) 4–2	Division Two	Boyd, Leighton, Smith 2	14000

Debut for Norman Tapken, in goal.

1935	Bobby Cummings born, Ashington.				
1951	Arsenal	(h) 2–0	Division One	G. Robledo, OG	61192
1956	Everton	(h) 0–0	Division One	No Scorer	32263
1958	Orgryte (Sweden)	(h) 5–2	Friendly	Allchurch 2, White, Eastham, Curry	18356
1962	Southampton	(a) 0–3	Division Two	No Scorer	13582

Another disaster at the Dell, as Southampton led 1–0 at the break through Sydenham, with Burnside and O'Brien adding further goals in the second half. Top scorer Barrie Thomas missed out for United, and such was the injury crisis that reserve inside-forward Charlie Woods almost played his first game since the previous February. Woods had actually travelled south to join Bournemouth, but was placed on standby until Alan Suddick was cleared by the referee to play with a plaster cast on his right hand. Woods then signed for Bournemouth for a fee of £6,000, was rushed by car to Eastville and played for his new club that afternoon against Bristol Rovers. Of course, he scored the first goal in a 2–1 victory.

1973	Manchester United	(h) 3–2	Division One	Cassidy 2, Hope	42474

Lou Macari and George Graham were on target for the visitors but George Hope scored the only goal of his short career at St James' to win it, with a header at the Gallowgate end.

1979	Bristol City	(a) 1–1	Division Two	Shoulder	7626
1990	Barnsley	(h) 0–0	Division Two	No Scorer	15548

Just rubbish. An absolutely miserable performance that reduced the crowd to silence.

1991	Sunderland	(a) 1–1	Division Two	O'Brien	29224

The early kick-off on a Sunday did little to dampen the emotions – or thirsts – of both sets of fans, and local bars simply opened (illegally) from early morning to compensate. However, the only pitch invasion took place as a small child danced across the turf waving a black-and-white scarf after the match, to the delight of the away fans locked in the Roker End.

1993	Swedish trialist Mat Elison played in a 1–0 reserve home defeat by Sheffield Wednesday and was shown the door.				

NOVEMBER 18TH

1893	Northwich Victoria	(a) 3–5	Division Two	Crate, Thompson, OG	400

Believed to be the oldest continually used football ground, the Drill Field hosted League football for only two seasons. This was United's only visit in the final campaign the Vics took part in before their relegation.

1899	Burnley	(a) 3–1	Division One	Fraser, Wardrope, Rogers	5000
1905	Aston Villa	(a) 3–0	Division One	Orr 2, Veitch	30000
1908	Middlesbrough	(h) 5–1	Friendly	Stewart 3, Higgins, Wilson	3000

A benefit match against local opposition to raise funds for Newcastle's Royal Victoria Infirmary.

1911	Notts County	(h) 3–2	Division One	Low, Rutherford 2	18000
1922	Tottenham Hotspur	(a) 1–0	Division One	McDonald	30300
1933	Leicester City	(h) 1–1	Division One	McMenemy	8000
1950	Tottenham Hotspur	(a) 0–7	Division One	No Scorer	70026

Les Medley grabbed a hat-trick for the Londoners.

1961	Bristol Rovers	(h) 5–2	Division Two	J. Wilson, Allchurch, White 3	23215
1967	Burnley	(a) 0–2	Division One	No Scorer	15546
1967	Gavin Peacock born, Welling, Kent.				
1969	FC Porto (Portugal)	(a) 0–0	Fairs Cup 2nd Round 1st Leg	No Scorer	25000

An uneventful game at the Antas Stadium, Oporto. Moncur recovered from a fever to take his place in the defence.

1970	Ayr United	(a) 0–2	Friendly	No Scorer	5000
1972	Liverpool	(a) 2–3	Division One	Tudor, Macdonald	46153

1977 Newcastle appointed Bill McGarry as their new manager, replacing the recently dismissed Richard Dinnis.

1978	Luton Town	(a) 0–2	Division Two	No Scorer	10434
1984	Liverpool	(h) 0–2	Division One	No Scorer	27015

St James' Park hosted its first Sunday game for this televised encounter.

1989	Barnsley	(a) 1–1	Division Two	Quinn	10475

1988 No match at St James' Park, but it was a measure of the plight of the team that nearly 20,000 fans turned up for an open day, 5,000 more than had suffered the previous day's goalless draw. Charitable observers saw the open day as a thank you to the fans, while the more cynical among us noted that the deadline for the share issue was less than a week away.

1995	Aston Villa	(a) 1–1	Premier League	Ferdinand	39167

Gateshead-born United fan Tommy Johnson put Villa ahead.

1997	Derby County	(a) 1–0	League Cup	Tomasson	27364

Newcastle became the first team to beat Derby in a competitive match in their new Pride Park stadium, although Sampdoria had triumphed 1–0 in a pre-season friendly to open the ground.

NOVEMBER 19TH

1898	Bolton Wanderers	(h) 4–1	Division One	Peddie 2, MacFarlane, Rogers	20000
1902	Middlesbrough	(a) 3–1	Friendly	Gardner, Graham, Unknown Scorer	1000
1904	Bury	(h) 3–1	Division One	Gosnell, Appleyard, Veitch	18262
1910	Sunderland	(h) 1–1	Division One	Shepherd	57416
1921	Sunderland	(h) 2–2	Division One	McDonald, McIntosh	46000

An interested spectator at Gallowgate was the Duke of York, future King George.

1927	Burnley	(h) 1–1	Division One	Gallacher	28000
1932	Manchester City	(h) 2–0	Division One	Cape 2	24000
1938	Blackburn Rovers	(a) 0–3	Division Two	No Scorer	21300

Sole senior appearance of George Bradley, although he did feature in wartime United teams. Benny Craig, who had a rather longer career at St James Park, also made his entrance.

1949	Derby County	(a) 0–1	Division One	No Scorer	29973

With just 15 minutes left, the Rams looked set for a win until the fog descended and the game was abandoned. The replay finished 1–1.

1955	Cardiff City	(h) 4–0	Division One	Milburn 2 (1 pen), Keeble, Crowe	35603

1955 United signed Mickley-born twin brothers Alan and Norman Breen, who failed to make the grade.

1957 Death of Jack Allen, 54.

1959	Torpedo Moscow (USSR)	(h) 4–4	Friendly	White 2, Allchurch, Eastham (pen)	7921

The Russian first division side Torpedo visited Tyneside as part of a three-match tour of England, also being entertained by Tottenham and Sheffield United. The second half of this match was televised by ITV.

1960	Everton	(a) 0–5	Division One	No Scorer	41123

1965 Death of Tom Phillipson, 67.

1966	West Ham United	(a) 0–3	Division One	No Scorer	31285

1975 England's chances of European Championship qualification were virtually ended by a 1–1 draw with Portugal in Lisbon. It was to be Malcolm Macdonald's final England appearance.

| 1977 | Arsenal | (h) 1–2 | Division One | Cassidy | 23679 |
| 1983 | Sheffield Wednesday (a) 2–4 | | Division Two | McDermott, Keegan (pen) | 41134 |

A magnificent show of support for United, around 15,000 travelling to cheer them on. Unfortunately they were to witness former and future Magpies on target for the Owls, Varadi and Cunningham. Varadi stood almost apologetically in front of the travelling masses after scoring at the Leppings Lane end, and was given a sporting reception.

| 1988 | Millwall | (a) 0–4 | Division One | No Scorer | 15767 |

A team coached by Mick Martin and featuring the talents of Liam O'Brien and Rob McDonald for the first time were hammered by the Lions. McDonald almost scored with a header, but the 'goal' was ruled out. The unloved Terry Hurlock was among the scorers for the Lions.

| 1993 | Sir John Hall named the new Leazes end stand after himself and buried a time capsule including a bottle of broon. |

| 1994 | Wimbledon | (a) 2–3 | Premier League | Beardsley, Kitson | 14203 |

The inevitable failure at Selhurst Park, this year's twist being a future Magpie (Barton) setting up a former Magpie (Harford) for the winner.

| 1996 | Metz (France) | (a) 1–1 | UEFA Cup 3rd Round 1st Leg | Beardsley (pen) | 23000 |

NOVEMBER 20TH

1897	Stockton	(a) 4–1	FA Cup Qualifier	Campbell, Harvey, Ghee, Jackson	8000
1909	Notts County	(h) 1–3	Division One	Rutherford	18000
1912	Thackery's XI	(a) 2–3	Friendly	Fleming 2	
1920	Liverpool	(h) 2–0	Division One	Seymour, Ward	50000
1926	Birmingham	(h) 5–1	Division One	Gallacher, Hudspeth, McDonald, McKay, Seymour	20000
1937	Plymouth Argyle	(h) 3–1	Division Two	Mooney, Smith, Imrie (pen)	21000
1948	Arsenal	(a) 1–0	Division One	OG	62000

The winner came from the only own goal Joe Mercer conceded in 18 years. An estimated 30,000 supporters were locked out of Highbury.

1954	Bolton Wanderers	(a) 1–2	Division One	Curry	27000
1957	Hearts	(a) 2–2	Friendly	Bell, White	14500
1965	Leicester City	(h) 1–5	Division One	Robson	27603
1968	Sporting Lisbon (Portugal)	(h) 1–0	Fairs Cup 2nd Round 2nd Leg	Robson	53747
1968	Bill McGarry quit Ipswich Town to take over at Wolves from Ronnie Allen.
1971	Nottingham Forest	(h) 2–1	Division One	Macdonald 2	24583

Debut for Alex Reid, who briefly deputised for Tommy Gibb in midfield.

1973	Sad news as surgeons confirmed that Tony Green's football career was over.
1975	Death of Robert Roxburgh, 78.
1976	West Ham United	(a) 2–1	Division One ·	Burns, Nulty	21324
1979	Paul Robinson born, Sunderland. Kenny Dalglish acted quickly in March 1998 to capture Darlington's striking prodigy at an initial cost of £250,000. After having made his debut for the Quakers' first team at the age of 16, Robinson played for both Newcastle reserve and junior sides in the successful conclusion to the season.
1982	Carlisle United	(a) 0–2	Division Two	No Scorer	16276
1991	Southend United	(h) 3–2	Division Two	Peacock 2 (1 pen), Hunt	14740

NOVEMBER 21ST

| 1896 | Leith Athletic | (a) 2–1 | Friendly | Aitken, Smellie | 1200 |
| 1903 | Liverpool | (a) 0–1 | Division One | No Scorer | 9000 |

1908	Aston Villa	(h) 0–2	Division One	No Scorer	35000
1914	Oldham Athletic	(h) 1–2	Division One	Hudspeth (pen)	12000
1925	Cardiff City	(a) 0–0	Division One	No Scorer	25000
1931	West Bromwich Albion	(h) 5–1	Division One	Allen, Boyd, J.R. Richardson 2, Weaver	36000
1936	Fulham	(a) 4–3	Division Two	Pearson, Rogers 2, Smith	20000
1950	Tommy Craig born, Penilee, Scotland.				
1953	Portsmouth	(h) 1–1	Division One	Milburn	48853
1959	Blackburn Rovers	(h) 3–1	Division One	Eastham, White 2	31368
1964	Derby County	(h) 2–2	Division Two	Cummings, McGarry	31041
1968	Mark Robinson born, Manchester.				
1970	Tottenham Hotspur	(a) 2–1	Division One	Gibb, Craig	38873
1981	Luton Town	(h) 3–2	Division Two	Brown 2, Varadi	21084

A classic encounter, with the quicksilver front combination of Brown and Varadi leading the Hatters a merry dance and taking a 2–0 interval lead. Second-half goals from Ricky Hill and David Moss, together with Brown limping off injured, appeared to have blown it, but a late strike from Varadi sent the crowd berserk. Brown later commented, 'I heard the cheers as I came back down the tunnel, and when I saw the crowd on the pitch, I knew we'd won it.'

1987	Queens Park Rangers	(a) 1–1	Division One	P. Jackson	11794
1990	Nottingham Forest	(a) 1–2	Zenith Data Systems Cup	Scott	9567
1992	Watford	(h) 2–0	Division One	Peacock, Lee	28871

Hornets player Gerard Lavin was sent off for two bookable offences within seconds, firstly kicking the ball away at a free-kick and then encroaching from the wall before it was taken. Robert Lee scored his first goal at St James' in a Newcastle shirt after Peacock had seen a penalty saved at the Leazes end and Lee pounced on the rebound.

1993	Liverpool	(h) 3–0	Premier League	Cole 3	36246

A demolition of the Reds by Cole, who hit three identical goals from three identical left-wing crosses past a bemused Bruce Grobbelaar in the first half. Footage of this match was later shown in court as the goalkeeper and his accomplices stood accused of match rigging. What was never questioned was the complicity of the whole Liverpool team in letting United rip through them at will and being utterly hopeless in front of goal until three down.

NOVEMBER 22ND

1902	Grimsby Town	(h) 1–0	Division One	Rutherford	11000
1913	Liverpool	(a) 0–0	Division One	No Scorer	30000
1919	Sunderland	(a) 0–2	Division One	No Scorer	47148
1924	Birmingham	(h) 4–0	Division One	Cowan, Harris 3	18000
1930	Sunderland	(a) 0–5	Division One	No Scorer	26303
1947	Cardiff City	(h) 4–1	Division Two	Milburn 2, Shackleton, Stobbart	56904

An opening goal from Milburn after ten seconds paved the way for a comfortable win. The crowd were treated to an exhibition of trickery from Shackleton including attempts to play one-twos with a corner flag and sitting on the ball in the manner later repeated by Kenny Wharton.

1952	Manchester United	(a) 2–2	Division One	Keeble, G. Robledo	33528
1958	West Bromwich Albion	(h) 1–2	Division One	Allchurch	51636

A debut for John Mitten, son of manager Charlie Mitten. Rather cruelly, he was given the job of penalty-taker on his debut and missed.

1965	Dinamo Moscow (USSR)	(h) 1–4	Friendly	Moncur	11130

1969	Coventry City	(a) 0–1	Division One	No Scorer	31825
1975	Norwich City	(a) 2–1	Division One	Nulty 2	19036
1978	Cambridge United	(h) 1–0	Division One	Bird	20004

Debut for Gary Nicholson.

| 1980 | Wrexham | (h) 0–1 | Division Two | No Scorer | 15941 |

Another goal from Dixie McNeil took the points back to Wales. Their other hero was Dai Davies, who saved a penalty from Alan Shoulder. One fan staged a centre-spot sit-in and was led away to a chorus of boos.

| 1986 | Chelsea | (a) 3–1 | Division One | A. Thomas 2, Beardsley | 14544 |
| 1996 | | | | | |

Newcastle's Darren Huckerby travelled to Coventry City after the two clubs agreed a £1 million fee.

| 1997 | Southampton | (h) 2–1 | Premier League | Barnes 2 | 36759 |

NOVEMBER 23RD

1895	Rendal	(h) 5–0	FA Cup Qualifier	Wardrope, Aitken 2, Logan, Thompson	3000
1901	Liverpool	(h) 1–0	Division One	McColl	20000
1907	Birmingham	(h) 8–0	Division One	Appleyard, Howie 2, Rutherford 3, Veitch 2	16000
1909	Tom Russell born, Cowdenbeath, Scotland.				
1910	Norwich City	(a) 3–0	Friendly	Shepherd 3	5944

Hospital Cup match.

| 1912 | Tottenham Hotspur | (a) 0–1 | Division One | No Scorer | 25000 |

Debutant James Fleming obviously impressed the victors of this match, who payed £300 for his services within six months.

1924	Death of Charlie Watts, 52, reported as having taken his own life.				
1929	Portsmouth	(h) 4–1	Division One	Gallacher 4	15000
1935	Sheffield United	(a) 1–5	Division Two	Livingstone	32000

Debut for Archie Livingstone.

1946	Bury	(h) 1–1	Division Two	Bentley	49656
1957	Manchester United	(h) 1–2	Division One	R. Mitchell	53950
1963	Manchester City	(h) 3–1	Division Two	Penman, Thomas 2	22557
1968	Wolverhampton Wanderers	(a) 0–5	Division One	No Scorer	25425

Two goals apiece from Derek Dougan and Peter Knowles and one from Frank Wignall.

1974	Burnley	(a) 1–4	Division One	Barrowclough	19523
1982	Dynamo Kiev (USSR)	(h) 2–1	Friendly	Waddle, Varadi	12572
1985	Manchester City	(a) 0–1	Division One	No Scorer	25179
1991	Blackburn Rovers	(h) 0–0	Division Two	No Scorer	23639

The chief attractions of this game were the moaning and cheating antics of David Speedie, which wound up the crowd as usual, and the appearance of Kevin Keegan, who launched a new book about United. After the match ended, occupants of the Milburn Stand boxes and bars included the film crew of the BBC drama *Spender*, who were waiting for the ground to empty before filming a number of scenes.

| 1994 | Newcastle gave a short trial to Sam Hyypia, a 20-year-old Finnish central defender. | | | | |
| 1996 | Chelsea | (a) 1–1 | Premier League | Shearer | 28401 |

Batty was sent off for elbowing Mark Hughes.

NOVEMBER 24TH

1894	Woolwich Arsenal	(h) 2–4	Division Two	Dickson 2	3000
1900	Liverpool	(h) 1–1	Division One	Laidlaw	19000
1906	Bristol City	(a) 1–2	Division One	Brown	25000
1923	Preston North End	(h) 3–1	Division One	Seymour, Cowan 2	25000

1928	Portsmouth	(a) 1–0	Division One	Harris	18000
1934	Notts County	(a) 1–0	Division Two	Smith	10000
1951	Manchester City	(a) 3–2	Division One	Milburn, Mitchell, G. Robledo	39358

1952 David Crosson born, Bishop Auckland.
1952 David McLean born, Newcastle.

| 1956 | Blackpool | (a) 3–2 | Division One | Casey, Milburn, White | 18248 |

1958 Roy Aitken born, Irvine, Scotland.

| 1962 | Scunthorpe United | (h) 1–1 | Division Two | Hale | 25864 |

1967 Gavin Maguire born, Hammersmith.

| 1971 | Derby County | (a) 0–1 | Texaco Cup | No Scorer | 20201 |
| 1973 | Everton | (a) 1–1 | Division One | Gibb | 34376 |

Mike Lyons scored for the Toffees.

1976	Everton	(h) 4–1	Division One	T. Craig, Gowling 2, Cannell	31203
1979	Swansea City	(a) 3–2	Division Two	Hibbitt, Rafferty, Shoulder	15442
1981	Orient	(a) 0–1	Division Two	No Scorer	4026
1984	Southampton	(a) 0–1	Division One	No Scorer	18895

Debut for Gary Megson.

1989 Crystal Palace agreed to pay £650,000 for United defender Andy Thorn.

| 1990 | Watford | (h) 1–0 | Division One | Quinn (pen) | 13774 |

On-loan striker Tommy Gaynor made his debut, in place of the injured McGhee. The seven-match run without victory came to an end thanks to a pair of penalties: Quinn scored, but Wearsider Gary Porter missed for the Hornets.

| 1992 | Ascoli (Italy) | (h) 0–1 | Anglo-Italian Cup | No Scorer | 9789 |

David Kelly was sent off in this exceptionally violent game after launching a pre-emptive strike as an Italian player homed in on him. Keegan and a policeman had to restrain the Ascoli coach, who made a grab for the departing striker as he headed down the tunnel. The Newcastle manager later commented, 'If I ever get like that, shoot me.' He also refused to fine Kelly for being dismissed. In the match itself, future German star Oliver Bierhoff scored the only goal and Benito Carbone, later to appear with Sheffield Wednesday, made a brief appearance.

| 1993 | Sheffield United | (h) 4–0 | Premier League | OG, Beardsley 2 (1 pen), Cole | 35029 |

Sellars claimed a goal, but it was later deemed an own goal from Ward by a special Premier League body who meet to decide such matters.

NOVEMBER 25TH

| 1893 | Liverpool | (h) 0–0 | Division Two | No Scorer | 2000 |

Debut for Scotsman Tom Rogers, at left-back.

1897 James Keen born, Walker.

| 1899 | Preston North End | (h) 0–0 | Division One | No Scorer | 15000 |

Debut for Scotsman Alex Gardner, who played for United in a variety of positions in his 11 years with the club.

1905	Liverpool	(h) 2–3	Division One	Orr, McWilliam	32000
1911	Tottenham Hotspur	(a) 2–1	Division One	Hay, Hibbert	37541
1922	Tottenham Hotspur	(h) 1–1	Division One	McDonald	25000
1933	Aston Villa	(a) 3–2	Division One	Lang, Williams, Weaver	40000

Goal on his debut for centre-forward Ron Williams.

| 1950 | Charlton Athletic | (h) 3–2 | Division One | Milburn 2, Walker | 48670 |

With ten minutes remaining, a second successive home defeat looked inevitable as the visitors led 2–0, but some Milburn magic won it for United.

1959 Death of Bob McColl, 83. His name lives on in the chain of newsagents he founded.

| 1961 | Stoke City | (a) 1–3 | Division Two | Hale (pen) | 22009 |

1965 David Kelly born, Birmingham.

| 1967 | Sheffield Wednesday | (h) 4–0 | Division One | Bennett 2, Davies, Elliott | 28101 |

1978	Oldham Athletic	(h) 1–1	Division Two	McGhee	20563
1987	Shrewsbury	(h) 2–1	Full Members Cup	Mirandinha, Bogie	7787
1989	Sheffield United	(h) 2–0	Division One	Gallacher, Quinn	27170
1995	Leeds United	(h) 2–1	Premier League	Beardsley, Watson	36572

NOVEMBER 26TH

1898	Derby County	(a) 1–3	Division One	Wardrope	7000

Two goals for the prolific Steve Bloomer, a Derby goalscoring legend who was to haunt United for two decades.

1904	Aston Villa	(a) 1–0	Division One	Appleyard	13000
1910	Woolwich Arsenal	(a) 2–1	Division One	Shepherd, Duncan	13000
1921	Sunderland	(a) 0–0	Division One	No Scorer	49483
1927	Leicester City	(a) 0–3	Division One	No Scorer	35000

Inside-left Billy Halliday made his only Newcastle appearance.

1932	Sunderland	(a) 2–0	Division One	Allen, Lang	39000
1938	Millwall	(h) 2–2	Division Two	Clifton, Mooney	37000
1949	West Bromwich Albion	(h) 5–1	Division One	Houghton, Milburn 2, G. Robledo, Walker	32415
1955	Manchester City	(a) 2–1	Division One	Hannah, Keeble	22860
1956	Hibernian	(a) 3–1	Friendly	Milburn 2, White	8000
1960	Blackburn Rovers	(h) 3–1	Division One	Mitchell, White 2	22623

The immense Herbert Garrow made his debut in goal, lasted three games and was then dropped following a 5–5 draw with West Ham. Albert Scanlon, a Munich air disaster survivor and nephew of United boss Mitten, also made his first appearance.

1966	Sheffield Wednesday	(h) 3–1	Division One	Bennett, Davies, Robson	26873
1968	Barnsley	(a) 1–5	Friendly	Hindson	10000

Testimonial match.

1969	FC Porto (Portugal)	(h) 1–0	Fairs Cup 2nd Round 2nd Leg	Scott	44833
1983	Cambridge United	(h) 2–1	Division Two	Beardsley, Keegan (pen)	25065
1994	Ipswich Town	(h) 1–1	Premier League	Cole	34459
1997	Barcelona (Spain)	(a) 0–1	Champions League	No Scorer	26000

What being a Newcastle supporter is all about: travelling with thousands of companions to one of the best grounds in the world, getting soaked, witnessing a miserable performance, being ignored by the team and still singing. Giovanni got the only goal and Aaron Hughes made his first senior start.

NOVEMBER 27TH

1897	Small Heath	(h) 4–0	Division Two	Wardrope, Peddie, Campbell 2	11000
1909	Middlesbrough	(h) 2–0	Division One	Shepherd, Howie	28000
1920	Liverpool	(a) 1–0	Division One	Smailes	25000
1926	Tottenham Hotspur	(a) 3–1	Division One	Gallacher 3	35015
1937	Fulham	(a) 2–1	Division Two	Park, Smith	14000
1948	Huddersfield Town	(h) 2–4	Division One	Hair, Milburn	49332
1954	Huddersfield Town	(h) 2–2	Division One	Curry, White	36409
1957	Hearts	(h) 2–0	Friendly	White, Eastham	10260
1965	Sheffield United	(a) 2–3	Division One	Thompson, Iley	13880
1965	Scott Sellars born, Sheffield.				
1969	David Robinson born, Walkergate.				
1971	Stoke City	(a) 3–3	Division One	Macdonald 2, D. Craig	16855
1974	Southampton	(a) 0–1	Texaco Cup	No Scorer	17100
1976	Queens Park Rangers	(h) 2–0	Division One	Burns, Cannell	39045

1982   Cambridge United   (h) 2–0   Division Two   McDermott, Martin   20385
        Debut for Howard Gayle.
1988   Manchester United (h) 0–0   Division One   No Scorer   20234
        A tedious Sunday afternoon. Newcastle never looked in danger of breaking their four-
        match scoring drought in this televised game, and their visitors were equally inept.
1989   After a year in the manager's chair at the Victoria Ground, Bobby Moncur resigned as
        manager of struggling Hartlepool United.
1993   Arsenal   (a) 1–2   Premier League   Beardsley   36091
        United were undone by set-piece goals from Wright and Smith, but Beardsley got one back
        in front of the travelling army of away supporters seated in the Clock End.
1996   Middlesbrough   (a) 1–3   League Cup 4th   Shearer   29831
                                      Round

NOVEMBER 28TH

1891   Jack Alderson born, Crook, Durham.
1896   Loughborough Town (h) 4–1   Division Two   Wardrope, Aitken, Connen, 7000
                                                          Lennox
1903   Bury   (h) 3–2   Division One   Appleyard, Howie 2   8000
        Debut for Kilmarnock-born Thomas Wills, at left-back.
1903   Alec Betton born, New Tupton, Derbyshire.
1908   Nottingham Forest (a) 4–0   Division One   Wilson, Shepherd, Higgins, 8000
                                                          Liddell
        Goalscoring debut for United's new striker Albert Shepherd, signed from Bolton
        Wanderers with a reputation for finding the net regularly.
1914   Manchester United (a) 0–1   Division One   No Scorer   5000
1931   Sunderland   (a) 4–1   Division One   Boyd, Lang, McMenemy, 40000
                                                          J.R. Richardson
1933   Alex Tait born, West Sleekburn, Northumberland.
1936   Burnley   (h) 3–0   Division Two   Garnham, Leighton, Smith 27000
1948   Mick Channon born, Orcheston, Wiltshire.
1953   Arsenal   (a) 1–2   Division One   Milburn   62456
1955   Carlisle lost 3–1 to Darlington in an FA Cup first-round match held at St James' Park
        which attracted 34,257 onlookers. This was also the first time the Gallowgate floodlights
        had been used for an FA Cup tie.
1959   Manchester City   (a) 4–3   Division One   Allchurch, Bell, White, OG 29416
        The winning goal was an own goal scored by City centre-half McTavish, his third in four
        games. City went down despite the heroics of Bert Trautmann in goal and a hat-trick from
        Billy McAdams.
1959   Martin Thomas born, Senghenydd, Wales.
1960   Kenny Wharton born, Blakelaw.
1964   Swindon Town   (a) 6–1   Division Two   Suddick, Penman 2, Hilley, 15866
                                                          Anderson 2
1970   Burnley   (h) 3–1   Division One   Ford, Robson, Moncur 20994
1973   Birmingham City   (h) 1–1   Texaco Cup   Tudor   5529
        Abandoned due to bad light after ten minutes of extra time.
1981   Grimsby Town   (a) 1–1   Division Two   Wharton   9256
1987   Charlton Athletic (h) 2–1   Division One   Mirandinha, Cornwell 19453
        Unlucky day for Charlton striker Colin Walsh, who broke his leg. Cornwell scored the only
        goal of his United career, at the Leazes end.
1989   Oldham Athletic   (h) 2–0   Full Members Cup   Quinn 2   6167
1990   Cash-strapped United continued their search for bargain signings, giving a trial to local
        striker John Richardson, who had been playing in New Zealand. He lasted 65 minutes of
        a reserve game at St James', which United lost 2–1 to Aston Villa. Steve Watson got the
        United goal.

1992   Cambridge United   (h) 4–1   Division One   Kelly 3, Peacock   27991
The visitors lost Andy Fensome, sent off for whacking Alan Thompson, but the result was never in much doubt. Fensome had actually been on trial at United for a short spell in 1988. With the score at 2–0, United were awarded a penalty at the Gallowgate end. Usual taker Peacock moved to gather the ball but had it snatched from him by David Kelly, who completed his hat-trick from the spot. A late chance converted by Peacock made sure everyone ended up satisfied. Cambridge scored a late goal through Steve Claridge, who had already played at Gallowgate earlier in the season for Luton Town.

1995   Newcastle allowed midfielder Richie Appleby to go on loan to Ipswich Town, a move that was later made permanent.

NOVEMBER 29TH

1902   Aston Villa   (a) 0–7   Division One   No Scorer   10000
Inauspicious debut for Harry Stenhouse at outside-right. Harry joined United from his hometown club Blyth Spartans.

1913   Aston Villa   (h) 2–2   Division One   Low, Hudspeth (pen)   34000
1919   Sunderland   (h) 2–3   Division One   Hibbert, Robinson   61761
1924   West Bromwich   (a) 0–2   Division One   No Scorer   15000
        Albion
1930   Blackburn Rovers   (h) 2–3   Division One   Boyd, Lindsay   18000
1947   Sheffield Wednesday (a) 0–1   Division Two   No Scorer   41355
The only goal of the game came from the memorably named Redfern Froggatt as United failed to record their fourth consecutive win away from home.

1952   Portsmouth   (h) 1–0   Division One   G. Robledo   46721
1958   Leeds United   (a) 2–3   Division One   Allchurch 2   23500
1972   Malcolm Macdonald was in blistering form, netting a first-half hat-trick as England Under-23 beat their Welsh counterparts at the Vetch Field, Swansea.

1975   Manchester United   (a) 0–1   Division One   No Scorer   52264
1980   Orient   (a) 1–1   Division Two   Shinton   5800
Thin times for United. This goal by Bobby Shinton was his seventh of the season in all competitions. He didn't find the net again that season, but still finished top scorer.

1995   Liverpool   (a) 1–0   League Cup 4th   Watson   40077
                                 Round
One of the best goals scored by any United player in recent years, a mesmerising solo run and chip by stand-in striker Steve Watson. Les Ferdinand had earlier departed with a head injury.

1997   Crystal Palace   (a) 2–1   Premier League   Tomasson, Ketsbaia   26085

NOVEMBER 30TH

1895   Sunderland   (h) 0–4   Friendly   No Scorer   12000
1901   Grimsby Town   (h) 5–1   Division One   Roberts, Peddie 3, Orr,   15000
1907   Aston Villa   (a) 3–3   Division One   Appleyard, Howie, Orr   25000
1912   Middlesbrough   (h) 3–1   Division One   G. Wilson, Peart, Hay   25000
1929   Arsenal   (a) 1–0   Division One   Weaver   25000
Goalscoring debut for Sammy Weaver.

1935   Nottingham Forest   (h) 5–1   Division Two   Fairhurst 2, Harris,   24000
                                                       J. Smith 2

Debut in defence for Hugh Bulloch.

1946   Luton Town   (a) 3–4   Division Two   Bentley, Shackleton, Wayman 25410
1953   Portsmouth   (a) 1–1   Friendly   Mitchell   14379
Testimonial match.

1957   Arsenal   (a) 3–2   Division One   Hughes, R. Mitchell 2   41649
1963   Bury   (a) 2–1   Division Two   Thomas, OG   9848
1968   Southampton   (h) 4–1   Division One   Dyson, Foggon, Robson 2   29515
1974   Manchester City   (h) 2–1   Division One   Macdonald, Howard   37684

Celebrity spectators at St James' were boxing champion John Conteh and pop singer David Essex, who presented Pat Howard with a player-of-the-month award on the pitch.

1985	Leicester City	(h) 2–1	Division One	Clarke, Beardsley	17311
1986	West Ham United	(h) 4–0	Division One	A. Thomas 2, McDonald, D. Jackson	22077
1991	Barnsley	(a) 0–3	Division Two	No Scorer	9648
1994	Manchester City	(a) 1–1	League Cup 4th Round	Jeffrey	25162
1996	Arsenal	(h) 1–2	Premier League	Shearer	36565

Tony Adams was sent off for the Gunners.

DECEMBER 1ST

1894	Grimsby Town	(a) 1–4	Division Two	Thompson	1500
1900	Sheffield Wednesday	(a) 2–2	Division One	Peddie, Niblo	12000
1902	Aberaman	(a) 1–1	Friendly	Stenhouse	

In the absence of League opposition, United travelled to the Welsh coalfields for this friendly encounter.

1905	Allan Taylor born, North Shields.				
1906	Notts County	(h) 4–3	Division One	Appleyard 2, Speedie, Veitch	20000
1915	Arthur Frost born, Walton, Liverpool.				
1923	Burnley	(a) 2–3	Division One	Seymour, Harris	8000
1928	Bolton Wanderers	(h) 4–1	Division One	Boyd, McCurley, MacKenzie, Wilkinson	30000
1934	Southampton	(h) 1–0	Division Two	Lang	16000

1948 A second international goal for Milburn as England routed Switzerland 6–0 at Highbury.

1951	Derby County	(h) 2–1	Division One	G. Robledo 2	49880
1956	Wolverhampton Wanderers	(h) 2–1	Division One	Curry, White	37562
1962	Bury	(a) 0–0	Division Two	No Scorer	12633

Sole appearance of George Watkin at centre-forward, in for the absent Barrie Thomas.

1978 United manager Bill McGarry continued his rebuilding programme with the signing of Mick Martin from West Bromwich Albion for £100,000.

1979	Fulham	(h) 2–0	Division Two	Rafferty, Withe	23485

Debut for Steve Carney, at right-back.

1984	Stoke City	(h) 2–1	Division One	Waddle, Anderson (pen)	21564

Debut for Joe Allon.

1990	Leicester City	(a) 4–5	Division Two	Quinn 3, O'Brien	11045

Debut for Gavin Peacock, who almost marked the occasion with an opening goal in the first seconds. Future Newcastle striker David Kelly claimed the match ball after hitting a hat-trick, while Mick Quinn was left to rue defensive lapses from his colleagues, Aitken especially.

1997	Bolton Wanderers	(a) 0–1	Premier League	No Scorer	24494

A first visit to the new Reebok stadium and a thoroughly miserable night ensued. Sky TV were on hand to show the game live, and such was the lack of interest from United fans that payment could even be made on the night, although there were few takers. Blake hit the only goal for the home side.

DECEMBER 2ND

1893	Dipton Wanderers	(a) 2–0	Friendly	Crate, Quinn	500
1899	Nottingham Forest	(a) 0–1	Division One	No Scorer	9000

First of 278 senior games for Jack Carr, who joined Newcastle from his home side of Seaton Burn and gave 13 seasons of great service at left-half and left-back. He never played for any other club, although he endured a poor spell as Blackburn boss.

1905	Sheffield United	(a) 0–2	Division One	No Scorer	15000

Solitary appearance of Glaswegian Hugh Bolton. However, he went on to play a more crucial role in United's season, gaining an FA Cup winners' medal for his new club Everton at the expense of his former colleagues.

1911	Manchester United	(h) 2–3	Division One	Stewart, McCracken (pen)	25000
1922	Liverpool	(a) 2–0	Division One	Harris, McIntosh	35000
1933	Huddersfield Town	(h) 3–3	Division One	Lang, Williams 2	26000
1935	Jimmy Kerray born, Stirling.				
1950	Manchester United	(a) 2–1	Division One	Hannah, Walker	40000
1958	Nottingham Forest	(h) 1–3	Division One	Curry	49447
1961	Sunderland	(h) 2–2	Division Two	McGuigan, White	53991

Brian Clough hit both goals for the visitors but by the end of the month had seen his career wrecked by injury.

1967	Tottenham Hotspur	(a) 1–1	Division One	Davies	34494
1968	David Batty born, Leeds.				
1972	West Ham United	(a) 1–1	Division One	Craig	23785
1978	Crystal Palace	(a) 0–1	Division Two	No Scorer	19761

Mick Martin made his debut.

| 1987 | Bradford City | (a) 1–2 | Full Members Cup | Scott | 8866 |
| 1989 | Leeds United | (a) 0–1 | Division One | No Scorer | 31715 |

A horrible game settled by an Ian Baird header. Leeds gave out only 900 away tickets and the game took place in a menacing atmosphere, stoked up further by the pre-match antics of Vinnie Jones, who climbed the perimeter fence and incited the home fans still further. Numerous fights broke out throughout the game and the away enclosure was repeatedly showered with coins and rocks.

DECEMBER 3RD

| 1898 | West Bromwich Albion | (h) 3–0 | Division One | Aitken, Peddie, Rogers | 16000 |
| 1904 | Blackburn Rovers | (h) 1–0 | Division One | McClarence | 20000 |

Goalscoring debut for locally born centre-forward Joe McClarence.

| 1910 | Bradford City | (h) 6–1 | Division One | Stewart, Shepherd 3, Higgins 2 | 18000 |

A memorable score to mark the first appearance of a Newcastle legend, Frank Hudspeth. In nearly 20 years at United he made no fewer than 472 starts.

| 1919 | Middlesbrough | (h) 0–0 | Division One | No Scorer | 40000 |
| 1921 | Middlesbrough | (h) 0–0 | Division One | No Scorer | 50000 |

Debut for Jimmy Low, at outside-right.

| 1927 | Liverpool | (h) 1–1 | Division One | McKay | 20000 |

William Carlton made his debut at right-half.

1932	Leeds United	(h) 3–1	Division One	Allen 2, Lang	22000
1938	Manchester City	(a) 1–4	Division Two	Cairns	45000
1941	Death of Neil Harris, 47.				
1949	Manchester United	(a) 1–1	Division One	Walker	38000
1951	John Burridge born, Workington.				
1955	Bolton Wanderers	(h) 3–0	Division One	Davies, Keeble 2	36856
1958	Bucharest XI (Romania)	(h) 4–1	Friendly	Curry, Allchurch, Eastham, Hughes	20862
1960	Bolton Wanderers	(a) 1–2	Division One	White	12921
1966	Southampton	(a) 0–2	Division One	No Scorer	21488
1975	Notts County	(h) 1–0	League Cup 5th Round	OG	31114

United won a place in the League Cup semi-finals courtesy of County keeper Eric McManus, who dropped a long throw from Malcolm Macdonald into his own net.

| 1977 | Leicester City | (h) 2–0 | Division One | Burns, Nattrass | 20112 |

Debut for left winger Stuart Robinson.

1979	North Shields	(a) 4–1	Friendly	Rafferty 2, Martin, Withe	1100
1983	Derby County	(a) 2–3	Division Two	Waddle, Keegan	18691
1986	Everton	(a) 2–5	Full Members Cup	A. Thomas 2	7530
1988	Luton Town	(a) 0–0	Division One	No Scorer	8338

Archie Gourlay made his debut, replacing Mirandinha, but was unable to fashion a winner.

1994	Tottenham Hotspur	(a) 2–4	Premier League	Fox 2	28002

A Sheringham hat-trick and a winner from Popescu.

1995	Wimbledon	(a) 3–3	Premier League	Ferdinand 2, Gillespie	18002

United were led out by Warren Barton, returning to his former club, but on a frosty pitch they were denied victory by two Dean Holdsworth goals and, almost inevitably, one from Mick Harford.

1996	Metz (France)	(h) 2–0	UEFA Cup 3rd Round 2nd Leg	Asprilla 2	35641

Two late goals from Tino sent United through to the next round and he celebrated in original style by uprooting the corner flag and hoisting his shirt from it. The unimpressed referee promptly booked him. Asprilla then contrived to injure himself and was taken from the field on a stretcher to thunderous applause, which he milked as he made slow progress around the perimeter of the pitch.

1996   The Cat crept in, as Newcastle revealed that their new goalkeeping coach was to be Peter Bonetti.

DECEMBER 4TH

1897	Gainsborough Trinity	(a) 3–1	Division Two	Campbell, Harvey, Ostler	700

One of only two visits to the Northolme for United, as Gainsborough enjoyed a two-season spell in League football.

1899   Charlie Spencer born, Washington, Tyne and Wear.

1900   Chris Swan born, Byker.

1909	Liverpool	(a) 5–6	Division One	Shepherd 4, Howie	20000

Unbelievably, United were 5–2 ahead at half-time but wilted under tremendous pressure, as former United player Ronald Orr hit two goals and Goddard headed a late winner for the home side.

1920	Aston Villa	(h) 2–1	Division One	Seymour, Smailes	25000

One of only two runouts for reserve outside-right Andrew Gray.

1926	West Ham United	(h) 2–0	Division One	Gallacher, Seymour	36000
1937	Sheffield Wednesday	(h) 1–0	Division Two	Mooney	9500

1943   Les O'Neil born, Hartford.

1948	Manchester United	(n) 1–1	Division One	Stobbart	70787

This match was played at Maine Road, Old Trafford still being repaired following extensive bomb damage sustained during the war.

1954	Sheffield Wednesday	(a) 3–0	Division One	Broadis, Mitchell, White	15000
1971	Chelsea	(h) 0–0	Division One	No Scorer	37586
1974	Chester	(h) 0–0	League Cup 5th Round	No Scorer	31656

Debut at right-back for Peter Kelly.

1976	Arsenal	(a) 3–5	Division One	Gowling, Burns 2	35000

Three goals for Supermac as he reminded the travelling supporters of what they were missing.

1982	Charlton Athletic	(a) 0–2	Division Two	No Scorer	10381

1988   At last a new manager, as Jim Smith agreed to leave Queens Park Rangers for Tyneside.

1993	Tottenham Hotspur	(a) 2–1	Premier League	Beardsley 2	30780

A debut for Mike Jeffrey as two pieces of Beardsley genius won it. After being pegged back by a Barmby penalty, Hooper made a crucial stop and Beardsley jinked past three defenders to wallop a winner in the last seconds.

DECEMBER 5TH

1894	Bedlington Turks	(a) 4–2	Friendly	Thompson, McNee, Dickson 2	1200
1896	Burton Wanderers	(a) 1–0	Division Two	Aitken	
1903	Blackburn Rovers	(a) 0–4	Division One	No Scorer	
1908	Sunderland	(h) 1–9	Division One	Shepherd (pen)	56000

A goal on his home debut for Albert Shepherd in this humiliation. However, United still went on to win the title the following April. The *Football Echo* commented, 'As to the cause of the collapse of the Newcastle team, it was quite evidently due to their being useless as a combination.'

1914	Bolton Wanderers	(h) 1–2	Division One	Hibbert	15000
1922	Bobby Cowell born, Trimdon Grange.				
1925	West Bromwich Albion	(a) 0–4	Division One	No Scorer	10000
1931	Portsmouth	(h) 0–0	Division One	No Scorer	30000

Neither side could even muster a corner in this drab game.

1936	Southampton	(a) 0–2	Division Two	No Scorer	16000
1937	Ron McGarry born, Whitehaven, Cumbria.				
1953	Chelsea	(h) 1–1	Division One	Mitchell	41728
1959	Arsenal	(h) 4–1	Division One	Allchurch 2, White 2	40031
1961	Alan Davies born, Horton, Wales.				
1964	Portsmouth	(h) 3–0	Division Two	Hockey, Iley, Anderson	29135
1970	Chelsea	(a) 0–1	Division One	No Scorer	39413
1973	Birmingham City	(h) 3–1	Texaco Cup	Tudor 2, Clark	9762

Jimmy Smith lasted less than a minute before being ordered off after a vicious tackle.

1981	Blackburn Rovers	(h) 0–0	Division Two	No Scorer	18775
1987	Oxford United	(a) 3–1	Division One	McDonald (pen), O'Neill, Mirandinha	8190
1992	Notts County	(a) 2–0	Division One	Sheedy, Peacock	14840

United faced ten men for the third successive match when Chris Short was sent off after 73 minutes for launching himself at O'Brien. A large travelling support made up half the Meadow Lane crowd.

DECEMBER 6TH

1899	Hearts	(h) 4–1	Friendly	Macfarlane 3, Rogers	4000
1902	Nottingham Forest	(h) 0–2	Division One	No Scorer	12000
1913	Middlesbrough	(a) 0–3	Division One	No Scorer	17000
1915	Benny Craig born, Leadgate, Durham.				
1919	Sheffield United	(a) 1–2	Division One	Hall	35000

Debut for Andy Smailes, a goalscoring forward signed from Blyth Spartans.

1924	Tottenham Hotspur	(h) 1–1	Division One	Seymour	28000
1930	Manchester City	(a) 0–2	Division One	No Scorer	20000
1947	Tottenham Hotspur	(h) 1–0	Division Two	Milburn	57950
1951	David Mills born, Whitby.				
1952	Bolton Wanderers	(a) 2–4	Division One	Keeble, Walker	41420
1956	Peter Kelly born, East Kilbride, Scotland.				
1958	Burnley	(h) 5–2	Division One	Allchurch 2, White, Eastham, Bell (pen)	42561
1967	Ian Bogie born, Walker.				
1969	Stoke City	(a) 1–0	Division One	Robson	17767
1970	Death of Ted Robledo, 52, in mysterious circumstances while serving on an oil tanker in the Persian Gulf.				

1975	Coventry City	(h) 4–0	Division One	T. Craig 2 (1 pen), Burns,	27172
				D. Craig	
1983	Bristol Rovers	(a) 4–5	Friendly	Waddle, Trewick,	4107
				McDermott, Mills	
1986	Charlton Athletic	(a) 1–1	Division One	Goddard	7333

A late equaliser and first United goal from Paul Goddard, right in front of a large Geordie following on the then-standing Holmesdale Terrace at Selhurst Park. Tony Nesbit made his first appearance, as a substitute.

| 1995 | Scott Sellars joined Bolton Wanderers for a fee of £750,000. | | | | |
| 1997 | Arsenal | (h) 0–1 | Premier League | No Scorer | 36751 |

Ian Wright ended his long goal famine and ran the length of the pitch with his shirt over his head to reveal a T-shirt with the words 'At last' on it.

DECEMBER 7TH

1895	Burton Swifts	(a) 1–3	Division Two	Wardrope	2000
1901	Aston Villa	(a) 0–0	Division One	No Scorer	20000
1907	Everton	(h) 2–1	Division One	Appleyard (pen), Rutherford	30000

Debut for James Ridley, at outside-left.

| 1912 | Notts County | (a) 1–0 | Division One | Peart | 10000 |
| 1929 | Aston Villa | (h) 2–2 | Division One | Gallacher (pen), Weaver | 35000 |

After scoring the previous week at Highbury on his debut, Sammy Weaver repeated the feat on his first home appearance. Joseph Wilson made his only appearance for the first team, at centre-half.

| 1935 | Norwich City | (a) 0–1 | Division Two | No Scorer | 12000 |

Debut for Alf Garnham.

| 1946 | Plymouth Argyle | (h) 3–2 | Division Two | Bentley 3 | 47661 |

Debut for Dick Burke.

1957	Bolton Wanderers	(h) 1–2	Division One	Eastham	29886
1963	Scunthorpe United	(h) 3–1	Division Two	Suddick, Penman, Thomas	24988
1968	Stoke City	(a) 0–1	Division One	No Scorer	11594
1974	Tottenham Hotspur	(a) 0–3	Division One	No Scorer	23422

The one and only appearance of keeper Tony Bell for the first team, unfortunately caught on film.

| 1985 | Luton Town | (a) 0–2 | Division One | No Scorer | 10319 |

Debut for Billy Whitehurst.

| 1988 | New manager Jim Smith lived up to his wheeler-dealer reputation within hours of arriving at St James'. Back to Hearts went unhappy striker John Robertson for £625,000, and £500,000 was paid to Queens Park Rangers, £350,000 for midfielder Kevin Brock and the remainder as compensation for Smith's departure. | | | | |
| 1991 | Port Vale | (h) 2–2 | Division Two | Makel, Peacock (pen) | 18162 |

Debuts for loan signing Paul Bodin at left-back and striker David Kelly. Kelly endeared himself to United fans before he kicked a ball, by turning down the chance to sign for Sunderland. He did later join them, and could be seen in a couple of episodes of the hilarious BBC series *Premier Passions*, looking suitably embarassed.

| 1995 | Newcastle youngster Chris Holland, after a string of impressive performances at Under-21 level, was invited to train with the England senior squad. | | | | |

DECEMBER 8TH

1884	Wilf Lawson born, Aberdeen.				
1896	Manchester City	(a) 2–5	Division Two	McKay, Lennox	10000
1900	Sheffield United	(h) 0–2	Division One	No Scorer	15000

Debut for Matt Scott, at left-back.

| 1906 | Sheffield United | (a) 0–0 | Division One | No Scorer | 16000 |

Debut for Jarrow lad Chris Duffy, at outside-left.

1912	Cam Theaker born, Spalding, Lincolnshire.				
1914	Billy Leighton born, Walker.				
1923	Burnley	(h) 2–0	Division One	Seymour, McDonald	25000
1928	Sheffield Wednesday	(a) 1–3	Division One	Gallacher (pen)	25000
1934	Bolton Wanderers	(a) 0–1	Division One	No Scorer	21000
1951	Aston Villa	(a) 2–2	Division One	Duncan 2	35000
1951	Terry McDermott born, Kirby.				
1956	Bolton Wanderers	(a) 1–3	Division One	Davies	25131
1962	Rotherham United	(h) 4–1	Division Two	Tuohy, Kerray, Hale 2	21955
1966	Les Ferdinand born, Notting Hill.				
1971	Derby County	(h) 2–3	Texaco Cup	Macdonald, Barrowclough	37000
1973	Birmingham City	(a) 0–1	Division One	No Scorer	25428

Debut for Dennis Laughton. Kenny Burns struck the only goal of the game.

1979	Luton Town	(a) 1–1	Division Two	Rafferty	14845

The medial ligament injury sustained by Mick Martin was a turning point in the season, as United gradually lost form and dropped out of the promotion race.

1980	Scheduled home game with Bristol Rovers postponed due to a frozen pitch.				
1984	Tottenham Hotspur	(a) 1–3	Division One	Waddle	29695
1992	Bari (Italy)	(a) 0–3	Anglo-Italian Cup	No Scorer	1229

Roger Milford refereed this weekday afternoon encounter at the San Nicola Stadium which saw United well beaten and thankfully eliminated from the competition. Brian Kilcline 'scored' with a header from a corner but saw it disallowed, and both Appleby brothers played in the team for the first time.

DECEMBER 9TH

1884	Sandy Mutch born, Inveraray, Scotland.				
1892	At a meeting in Bath Lane Hall, it was agreed that the club be renamed Newcastle United from the former East End. Suggestions for City and Rangers were not taken up.				
1893	Notts County	(h) 3–0	Division Two	Wallace 2, Thompson	4000

Debut for locally born inside-left Thomas 'Knocker' Barker.

1899	Dundee	(h) 2–2	Friendly	Peddie, Stevenson	2000
1905	Notts County	(h) 3–1	Division One	Appleyard, J. Rutherford, Veitch	17073
1911	Liverpool	(a) 1–0	Division One	Stewart	15000
1916	Eddie Connelly born, Dumbarton, Scotland.				
1922	Liverpool	(h) 0–1	Division One	No Scorer	30000
1925	Sheffield United	(h) 3–1	Division One	Mordue, Cowan, Hudspeth (pen)	13000

A debut goal for Tom Mordue.

1933	Wolverhampton Wanderers	(a) 1–2	Division One	J.R. Richardson	17000
1950	Wolverhampton Wanderers	(h) 1–1	Division One	Walker	48492

Despite the fact that United went ahead through Tommy Walker after only 15 seconds, the points were shared.

1961	Peter Haddock born, Newcastle.				
1963	Dunfermline Athletic	(a) 0–2	Friendly	No Scorer	10000

Testimonial match.

1967	Manchester United	(h) 2–2	Division One	Iley, T. Robson	48639
1970	Newcastle agreed a £45,000 fee with Burnley for midfielder Doug Collins, and he travelled to Tyneside to sign. However, the deal was never completed after Burnley refused to pay the player his share of the proceeds.				
1972	Southampton	(h) 0–0	Division One	No Scorer	20436

1978	Stoke City	(h) 2–0	Division One	Connolly, Withe	23459

Debut for Alan Shoulder.

1989	Oxford United	(h) 2–3	Division Two	Stimson, Quinn (pen)	16645
1995	Chelsea	(a) 0–1	Premier League	No Scorer	31098

United made a goalkeeping substitution as Chelsea shaped to take a free-kick with the injured Hislop going off. Replacement Srnicek's first job was to pick the ball out of the net as Dan Petrescu scored the only goal of the game.

1996	Nottingham Forest	(a) 0–0	Premier League	No Scorer	25762

DECEMBER 10TH

1872	Billy Lindsay born, Stockton.				
1898	Blackburn Rovers	(a) 2–4	Division Two	Stevenson 2	7000
1904	Nottingham Forest	(a) 3–1	Division One	Gosnell, Appleyard, Veitch	10000
1910	Blackburn Rovers	(a) 1–3	Division One	Duncan	12000
1921	Middlesbrough	(a) 1–1	Division One	Harris	36000
1926	John Duncan born, Glasgow.				
1927	Arsenal	(a) 1–4	Division One	Seymour	35000

A testing debut for Tom Evans, at left-back.

1932	Blackburn Rovers	(a) 1–2	Division One	Lang	7000
1938	Bury	(h) 6–0	Division Two	Mooney 3 (1 pen), Clifton 3	28000
1949	Chelsea	(h) 2–2	Division One	Milburn, Mitchell	43239
1951	Merthyr Tydfil	(a) 6–4	Friendly	Davis, Cowell, Foulkes 2, Duncan 2	5200
1955	Chelsea	(a) 1–2	Division One	Milburn (pen)	37327
1960	West Ham United	(h) 5–5	Division One	Bell, McGuigan, R. Mitchell, White 2	20106
1966	Chelsea	(h) 2–2	Division One	Davies, Robson	32529
1977	Queens Park Rangers	(a) 1–0	Division One	Robinson	15251

A clean sheet on his debut for 19-year-old Kevin Carr.

1980	Arthur Cox dispensed with the services of Billy Rafferty, who signed for Portsmouth in an £80,000 move.				
1983	Huddersfield Town	(h) 5–2	Division Two	McDermott, Waddle 2, Beardsley, Keegan	25747

Not as convincing as the scoreline suggests. Goals from Phil Watson and Paul Jones had tied the scores at 2–2 by half-time before United stepped up several gears.

1988	Wimbledon	(h) 2–1	Division One	Hendrie 2	20292

Debut for Kevin Brock and at last something to cheer about as United scored their first goal in over nine hours.

1994	Leicester City	(h) 3–1	Premier League	Albert 2, Howey	34400

David Oldfield scored for the Foxes as Albert demonstrated his shooting prowess from free-kicks.

1997	Dynamo Kiev (Russia)	(h) 2–0	Champions League	Barnes, Pearce	33694

An academic game for United, who had already missed the chance to qualify from the group stages of the Champions League. Pearce struck his first goal for the club with a swerving free-kick at the Leazes end.

DECEMBER 11TH

1897	Middlesbrough	(a) 2–0	FA Cup Qualifier	Wardrope, Harvey	6000
1909	Aston Villa	(h) 1–0	Division One	Higgins	19000

Debut for Bob Waugh, at right-back.

1920	Aston Villa	(a) 0–0	Division One	No Scorer	35000
1926	Sheffield Wednesday	(a) 2–3	Division One	McDonald, McKay	35000

1928   George Hannah born, Liverpool.

1937   Chesterfield   (a) 0–1   Division Two   No Scorer   10000
Abandoned after 76 minutes due to failing light at Saltergate.

1948   Sheffeld United   (h) 3–2   Division One   Milburn, Stobbart, OG   42862
Only appearance of Albert Clark for United, standing in for Joe Harvey.

1954   Portsmouth   (h) 2–1   Division One   Keeble 2   33414

1965   West Ham United   (a) 3–4   Division One   Robson, Bennett, Iley   23758
Three-nil down within 18 minutes, skipper Jim Iley led by inspiration to make a game of it with a gallant fightback that fell just short. Geoff Hurst scored a hat-trick for the Hammers.

1971   West Bromwich   (a) 3–0   Division One   Busby, Macdonald 2   18036
      Albion

1974   Southampton   (h) 3–0   Texaco Cup   Tudor, Bruce, Cannell   20615

1976   Ipswich Town   (h) 1–0   Division One   Barrowclough   39257
The icy conditions underfoot forced the postponement of this match at half-time. The restaged game ended in a 1–1 draw.

1982   Wolverhampton   (h) 1–1   Division Two   Wharton   19595
      Wanderers

1989   Steve Howey signed his first professional contract with the club.

1993   Manchester United (h) 1–1   Premier League   Cole   36332
United coach Derek Fazackerley collected Keegan's Carling Manager of the Month award before the game, while Cole deservedly equalised Ince's shot.

DECEMBER 12TH

1880   Jimmy Hay born, Beith, Scotland.

1896   Notts County   (h) 2–2   Division Two   Wardrope, Aitken   17000

1897   Norman Smith born, Newburn.

1903   Nottingham Forest (h) 3–1   Division One   McColl, Appleyard, Howie 15000

1908   Chelsea   (a) 2–1   Division One   Allan, Veitch (pen)   30000

1914   Blackburn Rovers (a) 3–2   Division One   King 2, Hudspeth (pen)   5000

1925   Everton   (h) 3–3   Division One   Gallacher 2, Seymour   36000
Clash of the striking legends, as Gallacher scored two and made the other for Seymour. Dixie Dean scored all three of the visitors' goals.

1931   Blackpool   (a) 1–3   Division One   Lang   15000

1936   Swansea Town   (h) 5–1   Division Two   Pearson, Rogers 2, Smith 2 14000

1952   Irving Nattrass born, Fishburn, Durham.

1953   Blackpool   (a) 3–1   Division One   Broadis, Hannah, Mitchell 19896

1959   Luton Town   (a) 4–3   Division One   Eastham 2, Hughes, Luke 14524

1964   Northampton Town (h) 5–0   Division Two   McGarry 3, Hockey, OG   40376
Future Magpie Tommy Robson limped out of the game early on, and his colleague Mike Everitt put through his own goal.

1966   Lee Payne born, Luton.

1970   Huddersfield Town (h) 2–0   Division One   Dyson, Robson   21254
The game kicked off at 2 p.m. in order to conserve electricity by minimising the time the floodlights were used.

1973   Dundee United   (a) 0–2   Texaco Cup   No Scorer   8500

1987   Portsmouth   (h) 1–1   Division One   Mirandinha   20255
The game was marked by the double sending off of Peter Jackson and Kevin Dillon, then of the visitors.

1990   Newcastle reserves got a good 4–0 pasting at St James' from Manchester City. Twenty-four-year-old Danish striker Ove Hansen was on trial for United but was sent packing immediately after.

DECEMBER 13TH

1902	Bury	(a) 0–1	Division One	No Scorer	8000

First of four first-team runouts for right-back Billy Wilson. Unfortunately United lost three of them.

1913	Sheffield United	(h) 2–1	Division One	Hibbert, Hudspeth (pen)	25000

Debut for the unfortunate Stan Hardy, a locally born inside-left who was gassed in the trenches during the Great War but survived.

1914	Stan Docking born, Chopwell.				
1919	Sheffield United	(h) 2–1	Division One	Robinson, Smailes	30000
1924	Bolton Wanderers	(a) 2–3	Division One	Keating, Low	15000
1930	Leicester City	(h) 5–2	Division One	Bedford, Boyd, Hutchinson 2, OG	25000

Goalscoring debut for Harry Bedford.

| 1944 | Tommy Gibb born, Bathgate, Scotland. | | | | |
| 1947 | Millwall | (n) 1–2 | Division Two | Pearson | 30000 |

Played at Selhurst Park.

1952	Aston Villa	(h) 2–1	Division One	Keeble, OG	38046
1955	Glenn Roeder born, Woodford, Essex.				
1956	Malcolm Brown born, Salford.				
1958	Bolton Wanderers	(a) 1–1	Division One	White	23020
1969	Derby County	(a) 0–2	Division One	No Scorer	30057
1970	David Roche born, Daisy Hill, Wallsend.				
1975	Leicester City	(a) 0–1	Division One	No Scorer	18130
1980	Swansea City	(a) 0–4	Division Two	No Scorer	11672

More misery beamed to the nation, courtesy of *Match of the Day* and Jonah Motson.

1986	Nottingham Forest	(h) 3–2	Division One	Wharton, A. Thomas, Beardsley	26191
1988	Watford	(a) 1–2	Full Members Cup	R. McDonald	6186
1992	Barnsley	(a) 0–1	Division One	No Scorer	13263
1995	Former Newcastle striker Mark McGhee incurred the wrath of Leicester fans by walking				

out to become the new manager of Wolverhampton Wanderers.

| 1997 | Barnsley | (a) 2–2 | Premier League | Gillespie 2 | 18687 |

DECEMBER 14TH

1901	Sheffield United	(h) 1–1	Division One	Peddie (pen)	18000
1907	Liverpool	(a) 5–1	Division One	Appleyard, Rutherford 2, Wilson 2	20000

Two goals on his debut for outside-left George Wilson, signed from Everton.

1912	Manchester United	(h) 1–3	Division One	Rutherford	20000
1918	Death of Angus Douglas, 29, after contracting pneumonia.				
1921	South Shields	(a) 0–3	Friendly	No Scorer	6000

Ingham Cup match.

1929	Leeds United	(a) 2–5	Division One	Gallacher 2	12000
1935	Southampton	(h) 4–1	Division Two	Imrie, Pearson, J. Smith 2	18000
1939	Arthur Cox born, Southam, Warwickshire.				
1946	Leicester City	(a) 4–2	Division Two	Bentley, Pearson, Shackleton, Wayman	35262
1957	Leeds United	(a) 0–3	Division One	No Scorer	23500
1960	Brian Ferguson born, Irvine, Scotland.				
1960	Chris Waddle born, Heworth.				
1963	Derby County	(a) 2–1	Division Two	Thomas, Hilley	9237
1967	Scott Sloan born, Wallsend.				
1968	Ipswich Town	(h) 2–1	Division One	Davies 2	26454

| 1974 | Coventry City | (a) 0–2 | Division One | No Scorer | 15562 |
| 1985 | Southampton | (h) 2–1 | Division One | Beardsley, Roeder | 19340 |

Debut for Paul Stephenson.

| 1991 | Brighton and Hove Albion | (a) 2–2 | Division Two | Peacock, Kelly | 7658 |

David Kelly netted his first goal for Newcastle with a brilliant header, but following the loss of O'Brien, a point was a fair return.

DECEMBER 15TH

1894	Rotherham Town	(h) 5–2	Division Two	Dickson 2, Willis 2, Graham	4000
1900	Manchester City	(h) 2–1	Division One	Laidlaw, Peddie	14500
1906	Bolton Wanderers	(h) 4–0	Division One	McClarence, Orr, Speedie 2	22000
1923	Sunderland	(a) 2–3	Division One	Seymour, Harris	45000
1928	Derby County	(h) 4–1	Division One	Boyd, Chalmers, Gallacher, McCurley	28000
1934	Oldham Athletic	(h) 4–2	Division Two	Lang, McMenemy, Smith 2	13000

1935   Jim Iley born, South Kirby, Yorkshire.

1950   Newcastle manager George Martin left the club and became the new boss of Aston Villa.

1951	Stoke City	(a) 5–4	Division One	Davies 2, Duncan, G. Robledo 2	30000
1956	Portsmouth	(a) 2–2	Division One	Davies 2	18453
1962	Cardiff City	(h) 2–1	Division Two	Fell 2	27916

Ron McGarry made his debut.

| 1973 | Derby County | (h) 0–2 | Division One | No Scorer | 19470 |
| 1979 | Queens Park Rangers | (h) 4–2 | Division Two | Shoulder, Cassidy, Withe 2 | 25027 |

A fantastic game in which United took an early lead through a looping Shoulder shot but fell behind to goals from Paul Goddard and Glenn Roeder by half-time. In the second half a black-and-white dog appeared on the pitch as Hibbitt prepared to take a free-kick, and he resisted attempts at capture, including a rugby tackle from Peter Withe. When the game restarted with the free-kick, Withe headed an equaliser, to his great delight, before shots from Cassidy and Withe again sealed a memorable victory.

1981   Death of Tom Mooney, 71.

| 1984 | Norwich City | (h) 1–1 | Division One | Waddle | 20423 |

DECEMBER 16TH

1876   Death of Tosh Hope, 73.

1880   William Agnew born, New Cumnock, Scotland.

| 1893 | Small Heath | (a) 4–1 | Division Two | Crate, Wallace, Willis, Graham | 8000 |

Debut for locally born Bobby Willis, at inside-right.

1895	Tow Law Town	(h) 4–0	FA Cup Qualifier	Wardrope, Thompson, Lennox, Stott	3000
1899	Stoke	(a) 2–2	Division One	A. Gardner, Higgins	3000
1905	Stoke	(a) 0–1	Division One	No Scorer	8000

1907   George Nevin born, Lintz, Durham.

| 1908 | Middlesbrough | (a) 2–1 | Friendly | Stewart, Liddell (pen) | 1000 |

Another fundraiser, this time for the Medical Charities Fund.

| 1911 | Aston Villa | (h) 6–2 | Division One | Higgins, Hibbert, Stewart, Rutherford, Hay, McCracken (pen) | 30000 |
| 1922 | Aston Villa | (a) 1–1 | Division One | Harris | 16000 |

1929   Ivor Allchurch born, Swansea.

1933	Stoke City	(h) 2–2	Division One	J.R. Richardson,	20000
				Weaver (pen)	
1944	John Markie born, Bo'ness, Scotland.				
1950	Stoke City	(h) 3–1	Division One	Hannah, Mitchell,	29505
				G. Robledo	
1961	Leyton Orient	(a) 0–2	Division Two	No Scorer	13261
1962	Andy Thomas born, Eynesham, Oxfordshire.				
1967	Southampton	(a) 0–0	Division One	No Scorer	19498

1970 On the eve of United's Fairs Cup encounter with Southampton, Joe Harvey signed David Ford from Sheffield Wednesday in an exchange deal with Jackie Sinclair. Ford was ineligible for the cup game due to a 48-hour qualification rule.

| 1972 | Derby County | (a) 1–1 | Division One | Tudor | 28826 |

1975 United's Tommy Craig captained the Scotland Under-23 side to a 4–0 victory over Romania at Falkirk's Brockville ground. Craig hit the fourth goal from the penalty spot.

| 1978 | Fulham | (a) 3–1 | Division Two | Connolly, Withe, Shoulder | 8575 |

The home side's goal was scored by former United striker Chris Guthrie.

| 1990 | Plymouth Argyle | (a) 1–0 | Division Two | Peacock | 7845 |

This game kicked off at noon on a Sunday because Plymouth decided to rent their car park out for a Christmas shoppers' park-and-ride facility. A quite dreadful game was scant reward for the intrepid travellers who spent most of the weekend getting to and from the game, but a last-minute goal from Gavin Peacock provided a measure of warped justice.

| 1992 | Cesena (Italy) | (h) 2–2 | Anglo-Italian Cup | Peacock 2 | 4609 |

A meaningless match for already-eliminated United during which they experimented with a 3–4–3 formation, Neilson, Howey and Matty Appleby forming the rearguard. The Italians wore gloves and should have lost when they conceded a last-minute penalty. However, Peacock contrived to miss it and failed to complete his hat-trick.

| 1995 | Everton | (h) 1–0 | Premier League | Ferdinand | 36557 |

Ten-man United held out for an hour against the Toffees after Beresford had been dismissed for hauling down Kanchelskis.

DECEMBER 17TH

| 1898 | Sheffield Wednesday (h) 2–2 | Division Two | Peddie, MacFarlane | 15000 |

In three spells with Newcastle, this was the only time outside-right Archie Mowatt made the first XI.

1904	Sheffield Wednesday (h) 6–2	Division One	Orr, Appleyard, Howie,	18000
			Rutherford 2, McWilliam	
1910	Nottingham Forest	(h) 4–1	Division One	Shepherd 4	15000
1921	Aston Villa	(h) 1–2	Division One	Mooney	30000

Sole appearance of Pelaw-born John Thain, at outside-right.

1927	Portsmouth	(h) 1–3	Division One	McDonald	20000
1932	Derby County	(h) 0–0	Division One	No Scorer	23000
1933	George Luke born, Newcastle.				
1938	Swansea Town	(a) 1–0	Division Two	Clifton	15000
1949	Portsmouth	(a) 0–1	Division One	No Scorer	30455
1955	Sheffield United	(a) 1–2	Division One	Milburn	23000
1960	Preston North End	(h) 0–0	Division One	No Scorer	21514
1966	Aston Villa	(h) 0–3	Division One	No Scorer	25406

The final straw for Joe Harvey, as United's perilous position at the bottom of Division One demanded drastic measures. Alan Suddick played his final game, being sacrificed to provide funds for Dave Elliott, John McNamee and Tommy Robson.

1966	Kevin Scott born, Easington, Durham.				
1969	Southampton	(h) 0–0	Fairs Cup 3rd	No Scorer	38163
			Round 1st Leg		

The winning run in home Fairs Cup matches came to an end, partly due to the early departure of former Magpie John McGrath with a broken cheekbone following a challenge by Wyn Davies. After this the Saints withdrew into defence and played for the draw.

1977	Wolverhampton Wanderers	(h) 4–0	Division One	T. Craig, Mitchell, Cassidy, Nattrass	22982
1983	Brighton and Hove Albion	(a) 1–0	Division Two	Waddle	13896
1988	Southampton	(h) 3–3	Division One	Brock, O'Neill 2	20103

Two goals from Matthew Le Tissier looked to have put the Saints on the way to a comfortable win, but substitute O'Neill first got one back, then forced in the equaliser deep into injury time.

| 1991 | Death of Ron Starling, 82. | | | | |
| 1994 | Coventry City | (a) 0–0 | Premier League | No Scorer | 17237 |

In the final minutes, Kitson tumbled in the box and the referee charitably pointed to the spot. With Beardsley off the pitch, nobody appeared to want to take it, and a clearly reluctant Cole saw his effort saved by Ogrizovic.

1995 United striker Malcolm Allen announced his retirement from professional football following a number of operations on his injured knee and abortive comebacks. Apparently, Allen knew his career was over when he was caught by a Durham taxi driver after attempting to escape without paying his fare. He later appeared in court and was fined.

| 1996 | Coventry City | (a) 1–2 | Premier League | Shearer | 21538 |
| 1997 | Derby County | (h) 0–0 | Premier League | No Scorer | 36289 |

An unbelievably boring game, the only highlight of which was the dismissal of Eranio, who for some reason took exception to Albert pulling him up by the ears.

DECEMBER 18TH

1897	Burton Swifts	(a) 1–3	Division Two	White	
1909	Sheffield United	(a) 0–4	Division One	No Scorer	20000
1920	Manchester United	(a) 0–2	Division One	No Scorer	30000
1922	Ivor Broadis born, Isle of Dogs.				
1926	Leicester City	(h) 1–1	Division One	Seymour	25000

Profligacy from the penalty spot as both Hughie Gallacher and Frank Hudspeth missed for United.

1937	Swansea Town	(h) 1–0	Division Two	Imrie (pen)	16000
1948	Everton	(h) 1–0	Division One	Taylor	43515
1954	Arsenal	(h) 5–1	Division One	Mitchell 2 (1 pen), Keeble 2, Milburn	35122
1955	Micky Barker born, Bishop Auckland.				
1959	Kevin Dillon born, Sunderland.				
1965	Liverpool	(h) 0–0	Division One	No Scorer	34153
1971	West Ham United	(a) 1–0	Division One	Busby	21991
1974	Chester	(a) 0–1	League Cup 5th Round Replay	No Scorer	19000
1976	Aston Villa	(a) 1–2	Division One	Gowling	33982
1982	Sheffield Wednesday	(a) 1–1	Division Two	Varadi	16310

1990 Newcastle reserves beat Leicester 2–0 with goals from Michael Parkinson and John Gallacher. The game marked the only appearance of trialist defender Chris Zoricich, a New Zealander who came to England to be a professional footballer. He was eventually signed by Leyton Orient.

| 1993 | Everton | (a) 2–0 | Premier League | Cole, Beardsley | 25362 |

Peter Beardsley was warmly welcomed on his return to Goodison Park and marked the occasion with a fine individual goal.

DECEMBER 19TH

1903	Sheffield Wednesday (a) 1–1	Division One	McColl	10000
1908	Blackburn Rovers (h) 2–0	Division One	Anderson, Duncan	22000
1914	Notts County (h) 1–1	Division One	Hibbert	15000
1919	George Lowrie born, Tonypandy, Wales.			
1925	Manchester City (a) 2–2	Division One	McDonald (pen), Gallacher	35000
1931	Sheffield United (h) 5–3	Division One	Bedford 3, Boyd, Lang	27000
1936	Bradford City (a) 0–2	Division Two	No Scorer	10000
1953	Sunderland (a) 1–1	Division One	Broadis	49923
1959	Tottenham Hotspur (a) 0–4	Division One	No Scorer	32824
1963	Derek Bell born, Fenham.			
1964	Southampton (a) 1–0	Division Two	Suddick	22365
1970	Crystal Palace (h) 2–0	Division One	Robson 2 (1 pen)	21779
1973	Dundee United (h) 4–1	Texaco Cup	Robson, Tudor, Macdonald, Cassidy	5009
1980	John Trewick joined United from West Bromwich Albion for a record fee of £250,000.			
1987	West Ham United (a) 1–2	Division One	Mirandinha	18679

DECEMBER 20TH

1902	Blackburn Rovers (h) 1–0	Division One	Caie	12000
1909	George Mathison born, Walker.			
1913	Derby County (a) 0–2	Division One	No Scorer	15000
1919	Manchester United (a) 1–2	Division One	Hagan	20000

Consolation goal for Alf Hagan on his debut.

1924	Notts County (h) 1–0	Division One	McDonald	25000
1930	Arsenal (a) 2–1	Division One	Bedford, Hutchinson	50000
1938	Dave Hilley born, Glasgow.			
1947	Plymouth Argyle (a) 0–3	Division Two	No Scorer	25000
1949	Alan Duffy born, Stanley.			
1952	Sheffield Wednesday (h) 1–5	Division One	Mitchell (pen)	37927

Wednesday became the first team to take maximum points from St James' Park since the previous April, as Derek Dooley and Jackie Sewell hit two apiece and Jack Marriott the other.

1958	Blackburn Rovers (a) 0–3	Division One	No Scorer	25100
1968	Alex Mathie born, Bathgate, Scotland.			
1969	Ipswich Town (h) 4–0	Division One	Ford, Dyson, Robson 2	19411

Debut goal for David Ford.

1974	A double arrival at St James', as Tommy Craig joined for £110,000 from Sheffield Wednesday and Geoff Nulty came from Burnley for £120,000.			
1975	Ipswich Town (h) 1–1	Division One	Nulty	26152
1980	Bristol City (h) 0–0	Division Two	No Scorer	14131

Debut for John Trewick, in midfield. St James' Park entered the digital age, as a new electronic scoreboard was unveiled at the Gallowgate end. Half-times were never the same again, as hitherto unknown teams and incorrect scores were beamed to the crowd (remember 'Derby City'?), as well as, one year, the wrong winner of the Grand National!

1989	Derby County (h) 3–2	Full Members Cup	O'Brien, Gallacher, OG	6704
1991	Plymouth Argyle (a) 0–2	Division Two	No Scorer	5048

A Friday night kick-off and a shocking performance from United in front of a handful of loyal fans, many of whom stood stoically on the open terrace in shirt sleeves, oblivious to the rain. The fact that Plymouth were absolute garbage as well just made things worse.

1992	Millwall (h) 1–1	Division One	Kelly (pen)	26089

Ian Bogie appeared for the visitors, while Malcolm Allen was a substitute. The referee gave a late penalty for a combination of handball and a foul, much to the disgust of Lions boss Mick McCarthy.

DECEMBER 21ST

1895	Rotherham Town	(h) 6–1	Division Two	Wardrope 2, McKay, Lennox 2, Stott	5000
1907	Sunderland	(a) 4–2	Division One	Rutherford, Veitch, Wilson 2	30000
1912	Aston Villa	(a) 1–3	Division One	Hudspeth (pen)	30000
1929	Derby County	(h) 2–3	Division One	Chalmers, Hill	20000
1935	Death of Ted Birnie, 57.				
1946	Chesterfield	(h) 2–1	Division Two	Wayman 2	53675
1946	Micky Burns born, Preston.				
1957	West Bromwich Albion	(h) 3–0	Division One	Davies, White 2	31699
1963	Plymouth Argyle	(h) 1–1	Division Two	Thorn	23572
1968	Queens Park Rangers	(a) 1–1	Division One	Foggon	16444
1974	Leeds United	(h) 3–0	Division One	Tudor, Kennedy, Howard	34054
1985	Liverpool	(a) 1–1	Division One	Beardsley	30746
1986	Sheffield Wednesday	(a) 0–2	Division One	No Scorer	28897
1988	More frantic transfer activity at Gallowgate as Jim Smith brought in a new full-back pairing of Ray Ranson from Birmingham City and Kenny Sansom from Arsenal.				
1994	Manchester City	(h) 0–2	League Cup 4th Round Replay	No Scorer	30156
1997	Manchester United	(h) 0–1	Premier League	No Scorer	36767
	Andy Cole against his old club.				

DECEMBER 22ND

1894	Walsall Town Swifts	(h) 7–2	Division Two	Crate 2, Smith 3, Willis, OG	1500
	Debut for Pat O'Brien.				
1900	Bury	(a) 0–1	Division One	No Scorer	5000
1906	Manchester United	(a) 3–1	Division One	Speedie, McClarence, Veitch (pen)	18000
1923	Sunderland	(h) 0–2	Division One	No Scorer	50000
1928	Everton	(a) 2–5	Division One	Chalmers, Lang	20000
1934	Burnley	(a) 3–0	Division One	McMenemy, Pearson, Smith	14000
1951	Manchester United	(h) 2–2	Division One	Foulkes, Milburn	45414
1956	Sunderland	(h) 6–2	Division One	Tait 3, Davies, White, Casey (pen)	29727

A thick blanket of fog covered the pitch throughout, but it didn't prevent Alec Tait from making his mark in place of the absent Milburn.

1962	Portsmouth	(a) 1–3	Division Two	McGarry	18373
1973	Queens Park Rangers	(a) 2–3	Division One	Moncur, McDermott	15757
1973	Alan Thompson born, Newcastle.				
1979	Notts County	(a) 2–2	Division Two	Shoulder, Connolly	11224
1984	Aston Villa	(a) 0–4	Division One	No Scorer	14491
	Ian Baird made his debut, on loan from Southampton.				
1990	Bristol Rovers	(a) 1–1	Division Two	Gaynor	6643

Tommy Gaynor scored the only goal of his brief career on Tyneside to earn a point, while at the other end Kevin Scott was sent off after some disgraceful injury-feigning antics from the Rovers front men. One local radio reporter who shall remain nameless (initials CH) surpassed even his low standards by confusing sports and announcing Devon Malcolm as the Rovers dangerman.

1993 Leeds United (h) 1–1 Premier League Cole 36388
Peter Beardsley saw his penalty saved by Mark Beeney but Cole hit a powerful equaliser after Wallace had scored.

DECEMBER 23RD

1893 Royal Scots Regiment (h) 3–0 Friendly Crate 2, Willis 2000
1899 Sunderland (h) 2–4 Division One MacFarlane, A. Gardner 21000
The honour of hitting the first hat-trick in a Tyne–Wear league match fell to Robert Hogg of Sunderland.
1905 Bolton Wanderers (h) 2–1 Division One Orr, McClarence 20000
Debut at right-half for Scotsman John Findlay.
1911 Preston North End (a) 1–2 Division One Hibbert 12000
Debut for Tommy Lowes.
1922 Aston Villa (h) 0–0 Division One No Scorer 20000
1933 Liverpool (a) 2–1 Division One J.R. Richardson, Williams 20000
1935 St James' Park hosted a second-round FA Cup match, when Hartlepools United beat Halifax Town 4–1. Five thousand fans turned up.
1950 Everton (a) 1–3 Division One Taylor 30000
1952 Alex Bruce born, Dundee.
1961 Preston North End (h) 0–2 Division Two No Scorer 18775
1967 Liverpool (h) 1–1 Division One Scott 46204
United took the lead when Wyn Davies saw his header parried and Jimmy Scott swept in the loose ball. Ian St John equalised.
1972 Manchester City (h) 2–1 Division One Macdonald (pen), Barrowclough 28274
1978 Burnley (h) 3–1 Division Two Withe, Shoulder, Cassidy 23639
1980 Arthur Cox got his cheque book out again, this time for striker Mick Harford, a £216,000 signing from Lincoln City.
1995 Nottingham Forest (h) 3–1 Premier League Ginola, Lee 2 36531
Ian Woan got the first of many goals against United.
1996 Liverpool (h) 1–1 Premier League Shearer 36570

DECEMBER 24TH

1892 Middlesbrough (h) 2–1 Friendly McIntosh, Reay 1200
Following FA approval of the name change, the newly named Newcastle United took to the field for the first time.
1898 Sunderland (a) 3–2 Division Two Wardrope, Peddie 2 25000
The first Tyne–Wear league meeting and the first time the two sides had met at Roker Park. In a typical move, the home side cashed in by raising admission charges.
1904 Sunderland (a) 1–3 Division One McWilliam 35000
Contemporary press reports claimed that Appleyard of Newcastle missed a penalty by 'at least 20 yards'.
1909 David Bell born, Gorebridge, Scotland.
1910 Manchester City (a) 0–2 Division One No Scorer 15000
1921 Aston Villa (a) 0–1 Division One No Scorer 32000
1927 West Ham United (a) 2–5 Division One Boyd, Evans 22000
1932 Blackpool (a) 4–0 Division One Allen 2, Boyd, Lang 15000
1938 Plymouth Argyle (a) 1–0 Division Two Mooney 17861
1949 Wolverhampton Wanderers (h) 2–0 Division One Taylor, OG 56048
1955 Preston North End (h) 5–0 Division One Mitchell (pen), Keeble 2, Milburn 2 32976
1960 Birmingham City (h) 2–2 Division One Mitchell, Scanlon 20354

1966	Leeds United	(h) 1–2	Division One	Craggs	29165

Debut for Tot Winstanley, at centre-half.

1978	Death of Stan Seymour, 85.

DECEMBER 25TH

1893	Middlesbrough Ironopolis	(a) 1–1	Division Two	Crate	2000

A Yuletide visit to the Paradise Ground to face the Nops, who played in red-and-white striped shirts.

1894	Crewe Alexandra	(h) 6–0	Division Two	Wallace, O'Brien, Willis, Smith 3	7000
1895	Crewe Alexandra	(h) 6–0	Division Two	Wardrope, Aitken, McKay 2, Collins, Lennox	8000

Local lad John Carr made his debut, at left-half.

1896	Dundee	(h) 3–1	Friendly	Wardrope, Thompson, Milne	10000
1897	Blackpool	(a) 3–2	Division Two	Wardrope, Campbell, Stott	4000
1899	Kilmarnock	(h) 4–1	Friendly	Fraser, Rogers 2, Wardrope	2500
1900	Glasgow Rangers	(h) 4–1	Friendly	Niblo 2, MacFarlane, Peddie	5000
1901	Dundee	(h) 1–1	Friendly	Graham	1000
1902	Hibernian	(h) 1–0	Friendly	Stenhouse	3000

1902	In a Northern League match at Roker Park in front of 5,000, Sunderland 'A' overcame Newcastle 'A' 3–2. Newcastle's second goal came from Willie Wilson, who shot from inside the centre circle.

1903	Sheffield United	(a) 2–2	Division One	Appleyard, Howie	20000
1905	Woolwich Arsenal	(a) 3–4	Division One	Howie 2, J. Rutherford	20000
1906	Blackburn Rovers	(a) 0–4	Division One	No Scorer	35000
1907	Woolwich Arsenal	(a) 2–2	Division One	Appleyard, Higgins	30000
1908	Manchester United	(h) 2–1	Division One	Shepherd, Wilson	40000
1909	Woolwich Arsenal	(a) 3–0	Division One	Shepherd 2, Rutherford	25000
1911	Oldham Athletic	(a) 4–2	Division One	Hay, Hibbert 2, Low	25000
1912	Sheffield United	(h) 1–2	Division One	Higgins	18000
1913	Bradford City	(h) 0–0	Division One	No Scorer	25000

1913	William Gallantree born, East Boldon.

1914	Sunderland	(h) 2–5	Division One	OG 2	40000
1920	Tottenham Hotspur	(h) 1–1	Division One	Harris	45000
1922	Middlesbrough	(h) 1–1	Division One	Aitken	30000
1923	Liverpool	(a) 1–0	Division One	R. Clark	25000
1924	Everton	(a) 1–0	Division One	Keating	30000

Winning debut for Alf Maitland, at right-back.

1925	Liverpool	(a) 3–6	Division One	Gallacher 3	35000

An eventful game for Joe Harris to make his debut, following a transfer from Middlesbrough.

1926	Cardiff City	(h) 5–0	Division One	Gallacher 2, McDonald 3	
1928	West Ham United	(a) 0–1	Division One	No Scorer	15000
1929	Middlesbrough	(h) 3–2	Division One	Chalmers, Gallacher, Weaver	40000

Left winger George Scott made his debut, after joining from South Shields.

1931	Huddersfield Town	(h) 2–1	Division One	Bedford, McMenemy	44000
1933	Everton	(h) 1–2	Division One	Williams	50000
1934	Hull City	(h) 6–2	Division Two	Gallantree, Pearson 2, Smith 2, Wilson	26000

Goalscoring debut for Joe Wilson, at inside-right.

1936	Norwich City	(h) 0–1	Division Two	No Scorer	40000
1937	Stockport County	(h) 0–0	Division Two	No Scorer	
1946	West Bromwich Albion	(h) 2–4	Division Two	Shackleton, Stobbart	44722

1948	Birmingham City	(a) 0–2	Division One	No Scorer	42000
1950	Middlesbrough	(a) 1–2	Division One	Stokoe	48000

Debuts for Matthew McNeil at centre-half and Tom Patterson at outside-left. Bob Stokoe got his first start as an emergency forward and netted United's only goal.

1951	Sunderland	(a) 4–1	Division One	Foulkes, Milburn, G. Robledo 2	52274
1952	Cardiff City	(h) 3–0	Division One	Mitchell (pen), Foulkes 2	36143

Yuletide debut for Tommy Cahill.

1953	Middlesbrough	(a) 3–2	Division One	Mitchell, Monkhouse, Scoular	40000
1954	Manchester City	(a) 1–3	Division One	Keeble	26664
1956	West Bromwich Albion	(a) 0–1	Division One	No Scorer	13730
1957	Nottingham Forest	(h) 1–4	Division One	Hughes	25214
1973	Robbie Elliott born, Gosforth.				

DECEMBER 26TH

1892	Sheffield Wednesday	(a) 0–1	Friendly	No Scorer	
1893	Walsall Town Swifts	(a) 2–1	Division Two	Wallace 2	5000

Debut for Scottish striker John Law, who had signed for Everton after leaving Glasgow Rangers but never actually appeared for the Merseyside club, joining Newcastle instead.

1894	Rotherham Town	(a) 0–1	Division Two	No Scorer	2000
1895	Grimsby Town	(a) 1–2	Division Two	Collins	4000
1896	Grimsby Town	(a) 2–3	Division Two	Wardrope, Stott	7000

Debuts for Jack Ostler at centre-half and Tom Stewart at right-back.

1898	Aston Villa	(a) 0–1	Division Two	No Scorer	30000
1899	Third Lanark	(h) 1–1	Friendly	Peddie	2500
1900	Woolwich Arsenal	(a) 1–1	Friendly	Niblo	8000
1901	Derby County	(a) 0–1	Division One	No Scorer	20000

The season of good cheer interrupted by Steve Bloomer of Derby.

1902	Dundee	(h) 1–1	Friendly	Rutherford	3000
1903	Sunderland	(h) 1–3	Division One	Rutherford	30000
1905	Manchester City	(a) 4–1	Division One	Gosnell, McClarence, J. Rutherford, Veitch	5000
1906	Stoke	(a) 2–1	Division One	Howie, Speedie	10000
1907	Sheffield United	(h) 2–3	Division One	Appleyard, Howie	35000

Debut of John McCormack, at centre-half.

1908	Manchester United	(a) 0–1	Division One	No Scorer	45000
1910	Everton	(h) 1–0	Division One	Shepherd	40000
1911	Sheffield United	(h) 2–2	Division One	Hibbert, Rutherford	40000
1912	Liverpool	(a) 1–2	Division One	G. Wilson	35000

Debut for Dick Little, at right-back.

1913	Bradford City	(a) 0–2	Division One	No Scorer	18000
1914	Sunderland	(a) 4–2	Division One	Higgins, Hibbert 2, Hudspeth	20000
1919	Burnley	(h) 0–0	Division One	No Scorer	45000
1921	Liverpool	(a) 0–1	Division One	No Scorer	45000
1922	Middlesbrough	(a) 1–1	Division One	Woods	40000
1923	Liverpool	(h) 2–1	Division One	McDonald 2	23000
1924	Everton	(h) 1–1	Division One	Seymour	25000
1925	Liverpool	(h) 3–0	Division One	Clark, Gallacher, Urwin	50000
1927	Middlesbrough	(a) 1–1	Division One	Gallacher	35000
1928	West Ham United	(h) 1–0	Division One	McCurley	43000
1929	Middlesbrough	(a) 2–2	Division One	Scott, Hutchinson	45000
1930	Huddersfield Town	(a) 3–0	Division One	Boyd 2, Starling	20000

1931	Huddersfield Town	(a) 2–1	Division One	Allen, OG	25000
1932	Birmingham	(h) 2–1	Division One	Boyd, J.R. Richardson	43000
1933	Everton	(a) 7–3	Division One	Lang, Weaver (pen), Williams 3, J.R. Richardson, Boyd	40000
1934	Hull City	(a) 1–1	Division Two	Pearson	25000
1935	Bradford City	(h) 3–2	Division Two	McMenemy, J. Smith, Weaver	14000
1935	Terry Marshall born, Wisbech.				
1936	Barnsley	(a) 0–1	Division Two	No Scorer	22000
1946	West Bromwich Albion	(a) 2–3	Division Two	Wayman 2	31794
1947	West Bromwich Albion	(a) 1–0	Division Two	OG	48322
1949	Middlesbrough	(h) 0–1	Division One	No Scorer	61184
1951	Sunderland	(h) 2–2	Division One	Milburn 2 (1 pen)	63665
1953	Middlesbrough	(h) 2–3	Division One	Broadis, Mitchell	43750

The missing Jackie Milburn was replaced by Alex Gaskell, who never got another chance.

1955	Sunderland	(a) 6–1	Division One	Curry 2, Keeble 2, Milburn 2	55723
1956	West Bromwich Albion	(h) 5–2	Division One	Punton, Davies 2, Casey (pen), Scoular	20319
1957	Nottingham Forest	(a) 3–2	Division One	Casey, R. Mitchell, White	32359
1958	Nottingham Forest	(h) 1–3	Division One	Curry	

United manager Charlie Mitten was so incensed by the deplorable refereeing he witnessed that he wrote to the Football League demanding the appointment of professional officials.

1959	Chelsea	(a) 2–2	Division One	Allchurch, White	7462
1960	Birmingham City	(a) 1–2	Division One	Woods	29435
1961	Middlesbrough	(h) 3–4	Division Two	Tuohy, Allchurch, McGuigan	21038
1963	Huddersfield Town	(h) 2–0	Division Two	Thomas, Hilley	37898
1964	Middlesbrough	(a) 2–0	Division Two	Hilley, OG	38184
1966	Leeds United	(a) 0–5	Division One	No Scorer	40680
1967	Sunderland	(h) 2–1	Division One	Bennett, Davies	59579
1968	Leeds United	(a) 1–2	Division One	McNamee	44995
1969	Leeds United	(h) 2–1	Division One	Davies, Robson	54517
1970	Leeds United	(a) 0–3	Division One	No Scorer	46758

Plenty of exercise for Martin Burleigh on his full debut, replacing McFaul. Frank Clark gave away two penalties, both of which were converted by Johnny Giles. Allan Clarke scored the other goal.

1972	Leeds United	(a) 0–1	Division One	No Scorer	45486
1973	Leeds United	(h) 0–1	Division One	No Scorer	55638

The points returned to Yorkshire thanks to a Paul Madeley goal.

1974	Carlisle United	(a) 2–1	Division One	Tudor, Macdonald	20605

Debuts for Tommy Craig and Geoff Nulty.

1975	Burnley	(a) 1–0	Division One	T. Craig (pen)	22458

More bad luck for John Tudor, who lasted two minutes of his comeback match before breaking down again. On a previous visit to Turf Moor, he had been struck by a brick hurled at the Newcastle team bus.

1977	Manchester City	(a) 0–4	Division One	No Scorer	45811

The briefest of debuts for Martin Gorry, as substitute for John Blackley, when the game was already lost.

1978	Sheffield United	(a) 0–1	Division Two	No Scorer	23200
1979	Burnley	(a) 2–3	Division Two	Shoulder, Barton	16433
1980	Grimsby Town	(a) 0–0	Division Two	No Scorer	17623

Debutant Mick Harford came the closest to breaking the deadlock, hitting the bar with a header.

1983 Blackburn Rovers (h) 1–1 Division Two Waddle 33622
Debut for Glenn Roeder, who signed for United when the other Magpies, Notts County, failed to raise the £150,000 transfer fee to make his loan move permanent, despite a supporters' appeal. Future United coaches Terry Gennoe and Derek Fazackerley were in the Rovers side who opened the scoring through 19-year-old debutant Simon Barker.

1984 West Bromwich (a) 1–2 Division One Baird 20248
Albion

1985 Sheffield Wednesday (a) 2–2 Division One Beardsley, Roeder 30269

1986 Everton (h) 0–4 Division One No Scorer 35079
Debut for Jeff Wrightson in midfield, in the absence of injured David McCreery.

1987 Manchester United (h) 1–0 Division One Roeder 26461

1988 Sheffield Wednesday (a) 2–1 Division One McDonald, O'Neill 25573
Injury to John Anderson and the poorness of Brian Tinnion prompted Jim Smith to bring in a vastly experienced full-back pairing of Ray Ranson and Kenny Sansom.

1989 Stoke City (a) 1–2 Division Two Scott 14878

1990 Swindon Town (h) 1–1 Division Two Quinn 17003

1991 Middlesbrough (h) 0–1 Division Two No Scorer 26563

1992 Wolverhampton (h) 2–1 Division One Kelly 2 30137
Wanderers
An inspirational performance from David Kelly, including a tremendous volley which, no doubt, influenced Wolves to pay £750,000 for him the following summer.

1994 Leeds United (a) 0–0 Premier League No Scorer 39337

1996 Blackburn Rovers (a) 0–1 Premier League No Scorer 30398

1997 Derby County (a) 0–1 Premier League No Scorer 30232

DECEMBER 27TH

1893 Crewe Alexandra (a) 1–1 Division Two Graham 2000

1897 Burnley (h) 0–1 Division Two No Scorer 24959

1898 Coventry City (a) 2–0 Friendly Wardrope, Stevenson 2000

1902 Sunderland (a) 0–0 Division One No Scorer 24000

1909 Chelsea (a) 1–2 Division One Veitch 70000

1910 Sheffield Wednesday (a) 2–0 Division One Shepherd 2 20000

1913 Sunderland (h) 2–1 Division One Goodwill, Hibbert 50000

1919 Manchester United (h) 2–1 Division One Hibbert, Smailes 35000

1920 Tottenham Hotspur (a) 0–2 Division One No Scorer 54500

1924 Huddersfield Town (a) 0–0 Division One No Scorer 15000
Debut for Jimmy Loughlin, at centre-forward.

1926 Leeds United (a) 2–1 Division One Seymour, Urwin 48620

1927 Middlesbrough (h) 3–3 Division One Boyd, Gallacher, McDonald 40000

1930 Sheffield Wednesday (h) 1–2 Division One Bedford 38000

1932 Birmingham (a) 2–1 Division One Lang, Murray 40000

1936 Billy Day born, Middlesbrough.

1937 Stockport County (a) 2–2 Division Two Smith, Park 19000
Abandoned after 77 minutes due to failing light.

1938 Norwich City (h) 4–0 Division Two Mooney 2 (2 pens), Clifton 2 46000

1948 Birmingham City (h) 1–0 Division One Milburn 49457

1949 Middlesbrough (a) 0–1 Division One No Scorer 53802
Ayresome Park's record attendance crowded into this game and saw an inspired display by Jamaican-born winger Lindy Delaphena for the 'Boro.

1952 Cardiff City (a) 0–0 Division One No Scorer 40000

1954 Manchester City (h) 2–0 Division One Mitchell 2 (1 pen) 52874

1955 Sunderland (h) 3–1 Division One Keeble, Milburn, White 61058

After the previous day's hammering at Roker, Sunderland signed Burnley striker Bill Holden, who scored their only goal as they lost again.

1958	Nottingham Forest	(a) 0–3	Division One	No Scorer	39907
1967	Mark Stimson born, Plaistow.				
1969	Arsenal	(a) 0–0	Division One	No Scorer	39646
1971	Sheffield United	(h) 1–2	Division One	Hibbitt	53079
1975	Sheffield United	(h) 1–1	Division One	Macdonald	31762
1976	Sunderland	(h) 2–0	Division One	Cannell, Kennedy	49664
1980	Derby County	(h) 0–2	Division Two	No Scorer	20886

Never any doubt about the result after Boam headed past his own keeper in the second minute of the match. Roy McFarland added a second to make sure.

| 1982 | Derby County | (h) 1–0 | Division Two | Gayle | 30559 |
| 1983 | Carlisle United | (a) 1–3 | Division Two | Waddle | 14756 |

After Waddle had opened the scoring, this should have been easy, but three goals passed by United keeper Martin Thomas in such a fashion that a Newcastle fan got to him and started swinging punches before being dragged away.

| 1986 | Watford | (a) 0–1 | Division One | No Scorer | 18011 |

John Barnes hit the only goal.

| 1995 | Manchester United | (a) 0–2 | Premier League | No Scorer | 42024 |

Andy Cole and Roy Keane scored the goals on a rock-hard pitch, while Keith Gillespie was badly injured for United.

DECEMBER 28TH

| 1886 | Stanley Allan born, Wallsend. | | | | |
| 1895 | Lincoln City | (a) 0–4 | Division Two | No Scorer | 1500 |

United player William Miller was disciplined by the club after he admitted the theft of jewellery from his colleagues in the dressing-room at this match.

| 1896 | Gainsborough Trinity | (a) 0–2 | Division Two | No Scorer | 7000 |
| 1901 | Bury | (h) 1–1 | Division One | Roberts | 7000 |

Debut for local lad John Graham, at outside-left.

| 1907 | Middlesbrough | (h) 1–1 | Division One | McCormack | 20000 |

Forty-eight hours after his debut, centre-half John McCormack made his second and final appearance and saved a point with a second-half leveller.

| 1912 | Sunderland | (a) 0–2 | Division One | No Scorer | 35000 |
| 1921 | Corinthians | (h) 5–4 | Friendly | Dixon 2, Patten 2, McDonald | 5000 |

This game had to be abandoned with ten minutes remaining due to drifting snow.

1929	Manchester United	(a) 0–5	Division One	No Scorer	10000
1931	Aston Villa	(a) 0–3	Division One	No Scorer	45000
1935	Bradford City	(a) 2–3	Division Two	Pearson 2	12500
1936	Norwich City	(a) 5–1	Division Two	Pearson, Smith 3, Leighton	19300
1946	Millwall	(h) 0–2	Division Two	No Scorer	53305
1957	Tottenham Hotspur	(a) 3–3	Division One	R. Mitchell (pen), White 2	51649

Debuts for Ken Hale at inside-right and Bill McKinney at right-back.

1959	Chelsea	(h) 1–1	Division One	Eastham	43295
1963	Huddersfield Town	(a) 0–3	Division Two	No Scorer	12832
1964	Middlesbrough	(h) 2–1	Division Two	Hilley 2	54750
1977	Nottingham Forest	(h) 0–2	Division One	No Scorer	41612
1982	Grimsby Town	(a) 2–2	Division Two	Varadi, Gayle	14983
1987	Liverpool	(a) 0–4	Division One	No Scorer	44637
1991	Bristol Rovers	(h) 2–1	Division Two	Brock, Kelly	19329

The Hall era at United got off to a bad start when Devon White scored for Rovers, Thompson having gifted him the ball. However, a second-half revival saw Brock grab his first of the season and David Kelly win it with eight minutes to go, Howey guiding the ball safely over the line. Kevin Scott was deservedly booked for a savage tackle on Carl Saunders that was a legacy from a previous encounter, when 'gamesmanship' from the Rovers player had resulted in Scott's dismissal.

1992	Oxford United	(a) 2–4	Division One	O'Brien, Clark	9293

1992   Death of Duggie Wright, 75.

1993	Chelsea	(a) 0–1	Premier League	No Scorer	23133
1996	Tottenham Hotspur	(h) 7–1	Premier League	Shearer 2, Ferdinand 2, Lee 2, Albert	36308

The game at which Kevin Keegan decided to leave Newcastle, according to one version of his 'exclusive' story granted to a tabloid newspaper.

1997	Liverpool	(h) 1–2	Premier League	Watson	36702

DECEMBER 29TH

1894	Walsall Town Swifts	(a) 3–2	Division Two	Willis 3	2000

William Milne made his debut for United in this match played at Walsall's notoriously muddy West Bromwich Road ground, which they used only for a brief spell. The home team walked off the pitch with ten minutes left over a payment wrangle, the match ending with the score at the time being taken as final.

1900	Nottingham Forest	(a) 2–1	Division One	Peddie 2	10000
1923	Nottingham Forest	(a) 0–0	Division One	No Scorer	12000
1928	Cardiff City	(a) 0–2	Division One	No Scorer	10000
1934	Nottingham Forest	(h) 2–0	Division Two	Murray, Pearson	24000
1951	Tottenham Hotspur	(a) 1–2	Division One	G. Robledo	55219

Debut for George Lackenby, at right-half.

1954   Martin Gorry born, Derby.

1956	Sheffield Wednesday	(h) 1–2	Division One	Curry	42649

Sole appearance for Bill Redhead, who had a traumatic afternoon at left-half.

1967   Joe Harvey travelled to Leicester and returned with Jackie Sinclair, acquired for a fee of £67,500.

1973	Sheffield United	(h) 1–0	Division One	Tudor	27943

1977   Panic buying by United boss McGarry, as he splashed out on two unknown Scottish strikers without ever having seen them play. Mike Larnach arrived from Clydebank for £100,000 and Mark McGhee from Morton for £150,000. Had it come off, McGarry would have been a hero, but Larnach was out of his depth and McGhee only showed his worth to United when he rejoined them over a decade later.

1978   Brian Pinas born, Rotterdam, Holland. A slightly built winger, he left Feyenoord under freedom of contract to try his luck in England. Within days of signing, he played for the first team in a friendly at Birmingham City but was restricted to junior and reserve matches before returning to Holland in July 1998.

1979	Charlton Athletic	(h) 2–0	Division Two	Shoulder, Cassidy	26225
1984	Arsenal	(h) 1–3	Division One	Beardsley (pen)	27828
1990	Notts County	(h) 0–2	Division Two	No Scorer	17557

DECEMBER 30TH

1893	Burslem Port Vale	(h) 2–1	Division Two	Crate, Crielly	3000
1899	West Bromwich Albion	(h) 4–2	Division One	Fraser, Peddie, Stevenson 2	12000
1903	Corinthians	(h) 4–2	Friendly	Fraser 2, Birnie, Graham	10000
1905	Sunderland	(h) 1–1	Division One	Orr	56000
1911	Bolton Wanderers	(h) 5–2	Division One	Hay, Hibbert 3, Veitch	28000
1912	Sheffield United	(a) 1–1	Division One	McTavish	22000
1922	Nottingham Forest	(a) 1–0	Division One	Mitchell	12000
1933	Portsmouth	(a) 0–2	Division One	No Scorer	15000

1948   Colin Suggett born, Washington, Tyne and Wear.

1950   Billy Rafferty born, Glasgow.
1967   Sunderland   (a) 3–3   Division One   Burton 2 (2 pens), McNamee 46030
In a well-remembered Tyne–Wear derby, John McNamee hung from the net after equalising for United. Ian Porterfield made his Sunderland debut and Colin Suggett grabbed two to begin a habit of scoring against the Magpies.
1972   Sheffield United   (h) 4–1   Division One   Macdonald, Tudor, Nattrass, 28620
                                                         Craig
1978   Brighton and Hove   (a) 0–2   Division Two   No Scorer   25812
Albion
Keith Mulgrove made his only first-team appearance, replacing Colin Suggett. Goals from Malcolm Poskett and Peter O'Sullivan won it for the Seagulls.
1989   Swindon Town   (a) 1–1   Division Two   Quinn   11657
Debut for Darren Bradshaw.

DECEMBER 31ST

1892   Corinthians   (h) 8–1   Friendly   McKane, Sorley, McIntosh 2, 1500
                                                         Thompson 3, Reay
1897   Willie Bertam born, Brandon, Durham. Inside-left who briefly appeared for the first team.
1898   Wolverhampton   (a) 0–0   Division Two   No Scorer   6000
Wanderers
1904   Woolwich Arsenal   (a) 2–0   Division One   Rutherford, Veitch   30000
1910   Bristol City   (a) 0–1   Division One   No Scorer   14000
1921   Manchester United   (h) 3–0   Division One   Harris 2, McDonald   30000
1927   Huddersfield Town   (h) 2–3   Division One   Gallacher 2   30000
1932   Bolton Wanderers   (h) 3–1   Division One   Allen, Boyd 2   15000
1938   Sheffield United   (h) 0–0   Division Two   No Scorer   47000
1949   Aston Villa   (a) 1–0   Division One   Hannah   40000
Debut for Ted Robledo, who joined his brother George in the first team.
1950   Ray Ellison born, Newcastle.
1955   Burnley   (a) 1–3   Division One   Keeble   29032
1960   Burnley   (a) 3–5   Division One   White, Hughes 2   24972
1966   Tottenham Hotspur   (a) 0–4   Division One   No Scorer   27948
A baptism of fire for Joe Harvey's new recruits Tommy Robson, Dave Elliott and John McNamee, as the quest for points to move away from the relegation zone continued. All three had been signed since the Boxing Day defeat by Leeds following frantic negotiations.
1977   Liverpool   (h) 0–2   Division One   No Scorer   36499
A debut for Mike Larnach as United vainly attempted to spend their way out of relegation trouble.
1983   Oldham Athletic   (a) 2–1   Division Two   Keegan 2   8518
1988   Tottenham Hotspur   (a) 0–2   Division One   No Scorer   27739
1994   Norwich City   (a) 1–2   Premier League   Fox (pen)   21172